THE SOUTHERN
PHILOSOPHER

Collected Essays of John William Corrington

THE SOUTHERN
PHILOSOPHER

Collected Essays of John William Corrington

EDITED BY ALLEN MENDENHALL

UNG

UNIVERSITY *of*
NORTH GEORGIA™
UNIVERSITY PRESS

Blue Ridge | Cumming | Dahlonega | Gainesville | Oconee

Published by:
University of North Georgia Press
Dahlonega, Georgia

Printing Support by:
Lightning Source Inc.
La Vergne, Tennessee

Cover Image and Frontispiece: John William Corrington, courtesy of Joyce Corrington

Book design by Corey Parson

ISBN: 978-1-940771-37-3

Printed in the United States of America
For more information, please visit: http://ung.edu/university-press
Or e-mail: ungpress@ung.edu

For Joyce Corrington

Contents

Preface

Most of this book consists of John William Corrington's previously-neglected essays and lectures. Because Corrington did not prepare each of these essays and lectures for publication, each required the predictable revisions: spelling and punctuation corrections, citation and footnote corrections, and the location and addition of secondary sources to which the essays and lectures referred. I have added quotation marks where Corrington was quoting other authors and have made grammatical revisions where they seemed necessary. Some of these essays and lectures were handwritten so had to be typed for the first time. I owe thanks to Joyce Corrington for her assistance in transcribing some longhand essays and to Centenary College for mailing me copies of archived documents. Corrington's handwriting was not a model of clarity; at times only Joyce was able to decipher it. I am grateful for her patience and openness with me and admiring of her continued devotion to her late husband. I dedicate this book to her.

I have attempted to achieve consistency where Corrington was inconsistent. For instance, I have capitalized words that Corrington consistently capitalized and have maintained Corrington's spelling if he employed it consistently, even if it is at odds with the common spelling. For example, Corrington alternated between "uroborotic" and "uroboric," so I have noted inconsistencies in such moments. I have made many minor changes—such as adding a missing "and" or capitalizing a proper noun—without noting them, but I did explain minor changes if I believed an explanation would benefit future scholars. For purposes of reference and study, I have written an introduction to each chapter.

Each essay required its own special attention. "Recovery of the Humanities," for instance, used many Indian names that have multiple spellings in English, and because Corrington did not always use the common spellings for these Indian names, I left his spellings—with some exceptions—alone. I have noted major changes wherever I made them. The most difficult editorial task involved tracking down Corrington's sources. He was prone to quoting obscure sources and occasionally attributed a remark to the correct author but to the incorrect work or title by that author. He also tended to summarize or alter the quotations of others rather than maintaining the original quotation. He took liberties with punctuation and even diction when he quoted from sources. I have either corrected Corrington's mistakes and alterations in such moments or have noted these mistakes and alterations in a footnote.

Some of Corrington's own footnotes consisted of nothing more than the author's name or the title of the work he was citing; others contained errors or only partial information. These are not shortcomings; rather, in my view they reveal an impressive mind that could recall sources without having to look them up. I used Corrington's references as a starting point for locating the proper sources.

I have also integrated his footnotes with my own footnotes for two important reasons. First, for ease of reference, I wanted the footnotes in this book to appear on the same page as the text being footnoted. Second, Corrington's footnotes sometimes contained errors or required additional context or explanation. Rather than awkwardly footnoting a footnote to provide such context or explanation, I added my own commentary either preceding or following Corrington's note, with Corrington's language appearing within quotation marks. I have indicated Corrington's notes with the phrase "Corrington's note," followed by a quotation of Corrington's note. For the most part, I have maintained the originality and integrity of Corrington's work, including the footnotes.

A final note of thanks is in order: Nathalie Marcus assisted me with this project and deserves special recognition. She read the entire manuscript, recommended changes, and suggested footnotes and revisions. Without her, this book would not exist.

Finally, I am grateful to James "Jim" R. Elkins at West Virginia University College of Law—and not just for his encouragement and support of this book. He is the reason I attended WVU for my M.A. and J.D. and the reason I became interested in Corrington to begin with. I miss our conversations at the little coffee shop in Morgantown, West Virginia. Of the essays and lectures in this book, Jim has published four in *The Legal Studies Forum*: "Science, Symbol, and Meaning" (published in *LSF* as "The Wind Is Rising and the Rivers Flow"), "The Mystery of Writing," "Law and the Prophets," and "The Recovery of the Humanities." "A Poets Credo" originally appeared in the journal *Midwest*. "A Rebirth of Philosophical Thought" first appeared in *The Southern Review*. "Philosophies of History: An Interview with Eric Voegelin" first appeared in the *New Orleans Review*. "Law and the Prophets" first appeared in Tulane Law School's *Law Forum*. The remaining essays and lectures are published for the first time in this book with the gracious permission of Joyce Corrington.

Introduction

It was the spring of 2009. I was in a class called Lawyers and Literature. My professor, Jim Elkins, a short, thin man with long-white hair, gained the podium. Wearing what might be called a suit—with Elkins one never could tell—he recited lines from a novella, *Decoration Day*. I had heard of its author John William Corrington but only in passing.

"Paneled walnut and thick carpets," Elkins beamed, gesturing toward the blank-white wall behind him, "row after row of uniform tan volumes containing between their buckram covers a serial dumb show of human folly and greed and cruelty."

The students, uncomfortable, began to look at each other, registering doubt. In law school, professors didn't wax poetic. But this Elkins—he was different. With swelling confidence, he pressed on: "The *Federal Reporter, Federal Supplement, Supreme Court Reports.* Two hundred years of our collective disagreements and wranglings from Jay and Marshall through Taney and Holmes and Black and Frankfurter—the pathetic often ill-conceived attempts to resolve what we have done to one another."

Elkins paused. The room went still. Awkwardly profound, or else profoundly awkward, the silence was there, all too there. No one knew how to respond. Law students, most of them, can rattle off fact patterns or black-letter law whenever they're called on. But what were we to do with *this*?

What I did was find out more about Corrington. Having studied literature for two years in graduate school, I was surprised to hear the name "Corrington" in law school. I booted up my laptop, right where I was sitting and, thanks to Google, found a few biographical sketches of the man, who, it turned out, was perplexing and riddled with contradictions: a Southerner from the North, a philosopher in cowboy boots, a conservative *litterateur*, a lawyer poet. This introduction to Corrington led me to more books, more articles, and more research. Before long I'd spent over $300 on Amazon.com. And I wasn't done yet.

Born in Cleveland, Ohio, on October 28, 1932, Corrington—or Bill, as his friends and family called him—was a Southerner through and through and spent most of his life celebrating that fact. Although Corrington's curriculum vitae maintained that he was born in Memphis, he was actually born in Cleveland because his parents, who were from Memphis, Tennessee, had traveled to Ohio to find work during the Depression. Corrington was fascinated by Louisiana and cherished his connections with Shreveport and New Orleans, which served as settings for his fiction.

Corrington lived most of his life below the Mason-Dixon Line, moving to Shreveport at age ten. Raised Catholic, he attended a Jesuit high school in Louisiana but was expelled for, in his words, "having the wrong attitude." The Jesuit influence would nevertheless remain with him. At the beginning of his books he scribbled, "AMDG," which stands for *Ad Majorem Dei Gloriam*—"for the greater glory of God." "It's just something that I was taught when I was just learning to write," he explained in an interview in 1985, "taught by the Jesuits to put at the head of all my papers."

Corrington authored or edited, or in some cases co-edited, twenty books of varying genres. He earned his B.A. from Centenary College and his M.A. in Renaissance literature from Rice University, where he met Joyce Hooper, whom he married on February 6, 1960. In September of that year, he and Joyce moved to Baton Rouge where he became an instructor in the Department of English at Louisiana State University (LSU). At that time, LSU's English department was known above all for *The Southern Review*, the brainchild of Cleanth Brooks and Robert Penn Warren, but also for such literary luminaries as Robert B. Heilman, who would become Corrington's friend.

Corrington had been married once before. Joyce once confided to me that he had married "Floice somebody" and that the marriage had been quickly annulled because Corrington was Catholic and Floice's father was a Protestant minister. Corrington and Floice were young at the time, either still in high school or in their freshman or sophomore year of college, and Corrington would later say that Floice, a fellow musician, was the only person he'd ever met who had perfect pitch. He also claimed their union was never consummated because sex was too painful for her.

In 1965, *The Southern Review* was revived. It had been closed in 1942 due to the tightening budgets occasioned by World War II. Corrington and Miller Williams, his colleague at LSU, lobbied hard and successfully for the reinstatement of the journal, and Corrington pushed the editors to feature fiction and poetry and not just literary criticism. Corrington and Williams expected to be named the editors of the journal, but that honor fell to Lewis P. Simpson and Donald E. Stanford.

During this time, Corrington carried out a sprightly correspondence with the poet Charles Bukowski. A year after joining the LSU faculty, Corrington published his first book of poetry, *Where We Are*. With only eighteen poems and 225 first edition printings, the book hardly established Corrington's reputation as a Southern man of letters, but it did bring him recognition. Corrington had always wanted to be a novelist, and reading Hodding Carter's *The Angry Scar* (1959) inspired him to complete his first novel *And Wait for the Night* in 1964.

Corrington and Joyce spent the 1963-64 academic year in Sussex, England, where Corrington took his D.Phil. from the University of Sussex in 1965. In the summer of 1966, at a conference at Northwestern State College, Mel Bradford, the so-called Dean of Southern Letters, pulled Corrington aside and enthusiastically told him that *And Wait for the Night* rivaled Faulkner's *The Unvanquished* in the enormity of its themes and approaches.

Corrington agreed. And happily.

Jo LeCoeur, a poet and literature professor, once said of Corrington and Williams, "Both men had run into a Northern bias against what was perceived as the culturally backward South. While at LSU they fought back against this snub, editing two anthologies of Southern writing and lecturing on 'The Dominance of Southern Writers.' Controversial as a refutation of the anti-intellectual Southern stereotype, their joint lecture was so popular [that] the two took it on the road to area colleges."

In this respect, Corrington was something of a latter-day Southern Fugitive—a thinker in the tradition of Donald Davidson, Allan Tate, Andrew Nelson Lytle, and John Crowe Ransom. Corrington, too, took his stand; his feelings about the South were strong and passionate but also mixed and complex. "[T]he South was an enigma," Corrington wrote to Bukowski, "a race of giants, individualists, deists, brainy and gutsy: Washington, Jefferson, Madison, Jackson (Andy), Davis, Calhoun, Lee, and on and on. And yet the stain of human slavery on them."

Corrington was interested not in hagiographic renderings of Southern figures but in the rich complexities of Southern people and experience. In the end, though, there was no doubt where his allegiances lay. "You strike me as the most unreconstructed of all the Southern novelists I know anything about," said one interviewer to Corrington. "I consider that just about the greatest compliment anyone could give," Corrington responded.

Corrington resisted categories and defied simple classification. He informed Bukowski, for instance, that he had taken up the sonnet just to throw "dirt in the eyes of those would love to put some label on my ass." While on tour with Williams, Corrington remarked in a presentation that "we are told that the Southerner lives in the past. He does not. The past lives in him, and there is a difference." The Southerner, Corrington continued, "knows where he came from, and who his fathers were" and "knows still that he came from the soil, and that the soil and its people once had a name." The Southerner knows that this is not only "true" but also "a myth." And the Southerner "knows the soil belonged to the black hands that turned it as well as it ever could belong to any hand." In short, in Corrington's view, the Southerner knew that his history was tainted but that it retained virtues worth sustaining—that a fraught past is not reducible to sound bites or political abstractions but is, as Whitman said of himself, vast and multitudinous.

In 1966, Bill and Joyce Corrington moved to New Orleans, where the English Department at Loyola University, housed in a grand Victorian mansion on St. Charles Avenue, offered him a chairmanship. Joyce earned her M.S. in chemistry from LSU that same year. By this time, Corrington had written four additional books of poetry, the last of which, *Lines to the South and Other Poems* (1965), benefited from Bukowski's influence. Corrington and Bukowski had become regular correspondents. Bukowski moved to New Orleans after Corrington returned from England with his doctorate. When the two men finally met in person, Bukowski, apparently insecure about his inadequate education, resented Corrington's collegiate style and ended their relationship.

Corrington's books of poetry earned him a few favorable reviews but not as much attention as was won by his novels, *And Wait for the Night* (1964), *The Upper Hand* (1967), *The Bombardier* (1970), and *Shad Sentell* (1984). Writing in *The Massachusetts Review*, Beat poet and critic Josephine Miles approvingly noted alongside poetry by James Dickey two of Corrington's poems from *Lines*, "Lucifer Means Light" and "Algerien Reveur," but her comments were more in passing than in depth. Dickey himself admired Corrington's writing, saying, "A more forthright, bold, adventurous writer than John William Corrington would be very hard to find."

Joyce Corrington earned her Ph.D. in chemistry from Tulane in 1968. Her thesis, which she wrote under the direction of L. C. Cusachs, was titled "Effects of Neighboring Atoms in Molecular Orbital Theory." She began teaching chemistry at Xavier University, and her knowledge of the hard sciences brought about engaging conservations between her and Corrington about the New Physics. "Even though Bill only passed high school algebra," Joyce would later say, "his grounding in Platonic idealism made him more capable of understanding the implications of quantum theory than many with more adequate educations."

By the mid-70s, Corrington had become enthralled with the philosophy and personality of Eric Voegelin. A German historian, philosopher, and *émigré* who had fled statist Germany and the Third Reich, Voegelin taught in LSU's history department and lectured for the Hoover Institution at Stanford University. Voegelin's philosophy, which is known for its warnings against "immanentizing the eschaton"—i.e., against attempting to bring about a heaven on earth within history—inspired Corrington to study Gnostic texts and teachings, subject matter that reawakened his Catholic imagination. Voegelin made such a lasting impression on Corrington that, at the time of Corrington's death, he was working on an edition of *The Nature of the Law and Related Legal Writings*. After Corrington's death, two men—Robert Anthony Pascal and James Lee Babin—finished what Corrington had begun, and the completed edition appeared in 1991. Corrington thus contributed as a co-editor to one volume of the thirty-four-volume *Collected Works of Eric Voegelin* (University of Missouri Press).

In an essay entitled "The Evolution of Bill Corrington's Metaphysics," Joyce Corrington mapped her husband's shifting philosophical interests as he gradually integrated, in sometimes strange and unpredictable ways, his fascination with the American Civil War, Voegelin's studies of Christian and Hellenist thought, Heidegger, modern physics, and Indian philosophy. Corrington was, she said, developing "his own personal concept of the divine." According to Joyce's sweeping summary, Corrington sought to recover the values and sense of historical consciousness that he believed had been lost to Western Civilization since the Enlightenment. He saw in the American South the organizing poetic elements of myth and symbol that stood in contradistinction to disordered modernity.

Although conservative—one of his friends insists that he preferred the term "Voegelinian"—Corrington came to dislike certain members of the mainstream conservative movement. He did not take to George Will, for instance, because of the controversy ignited by Reagan's nomination of Bradford as the chair of the National Endowment for the Humanities in 1981. In the pages of *The Washington Post*, Will had decried Bradford's attachment to the "nostalgic Confederate remnant within the conservative movement." Bradford's singular offense was proposing that Lincoln was a "Gnostic" in the sense that Voegelin used the term. Corrington did not think Lincoln was a Gnostic. In a 1964 letter to Anthony Blond, the British editor who had published *And Wait for the Night*, Corrington asserted that Lincoln stood "in relation to the South very much as Khrushchev did to Hungary, as the United Nations *apparatchiks* did to Katanga." Corrington covered for Bradford but did not agree with him, at least not fully. In one letter, Bradford rebuffed Corrington because Corrington allegedly did not want to be publically associated with attacks on Lincoln.

Corrington was one of those conservatives whom Will decried for having a not unfavorable view of the Confederate States of America. He named his sons after General Robert E. Lee and General Stonewall Jackson and once dashed off a missive to Bukowski that referred to Lee as "the greatest man who ever lived." A statue of General Sherman on a horse inspired—or, rather, provoked—Corrington's collection of poems *Lines to the South*. Heilman observed that seventy-five percent of Corrington's short stories involved the Civil War. Asked whether he was a Southern writer, Corrington quipped, "If nobody else wants to be, that's fine; then we would have only one: me."

Unlike Will, Corrington was not about to let Lincoln mythology become a condition for conservative office or to disregard the different historical circumstances that shaped political theories about the role of the central government in relation to the several states. "Will's stance," Corrington announced with bravado in an article about Southern conservatism, "comes close to requiring a loyalty oath to the Great Emancipator, and I for one will not have it. It is one thing to live one's life under the necessity of empirical events long past; it is quite another to be forced to genuflect to them."

Shortly after discovering Voegelin, Corrington began to read Russell Kirk. Bruce Hershenson, then a producer with a Los Angeles television station who had come to prominence through a documentary on the funeral of John F. Kennedy, commissioned Corrington to write a screenplay of Kirk's *Roots of American Order*. Corrington drew up the script, but it was never produced. Kirk later entrusted the script to Richard Bishirjian, who supplied me with a copy of it a few years ago. (I made additional copies for Annette Kirk; the script is now on file in the archives at the Russell Kirk Center for Cultural Renewal.) I don't know why the script failed, but according to Bishirjian, it had something to do with "the new political appointees at NEH that Bennett recruited." These appointees were, Bishirjian says, "ideologues for whom John Locke, the Declaration of Independence, Abraham Lincoln, and Harry Jaffa define America."

Corrington believed that social orders were structured around states of consciousness or experience that both generated and reflected symbols of reality. Reality in this sense was the existing rather than the imagined state of actual things. Because all things actually existing cannot be comprehensively or fully known by acting agents, not all reality can be apprehended; therefore, myth, poetry, typology, and cosmological symbolization were necessary to make sense of the mysteries and ambiguities that order our experience even in spite of our cognitive limitations. Studying symbols as representations of experience or consciousness was, for Corrington, essential to understanding the political categories within any system because it revealed the restrictions and possibilities of the knowledge on which social order was predicated. Corrington looked at the phenomenal world through the lens of premodern man, thereby seeking to understand politics and science and their subjects mythopoetically and as elements of divine cognition. He adopted the notion that all acting agents operated in a state of *metaxy* between the human and the divine, with human knowledge originating from the reality that is evidence of cosmic unity or transcendent design. Human consciousness made history intelligible and communicable from person to person and informed our views of divine purpose. Corrington's philosophy, like Voegelin's, is demanding and complex with its free use of obscure theological lexica and esoterica derived from classical and scholastic thought. Nevertheless, with remarkable consistency and depth, he challenged his readers to return to such fundamental questions of philosophy as time, existence, reality, infinitude, divinity, consciousness, and the cosmos within the framework of early Christian theology.

Gnosticism was central to Corrington's politics. Seeking answers for why and how Nazism, fascism, Marxism, communism, and other totalizing ideologies had developed during the twentieth century, Corrington explored the psychological and metaphysical dimensions of Gnosticism which maintained that personal intuition and experience could achieve a certain Gnosis ("knowledge") or transcendence whose description was possible only through myth and poetry. The Gnostics considered themselves to be set apart or alienated from the social order and assumed that their access and understanding of the transcendent were superior to that of non-Gnostics. Corrington adjudged modern ideology and utopianism to have advanced a distorted form of Gnosticism insofar as they proposed that the disorder of the phenomenal cosmos could be transcended and overcome by those with superior knowledge, or with visions for human salvation on earth rather than in the Christian eschaton. According to this portrayal of Gnosticism, a privileged and enlightened few enjoyed an unqualified duty and power to control and direct the activities of the unenlightened masses. Such Gnosticism inhered in the radical totalitarianism of the twentieth century when centralized governments amassed vast powers in the hands of a few individuals who possessed a remarkable facility with symbolism and poetics as manifest in political literature, propaganda, oration, iconography, and other styles of semiotics and communication.

By 1975, the year in which he earned his law degree from Tulane, Corrington had penned three novels, a short story collection, two editions (anthologies), and four books of poetry. His writing, however, earned him little money. He also had become increasingly disenchanted with the "political correctness" on campus.

> By 1972, though I'd become chair of an English department and offered a full professorship, I'd had enough of academia. You may remember that in the late sixties and early seventies, the academic world was hysterically attempting to respond to student thugs who, in their wisdom, claimed that serious subjects seriously taught were "irrelevant." The Ivy League gutted its curriculum, deans and faculty engaged in "teach-ins," spouting Marxist-Leninist slogans, and sat quietly watching while half-witted draft-dodgers and degenerates of various sorts held them captive in their offices. Oddly enough, even as this was going on, there was a concerted effort to crush the academic freedom of almost anyone whose opinions differed from that of the mob or their college-administrator accessories. It seemed a good time to

get out and leave the classroom to idiots who couldn't learn and didn't know better, and imbeciles who couldn't teach and should have known better.

Having left the academy behind, Corrington joined the law firm of Plotkin & Bradley, a small personal injury practice in New Orleans, and continued to publish in such journals as *The Sewanee Review* and *The Southern Review*, and in such conservative periodicals as *The Intercollegiate Review* and *Modern Age*. His stories took on a legal bent, peopled as they were with judges and attorneys, but neither law nor legal fiction brought him fame or fortune.

So he turned to screenplays and, at last, earned the profits for which he had labored for so long. Viewers of the film *I am Legend* (2007), starring Will Smith, might be surprised to learn that the Corringtons wrote the screenplay for the earlier version *Omega Man* (1971), starring Charlton Heston. And viewers of *Battle for the Planet of the Apes* (1973), which has only recently been remade, might be surprised to learn that Corrington wrote the film's screenplay while he was still a law student. All told, the Corringtons wrote five screenplays and one television movie. Free from the constraints of university committees, politics, and bureaucracy, they collaborated on various television daytime dramas, less kindly known as soap operas, including *Search for Tomorrow, Another World, Texas, Capitol, One Life to Live*, and *General Hospital*. They eventually moved to Malibu, California, to write *Superior Court*, a job that required their attending weekly brainstorming meetings in Los Angeles.

Throughout his career, Corrington molded and remolded his image, embracing Southern signifiers while altering their various expressions. His early photos suggest a pensive, put-together gentleman wearing ties and sport coats and smoking pipes; he looked like Robert Penn Warren or T. S. Eliot, both of whom he admired. Later photos conjure up the likes of Elvis and Roy Orbison, what with Corrington's greased hair, cigarettes, and dark sunglasses. Still later photos depict a rugged man clad in western wear, the look of John Wayne or Charlton Heston. Corrington joined together the disparate characters of a Beat poet, a Voegelinian philosopher, a Southern man of letters who called Louisiana his home, a struggling lawyer, and a Hollywood habitué.

Whatever his looks and occupation, Corrington was a stark, provocative, and profoundly sensitive writer. His impressive *oeuvre* has yet to receive the critical attention it deserves. That scholars of conservatism, to say nothing of scholars of Southern literature or American literature, have ignored this man seems to me almost inconceivable. There are no doubt many aspects of Corrington's life and literature left to be discovered. His friend William Mills stated, "I believe there is a critique of modernity throughout [Corrington's] writing that will continue to deserve serious attentiveness and response."

On Thanksgiving Day, November 24, 1988, Corrington suffered a heart attack and died. He was fifty-six. His last words, uttered as Joyce and others rushed him to the hospital, were, "It's all right."

Bishirjian once called Corrington "Solzhenitsyn as Southerner" and described him as "a bawdy speaker, a musician at college, a writer, attorney, philosopher, and raconteur." "How one person can command so many disciplines," Bishirjian added, "is a mystery of God's Providence. Bill fit Marian Montgomery's definition of human beings as rooted in place and time." Whatever Bishirjian meant, he was not just appreciative; he was amazed. "Bill was bigger than life," Bishirjian would later say to me, and that is why this volume is so important: it's the first of its kind since Corrington's death, indeed, the first to compile Corrington's literary, political, religious, jurisprudential, and philosophical writings in one place.

No edition of Corrington's essays and lectures exists; some of the works here have never been published in any form. My hope is that this work inspires further study of Corrington and his thought. Scholarship on Corrington focuses mostly on his fiction and poetry rather than his literary, political, religious, jurisprudential, and philosophical beliefs and interests. His nonfiction is ignored. Only Elkins has devoted considerable attention to Corrington's essays and lectures, most notably in "Fishing Deep Waters: John William Corrington (1932-1988)" in *Legal Studies Forum*, Vol. XXVI, No. 2, 2002. The essays and lectures contained in the present edition address a wide variety of topics that fall within the general rubrics of the humanities. While varying in complexity, formality, and detail, they share a commitment to humane and rigorous learning, myth criticism, symbology, and modernity. Corrington was a towering figure whose writing has not received adequate scholarly treatment. Dividing his essays and lectures by subject matter—writing, literature, history, and Gnosticism—this edition is a corrective: it seeks to give Corrington's nonfiction a wider audience and to reinstate him as a major figure in the literary and political scene of the latter half of the twentieth century.

Allen Mendenhall

Part I

WRITING

The Mystery of Writing

1985

This chapter consists of a lecture that Corrington delivered in 1985 at the Northwest Louisiana Writer's Conference in Shreveport, Louisiana, Corrington's hometown. The lecture is part memoir, part commentary on writing as a craft. Corrington explains that he wanted to be a musician before he wanted to be a writer. He discusses his education at Centenary College and the state of popular literature at the time. He explains that he left academia because he felt disenfranchised politically in the academy, thus causing him to enter law school. The lecture demonstrates that Corrington saw himself as a Southern author who bemoaned the state of current popular writing. He notes how his popular writing for film and television earned him money though his literary writing—novels and poetry—was not profitable. Although he wrote for film and television, he had contempt for those media and felt they did not challenge viewers intellectually, at least not in the way that literature challenged readers. Corrington's conservatism is evident in his emphasis on a discernable literary tradition and his disgust for the technologies that made possible his own career. His advice for his audience is that they write about what they know, just as he writes about the South; therefore, he advises his audience not to become professional writers but to find other employment as a source for writing. His discussion of good writing as an ongoing investigation of perennial themes calls to mind the controversial notion of the literary canon as developed by Harold Bloom, Allan Bloom, John Ellis, and E. D. Hirsch.

In the next two days, you all[1] will be hearing a great deal about the nuts and bolts of writing, how to write, how to sell what you write, how to hang in there with editors and publishers, and so on. All of that is good, and is, as I understand, the stuff of writers' conferences. I can't say from personal experience, since this is the first such conference I have attended since the 1960s.

In any case, since most of you are from North Louisiana, and from the South, it seemed to me that I should talk not about how to sell and how to get along and how to make a smashing career out of writing—but about what writing meant to me when I was a tow-headed redneck boy growing up in Shreveport thirty years ago, and how that dream has worked out. As my work shows, I am not given to

---

1   Originally read "youall."

autobiographical ravings, but each of us starts where we start, and that is all we really have to tell about. The rest is second-hand, and you could get it better in the *Writer's Digest* or some such thing.

To begin, writing was my second love, not my first. The thing I wanted to do more than anything else was to play lead trumpet with the Glenn Miller Orchestra. Those of you who remember those days and that orchestra may understand the passion.

But I was too late, and not good enough anyhow. Major Glenn Miller died in the winter of 1944, and I was just a pretty good trumpet player. The horn got me through high school and even got me a college scholarship and a place on the Symphony. But as much as I loved music, I simply didn't have the skills, the fundamental capacities to achieve what I wanted to achieve.

My mother had always suspected as much. "Be a writer," she said. "You can live where you want to live and be your own boss. Anyhow, that's what you're good at."

I think she must have been right. They had a short-story contest at Jesuit High here in town, and I won it till they stopped having it. Maybe that's why they stopped having it.

I was two years into college before I could bring myself to admit that I was never going to be good enough to be a professional musician. It was as painful an admission as I've ever had to make. But changing my major from music to English taught me something about reality. It is best to respect it, to move with it when you can, to find ways in which you and reality can work together. No dream, however deeply held, is worth a damn if you fail to achieve it, and you can break your heart in the process of failing.

In my third year of college, I learned the fundamental lesson about writing. If you want to write, read. Read everything. By the time I had graduated, I must have read two-thirds of the Modern Library, bought book-by-book on credit from J. B.'s bookshop[2] through the kindness of J. B. and Henry Meyer.

Aside from reading, you have to talk, to ask questions, to argue your way through things until you see—or think you see—what they mean. My years at Centenary College saw to that. I was lucky enough to have as my professors the best of the best in those years: Edward Murray Clark, John R. Willingham, Lee Morgan, and Bryant Davidson. There are debts beyond payment, and whatever success I've had is largely due to the hours those four men spent with me after class, when they had no further duty to me at all.

Even now, I return in memory to the dark study of Dr. Clark's house where we talked about religion and literature, about the truths of the heart and what they might mean, about what men had known and felt three thousand years ago, what

---

2   The 1955 edition of the Shreveport City Directory contains information about the J. B. Book and Gift Shop. The shop was located at 626 Marshall Street. The owners were Henry N. Meyer and Julia B. Meyer.

they were thinking just then, in 1954. I remember the living room of Professor Davidson's house where we met for our weekly Philosophy seminar. I can even recall the ongoing debate between Professor Davidson and me—the only argument I ever won with him—regarding his practice of skipping the Middle Ages in his Philosophy course, going from Plotinus to Descartes as if nothing had happened in between. I didn't know much, but I was smart enough to know that you couldn't skip 1400 years and make things come out right in the history of Western Philosophy.

Professor Davidson finally owned up that I was likely right, but that he just had no use for the Middle Ages, and hence not the sympathy needed to teach the style of medieval thinking.

My teachers at Centenary thought better of my work than I did, and proposed that I should go to graduate school when I was done with my BA. The idea of getting a PhD seemed pretty remote to me, and not even something I was especially interested in. By my senior year I'd reckoned on what I wanted to do with my life. I wanted to write. I was in the process of moving my spiritual and intellectual baggage from Artie Shaw and Glenn Miller to William Faulkner and Thomas Wolfe.

But I was smart enough to know that I had a choice to make right then. It had become obvious by the mid-fifties that there was an inverse proportion between the amount of money a man could make and the quality of his writing. If you wanted to make a lot of money, you wrote crap. If you wrote quality fiction, you weren't going to make any money. My junior year in college had given me an example. I was working at the *Shreveport Times* in those years, and when I wasn't on the police beat or doing general reporting, I did book reviews. They gave me a big thick novel to review. It was one of the finest novels I've ever read. It was called *The Recognitions*, by William Gaddis. It cost $7.95 when the average novel cost $3.95 or $4.95, and, of course, it made no money at all for its publisher.

Years later, I talked to an editor who had worked at Harcourt, Brace in 1955. He remembered the meetings surrounding the publication of *The Recognitions*. "We knew there was no money in it," he told me. "But everybody thought the book had to be published. In those days, there was still a thing called American literature, and we felt we had to publish a book as splendid as it. We just had to."

That was then. This is now. I think it safe to say that no American publisher would risk three dollars and ninety-five cents in the name of American literature. There is little reason to suppose that *Raintree County* would be published today. Less reason to think that any of Faulkner's major works would find print. Can you really imagine a contemporary publisher reading *As I Lay Dying* or *The Sound and the Fury* and, as they like to say, "committing corporate funds" to it? This is the age of Herman Wouk and John Updike, John Irvin, Stephen King, and, inevitably, James Michener. Some of you may have seen *Space* on network TV. It had one of the lowest mini-series ratings of recent years, and yet, believe me, the mini-series was better than the book.

One looks at the best seller list nowadays in amazement. There are sex novels, do-it-yourself books, diet techniques, spy fiction, thrillers. There is rarely any literature at all. And when there is, it comes from abroad—like D. M. Thomas's *The White Hotel*. It's likely that most of you know the sorry history of John Kennedy Toole's book *A Confederacy of Dunces*. Dozens of publishers are said to have turned it down before LSU Press published it—and won the Pulitzer Prize in fiction with it.[3] I will not argue that it is a great novel, but it is immeasurably superior to most of the tripe published each year by those who rejected it.

I suppose I had some intuition that things might go that way as far back as the late 1950s. That's why I went on to graduate school and entered college teaching. Not so much for love of teaching as for a little security while I got on with what it was I thought I should do in life.

I spent ten years teaching at LSU, Berkeley, and Loyola in New Orleans. During that time, I managed to publish eleven books and more pieces in magazines and journals than I care to remember. The three novels published during those years were well reviewed, picked up for publication in England, and, taken together, didn't make me enough money to pay for the books I needed to buy.

In 1972, though I'd become a department chairman and had been offered a full professorship, I'd had enough of academia. You may remember that in the late sixties and early seventies, the academic world was hysterically attempting to respond to student thugs who, in their wisdom, claimed that serious subjects seriously taught were "irrelevant." The Ivy League gutted its curriculum; deans and faculty engaged in "teach-ins," spouting Marxist-Leninist slogans, and sat quietly watching while half-witted draft-dodgers and degenerates of various sorts held them captive in their offices. Oddly enough, even as this was going on, there was a concerted effort to crush the academic freedom of almost anyone whose opinions differed from that of the mob or their college-administrator accessories.

It seemed a good time to get out and leave the classroom to idiots who couldn't learn and didn't know better, and imbeciles who couldn't teach and should have known better.

I went to law school at Tulane. At least in Southern schools, the lawyers were having none of this educational anarchy. The work there is simply too demanding and too competitive to allow for pretensions of any kind. It was a good time for me, and it produced a series of short stories dealing with life from the point of view of lawyers and the law that hasn't finished yet.

---

3   *A Confederacy of Dunces* was published posthumously at the urging of Walker Percy. Toole committed suicide in 1969 at the age of thirty-one. A carbon copy of the manuscript was recovered from Toole's home after his death. The novel did not appear until 1980. It received the Pulitzer Prize for Fiction the following year.

Meanwhile, in 1968, after I'd come back home to Louisiana after a term at the University of California, Berkeley, I got the strangest phone call. It was from a man named Roger Corman, whom I'd never heard of, and he'd read my second novel, *The Upper Hand*. He wanted me to write a movie for him—about Manfred, Baron von Richthofen, the great German air ace of World War I. I told Roger I didn't know how to write movies and wasn't especially interested. He said that was too bad, because he'd pay me $10,000 for a 125-page script. Since I was making $12,000 a year teaching at Loyola, it dawned on me suddenly that I sure as hell could learn how to write movies, and that, secretly, I'd always wanted to do just that.

Dr. Joyce Corrington and I together wrote the script *Richthofen and Brown*,[4] later re-titled *The Red Baron*. It marked the beginning of our work together as writers in film and television. After that came *The Omega Man*, *Boxcar Bertha*, *The Arena*, *Battle for the Planet of the Apes*, *Killer Bees*, and years of writing for television.

But even as I practiced law and wrote for what folks like to call "the movies," I kept in mind where I had started, what I had meant to do. Even when the work to pay the bills took almost all my time, I managed to do a short story or two each year. During a lull between jobs, I wrote a novel some of you may have seen called *Shad Sentell*. In almost all my work, Louisiana—Shreveport and New Orleans—has been central. It still is. Presently, I have three novels with my agent in New York, all laid in and around Shreveport.

Now I'd always wanted to write a mystery novel, because it's a classic American form almost as stylized as the Western. But it seemed to me it had never been used to carry much intellectual and emotional freight. The crimes all seemed pretty ordinary, the characters just a cut above cartoon figures. I thought it was possible to do better. So the first novel Jo[5] and I collaborated on, called *So Small a Carnival*, is a detective story set in New Orleans—but the protagonist is a redneck reporter from Shreveport who can't stand the place. That book has been purchased by Viking Press and is scheduled for publication next fall. The crime is anything but ordinary, and the reporter from Shreveport would never have believed he'd accidentally become involved in solving one of the great and memorable crimes of the century.

Plans for the future work range from two more mystery novels to go with *So Small a Carnival*, to a book dealing with the labor movement and its travails in the late nineteenth and early twentieth century in America. For those of you who know my work, *Under the Double Eagle* will fit chronologically in between my first book, *And Wait for the Night*, and my most recent, *Shad Sentell*, and tell the story of E. M. Sentell, II, in the 1880s and '90s. He is son of Major Edward Malcolm Sentell and father of E. M. III and Shad Sentell.

---

4   The full title is *Von Richthofen and Brown*.

5   Joyce Corrington.

So much by way of inventory. I've been gone from Shreveport for almost thirty years, but, as you can see, Shreveport has never left me. It remains the subject and matrix of my work, and it always will. Not because my recollections of it are without pain, or because I lived a golden untroubled childhood here. It wasn't that way. But the experiences I had here, the places I remember, the people I loved—and even the ones I despised—have been as useful to me, as evocative, as Paris of the 1880s and '90s was to Marcel Proust. Not in a direct sense, certainly. I have never written a *roman à clef*[6] about Shreveport, using real people with fake names. Yet, at the same time, all my characters live here. They fitted smoothly and anonymously into the interstices of time and space in the period between 1863 and 1960.

As I told a friend once, people in America, even in the South today, throw their pasts away. Graveyards and City Directories and old dance cards and flowers pressed in Bibles [where][7] no one remembers to enter births and deaths in any more—all of them are filled with thousands of pasts that are ignored, forgotten, thrown away. Nobody wants them, nobody sees any use in them. Who knows or cares who developed Broadmoor? Does anyone remember Dehan's Restaurant or Le Chat Noir or the Peerless Cleaners? Who remembers Worm's Hilltop House or The Chef, or the Rex Theatre or Mrs. Pat's Food Market? They belong to me now, and they have appeared—or will appear—in my work as it goes forward.

In a recent novella called "The Risi's Wife," I put it this way:

> Shreveport is not a contemporary city to me; it is a palimpsest, a transparency through which I can see to an overarching past standing beyond time where its borders were more narrow than today, in which a host of vanished men and women dominated its collective life.
>
> Put me on any street of this town, and I will raise up for you the structures that stood upon it a decade, two, three, four decades ago. I will evoke for you the houses, the business places, bars and brothels, schools and hospitals, and the people now long dead who lived and walked and plotted and loved and laughed amidst them.
>
> I have the power to draw forth from the stuff of memory an unreal city as it existed on some arbitrary summer day in 1937, 1942, 1956, or 1970. It is an awesome and terrible capability, and I use it for my own most inward purposes, uncertain as I am of the meaning, the use—even the propriety— of a nostalgia more powerful than avarice or cupidity or the awful sweat-drenched dreams of that *libido dominandi* that hustles us each and every one toward the commonest of graves as if we were on the path toward the eternal salvation that we demand and ignore and plead for and dread simultaneously.

6   Originally no accent on the "a," perhaps because Corrington didn't use accent marks with his typewriter.
7   "Where" added.

There is not a lot of use discussing the motives for serious writing. There may not be much use in talking about "serious writing" in that it seems to be an invention of modern times when the awesome power of the written word as understood by the archaic Greeks and Indians has been reduced to a mere vehicle for the transference of confusion.

Those of us who consider our writing more than a mere way to make money or an odd hobby should be aware that time—history, the opinion of generations—makes the decision as to what is serious work and what is not. I used to tell my university classes that they, not literary types, gave life to what we call literary classics. The *New York Review of Books* can make you immortal, for about fifteen minutes.

For example, I doubt that anyone in this room knows who the bestselling British novelist was in the nineteenth century, and it would be a safe bet that none of you has read more than one novel by him—if that.

The best-selling British novelist of the nineteenth century? Let's get at the answer by telling you who it wasn't. Not Dickens, or Thackeray. Not Jane Austen or one of the Brontës. Not George Eliot or Robert Smith Surtees, Anthony Trollope or even Sir Walter Scott. It was a gentleman named Sir Edward Bulwer-Lytton,[8] whose only surviving work that anyone has heard of is *The Last Days of Pompeii*.

In other words, there is no necessary connection between a bestselling writer and the best writers. One might extend the axiom by remembering that the overwhelming opinion of sixteenth–, seventeenth–, and even eighteenth–century critics listed Ben Jonson above Shakespeare, or that Bach's work was forgotten by the mid-nineteenth century and had to be recovered and re-popularized by the unselfishness and brilliance of Felix Mendelssohn.

Things get even more complex in regard to the writer's trade when we consider that pure capacity to write is no assurance of permanence, either. William Gaddis is unknown; George Meredith is unread—though either of them on the worst day he ever lived could write Margaret Mitchell or Carson McCullers into the ground. But *Gone with the Wind* and *The Heart is a Lonely Hunter* are great tales, and the compelling power they possess as stories overrides their authors' insensitivity to language, and the banal style in which they are told.

One reads a great deal about best sellers and their authors nowadays. Works of fiction and diet plans and exercise books and self-improvement manuals all seem to be lumped in together simply because the only determinant of literary success has come to be the amount of profit one can make from a book—or a film or a TV show, for that matter. The idea that there are qualities other than profitability that might reasonably be considered in evaluating a piece of work is not a notion held in high esteem.

---

8   There is now the Bulwer-Lytton Fiction Contest, which invites contestants to write the worst possible first line to a novel—in the "It was a dark and stormy night" vein.

The result of this attitude should give all of us pause to consider both the phenomenon and the result.

Joyce Corrington and I have consistently been paid best for our worst work. Neither of us could make a decent living writing what we want to write, writing in the great literary tradition that T. S. Eliot told us extends from the work of Homer to the present. If we are willing to write garbage and not complain, we can make thousands of dollars a week. If we insist on doing the best work we can do, we'll be lucky to make ten thousand a year.

Do not be deceived into thinking that we insist on taking an elitist position and want to write strange experimental stories. On the contrary, we want to write stories of adventure and romance, stories in which the past and present intersect to change the future. Stories about the most serious and deepest feelings and thoughts of people like the people in this room. Stories of the kind that Faulkner said were the only ones that mattered: stories of the human heart in conflict with itself.

One comes to believe that there is a fundamental flaw in mass societies like ours. We make much of our freedom to write and say what we wish. And yet, despite the legal rights we possess, the product of publishing houses, film studios, and TV networks is as effectively censored as if we lived in the Soviet Union. It is not a political censorship, and no one threatens us. It is a censorship founded in taste so debauched that even mass audiences of ordinary people have begun to turn away from network TV, from theatrical films, from trade fiction.

Twenty years ago, very few of us watched PBS. Today, most of the folks I know watched *The Jewel in the Crown* and *The Forsyte Saga*. We're watching *Reilly: Ace of Spies* now, and enjoying it thoroughly. Since we've gotten cable in New Orleans, we spend ninety percent of our time watching films like Michael Mann's *The Keep*, or *Sixteen Candles*—neither of which was successful in their theatrical releases. Even *Star Trek* in its umpteenth syndication holds more interest than the present junk on network TV.

What is true of TV and film has become true of publishing. I would be willing to argue that today there is no such thing as American literature. "Media standards," as they are humorously called, have taken over publishing as thoroughly as film and TV. The occasional triumph of talent and determination, such as that represented by the publication of Ellen Gilchrist's *In the Land Of Dreamy Dreams* and *Victory Over Japan*, or by the posthumous publication of *A Confederacy of Dunces* is not enough to establish—or re-establish—the kind of literary tradition that guided me in determining what direction my work should take, and what I should intend by it. Again, it is important to remember that Miss Gilchrist's first book and *A Confederacy of Dunces* were both originally published by university presses, and Southern university presses at that: Arkansas and Louisiana State, not by commercial publishing houses.

Young Americans today grow up with the bizarre notion that movies are an art form rather than, at best, an innocuous form of mindless entertainment. To my horror, my youngest son walked into my office a year or so ago and announced that he wanted to be a television producer. "For God's sake, think of your family," I answered. "Have you considered being a pimp instead? Among the various forms of prostitution currently available, I tend to prefer the old-fashioned kind."

Now I know that America's strengths and its weaknesses are two sides of the same coin. The national love affair with fad and tackiness also permits the endless fabrication of new forms, the working out of new ideas. I also know that the pendulum tends to swing back over time toward some kind of norm. I acknowledge this, and it is possible that we gain more than we lose by it. At least I like to think so.

But we are driven, carried along, by our own technology today, because that is easier than the alternatives. We seem to have reached a point in our national development where we are prepared to do anything rather than think, anything except examine our collapsing culture and try to determine what it is telling us—anything but face the reality that we have turned away from the heights and depths of life itself and settled into a kind of spiritual and intellectual fog from which no judgments worthy of the name can issue, and into which every new insight seems to vanish without a trace.

But perhaps I shouldn't be complaining. Perhaps it is precisely in these desperate circumstances that a writer in the great tradition finds his way and his meaning most readily. Because I know what it means to be from somewhere, to belong to a place and a people, and to possess the skill to recreate both in a form that may challenge time itself.

Even today, with 30 years and 400 miles between me and Shreveport, when someone asks where I'm from, I invariably answer without thinking, "Shreveport." When I start to put together a new story, I think of its setting here, or in New Orleans, or somewhere in between. Even when I write of New York or London or Los Angeles, the people are from Louisiana—simply because those are the people I know in the same way I know myself.

To know who you are and what you are about seems to be a rare thing today. But it is at the very center of serious writing. And if you have that sense, it is possible to shrug off the fads and the tackiness, the poor workmanship and stupidity of contemporary writing—even if, from time to time, you are forced to engage in it. Perhaps it is a little like the meditation practice of Zen Buddhism. You possess the capacity to withdraw into a real world of real people doing intelligible—even if terrible—things. You look at the world around you as an especially perverted illusion, and turn inward to a truth that expresses itself through the symbols of language, a truth that does not depend on a moment or a popular attitude or the deformed consciousness that supposes the end of language is to make money.

One morning just as we awoke, Joyce turned to me and told me of a dream she had. In that dream, it was clear to her that each one of us, every person alive, is a story told about God. She could tell me no more than that, but that was surely enough, for she had told me the tale she was told in dream. Some of us are destined to be triumphant stories, some tragic. Some of us may be epics, some lyrics. All that remains is the transition of what it means to be human into human language. The mystery of writing is the realization that in language carried from the heart, we possess the power to stand against any absurdity, to stand for any sublimity until, in time, that writing which speaks final words, which defines our humanity in some special way stands no longer challenged by the rubbish and stupidity that claimed a place some length of time ago.

There is a novel called *What Will He Do with It*, which you have never heard of. There is another novel called *Great Expectations*. The first is by Bulwer-Lytton, the other by Dickens. The first outsold the second when they were originally published. Today, you would have to go to a major university library to find a copy. *Great Expectations* can be bought almost anywhere.

Let me conclude with a quotation from another Southern writer, one of those whose work I have always revered, and who, as much as any, has served as a model for the kind of work I've always tried to do. This is a passage out of a letter from Thomas Wolfe to his mother:

> I know this now: I am inevitable. I sincerely believe The only thing that can stop me now is insanity, disease, or death . . . I want to know life and understand it and interpret it without fear or favor. This, I feel, is a man's work and worthy of a man's dignity . . . God is *not* always in his heaven, all is not always right with the world, it is not all bad, but it is not all good. It is not all ugly, but it is not all beautiful, It is life, life, life—the only thing that matters. It is savage, cruel, kind, noble, passionate, selfish, generous, stupid . . . painful, joyous—it is all these and more . . . I know there is nothing so commonplace, so dull, that it is not touched with nobility and dignity. And I intend to wreak out my soul on paper and express it all. This is what my life means to me: I am at the mercy of this thing, and I will do it or die . . . This is why I think I'm going to be an artist . . . I will go everywhere and see everything. I will meet all the people I can. I will think all the thoughts, feel all the emotions I am able, and I will write, write, write.[9]

9   Corrington's quotation of Wolfe's letter is very close to the original, albeit without some of Wolfe's capitalization: I know this now: I am inevitable. I sincerely believe The only thing that can stop me now is insanity, disease, or death . . . I want to know life and understand it and interpret it without fear or favor. This, I feel, is a man's work and worthy of a man's dignity . . . God is *not* Always in His Heaven, All is *not* always right with the world. It is not all bad, but it is

Six years after the letter was written, *Look Homeward, Angel*, one of the finest first novels ever written by an American, was published. Nine years after that, Thomas Wolfe was dead. But not before he had established his vision of American reality firmly and permanently, in such a way that a boy only six years old when Wolfe died saw the truth of that vision and determined that he would carry it forward— no matter what the cost. And, if a man is any kind of writer at all, that capacity to bequeath the mystery to another generation, to send the message onward, is the only thing that matters.[10]

Career of Writing

1. *No way to make a living*
   a. Fewer and fewer jobs for people who haven't already made it in one area or another.
   b. Media jobs call for one to live in New York or Los Angeles. Neither is a place to raise children or to live normally.
   c. Some people interested in "the writer's life," rather than writing itself. Very little glamour. Much hard work, very long hours, and constant frustration—if you care about the kind of stories you want to do.

2. *Describe* how a TV show is put on the air, how structured, how it becomes a success.
   a. Copy-cat procedures. *Hunter* failing, so it starts copying *Miami Vice*, which is successful.
   b. Nelson ratings are dominant over judgment.
   c. Network as determinant. Any show on CBS likely to have +3 share points over NBC. This changes in cycles, but slowly.

3. *Describe* the making of a film, especially what determines whether a film will be made or not.
   a. Requirements of a film script.
   b. Position of the writer in film vis-à-vis TV.

4. *Publishing*
   a. Has become nothing more than another arm of visual media. Books published to sell large numbers. Quality of no account at all.

---

not all good, it is not all ugly, but it is not all beautiful, it is life, life, life—the only thing that matters. It is savage, cruel, kind, noble, passionate, selfish, generous, stupid...painful, joyous—it is all these and more . . .
I know there is nothing so commonplace, so dull, that it is not touched with nobility and dignity. And I intend to wreak out my soul on paper and express it all. This is what my life means to me: I am at the mercy of this thing, and I will do it or die . . . This is why I think I'm going to be an artist . . . I will go everywhere and see everything. I will meet all the people I can. I will think all the thoughts, feel all the emotions I am able, and I will write, write, write. (Wolfe 2006)

10   This is the conclusion of the essay. It is unclear whether Corrington delivered the material that follows as part of his talk. Corrington did not give other talks, or participate in other panels, at the conference. Thus, the material at the end of the essay is not likely preparation for another panel or discussion. Because Corrington's handwritten notes are legible and there is something more intimate about reading handwritten notes, I have reproduced the original images of the notes.

    b. Cost constraints. Rarely 500 page books unless by pot-boiler writers.

    c. Bookstore chain buyers now able in some measure to control what books will sell, what books won't. Displays in windows, etc.

    d. General decline of audience for novels and serious fiction on account of TV, etc.

    e. University presses now considered as a first line for serious writers of poetry, short stories, and novels.

        i. Especially true for works strongly concerned with a given locale or area. Mention Sr. Dorothea[11] and her books on the Daughters of the Cross in Shreveport, published by LSU Press.

        ii. Quality must be high, because university presses accustomed to people who know what they're doing.

Writing best treated today as one's own private commitment, as a thing one has to do because it is a good thing to do, as an offering to the love of humanity and the glory of God.

If anyone has anything serious to say, writing should under no circumstances be undertaken as a way to make a living. Be a carpenter or a lawyer, a doctor or a teacher. Do something you like to do which leaves you time for the writing. I always thought running a fishing camp would be a great way to make a living. When Faulkner was asked what job would be best for a writer, he said he thought the ideal job would be to be the landlord of a bordello. You'd have all your time free, and everything you need close at hand.

Final Notes:

No writer is better than the sum of what he has read. Despite what people think, writing of the serious kind is not done in isolation—unless it is done badly. You are responsible to that long shadowy line of men and women who have gone before you, and who knew that language is God's special gift to our species, and that the word is sacred and should be realized as such by those who have the audacity to try to use it for something more than calling the dog, scolding the children, or lying about where you caught that 8-pound bass. To read is to educate yourself. Nothing that you read is ever lost or useless.

One can even profit from reading junk. After reading something by Sidney Sheldon or Tommy Thompson, you have at least seen how not to do it. Then, turning to Joseph Conrad or Henry James, you'll have a deeper appreciation of their accomplishment—and a sense of how far you still have to go.

---

11   Sister Dorothea Olga McCants was, among other things, the translator and editor of *Our People and Our History: Fifty Creole Portraits* by Rodolphe Lucien Desdunes.

When reading fiction, don't get put off by the distance in time or place or in manners and attitudes between you and Proust or Hawthorne or Goethe or Shakespeare. Remember that human nature is constant in the very diversity of its presentation in life. What human beings want and fear and love and trust may change, may shift in emphasis from the sixteenth century to now, or from France to here. But human beings will always want and fear, love and trust.[12]

It is the writer's task to tell stories that reveal that wanting and fearing, loving and trusting as it is in the secret hearts of his characters.

At last, writing has never been a career for anyone worthwhile. Few have made a living from it if their work was the kind that survives, and almost none has become rich from it. Absolutely none has become as rich as he might have in business or trade.

Writing is no more a career than loving, marrying, or raising one's children is a career. It is a way of living that entails seeing into the flow of one's own life and that of others—either close by or immeasurably far away—and then [making][13] use of one's hard gained skill to recreate that life in language. So that the life thus preserved enters into the ongoing life of generations—even nations—as yet unborn.

Not many people would think of referring to Homer's career, or Dante's, or Shakespeare's. When I think of Thomas Wolfe or William Faulkner, Ernest Hemingway or Scott Fitzgerald, I do not think of their careers. I think of their lives and how they spent them. Writing. Perhaps a better word for the writer's life is vocation—as a preacher has a call, or a priest a vocation. Surely what we do at our very best serves to contain and record the travail and triumph of the human spirit even as do the holy books of the world. As Dylan Thomas put it in dedicating one of his books, "These poems are written for the love of mankind and the glory of God, and I'd be a damned fool if they were not."[14]

---

12 In the handwritten manuscript, there is a line that seems to mark a section break before this paragraph.

13 The grammar was not parallel; therefore, "to make" was changed to "making."

14 This passage is from a note at the beginning of Dylan's Thomas's *Collected Poems, 1934–1952*, later republished as *Selected Poems, 1934–1952*. Corrington omits a phrase and misremembers a few words: "These poems, with all their crudities, doubts, and confusions, are written for the love of Man and in praise of God, and I'd be a damn' fool if they weren't" (New Directions 2003).

that the pendulum tends to swing back over time toward some
kind of norm. I acknowledge this, and it is possible that
we gain more than we lose by it. At least I like to think
so.

But we are driven, carried along, by our own technology
today, because that is easier than the alternatives. We
seem to have reached a point in our national development
where we are prepared to do anything rather than think,
anything except examine our collapsing culture and try to
determine what it is telling us--anything but face the
reality that we have turned away from the heights and depths
of life itself and settled into a kind of spiritual and
intellectual fog from which no judgements worthy of the name
can issue, and into which every new insight seems to vanish
without a trace.

But perhaps I shouldn't be complaining. Perhaps it is
precisely in these desperate circumstances that a writer in
the great tradition finds his way and his meaning most
readily. Because I know what it means to be from somewhere,
to belong to a place and a people, and to possess the skill
to recreate both in a form that may challenge time itself.

Even today, with thirty years and 400 miles between me
and Shreveport, when someone asks where I'm from, I
invariably answer without thinking, "Shreveport." When I
start to put together a new story, I think of its setting
here, or in New Orleans, or somewhere in between. Even when
I write of New York or London or Los Angeles, the people are

from Louisiana—simply because those are the people I know

in the same way I know myself.

To know who you are and what you are about seems to be

a rare thing today. But it is at the very center of serious

writing. And if you have that sense, it is possible to

shrug off the fads and the tackiness, the poor workmanship

and stupidity of contemporary writing—even if, from time to

time, you are forced to engage in it. Perhaps it is a

little like the meditation practice of Zen Buddhism. You

possess the capacity to withdraw into a real world of real

people doing intelligible—even if terrible—things. You

look at the world around you as an especially perverted

illusion, and turn inward to a truth that expresses itself

through the symbols of language, a truth that does not

depend on a moment or a popular attitude or the deformed

consciousness that supposes the end of language is to make

money.

One morning just as we awoke, Jo turned to me and told

me of a dream she had. In that dream, it was clear to her

that each one of us, every person alive, is a story told

about God. She could tell me no more than that, but that

was surely enough, for she had told me the tale she was told

in dream. Some of us are destined to be triumphant stories,

some tragic. Some of us may be epics, some lyrics. All

that remains is the translation of what it means to be human

into human language. The mystery of writing is the

realization that in language carried from the heart, we

posses the power to stand against any absurdity, to stand for any sublimity until, in time, that writing which speaks final words, which defines our humanity in some special way stands no longer challenged by the rubbish and stupidity that claimed a place some length of time ago.

There is a novel called, WHAT WILL HE DO WITH IT, which you have never heard of. There is another novel called GREAT EXPECTATIONS. The first is by Bulwer-Lytton, the other by Dickens. The first outsold the second when they were originally published. Today, you would have to go to a major university library to find a copy. GREAT EXPECTATIONS can be bought almost anywhere.

Let me conclude with a quotation from another Southern writer, one of those whose work I have always revered, and who, as much as any, has served as a model for the kind of work I've always tried to do. This is a passage out of a letter from Thomas Wolfe to his mother:

> I know this now: I am inevitable. I sincerely believe the only thing that can stop me now is insanity, disease, or death...I want to know life and understand it and interpret it without fear or favor. This, I feel, is a man's work and worthy of a man's dignity....God is not always in His heaven, all is not always right with the world. It is not all bad, but it is not all good. It is not all ugly, but it is not all beautiful. It is life, life, life—the only thing that matters. It

is savage, cruel, kind, noble, passionate,
selfish, generous, stupid...painful, joyous--it is
all these and more....I know there is nothing so
commonplace, so dull, that it is not touched with
nobility and dignity. And I intend to wreak out
my soul on paper and express it all. This is what
my life means to me: I am at the mercy of this
thing, and I will do it or die....This is why I
think I'm going to be an artist....I will go
everywhere and see everything. I will meet all
the people I can. I will think all the thoughts,
feel all the emotions I am able, and I will write,
write, write...

Six years after the letter was written, LOOK HOMEWARD,
ANGEL, one of the finest first novels ever written by an
American was published. Nine years after that, Thomas Wolfe
was dead. But not before he had established his vision of
American reality firmly and permanently, in such a way that
a boy only six years old when Wolfe died saw the truth of
that vision and determined that he would carry it forward--
no matter what the cost. And, if a man is any kind of
writer at all, that capacity to bequeath the mystery to
another generation, to send the message onward, is the only
thing that matters.

Career of writing

1. <u>No way to make a living</u>
   a. fewer & fewer jobs for people who haven't already made it in one area or another.
   b. media jobs call for one to live in New York or Los Angeles. Neither is a place to raise children or to live normally.
   c. Some people interested in "the writer's life," rather than in writing itself. Very little glamor. Much hard work, very long hours, & constant frustration — if you care about the kind of stories you want to do.

2. Describe how a TV show is put on the air, how structured, how it becomes a success.
   a. copy-cat procedures. Hunter failing, so it starts copying Miami Vice which is successful.
   b. Neilson ratings as dominant over judgement —
   c. network as determinant. Any show on CBS likely to have + 3 share points over NBC. This changes in cycles, but slowly.

3. Describe the making of a film, especially what determines whether a film will be made or not.
   a. requirements of a film script.
   b. position of the writer in film vis-a-vis TV.

4. publishing.
   a. has become nothing more than another arm of visual media. Books published to sell large numbers. Quality of no account at all.
   B. Cost constraints. Rarely 500 page books unless by pot-boiler writers.
   C. Bookstore chain buyers now able in some measure to control what books will sell, what books won't. Displays in windows, etc.
   D. General decline of audience for novels & serious fiction on account of TV, etc.

E. ~~vanity presses~~ university presses now considered
as a first line for serious writers of poetry,
short stories, novels.
  i. especially true for works strongly concerned
     with a given locale or area
  ii. Quality must be high, because university presses
      accustomed to people who know what they're
      doing.
         Mention of Sr. Dorothea & her books on the
         Daughters of the Cross in shreveport, published
         by LSU.

Writing best treated today as one's own private commitment,
as a thing one has to do because it is a good thing to
do, as an offering to the love of humanity & the
glory of God.

If anyone has anything serious to say, writing should
under no circumstances be undertaken as a way to
make a living. Be a carpenter or a lawyer, a
doctor or a teacher. Do something you like to do
which leaves you time for the writing. I always thought
running a fishing-camp would be a great way to
make a living. When Faulkner was asked what job
would be best for a writer, he said he thought
the ideal job would be to be the landlord of
a bordello. You'd have all your time free, &
everything you'd need close at hand.

3.

Final notes:

No writer is better than the sum of what he has read. Despite what people think, writing of the serious kind is not done in isolation — unless it is done badly. You are responsible to that long shadowy line of men & women who have gone before you, & who knew that language is God's special gift to our species, & that the word is sacred & should be realized as such by those who have the audacity to try to use it for something more than calling the dog, scolding the children, or lying about where you caught that 8-pound bass. To read is to educate yourself. Nothing that you read is ever lost or useless.

One can even profit from reading junk. After reading something by Sidney Sheldon or Tommy Thompson, you have at least seen how not to do it. Then, turning to Joseph Conrad or Henry James, you'll have a deeper appreciation of their accomplishment— & a sense of how far you still have to go.

When reading fiction, don't get put off by the distance in time or in place or in manners & attitudes between you & Proust or Hawthorne or Goethe or Shakespeare. Remember that human nature is constant in the very diversity of its presentation in life. What human beings want & fear & love & trust may change, may shift in emphasis from the 16th century to now or from France to here. But human beings will always want & fear, love & trust.

It is the writer's task to tell stories that reveal that wanting & fearing, loving & trusting as it is in the secret hearts of his characters,

1.

At last, writing has never been a career for anyone worthwhile. Few have made a living from it if their work was the kind that survives, & almost none have become rich from it. Absolutely none has become as rich as he might have in business or trade.

Writing is no more a career than loving, marrying, raising one's children is a career. It is a way of living that entails seeing into the flow of one's own life & that of others — either close by, or immeasurably far away — & then to make use of one's hard-gained skill to recreate that life in language. So that the life thus preserved enters into the ongoing life of generations, even nations — as yet unborn.

Not many people would think of referring to Homer's career, or Dante's or Shakespeare's. When I think of Thomas Wolfe or William Faulkner, Ernest Hemingway or Scott Fitzgerald, I do not think of their careers. I think of their lives, & how they spent them. Writing. Perhaps a better word for the writer's life is vocation — as a preacher has a call, or a priest a vocation. Surely what we do at our very best serves to contain & record the travail & triumph of the human spirit even as do the holy books of the world. As Dylan Thomas put it in dedicating one of his books, "These poems are written for the love of mankind & the glory of God, & I'd be a damned fool if they weren't."

The Uses of History and the Meaning of Fiction

1966

This chapter consists of a lecture that Corrington delivered in 1966 as part of a discussion series created by the National Defense Education Act. Corrington used the occasion to attack what he dubbed "realism" and to decry the use of verisimilitude in fiction. Corrington focuses on "dialogue" and suggests that, although his fiction is praised above all for its dialogue, the dialect spoken by his characters does not actually exist. He developed what he calls "synthetic speech," a mix of Southern or Appalachian dialect coupled with African-American dialect. Corrington surveys several "canonical" writers for the way in which they employed dialogue and speech in their work, e.g., whether they were after the sounds that are actually spoken or some form of manufactured speech that served the rhetorical function of fiction. Corrington believed that writers ought to strike a balance between actual and imaginary speech. Although primarily a commentary on craft, this essay reveals elements of Corrington's traditionalism. His use of such phrases as "the best literature in the Western world" indicates his abiding conservatism and his belief in a literary canon characterized by fixed and unchanging aesthetic standards.

To begin, fiction is, however one takes it, a question of illusion. Art is not life, Zola and the naturalist-realist schools to the contrary. A novel or a short story succeeds or fails not in terms of some preexistent journalistic standard of fidelity to "reality," but in terms of its appeal to certain cultural and aesthetic standards which centuries of writing and reading have pressed into convention. One must conceive of a piece of fiction as a magician shapes his mysteries. We do not give our audience life as it is, but life as our audience supposes it to be.

Some critics might argue that this is sophistry. That the writer's responsibility is to show life precisely as it is. My reply is that such a concept is invariably a screen for the propagandist who, when he speaks further, admits that he wishes us to write how life is—according to his own angle of vision.

To press the point only a little further, one need have no training in philosophy to note that life is not any certain way. It tends to conform admirably to the wishes of its observer. Thus, if one is a Marxist, all history—that is to say, all the records of past life—can be expressed as a war between classes. There is something to this. But not much. A Christian, like Mr. Deasy in *Ulysses*, will tell us all history is simply the slow working out, the gradual manifestation of God's will in the universe. Good. Personally, I believe it. But it is not demonstrable. It is like telling a chemistry[15] class that the hydrogen you are separating out of water by electrolysis will explode if ignited. It is a fair enough statement, but the students await the event.

And so on and on. I daresay my own vision of reality is vastly different from any of yours. Such differences may be ascribed to many things, but one fact is evident: it is impossible for any writer to bind himself to "reality" and think that by doing so he will be freed from the necessity of inventing a world and peopling it with his own brand of phantoms.

Some writers have become obsessed with physical detail, believing that verisimilitude is simply a matter of preparing lists and catalogues. Everyone who has attempted such shortcuts to supposed reality has suffered in ratio to the degree he has attempted to substitute details for art.

Today, I would like to discuss a single aspect of this reality-illusion dichotomy: that of dialogue. I was amused last year by the fact that almost every review of my novel, whether it was favorable or not, tended to compliment my dialogue as real, gripping, and all the usual tired reviewer's adjectives. The reason for my amusement is that I am certain beyond a doubt that no men anywhere, any time, ever spoke as do my characters. I remember the problem I had when I began to write a novel that extends from 1940 to 1965. The usual idiotic historical-novel jargon was, of course, out. But just as certainly the language of the 1960s would not serve. And so it was necessary to construct a synthetic speech. The basic element was what I call rural southern, a speech only beginning to change now, and that, in my boyhood, was pretty much what it had been for almost 300 years. It is the language of Appalachia, of English, Scotch, and Irish yeomen who were—and are—the backbone of the South's white population. To this basic speech I added a more modern syntax—freer,[16] more supple, less formal than that which is typical of surviving nineteenth-century writing in the South. That this honestly reflects the way Southerners talked—as opposed to how they wrote—is certain. There are a few surviving letters from Genl. Nathan Bedford Forrest of Memphis. He was completely unschooled, and thus wrote as he spoke. One such letter says:

> Cant you come up and lend a hand? This fite will do to hand down to your childrens children. We come on the Yankees Tuesday north of Memphis. We got in their rear. They dint know we was there. They run like suns of biches.[17]

---

15 Uppercase in original.

16 Changed punctuation from semi-colon to "em dash" after the word "syntax."

17 This passage may be out of order. See, for example, *Nathan Bedford Forrest: In Search of the Enigma*, by Eddy W.

Not much like Jefferson Davis's mannered Burkeian prose? No, more the way men spoke.

But even Bedford Forrest's language was not quite it. I wanted one other element which was not likely to be a common element in any white man's speech. The white man has manipulated too many abstractions for too long. His language has been leached almost dry of similes and metaphors based in the soil and in the commonest of rural and small-town experience. Sophistication has rendered his speech either effete or technical. And so I added a touch of the kind of language I'd heard in a dozen colored churches and amongst my colored friends when I caddied at the golf course or snuck into Freeman and Harris's restaurant with the Negro disc jockey who helped me in my first radio job.

Of course, this explanation is somewhat ex post facto. Because, as I found, the language was essentially my own. Being not only a writer but something of a worshipper of this English tongue, I have at least half a dozen languages—all English. Friends have told me that my accent thickens when I go North. Long enough in England and I'd probably sound like a South Carolinian. But the language of the novel is a modified form of the speech I use at home—a little more rural, somewhat more figurative, and, in the case of certain characters, more formal. But the roots of it are to be found between Memphis and Shreveport.

But there is one characteristic of the speech which is even beyond synthesis, and totally non-realistic. This is the average sentence length. That average length is shorter than Faulkner's, far shorter than Wolfe's, but still considerably longer than that in Hemingway or Fitzgerald or Steinbeck.

I cannot tell you why, but this essentially rhetorical sentence length, more suitable, one might think, to a Biblical epic than a novel, works for the Southerner. If someone cared to push fifty Southern and fifty non-Southern novels through a computer, I would be willing to bet that the Southern average would be notably longer.

My point, perhaps attenuated by the very rhetorical tendency I have mentioned, is that the dialogue of *And Wait for the Night* is not realistic, was not intended to be realistic, and, I maintain, has no business being realistic. One writes the language which will satisfy one's requirements—which will permit the saying of those things which the novel demands be said. Only a person without instinct would hamper his own purposes in the name of realism which at best is relative, at worst a nightmare of tedium.

Davison, Daniel Foxx (Gretna, Louisiana: Pelican, 2007), p. 75:

> I had a small brush with the Enamy on yesterday I Suceded in gaining thir rear and hot in to their entrenchments . . . and Burned a portion of thir camp . . . they wair not looking for me I taken them by Surprise they run like Suns of Biches. . . . this army is at this time in front of our Entrenchments I look for a fite soon and a big one. . . . Cant you come up and take a hand this fite wil do to hand down to your children.

Another edition has just this part: "cant you come up and take a hand. this fite will do to hand down to your childrens children. I feel confident of our success." See *Bedford Forrest and His Critter Company*, by Andrew Nelson Lytle (Nashville, Tennessee: J. S. Sanders & Company, 1992) p. 85. Lytle's original was first published in 1931.

I think it is relatively pointless to go into an historical account of the striving for realism and to show how, ironically, those who most gave lip service to it were also those whose examples most jarred with their precepts. Wordsworth and Dreiser will serve, and a glance at their works and preachments will indicate the intervening distance.

Now, if we agree the function of a novel is to create the *illusion*[18] of what we must call "real" people engaged in "real" conversation, we have come a long way. The operative word is *illusion*.[19] Thus we understand at once that we cannot seek to rear the vision of an oasis in the desert unless we grasp the principles by which such an unsubstantial—but convincing—simulacrum is produced. In fictional dialogue, the ways are many. My own choice of a master in this form of creation is Charles Dickens. I cannot think of any writer in any language so gifted in the art of evoking the illusion of human speech and at the same time staying leagues away from anything that truly resembles spoken language as we know it. This, from *Bleak House*:[20]

> Rev. Chadband: My friends, what is this which we now behold as being spread before us? Refreshment. Do we need refreshment then, my friends? We do. And why do we need refreshment, [my] friends? Because we are but mortal, because we are but sinful, because we are but of the earth, because we are not of the air. Can we fly, my friends? We cannot. Why can we not fly, friends? . . . I say, [my friends], . . . why can we not fly, my friends? Is it because we are calculated to walk? It is. Could we walk, my friends, without strength? We could not. What should we do without strength, my friends? Our legs would refuse to bear us, our knees would double up, our ankles would turn over, and we should come to the ground. Then from whence, [my friends], in a human point of view, do we derive the strength that is necessary to our limbs? Is it . . . from bread in various forms, from butter which is churned from the milk which is yielded unto us by the cow, from the eggs which are laid by the fowl, from ham, from tongue, from sausage, and from such-like? It is. Then let us partake of the good things which are set before us.[21]

This is clearly illusion; Dickens cannot mean us to believe in any journalistic sense that people speak in this way in nineteenth-century England—any more than young

---

18   Italics added to help emphasize Corrington's point.

19   The original has "illusion" in quotation marks; the word has been changed to italics because quotation marks around a single word could be misinterpreted.

20   Page numbers (pp. 204–205) removed from original because the editor could not locate which edition Corrington used.

21   This passage in the book is mostly a monologue with some narrative passages that Corrington removed. Ellipses have been added where Corrington cut the narrator's voice. In brackets are the words that Corrington dropped that seem important to his point about how this character talks. In addition, "that" has been changed to "which").

lovers sounded like Romeo and Juliet in the England of 1598. And yet, in Coleridge's term, we willingly suspend our disbelief and find ourselves immensely pleased with the dialogue of Dickens: its fire, its whimsy, its pell-mell and lively richness please us in a way no amount of tedious realism can hope to. And we accord Dickens the esteem due a genius—as reward for not boring us with human conversation as it is.

Let us quote another writer generally accepted in the first rank. Tune your ear, and tell me if this is the sound of a man—any man—talking:

(quote Faulkner)[22]

I think we would agree that few—if any—people can talk at such unbroken length and in such contorted syntax. And yet it pleases. It pleases because it suits the fictional frame into which it is placed. Can you imagine the effect of writing Hemingway-style dialogue into *Swann's Way*? Or, to make the point this side absurdity, can you picture Melville's *Moby-Dick* written with dialogue on the pattern of that in Hawthorne's *Blithedale Romance*? This is not so much a question of social-class distinction or time distinction as you may think. I believe the reason Hemingway's mode of dialogue could not be adapted to Proust is that it would mar rather than sustain or further the illusion. It does not complement the narrative style; it opposes the overriding nostalgia and gentle romanticism of Proust. While Hawthorne's *Blithedale* style would be grotesque in *Moby-Dick*, it is not far removed from the style—arch and sentimental—of *Pierre's* opening pages. The question in each case is determined not by class or temporal or social setting or even by the sort of people involved. (After all, is not Hollingsworth a demi-Ahab,[23] a creature whose flawed judgment is dreadfully complemented by a voracious will?)

It seems to me that the problem of reality in dialogue—and in the writing of fiction generally—is essentially a bogus issue. If fiction is composed of the stuff of life, that stuff is radically altered by the consciousness of the artist who distills it into a narrative. Last year, during a discussion of James Joyce's fiction in London, a noted Joyce scholar said he felt I had not given proper place to the "intensely autobiographical" element in Joyce's writing. I replied that, so far as I could tell, the biographical aspect of Joyce's writing was usually grossly overstated. Professor David Daiches concurs in this judgment. Stephen Dedalus may *look* like the young Joyce, their backgrounds, educations, and family life may be similar point for point. But all the biographical information we possess indicates that James Joyce was no Dedalus, that the young protagonist of *Portrait*[24] and *Ulysses* was an artistic

---

22   It is not clear why Corrington did not include the quotation in the manuscript. Perhaps he summarized the quotation or had it memorized and did not need to reproduce the exact words.

23   A character in *Blithedale*.

24   A Portrait of the Artist as a Young Man.

construct, and that part of the art was to produce an illusion of similarity which took in two decades of critics. But Joyce was far too fine a writer to fall into the realism trap. Art is too important to be left with no resources beyond the real.

This attitude I am pressing for is by no means contemporary, much less original with me. Both Browning and Conrad, for example, felt called upon to break the bonds of realism in narrative in order to pursue their ends. Browning's brilliant dramatic monologue, "Mr. Sludge, 'the Medium,'" occupies, in my edition, some twenty double-columned pages, during which time Mr. Sludge is apparently being strangled by a dissatisfied client. Conrad, on one occasion, felt called upon to defend his astoundingly long-winded narrator, Marlow, when it was suggested by a stickler for realism that Marlow's narration of *Heart of Darkness* aloud would have required his auditors to sit listening for five hours or more. I have heard it said that Faulkner's characters do not talk like anyone ever spawned in Mississippi. For whatever it may be worth, all of those charges are based in fact. And they would be damning if fact was our concern. But it is only a long step from the creed of realism to Plato's total condemnation of imaginative writing; only half a step to Boileau and the French neoclassical critics who clamped the theory of the unities on seventeenth-century drama until it collapsed under the weight of their inane prescriptions.

Perhaps this is the place for a cautionary word. I am not suggesting that either dialogue or fiction at large be divorced from the real world as each of us experiences and understands it. But there is a difference between observing life, and, like a medical technician, taking a slice of it. Life merely transcribed is rarely either revelatory or interesting. On the other hand, what can we write revealing and moving except what takes as its matrix the forms, the manners, the occasions and the situations of life, of reality?

If I were to suggest a rule for the balance of reality and imagination in the writing of dialogue, I would simply refer you to the best literature in the Western world. A writer learns, not, as some writing teachers would have you believe, by writing, but by reading. I would guess that I have read a book—possibly two—for every page I have written, and I mean to keep that ratio in effect. Since I hope to write a lot more pages, I expect the reading will occupy half my time, at least.

In closing, let me point out that the contemporary novel, particularly that sub-genre we call the picaresque novel, has moved rapidly in recent years away from old-fashioned realism and toward a new conception of what constitutes reality. Beginning with that splendid picaro Gulley Jimson of *The Horse's Mouth*, right up to J. P. Donleavy's *A Singular Man*, the trend is to use what the story requires, and let the reader exercise his "willing suspension of disbelief" or not, as he will. Ultimately, even the most rigorously realistic novel can claim no more.

Part II

LITERATURE
LITERARY CRITICISM
THE HUMANITIES
ACADEMIA

A Poet's Credo

1961

This essay originally appeared in the journal *Midwest* in 1961. Corrington writes that over the course of the twentieth century, poetry gradually became less "intellectual," a view he purports to share with Norman Mailer. Corrington decries as "love drivel" much of the poetry from the sixteenth to the twentieth century but considers the end of the nineteenth and the beginning of the twentieth century to have been a renaissance for poetry that is now in decline, with the notable exception of the poetry of Bukowski, Ginsberg, and Ferlinghetti. Corrington writes against the mass proliferation of quarterly journals that, he says, has resulted in the publication of more and more bad poetry. Corrington expresses appreciation for poets like Auden, Eliot, and Pound but wishes there were more room in anthologies for writers like Bukowski, Ginsberg, and Ferlinghetti, who, he says, represent "the new vision, the new lightning that is shaking on the west coast and in New Orleans, in New York and along the tidewater." Corrington is not against modernist poets like Auden, Eliot, and Pound; rather, he is against those who continue to imitate or copy these figures. What Corrington prizes in poetry is originality, which he considers to be lacking in the industry of literary periodicals in no small part because the editors of such periodicals publish only poems that copy the poetry of an earlier age rather than staking out new territory. Corrington calls this essay a "credo," perhaps because of its incantatory rhythms in addition to its statement of his belief that lasting poetry is, paradoxically, that which seems new. This essay is remarkable for revealing Corrington's early affiliation with Beat writers. Early in his career Corrington was known as a poet and interested mostly in poetry. Later in life he began to retreat from poetry as he grew more interested in philosophy, specifically in the thinking of Eric Voegelin and Gnosticism.

Without anyone's having planned it or wished it, the course of poetry in the latter half of the twentieth century has veered—and continues to veer—away from the sphere of cerebral activities the Learned Journals call "intellectual."

One has the option of writing for *Partisan Review*, or writing seriously. One can try assiduously to get printed in *Kenyon, Hudson, Sewanee*, etc., or he can try to write himself into the hearts and minds of readers who may not yet even be born. As Norman Mailer put it, "the shits are killing us." Mailer's shits are neither evil nor necessarily, in any very general sense, stupid. They teach classes, they edit periodicals;

they play pundit and they fancy themselves cultivated and sensitive readers—the kind of readers we should be writing for. The shits are telling us to write for the Trilling *ménage*. They tell us we will be famous and beloved and maybe, though not necessarily, impressive contributors to the American Way of Life—at least tax-wise.

And while they lurk and smile, beat the prevailing winds with their bludgeon eyebrows, we know what they mean: they mean for us to sell, piecemeal or whole, whatever fragment of honest vision our biology and our public heritage may have left us. They mean to con us into doing to ourselves what they find they cannot do to us: they want us to assume a shape.

It seems to me that, as some editor put it, "there is too much competent verse being written." I should know. I have written my share. It is the kind of verse that sees craftsmanship as an end, that imagines the difference between Trollope and Shakespeare, Costain[1] and Mailer to be one of degree rather than of kind. It is the kind of verse that clutters the pages of very nearly every academic quarterly in the country and that gluts every new anthology of "modern" poetry.

I believe one does not have to make Ginsberg an icon to prefer him to W. S. Merwin. I believe one does not have to claim Lawrence Ferlinghetti is the *only* poet writing today to see that he is alive and inventing and still has the kind of blood that circulates, and that Yvor Winters is as dead as the hell of our great-grandfathers.

What we owe to the dead is obvious: they pulled the carpet of phony sentiment from under us (though the century's very nature would have probably done the job as well); they taught us compaction and the value of a lean understated line that sounds like a brass gong. They taught us how impossibly wide the subject-matter of poetry really is compared to the endless love-drivel of English verse from the sixteenth century till 1900. For these things, we honor them.

But I wish someone would shovel the corpses out of the quarterlies so that there would be room for Bukowski and Corso, Ginsberg and Creeley, for Patchen and Ferlinghetti. I wish they would say: W. H. Auden, thank you. Here is the Nobel Prize (we will ignore the senility of your last book), now will you please get out of the way before the fresh air kills you. Then they could say: how pleasant to meet Mr. Eliot—on his way out.

I want courtesy here. I want Auden and Eliot and Pound and the rest of them to get the same shake Chaucer or Milton get. I want to see them in anthologies so that, like pictures of the old home town, like a US flag with forty-eight stars, we can leaf through them and enjoy our own past. But I want them to make room for the new vision, the new lightning that is shaking on the west coast and in New Orleans, in New York and along the tidewater.

But there is an end to courtesy. I do not care what method is used to clear the journals of Auden's apes and Eliot's pirates. I do not care whether the counterfeiters

1   Thomas B. Costain.

or the journals who publish them survive. I do not, deep down, care whether The Yale Younger Poets prints once more that same book they've been printing since 1948 or not. Great men, dated or not, deserve a salute in passing; the yahoos in their shadow are not worth a salute or a fulmination.

Most of us have taken the same course: they have given us English and history and philosophy, and when we have seen the implications of all or any of them, we have run, beat a retreat. Some of us have made it out still smiling: Ferlinghetti has. Some of us have been pinched: Ginsberg was. Some of us never even made the trip and may be the healthier for it; I think Corso fits here.

So now the battle lines are shaking themselves into recognizable shape: we can play the sewaneeeatlantickenyonhudsonpartisan[2] game, or we can play for keepsies and hold onto our nuts. We can rewrite Eliot's *Collected Poems*—for the seventh or eighth time—[3]or we can deny intellection, find the sensation that catches and growls, fix frenzies in their flights, as Rimbaud did. We can lie down in well-bred darkness gnawing on our own thesauruses, sending carbons[4] of the same poem to the force-feed journals, and pick up our juicy checks while they print the same carbon over and over in every issue—with a different title and a different author's name affixed—or we can accept the risks implied in being the first one to explore, to make our way across the watershed that separates all other poetry from the kind of thing Mallarmé was doing half a century ago, the kind of thing Rimbaud pioneered—the kind of thing that we are beginning to understand and exploit now in poems like Ferlinghetti's "And the Arabs asked terrible questions." For my part, I'll be satisfied when a poem of that caliber, by anyone, known now or still stewing toward the point of boiling over into print, appears in an American magazine with more than a handful of subscribers.

I expect to remain dissatisfied for quite a while.

---

2   Corrington's playful adjective appears this way in the original.

3   There is just one "em dash" in the typed essay, but the syntax appears to require a second one after "eighth time"; therefore, the editor added the second "em dash."

4   Carbon copy.

Intuition-Intellect

Approx. 1971

This chapter consists of Corrington's unpublished notes and sections of his unpublished lectures from the early 1970s that he maintained in one document. It demonstrates the shift in Corrington's interests in poetry as a craft to more philosophical concerns that were influenced by poetry or mythopoetics. His discussion of myth and his references to Eric Voegelin in these notes suggest that he had just begun to read Voegelin and to explore Gnosticism and myth criticism. Corrington questions the relationship between science and philosophy and hypothesizes about how the truths generated by science become mythologized to satisfy certain human desires. He proposes that science itself has a "mythic" character and claims that "the aftermath of every significant act of science is its mythologization." Corrington speculates whether myth is inevitable because it fulfills something basic or instinctive in human nature. Science amasses data for their predictive value, but asking what these data mean is the beginning of myth, which, properly understood, is another form of understanding and articulating truths about the world. However, myth can also, Corrington claims, have destructive implications at odds with truth. He warns about mismanaging myth, giving such examples as Nazism, Marxism, and free enterprise: ideological constructs that rely on abstract myth narratives to stamp out opposition. Corrington critiques the scientism that has developed since the Enlightenment because he considers its emphasis on empiricism and rationalism to mask its role in formulating mythic patterns or archetypes for governing the phenomenal world, including the human social order. These patterns or archetypes, despite their mythic nature, are taken as authoritative and valid because they are conflated with or understood as scientific truth; in this manner they are assumed to be separate and apart from myth when, in fact, they constitute myth. They are dangerous because they are presumed to be scientific truth subject to certain and definite application when they represent mythopoetic urges to satisfy innate and instinctual human impulses.

Corrington transitions from this discussion of myth and science into a discussion of twentieth-century poetry and its "overintellectualization," as evidenced by the implementation of supposedly scientific approaches to the study of poetry. Corrington considers the New Criticism to represent such a scientific approach to poetry. The turn to reason and science, Corrington suggests, has destroyed the aesthetics of poetry just as it has destroyed human civilizations in the sociopolitical context. In both contexts there has been, he believes, a failure to realize the distinction between science and the mythologization of science, a failure that has led certain groups to mistake what is unreasonable and irrational for absolute reason and rationality, to believe, that is, that what is merely a pattern or archetype—a human construct—is something given and definite even apart from human knowledge of it. Those who fail to understand the distinction between science and the mythologization of science embrace a potentially destructive psychic system that mistakes science for its opposite. This essay shows that, as Corrington begins to transition away from the writing of poetry, he is also trying to integrate his interest in poetry with his growing interest in philosophy.

The date of the material in this chapter is unknown; however, certain references suggest that Corrington wrote these notes in or around 1971. For example, he mentions a "new" album by the Rolling Stones, *Sticky Fingers*, which came out in 1971. It is possible that part of this material comes from a lecture that Corrington gave to the South-Central Modern Language Association in 1968. That lecture was titled "Cassirer's Curse, Keats's Urn, and the Poem Before the Poem." Some of the material may have come from the National Science Foundation Lecture that Corrington titled "Science and the Humanities" and delivered at Louisiana State University in 1966. Corrington began the essay with four discursive notes under the heading "Statements and Questions." Because the ideas in these notes are more fully developed in the text proper, I have moved them to the end of the essay.

Notes on the Mythic Character of Science.

Presuppositions of science include the prime value of knowledge and control of the phenomenological world; the absolute value of systematic and objective observation of phenomena; the capacity of mathematics to encompass all *real* occasions; the separateness and primacy of human intelligence as an instrument for probing and systematizing the real world. Science and observer are presumed not to interact.

This whole complex of ideas, their interlinkings and their implications are of very late origin, and possibly quite flimsy in a psychological sense. The power of scientific thought has always been proportionate to its ability to *deliver*, to predict, to repeat, to cure, to innovate through technology certain aspects of human life.

Satisfaction: science satisfies the mind—frequently at the cost of disturbing the emotions; myth satisfies the emotions—without reference, usually, to the mind. Voegelin suggests that the birth of critical intelligence (he uses Hesiod) is linked almost inextricably with the critique of myth. The first act of philosophy is not to construct either a system or a part-system, but to analyze current mythos and find it wanting.

Cassirer says myth is "not *what* we know, but *how* we know." Knowledge here cannot be construed, obviously, as simply intellectual information. It must be understood as covering the entire range of human cognition, emotional as well as intellectual.

If this is so, then the aftermath of every significant act of science is its mythologization. Is not the "mythologizing" of science really no more than either sensitive or stupid speculation upon the *meaning* of the scientific act, or emotional projection as to what the scientific act presages? Is it possible for anyone, sensitive or stupid, to encounter the proved results of a major scientific act without such speculation or projections? Is the very thing you find fault with in Schroedinger's[5]

---

5   Schrödinger is the more common spelling.

"God's own quantum system" the fact that he is both scientist ascertaining and man responding? Is his response *qua* man either less or more relevant than, say, the raft of *intelligent* responses made to Newton's world-view in the early eighteenth century?

Ideally, the scientist discovers, edits, theorizes his data and then sends it forth. There his function *qua* scientist stops. It has become virtually a matter of manners and of social decorum for him to then stand mute and let others do the mythologizing which is, in any case, inevitable, given that his work is of great importance. If he chooses to go beyond his work, to suggest what he (as man) feels it may mean in human terms, he risks his scientific standing and his reputation. Thus his role as scientist restricts his role as human being. Human beings speculate, often precipitately and foolishly, sometimes brilliantly. But they *do* speculate—and thus mythologize. The process is simply inexorable. Now is it best that the scientist deny himself the right to so speculate on his work (even to the extent of suggesting a transcendent meaning behind or in it) as a priest denies himself marriage? Or might it not be better if the scientist joins himself in the role of speculative philosopher and at least have his own opportunity to take part in the intricate process of establishing the world-view which must inevitably arise from his work?

Is it really a good idea that "division of labor" be carried quite so far in the intellectual world? Obviously a research scientist cannot now be also a philosopher (fully), a politician, a soldier, a priest, a poet, etc., etc. But *ideally* that is precisely what the increasingly complex human society—the world-society—calls for.

If myth is inevitable, it is becoming necessary for us to manage to control to some degree the nature and the vectors of myth. If we find ourselves in a position to control the biological nature and progress of mankind, we must, if there is to be any meaningful future for man, put ourselves in a position to control in some measure his psychic growth as well.

How much human misery is caused by what we might call "mismanaged myth"? Nazism is only a gross example. How about Marxism—or, for that matter, "free enterprise"? Once canonized, these peculiar approaches to life-style and to national destinies become myths beyond the effectual critique of either philosophy, poetry—or social science. Each form of mythos manages more or less to fulfill certain human needs. In this sense, there is an almost Darwinian characteristic to myth: those which most successfully and fully answer the widest range of human needs in a given timespan either crush or devalue their opponents.

One could study the progress of Marxism in this sense. It was Marx's speculation that the most fully industrialized countries would first make socialist revolutions and that certain more backward nations (Russia among them) would simply have to pass through the bourgeoisie phase before they could be ready for the socialist— and later the communist—phase. Now this has proved almost exactly wrong: it has *not* been the highly industrialized states which succumbed to the Marxist myth, but those most backward. This is partly explained by the fact that Marx presumed a certain course for capitalism, an almost static downward trend for the life of the proletariat, which has proven inaccurate. His other error was that he was too much of an esthete: he presumed that large human affairs would work out in an elegant fashion. They do not. One may well move from tribalism to socialism. The path does not inevitably lead through feudalism, nationalism, capitalism, etc. Or at least there is no substantial data to show this—unless one assumes that all such phases can be condensed and even run simultaneously.

Now the myth-structure of science is quite other from Marxism. It is not, essentially, speculative. It is not, as with Marx, a complex art form. The data of the Newtonian system is constant and time independent. It is probably for that reason that one's attention should be focused on the scientific myth forms. The only drift or alternation here is the question of how each generation interprets the identical data. Even there, the drift is minimal. The liberal of today is not so much different from the rationalist of the eighteenth century; the behaviorist is obviously a child of the logical positivist, and the parentage is not in doubt.

* * *6

Consider, if you will, that a work of fiction or poetry is essentially a theoretical construct of life—an analogue for that being in which we find ourselves, yet for which, as actually *experienced*, we can only construct metaphorical approximations. A person or a novel is as much a symbolic form as is the Schroedinger equation, or the mathematical description of a standing wave. It is a verbal construct, an organic mechanism which transfers one entity's knowing to another entity—from writer to reader.

Perhaps, as much human observation has suggested, there is a kind of exchange particle which mediates between the emotions of one human being and another across vast time and space—art in general—is the category of such particles.7

No aspect of the present human situation seems to me as crucial as that of morale. Nations and the women and men whose faith and commitment make up nations depend upon morale. Morale is the *tone* of a civilization when it is fit and willing and anxious to act within history. Its constituents are numerous: personal and public beliefs and intentions; personal and public self-control and restraint; personal and public valuations and judgments.

To the degree that those factors are totally internalized, the society in question suffers from the Imperial illness. Spiritual gangrene results from private and public

---

6   Archive document ends at this point and picks up with the text following the break.

7   Corrington has edited the end of this sentence. He marked out "and literature." The manuscript reads: "—and literature—art in general—is the category of such particles."

introspection and selfishness. Total externalization of such factors precipitates society into the totalitarian illness. Men bow to forces beyond their control, and become themselves instruments of those external forces. I do not suggest that those illnesses are mutually exclusive, or that there are no others. I *do* suggest that both deteriorate the spiritual capacities of individuals and the moral content of the society composed of the congeries of such individuals.

Now science as a generalized mode of human knowledge has a most interesting history, and is a prodigious child of the Enlightenment. It is the child of reason, gotten on empiricism, and its monolithic appearance, as we all know, is illusory. Its giants have been guided as much by creative as by analytical genius, and if it can make broad statistical claims to be foreknowledge, it remains balked by the unique—but possible—event. It bows before its own inability to reduce contingency to zero, but maintains that its insights will rule in a majority of cases.

One must differentiate most carefully between the rational and the empirical elements in modern science—between the mathematical and the experimental. If scientific method has been enthroned as the Decalogue of science, and so put forth to modern man as a carefully tested and derived empirical and hard-headed structure, those who *know* science realize that in numerous cases, scientific method has done no more than underwrite the prior creations of pure reason. I think, of course, of Einstein's relativity and Dirac's postulation of the positron.

Now there is an inherent cleavage between reason and empiricism, and their alliance within science has necessarily to be an uneasy one. For each mode of viewing phenomena has inherent in it certain preconceptions and certain evaluative mechanisms. Let us examine some of those.

What are the presuppositions of reason?

1. That the human mind, unaided, is capable of real knowledge—probably definitive knowledge—and that such knowledge either is, or at least is analogous to, reality. (quote Dirac)[8]

2. That any form of knowledge not reducible to rational statements—preferably mathematical statements—is not *real* knowledge, but simply opinion or emotion or some similar species of hallucination.

3. That propositional logic can derive the objective conditions of reality by use of its own internal mechanisms, providing only that the initial sensory observations are accurate. Reason, thus, renders more data *real*—or perhaps dispenses with it altogether if it does not serve the patterns dictated by reason.

This basic tendency is probably a gross oversimplification of Plato as misrepresented by Descartes. It effectively denies reality as an independent

---

8   This is a note from Corrington to himself.

entity, and absolutely minimizes the necessity for data-input as crucial to accurate description of reality. Given Descartes's formula *"cogito, ergo sum"* with all its ramifications, one arrives, logically, at a position not far from Dirac's. *Elegance*, understood as an almost mystical proportionality and propriety among relationships, becomes the hallmark of authentic reality. Impropriety, imbalance, lack of symmetry is the warning-sign of a rational world-picture gone wrong. From Newton's mechanistic cosmos to Bach's fugues and Haydn's *Water Music*, one sees the power of this particular mode of thought. It is a force of almost overwhelming seductiveness, since its determination to render the universe in the image of the enlightened, perhaps super-ego-related, primordial pattern appeals to a certain basic aspect of human cognition. The essence of rationalism is at last to forge a pattern of order upon phenomenological reality, and to respond to reality in terms of that pattern. The temptation offered the rationalist is to actually believe that his formulation has broken through the bounds of image and picture and metaphor expressing phenomena,[9] to the embodiment of numinal—ultimate—reality itself.

* * *10

Empiricism, on the other hand, is less dramatic. As the novel is to poetry, so empiricism is to rationalism. Its basic preconceptions seem to be these:

1. Accurate observation and experiment with painstakingly built instruments and careful use of control-subjects will yield, at last, an authentic insight into the nature of physical phenomena.

2. While such testing and experiment obviously require intelligence, reason's claims must not be exaggerated. Data is the warden of theory, and theory extended beyond or in a direction opposed to empirical determination is unscientific and fruitless.

3. There is no necessary correlation between accurate and precise data gathering and evaluation and any particular pattern or predetermined vision of phenomenological order. Data, in a sense, speaks for itself. Reason is no more than its card-sorter and high-speed printer.

Empiricism might be called, in a sense, the Dionysian alternative to Apollonian reason. It is sensuous, time-and-space bound, comparatively hard-headed, rigorously mechanistic, and, in a sense, humble. It presumes, in the phrase of Flip Wilson, that "what you see is what you get." It sees both the cosmos and man's capacity to know

---

9   As appears in the original. Corrington may have meant the following:
    Image- and picture- and metaphor-expressing phenomena.
Or he may have simply meant this construction:
    metaphor-expressing phenomena.

10   Archive document ends at this point and picks up with the text following the break.

that cosmos as finite and limited in terms of what is tangible, provable in material terms, and endlessly repeatable within laboratory circumstances. The essence of empiricism is the belief that reality is *quantifiable*, and that what cannot be reduced to an experimental procedure—indeed, in extreme cases, what has not actually been derived by such procedures—has no real existence, and falls properly into the field of abnormal psychology or mysticism. The temptation peculiar to empiricism is to conceive of the universe as *object* exclusively, rather than as process as well.

You will note that both rationalism and empiricism, while far apart as to each other, would join forces to deny the validity of any statement regarding reality which is based upon intuition, spiritual insight, myth, and so on.

Now at one level, of course, this is not true. Does not psychology deal with such forms of human conceptualization? Is not modern thought in large measure shaped by the work of Freud, Jung, Adler, and more recently Rollo May, Erik Erikson, and similar distinguished figures in psychology? Yes, it is. But on the one hand, psychology is not yet—and theoretically may never be—comparable to the exact sciences. Thus its claims are accepted with considerable qualification by many. On the other hand, psychology—like all social science—yearns to be recognized as a sister discipline to physics and chemistry, and thus, treats intuition or spiritual attitudes with little more sympathy than would chemistry. Psychology claims such phenomena for its own—and then tends to either reduce them to describable pathological states— neuroses, psychoses, and so on—or to stand as essentially hostile to them.

The tendency of modern science is to absorb all [. . .][11]

* * *[12]

This question of intuition or intellection is difficult to establish in "scientific" or even "scholarly" terms because, of course, both "science" and "scholarship" are instrumental constructs of the intellect—and, as in the Heisenberg effect, the examination of non-rational structure using a rational instrument yields either static, non-conclusive observations, and/or what appear to be—and, in intellectual terms, are—non-sequiturs. In other words, I can neither verify nor negate an intuitional structure authentically in intellectual terms. To claim an adequate exposition for an intuitional structure by use of intellect is, invariably, to suggest that a clever and exhaustive paraphrase of "Altarwise by owl-light"[13] is essentially to

---

11   Corrington appears to start a new paragraph here but does not complete the sentence; on the next page he moves on to a new topic.

12   Archive document ends at this point and picks up with the text following the break.

13   Poem by Dylan Thomas. The first 6 lines of the poem read:

    Altarwise by owl-light in the half-way house
    The gentleman lay graveward with his furies;
    Abaddon in the hang-nail cracked from Adam,

be co-valued with the poem itself—or to be preferred—since the paraphrase would presumably do away with much of the poem's "confusion" and "incoherence."

Few if any critics would allow such a gaucherie to pass unchallenged, and yet the very act of criticism—at any level—is essentially a first step toward such gaucherie. To comment on a poem via intellectual observation—even in the elucidation of a passage with footnotes as to historical or personal data—is to begin an invasion which, logically, ends with a gradual substitution of critical thought for intuitive poetry. Moreover, like it or not, every intellectual process of whatever kind is inexorably governed by logic in the long run. Criticism, well-directed, may hold its hand, pull back from the tendency to radical substitution of intellectual construct for intuitional artifact—but the drive of criticism is ultimately toward reduction of feeling to understanding, and, in the long run of which I speak, intellectual *coitus interruptus* is as painful as its physical and emotional counterpart.

Now the intuitional artifact—poetry, music, myth, whatever—is radically indefensible. How can the intuitional defend—or be defended, for that matter—against the intellectual? The success of Rationalism and Positivism is rooted in the fact that once a question is permitted regarding an intuitional artifact, no answer can be given but in rational terms. Thus Rationalism, like its model, mathematics, is a closed system. It plays, for better or worse, the onanistic game of answering its own questions. The beauty of such a system is that all the questions are brilliant, all the answers ultimately satisfactory. The ugliness of the system resides in the fact that frequently its brilliant questions regarding intuitional artifacts are not to the point, and the satisfactory answers utterly fail to join issue with the real problems—or mysteries—of the intuition. But in any case, a poem, a piece of music, a religious emotion, a feeling of romantic or filial love, a happiness or a misery—all are both beyond any meaningful intellectual analysis, and yet totally subject to the devastation of such analysis, should it be turned upon them.

One might observe that, with a friend like criticism, poetry or fiction needs no enemies. Even the best intentioned criticism tends to maul the integrity of the poem—and less well-intentioned analysis is quite capable of degenerating an intuitional experience into an unconscious economic exercise or a masked political polemic.

Worse, of course, in our own time has been the powerful tendency of criticism to dictate virtually the sort of poetry that would be written. The New Criticism, with its vast emphasis on irony, compression, tension, allusion, elliptical structures, tended, because of its powerful influence not only in academic circles but among young poets and would-be poets, to establish those *intellectual* values to the detriment

---

And, from his fork, a dog among the fairies,
The atlas-eater with a jaw for news,
Bit out the mandrake with to-morrows scream.

Excerpt from *Dylan Thomas: Selected Poems, 1934-1952* (New Directions Books, 2003), p. 76.

of intuitive values in American writing in the 1940s and early 50s. This, of course, became even an issue of literary politics, since the major literary journals, from *The Kenyon* and *Sewanee Reviews* to the *Partisan* and *Hudson Reviews* soon fell into the hands of the New Critics or those who tended, at one level or another, to support New Critical values. There a poet like Dylan Thomas tended to be underrated largely till the last half-decade of his life—while Wallace Stevens received perhaps an inordinate recognition from these journals and from critics committed to the New Criticism's values. Of course, this school of "academic poetry" was badly damaged by the Beat movement of the 50s, and though still holding to the academy and gaining literary prizes awarded by elderly scholars nostalgic for what are now the old values of the New Criticism, has been essentially displaced in influence by poets like Ginsberg and Ferlinghetti at one end, and James Dickey or Theodore Roethke at the other end of the spectrum.

One notes a certain similarity in the course of rock music over the past twenty years. Rock moves from the relatively unselfconsciousness of "Sixty-Minute Man" and "Sweet Little Sixteen," to the sophistication of *Sergeant Pepper's Lonely Hearts Club Band*, and then most recently toward the kind of retrospective represented by Bob Dylan's *Nashville Skyline* or *John Wesley Harding* albums. Of course, such apparent "return to the roots," repudiating over-intellectualization and abstraction, is always somewhat fraudulent. Neither an individual, a cultural artifact, nor a society can "go back." However Ginsberg may try to evoke Whitman, he remains a child of the twentieth century, Columbia educated, and versed in the advanced intellectualism of his age and milieu.[14] No matter how hard Bob Dylan attempts to find once more that feeling he had as a spiritual son of Woody Guthrie, he remains the artist who created *Highway 61*, that sardonic critique of modern mobile life, and *Desolation Row*, with its direct references to Eliot and Pound, both of whom could be said to have influenced it.

The point is that the movement from intuitional to intellectual knowledge seems to be a one-way street. What we don't know intellectually, we can presumably learn; what we feel can often—perhaps always—be rendered in some approximation as intellectual knowledge. But we cannot *unlearn, unknow* what we *know*. We cannot reverse the film, or the trend of entropy in which our feelings are reduced to ideas.

Thus, conscious romanticism like[15] that phenomenon which Spengler calls "the second religiousness"—or, I suspect, the current American fad toward super-patriotism—is not only fraudulent in intuitive terms, but is probably chiefly a kind of desperate attempt to hold at bay the increasing velocity of intellection and abstraction as they eat away at the intuitive roots of human experience.

Perhaps as students of the Humanities—not to even consider the application of these ideas to science, religion, philosophy, the social sciences, and other arts—we

---

14   Archive document ends at this point and picks up on the following page with the words "No matter."
15   "Em dash" deleted between "romanticism" and "like."

should be prepared to consider a most radical possibility: that the desire to *know*, to feed the intellect, is at last like any other appetite, and that as individuals or a society can be intellectually starved (so we say of the Black community, for example), so can they be glutted—and at last satiated, jaded, rendered either dull, brutalized, or effete by the endless digestion of all experience in terms of intellect. If the intellect feeds upon experience which is properly intuitive, will not the intuitive faculty starve and at last lose its power to function in terms of creative projection or creative response? And if such a situation goes on long enough, does not the human person, an amalgam of body, intuition, and intellect, finally lose one of his prime functions?

I would argue for our consideration of those possibilities, and for considering the further notion that intellectual self-restraint, prudence, and judiciousness need cultivating as surely as we require physical and emotional control. Aristotle pointed out that it was absurd to demand of a given discipline more exactitude, more precision, than the subject matter of the discipline allowed. By this rule, no one may reasonably expect the historian to rival the physicist in his specification of symbolic reality. As a matter of fact, those historians who have attempted the "scientizing" of the past have rarely managed to hold their own in general esteem with those who, less rigorous, make use of creative intuition in the evocation of the past.

Now this principle of Aristotle's may serve as guide in our present considerations. Is it possible that the tools of intellect not only are not suitable for handling and responding to a large range of human experience, but may actually be either misleading or actually destructive if used to handle experience which is properly within the realm of the intuitive?

Some illustrations: who are we to believe in the matter of a proper approach to Christian revelation? The Schoolmen, led by that supreme rationalist St. Thomas Aquinas, or the ancient church father Tertullian, who said of Christ's Godhood, "I believe it because it is absurd"? Is it possible that Tertullian's remark, echoing beforehand the thought and the ideas of Albert Camus, was wiser than the whole of Scholasticism, and that the decay of Christianity at the theoretical level was actually caused by the intervention of intellection into an area where its influence could only be debilitating?

Consider again the difference between the brilliant criticism of T. S. Eliot and Gregory Corso's definition of poetry as, "Fried shoes, I want fried shoes."

At last, is it of any particular significance that the Beatles, who drove farther and farther into musical experimentation with *Sergeant Pepper's Lonely Hearts Club Band*, *Magical Mystery Tour*, and the 1968 *White Album* are now disbanded—while their contemporaries the Rolling Stones, who have remained quite close to their Rhythm and Blues beginnings—even in their new album *Sticky Fingers*—are alive and doing well?[16]

---

16   *Sticky Fingers* was released in 1971.

Obviously, numerous intangible matters are involved with each of these illustrations, and no conclusions can possibly be drawn from them. Yet the questions are worth considering. Is it possible that there is—and has always been—a kind of subterranean intuitional history of man, counterpoised to that surface history which, by and large, shows the ongoing triumph of intellect and intellectual ends through the ages? In that history so well known to common wisdom, it is astronomy which is "valuable," not astrology; chemistry, not alchemy; Greek philosophy, not Egyptian magic—and science, not poetry.

Now it is time for a caveat. I do not argue for anti-intellectualism. Stupidity is not a remedy for too much abstraction. I am hardly unaware that the analysis I am presently making owes much to intellectual categories and constructs provided me by the past.[17]

Nor do I advocate censorship, burning of books, or an end to scholarship. I *do* suggest that intellectualism, in which we are all involved, owes itself and the humane values most of us presumably espouse a certain hesitation, a moment of silence in which we consider the course of past civilizations and past intellectual orders. I think that, specifically, criticism and its practitioners might pause and think once more about the nature of literature, its meaning, its functions—and determine honestly whether the current mode of setting literature before young audiences is calculated to make them rich in those intangible values we proclaim for it—or is simply a new impoverishment of their intuitive and emotional lives as we lay down the canons of scientific interpretation.

To be frank, I am not so much concerned with poetry or with the teaching of it. Though that has been and is yet a large part of my life, it remains only a portion of that larger mosaic of twentieth-century human experience in which all of us—and our students—are inextricably involved. No ground swell of literary concern for the emotional and intuitive values I speak of is going, in and of itself, to change the essential nature of this culture-wide phenomenon. At the same time, perhaps intellectual recognition of intellectual excess, wherever it begins, can be helpful and of some lasting use in a society which seems frequently bent upon reducing the bulk of its experiences to data fit for computer cards.

I think it is perhaps the most important part of our task as humanities teachers to simultaneously acknowledge the uses of science, intellection, and techniques produced by each, and yet to affirm solidly and without apology values which stand outside and independent not only of scientific method but of rationalist intellection as well. The *values* of literature are not finally susceptible to reduction or to ultimate elucidation by rationalist techniques—even those currently used by literary criticism and standing within the presumably generally accepted structures of organized scholarship. The ultimate values of literature—and, I believe, of mankind—remain,

17   Archive document ends at this point and picks up on the following page with the next paragraph that begins "Nor do I."

as they always have, intuitive. If they are transmitted by language, they are virtually transcendent to it. The values are rendered by language—they are not language values. They are, in a fundamental way, not discussable, and remain so despite every effort of criticism to somehow pry them loose from their linguistic matrix by the use of more and alternative words. Criticism may be considered, within this context, as a kind of anti-art—an alternative to art—or even an antidote to it.

This point will, of course, be argued. Nonetheless, elucidation of a work of art, modification of a basic form, amounts to a form of correction. To "explain" a communication is, inescapably, to say that it is not consistent, not fully communicative in itself. This is, largely, not a judgment that is rationally determinable—certainly not on a work of art. Consider the history of criticism and taste, for example, in regard to Keats's "Ode on a Grecian Urn." The ending is "flawed," does not "fit" the rest, etc. The small anthology of criticism "The Well-Read Urn" is enough to convince a careful reader that the vagaries of criticism are at least such as to put into serious question the whole intellectual process as it relates to a work of art.[18]

Still again, I am not setting myself against the act of criticism any more than I am attempting to recruit you for an anti-intellectual campaign. Rather I am trying to stress a point of view toward art—and toward the most basic of human experience: that of the intuition.[19]

Personally, I feel that it is past time to repudiate the fierce and dishonest pretensions of the Age of Reason, of scientism, and analysis. "The life of Reason" never existed, and when it most clearly showed itself, it was most frequently monstrous. Think of Robespierre, robed in white, blood-mad as the guillotine blade, prancing in pseudo-religious zeal before a bare altar dedicated to the goddess of Reason. Consider the unassailable Darwinian reason of Hitler's racial programs, the contemporary moral idiocy of East and West, each prepared to annihilate billions of human beings in the name of abstract ideas. What of the indisputable logic of Stalin's Terror, which cost some twenty million Russian lives?

Reason is no more than one of the soul's functions. It must work in tandem with the intuitions in order to function properly, in order to avoid that logical slide into madness and criminality which results whenever one of the soul's aspects breaks with the others and demands absolute control of the psyche.

Today, we are on the edge of what is called a "biological revolution" and biological scientists in every country are trying to determine how they may put the best public relations face on the fact that they intend to make a general practice of experimental research on human fetuses—in the name of science, reason, progress, and all the other "big words that hurt us so much," as James Joyce said. It

---

18   Harvey T. Lyon's *Keats' Well-Read Urn: An Introduction to Literary Method* (New York: Holt, 1958).

19   Archive document ends at this point and picks up with the following paragraph that begins with the word "Personally."

has occurred to me in recent months that perhaps Adolph Hitler's only error was in being born fifty years too soon. Many of his policies, refurbished and restated, are abroad today—and finding a more sympathetic audience than in the 1930s. I had always imagined Nazism a hideous bit of atavism. Now I begin to wonder if it was not, as George Orwell suspected, a hint of all our tomorrows. "War is peace," Orwell's *1984* tells us—which sounds much like the words of that American officer in Viet Nam[20] who observed, most reasonably, "We had to destroy the village in order to save it." But given the premises of Big Brother or the American power structure, both statements are unequivocally reasonable. *Because Reason itself is without premises. It is a system, not a valuator,* and when it attempts to establish values without reference to the intuitions—or, as in the case of Comte's logical positivism, a "value free" rationale—the result is an anarchy in which intuitional values—like love and honor and beauty and restraint—are swallowed up, and the reason itself destroyed in the ensuing chaos.

In Spengler's configuration, "The city is intellect. The Megalopolis is 'free' intellect. . . It upsets thrones and limits old rights in the name of reason."[21]

The fullness of abstraction, hypostatized in mechanism—perfected in the computer—is a kind of final state in the passing from intuition to intellectual life. It is in the great cities that men are homogenized, and in which their various values are concretized into that dominant intellectual abstraction: money. In these terms, money is not the root of evil at all: it is its blossom. When money-values dominate all others, one is simply made aware that the reduction of intuitional values has been virtually completed. In a very real sense, one who chooses to make war rather than love is not quite so desperately ill of abstraction as is the one who chooses money over love. The drive toward war has about it at least the dignity of basic human aggressive intention.

The final stage of draining intuitions away into impersonal abstractions is the breakdown of the abstract complex itself. Because, at last, the constructions of Reason and scientism, under conditions of stress, are as subject to collapse as are those of intuition. Suppose no one *cares* any longer about the presumed clarity, predictability and repeatability of scientific or pseudo-scientific formulations? Suppose those people—who have been reduced by abstraction to mere masses—no longer believe in the implied security and ongoing order of "the life of reason"? Suppose the dry stretches of abstraction have produced in a growing number of people an immense thirst for the *un*reasonable—or, more properly, the *non-reasonable*?

The result on, say, the relatively controlled level of art will be something like the phenomenon of the Beat Generation in poetry, Rock and Roll in music—

---

20   Vietnam.

21   Oswald Spengler, *The Decline of the West*, vol. 2, translated by Charles Francis Atkinson (London: George Allen & Unwin, 1928), 96.

both attempts to reestablish the balance between intellect and intuition, far more successful in music than in literature since music has not got that inescapably intellectual cognitive element which always threatens to drive written art into Cyril Tourneur's *The Transformed Metamorphosis*, Joyce's *Finnegans Wake*, or Robbe-Grillet's *The Voyeur*.

On a larger scale, this breaking out of an abstract order, as it begins to lose its grip on human imagination and needs, is likely to result in the kind of irrationality, a social upheaval,[22] we have seen growing over the past decade. Abstract rational orders and institutions no longer claim the faith of many people—especially the young, the poor, the Black, and the intellectuals themselves.

But pseudo-primitive poetry and music, like pseudo-primitive conduct, is not going to renew desiccated intuitions, although it may very well level the abstract structures which, while responsible in some measure for the devastation, are now nonetheless the *only* structures available within which any kind of ordered human life is currently possible. This is not, despite appearances, the slightest guarantee of the structures being able to maintain the status quo with impunity. That sort of response is more rationalism. Societal suicide is not only a possibility—it has excellent historical precedents.

Yet it is not inevitable. Only that bastard child of misunderstood Newtonian and Darwinian thought which we call behaviorism considers history-as-cycle an unbreakable order.

Statements and Questions:

1. If the facts of science are immutable, and the human mind is a biological computer, how is it that various human minds or minds of different periods can draw such varied inferences from the same scientific construct? Ruling out the differences caused by variant "programming" of minds by both genetic heritage and by acculturation, is it possible that the mythic speculations coming forth from scientific systems like Newton's actually *minimize* the scope of variation? Is it possible that common understanding of the implications of Newton's or Darwin's work is collectively less divergent than, say, understanding of the work of Shelley or Keats? Or Tillich or Barth?

2. Cassirer[23] maintains that every piece of human cognitive data is, *de facto*, a *mythologeme*—that is, part of a larger collective intellectual-emotional construct which is separated out by the intelligence only in an artificial way and for limited purposes. There is a similarity here with the text* sub-text[24]

---

22   Original document ends the page at this point and picks up on the following page with the word "we."

23   Ernst Cassirer.

24   Subtext.

notion.[25] A man may well intellectually agree that the life of his child is not as important as the life of one million people. When he acts, it is likely he will act for his son. Intellectual concurrence and emotional commitment are not unified. Science requires only intellectual concurrence; the question of emotional commitment remains free and indeterminate at this point. Thus the totality of human personality remains unfulfilled by "scientific truth," no matter how certain or how elegant. There is, finally, an emotional elegance as well as an intellectual one; the former is satisfied by myth, the latter by science or mathematics.

3. If all this is essentially so, then is it not inevitable that the more elaborate systems set up by science will be mythologized? That they *must* be in order to have any reality at the emotional level to most people—even scientists? Is it fair to say that only those objects of knowledge which admit of mythologizing can elicit serious response from human beings? Low-temperature physics, though studded by such marvels as superconductors, or quantum science, more astonishing than relativity actually, have not been "picked up" by even the most "intellectual" segments of the population. Because they do not admit of elegant mythologizing, as did Darwin and Newton, as does Einstein?

4. Each mythologized scientific concept must satisfy a pre-existent mythic appetite. A scientific concept in and of itself, as a function of natural order per se, divorced or set aside from human "archetypal" needs, is essentially meaningless in terms of total human personality. Only those which trigger human subconscious appetites assume the stature of myth, and thus become [. . .][26]

---

25 The asterisk appears in the original. Either a footnote is missing in the original text, or Corrington meant the asterisk to signal a backslash (as in "text / subtext").

26 Number 4 is handwritten and ends midsentence.

The "Message" as Art

1971?

This short essay is likely the written version of a lecture that Corrington delivered to the South-Central Modern Language Association in 1971. The title of that talk was "The Poetry of Rock & Roll." The "message" in art to which Corrington refers involves politics, or the role of "social consciousness" in works of poetry and fiction. Corrington suggests that, rather than generalize about the importation of politics to literature, one should examine each work on a case-by-case basis to determine whether it is art with a social theme or merely "a harangue disguised as art." Corrington is concerned with the distinction between art and propaganda, the latter of which, he suggests, is marked by cliché and the sort of troping that entails no clear political referent (i.e., no nameable, observable social examples) in the actual world. For this reason, Corrington criticizes art that employs such general types as "Big Business, the German Army, the Atomic Bomb, Big Labor, Hollywood, Mom, jingoistic patriotism, etc."

The dramatic resurgence of social consciousness as a <u>sine qua non</u>[27] of the intellectual in the 1960s has provided a need for renewal of the old dialogue concerning the "message" in art. Is poetry the proper—or even a reasonable—medium through which to voice horror at the arms-race? Is it possible to attack contemporary conformism by means of a short story, and still write a story? Is there a formula, a kind of intensity-determinate, that can be used to discern the difference in art that contains some propaganda and artful propaganda?

As usual, all answers to such questions have to be so extensively qualified as to make the answers almost meaningless. No important general specifications are possible. It is necessary to probe every poem, every story, every novel as an isolated entity in order to decide whether you have a work of art exemplifying thematically a social concern, or a harangue disguised as art.

A classic example of the second class is Kenneth Rexroth's "Thou Shalt Not Kill."[28] Rather than a poem dealing with the death of contemporary artists—

---

27   "Sine que non" underlined in original.

28   Corrington writes Rexroth's title as THOU SHALT NOT KILL (all capitalized letters, no quotation marks).

particularly Dylan Thomas—Rexroth has produced a rather bad tirade against the conformism and commercialism of contemporary America. As poetry, the demi-philippic has no value because it is undistinguished and indiscriminate indictment, and because the indictment itself is ludicrous.

Essentially, Rexroth credits those "sons-of-bitches in their Brooks Brothers suits" for having put Thomas under the sod.[29] The partisan reader is supposed to understand how and why the SOBs did this, and the response required of the reader is, I suppose, an outburst of lyric anger. It may be that such partisans exist. I doubt it.

Rexroth's failure is particularly absurd since, in it, he makes use of the "bogus entity" so long a figure in the history of American prejudice. If I were to make the statement "niggers are dirty and ignorant," Rexroth's howl of dissent would rend the California heavens—though it would be not [a][30] great task to find a number of Negroes who would exemplify the statement. But, obviously, no number of specifics can justify such a remark. Still, Rexroth is content to make use of this hate-monger's instrument in order to denigrate all wearers of Brooks Brothers suits. Thus the weight of his poem hangs by the denunciation of a Bogus Entity: the shadowy wearer of a certain kind of suit. Moreover, even if the Bogus Entity had real existence and was acceptable as a scape-goat (as for example, the Nazi SS was, to a certain extent), Rexroth would be hard put to show the manner in which these Brooks Brothers wearers contributed to Thomas's death. Discounting the possibility that Madison Avenue footed his liquor bill, the accusation seems a little thin. It is a shame that Thomas died; commercialism and conformism are contemptible. The nexus connecting the two remains for Rexroth or someone else to point out.

Rexroth's message-poem fails for at least two reasons (not taking into account whether or not Rexroth has any poetic talent). First, because it is based upon a reader's acceptance of a bogus entity, the wearer of Brooks Brothers suits. Second, because the stated connection between these "sons-of-bitches" and Thomas's death is, so far as anyone can tell, nonexistent. In this case, propaganda-as-poem fails for no deeper reason than that the entire proposition is fallacious from beginning to end.

Another reason for message-literature's failure is the inevitability of cliché in certain kinds of propaganda. No matter how true and salutary and essentially ethical certain propositions are, in and of themselves, no literature based upon them can be, except in rare cases discussed further on, more than disguised special

---

29   Kenneth Rexroth, "Thou Shalt Not Kill" (A Memorial for Dylan Thomas), lines 298–300. The actual lines conclude the poem and read as follows:

> You killed him! You killed him.
> In your God damned Brooks Brothers suit,
> You son of a bitch.

30   The article "a" was missing in the original.

pleading. Much anti-war literature fails for this reason. It is generally agreed by almost everyone that war is a bad thing—but to condemn *all* violence, *all* war,[31] no matter what the situation surrounding it, no matter what the issues involved, amounts to a simple-minded and essentially ignorant cliché. The same holds true of a novel or poem offering indiscriminate condemnation of Big Business, the German Army, the Atomic Bomb, Big Labor, Hollywood, Mom, jingoistic patriotism, etc. It requires a good deal less imagination to create a Gestapo beast than a Christian Diestl,[32] a lunatic tycoon than Tom in *The Great Gatsby*, a fat lecherous producer doing in country gals from Des Moines than Mailer's producer in *The Deer Park*. And the results of message-caricature are always predictable: the work invariably stinks, except in the case of satire, which rarely pretends to crusade seriously.

---

31   "All" placed in italics but underlined in the original.

32   Character in the 1958 war film *The Young Lions*. Diestl is a German ski instructor played by Marlon Brando. The plot takes place in Nazi Germany.

The Academic Revolution: Work in Progress

1969

This essay, which is part memoir, was delivered as a lecture at Centenary College in 1969. In it, Corrington seeks to develop what he calls his "ontologies," which he adopted in part while he was a student at Centenary. Corrington suggests that our lives are short and meaningless without an ontology and that our purposive acts ought to be guided by essential patterns of history. Corrington's conservativism and his belief in canonical greatness are apparent in his recommendation to "enter that vast communion of past, present, and future, of living, dead, and yet to be born that was recognized by the early church and called the communion of saints." One's sense of place and continuity, Corrington submits, is requisite to the production of great works of art. Corrington suggests that academic revolution is paradoxically tied to tradition in that the new necessarily springs from the old. He claims that the current academic revolution is rooted in the rejection of authority and the repudiation of materialism. He is concerned with the transitional ethic of the 1960s and the concomitant widespread questioning of the legitimacy of authority and institutions. He refers to this questioning as the New Politics. Corrington praises the academic revolution and encourages universities to serve as a matrix for that revolution. He believes that universities study the old disciplines to reveal new ways of forming constructive communities. Championing the drift of the university toward more student-centered objectives, toward more bottom-up rather than top-down power structures on campus, Corrington embraces and celebrates the reforming spirit of his students. He believes this spirit is in fact conservative in that custom and tradition and the complex, organic nature of social development teach that reform is necessary to ensure future growth. Corrington suggests that colleges and other institutions, to remain faithful to the past, must reform themselves; in other words, colleges and other such institutions must rework and reenergize the past for present purposes.

Contrary to what Dr. Morgan may have told you, I am not Centenary's oldest graduate still alive. I only feel like it when the authorities of Caddo Parish permit me back within their jurisdiction for 48-hour periods. In all seriousness, whenever I come home I think of those heartbreaking yet exultant lines which conclude *Swann's Way*:

The places that we have known belong now only to the little world of space on which we map them for our own convenience. None of them was ever more than a thin slice, held between the contiguous impressions that composed our life at that time; remembrance of a particular form is but regret for a particular moment; and houses, roads, avenues are as fugitive, alas, as are the years.[33]

This is not my Shreveport any longer: it is yours. This is not my Centenary College, though many of the people who made it the happiest memory of my life are still here. No, my town and my school began to blur and disassemble that morning in September on 1956 when I pointed my car south toward Houston and Rice University. This knowledge, this clear vision is the condition which permits nostalgia to have an honorable existence. Recollection of the past must be conditioned by recognition of the present—and by the prophetic vision of tomorrows yet to come. Otherwise, nostalgia is simply a refuge for the weak, an excuse for the torpid. And that kind of nostalgia is surely an intellectual crime—worse, it is probably a sin.

All of which bears most closely upon my topic for this evening, "The Academic Revolution: Work in Progress." I have not come here to diddle with you, to discuss the pros and cons of pass-fail courses, of an end to required curriculum and all the rest of the tactical business which could be dealt with in a single afternoon by men and women who had determined precisely what education in colleges and universities should and must be in the latter half of the twentieth century. John Crowe Ransom has said that every poet, every critic must first have an ontology, a view of Being, before he can set to work, and the same is true of those who commit together to the idea of education. It is axiomatic that you are unlikely to get what you want if you do not know what you want. So I come to bandy ontologies with you, to discuss the strategies and the ends of what has come to be called the Academic Revolution. I think it is obvious that those who know their strategies will find tactics ready to their hands.

Let me begin with something I learned in Mr. Hickox's course in historical geology, though he might be surprised to find out that I learned anything at all. I came to see that our lives, as Proust said in the quotation from *Swann's Way*, are so small, so fleeting, that they must be attached to some larger conception of things if they are not to be wasted. Consider that this room, in geologic terms, is a mirage, a fleck of time, and we ourselves ghosts who appear upon the film of world history for the least part of a second. The film goes on, leaving our passions and our acts behind, and only if our purposes have struck root in the largest and most essential patterns of our time can we aspire to be more than blips in the film. What can a man—or even a society—do

---

33   Corrington's footnote reads: "(Proust n.d.)." This quotation is accurate and seems to be from the "classic translation" of C.K. Scott-Moncrieff.

to sustain its reality, to fix its "having-lived" upon that onrushing pattern? I believe that we must become giants, and the only way to do that is to live for one another, to enter that vast communion of past, present, and future, of living, dead, and yet to be born that was recognized by the early church and called the *communion of the saints*. If we do not, as single persons and as a culture, come from something and tend toward something, then we are nothing. We are less than the trilobites that one can find stuck absurdly in the sediments left over from Devonian time. Is all this abstract metaphysics? Yes, but it is also the precise theme of a piece of contemporary poetry:

> We are but a moment's sunlight,
> fading in the grass. . .[34]

That is so. We are ephemeral, but we are, if we choose to be, in Schopenhauer's words, "Lords of eternity." And it is from this beginning that all great work, all meaningful revolution, springs.

Now for contemporary history. I have a battle-report to make. In the words of that great and honest revolutionary, Leon Trotsky, "All through history, mind limps after reality."[35]

"The day is a time for action, but at twilight feeling and reason come to take account of what has been accomplished."[36] So one day this epoch in American education, which began at Berkeley in 1964 with the Free Speech Movement, will be enshrined in nostalgia. Just now, however, the forces unleashed in that time and place still play like lightning across our lives and it is up to us who wish to act in our own time to understand and operate within the academic-political terms established during the last five years. It is of no use to regret the violence, the unreason—or appearances of unreason past and present. I leave that to the time of nostalgia.[37]

Let us dispose summarily with *Time-Life* idiocies. There is no generation-gap in terms of communications. Young and old alike watch each other a good deal more carefully than either cares to admit. There are young squares and old hippies. But there is certainly a gap. Yes. It existed twenty years ago, and it got me kicked out of Jesuit high school. It is the gap between those who believe in the concept of legitimate authority by imputation and those who do not. It is the gap between those who still live under the ideas put forward by the Congress of Vienna, the old divine-right notion, and those who demand that authority be judged upon its acts, its merits. Today when you say to most young people (and almost without exception the best young people—"you have to obey authority," the answer, if it is not a brick, is a question: "why?" I understand

---

34   This is a verse from The Youngblood's "Get Together" (originally written by Chet Powers).

35   From *Literature and Revolution*, originally published in 1925.

36   Trotsky, *Literature and Revolution* (1925).

37   In the original, this paragraph is part of the previous one.

both the statement and the reply. The statement is a cry for order—the old order. The question brings up the whole issue of whether legitimacy, the mere holding of an office, the mere historical role of an institution, or the printed catalog of a college, is any longer to be considered a warrant of authority. I believe that the issue is a real one, and that the old idea that authority resides in the uniform, the office, or the institution is, like it or not, essentially bankrupt. You say that it is awful that some attack the US presidency; very well, but what about the papacy? Ah, that is different. No, it is not. I see the presidency, the papacy—and the dean's office—as spatiotemporal points in which power is gathered. In the hands of John XXIII,[38] the papacy became for a few brief years an inspiration to the whole Christian world. Today, it is under attack from some of the most distinguished and intelligent princes of the Church. When a cardinal attacks papal power, it is hardly surprising that students attack the power invested in a college or university president or dean. For better or worse, the notion that respect is due an office, no matter what sort of boob occupies it, is as dead as . . . Spiro Agnew? I suggest that if you view the whole of our troubled society, you will find that this pattern is at the root of almost all the stir. Younger people simply reject the idea that a given office or institution possesses authority because it claims to possess it. In short, Paul VI is going to have a hard time of it, and so is the dean—unless they possess real authority, which is to say the wisdom, the strength, the articulateness to convince, to move their people to accept the standards and ideas they espouse. This is, whatever one thinks of it, the essence of the New Politics, and it is functional at every level from the presidency down to that of the family. It is very rough indeed for the official or institutional—or parental—misfit, the hack, the second-rater, the mechanic. But this seems to me to be in strict accord with reason, and to match the pattern of authentic revolution wherever we seek that pattern, from the time of Spartacus to Wesley to Lenin to Martin Luther King.

So much for the crisis of authority. But there is more, much more. For the reactionary, it is bad enough that people should question authority. But it is even worse when they question bed-rock values. Which is exactly what they are questioning. What values? Well, many values. Sexual values, personal-goals values, and so on. But much of this is overstressed by news media for its own obvious commercial purposes—which fact is directly related to the real value that is being assaulted head-on, and which has probably lost the battle already.

If you grab yourself a hippie, or a Berkeley activist, or a member of Weatherman, you will find general agreement on one point: a society which offers as its chief value [and] ultimate reward[39] the acquisition of money is a corrupt society. America is, and has been for the larger part of its past, just such a society. That theme is

---

38   John XXIII called the Second Vatican Council.

39   *Ultimate reward* is handwritten into the original. There is a word or mark before "ultimate" that may be a symbol for "and" or "or."

ubiquitous on American campuses. It is a source of general and sustained horror among business people that the cream of each year's graduating class is tending less and less to be interested in "making it" via Dow, IBM, U.S. Steel, etc. In increasing numbers, the sons and daughters of the affluent are going into social work, art, life sciences, and so on. They are turned off by the whole structure that insists that a man with a million dollars in the bank is a great man.

A year or so ago, *Time* magazine, the throbbing heart of American bourgeois society, discussed "the American aristocracy." What names were mentioned? I will not be invidious, but I will note that men like Michael DeBakey, Norman Mailer, James Dickey, Robert Motherwell, C. Vann Woodward were absent. In fact, we were told that "American aristocracy" was a collection of Rockefellers, Vanderbilts, Howard Hughes, etc. In other words, rich men, politicians, businessmen—all of whom shared a single characteristic. They possessed great power and money and notably little talent for anything that would have a chance of lasting much past the end of their lives.

Well, let me propose another list of American aristocracy—if by that term we can understand those people most influential among members of a given society. Eldridge Cleaver, Janis Joplin, Herbert Marcuse, Malcolm X, Albert Camus, The Doors, Julian Bond, Mark Rudd, Che Guevara, Hermann Hesse, and by adoption, Paul McCartney and colleagues. At a more sophisticated level, the list becomes one that only a few people past thirty can handle. It includes Joe Hill and Jimmy Rogers, John Reed and Big Bill Haywood, both Americans—buried in the Kremlin wall. It includes Ivan Kaliayev[40] and Trotsky, Colonel von Stauffenburg and Prince Kropotkin. It is, simply, a gallery of rebels; of those who, whether they got money or not, never aimed for it. It could by the old standard, be judged a list of losers. It does not include J. P. Morgan and Jay Gould.

In short, "making it" no longer makes it. Later for being "successful." One of the classic quotes from *Soul on Ice* has got to be where Eldridge Cleaver compares sex offenses against little children with wanting to be president of U.S. Steel. Do I concur with all this? You must understand that mine is a unique position: I am no longer young, but I am not quite old. Like Tiresias, I see both sides. So, do I concur? I will admit that I cannot accept either *Time*'s list of aristocracy, or that of my students. My own list would include Jefferson and Robert E. Lee, for example. But I note that no name appearing on *Time*'s list means anything to me, and that a large number of those names appearing on my students' lists mean a great deal to me. Horatio Alger's rule over the youthful American mind is over. Even those of my students who are interested in law and medicine—and the best young people going into business administration—are of a new breed. They mean to be creative; they mean to do their thing and to link their profession to the needs and hopes of the whole community. So, in summary, the campus revolution has at its roots a rejection of authority, a

40   This is Camus's spelling. The more common spelling is "Kalyayev."

repudiation of materialism. It goes without saying that racism, prudery, and dozens of other bug-bears are assaulted. But the twin pillars of the old order were authority separated from ability and materialism as an end in itself, and it is against these two fundamental concepts that the revolt is chiefly aimed.

But is there no positive side to the revolution? There is indeed, and I am endlessly amazed that no one—or very few—of my older colleagues has been able to see that positive side and name its elements. Consider the phrases that have been picked up by the news media and perverted into advertising: "Do Your Own Thing," "Tell it like it is," "Let it all hang out," and so on. Again, consider the lyrics of contemporary pop songs. Have you heard "Get down to Business Mr. Businessman"?[41] Or "Mother's Little Helper"? Or Donovan's "Atlantis"? And high on the charts right now, the Youngblood's "Get Together"? Or one of the most brilliant pieces of the last 20 years, Stonepillow's[42] "Eleazar's Circus"? If you do not listen, you will not hear. I seem to recall it said another way: Those who have ears, let them hear. My kids ask their parents, "How many times can a man turn away, pretending he just doesn't see . . . ?" Yes, and "How many times must the cannon-balls fly before they're forever banned?"[43] Yes, and "If I had a hammer, I'd hammer in the morning, I'd hammer in the evening all over this land. . . I'd hammer out love between my brothers and my sisters all over this land."

Whatever charge may be leveled at my students, the charge of non-communication cannot be. Every generation communicates in its own way. My kids use music and film, and what do they say? They say that they are sick of lies and dishonesty; they say that they are freaked out by old ways that do not work and that nobody has the guts or brains to change; they say that they intend to find or to build a family as large as the world itself; they say that loyalty is good—so long as it is freely given. They say that it is a sorry man who will not speak out against corruption and injustice and cruelty. They say that money is a nice thing, but not the only thing. They say that immorality is more a matter of lying to each other than lying with each other. They say all these things over and over again, and I for one am listening. And I could not be prouder of them. Forgive me my naiveté, but I believe that the best of my students are the best people who have ever drawn breath upon this continent.

But they are also troubled people, and it is on the campus that all these troubles get shaken out, yelled, talked, sung, written about. If the new order should not be aborted by the dead hand of authority and materialism, it will be on the campus that a new order arises. If that new order is to be sane and arrive at its own good

---

41   This is a line from the song "Mr. Businessman," by Ray Stevens (1968).

42   Corrington wrote "Stone Pillow's." Album covers for the band state "Stonepillow."

43   From Bob Dylan's "Blowin' in the Wind" (1962):

How many times can a man turn his head
Pretending he just doesn't see?

ends; if it is to be nurtured within constitutional patterns, then the college and university must grab hold, must cease its vaporings, its backing and filling, and establish itself as the very matrix of that shadowy new order.[44]

In short, American society within the next fifty years must either have the college and university at its very center, or there may not be any society. It is absurd to think that the campus today is a place where children go simply to learn. They are not children, and they go to the campus to find their kindred, those brothers and sisters who want to share in the task of putting together a new kind of life. Learning? Of course, but on a new scale: learning all the old disciplines, but learning also how to be part of the new community that is taking form in and around the campus.[45]

Let me point out quickly that my students are, as students, very good indeed. Within the next few years, we will be sending first-rate people to some of the best graduate schools in America and Europe; our people go to law school and into various professions, and they are almost uniformly better at what they do than I was at their age—as Dr. Morgan will doubtless be glad to witness.

What do these students want? Many things, but primarily the opportunity to take a real part in forming—and reforming—the most important institution in their lives: their college and university. They do not wish to be patronized by phony "consultation." That is simply another example of the old Legitimate Authority dodge. They wish to have power. They believe that they have a degree of special competency in the establishment of programs and curriculum, of college government, of degree requirements and disciplinary functions. They think that the university must, *must* become a place where things are done *with* them, not *to* them. They insist upon being our younger colleagues, not our day-nursery charges. Do they wish to dominate the university structure? No. Not one of the campus leaders at Loyola has ever suggested that he wished to replace the administrative oligarchy with a student dictatorship. Last year, a candidate for Student Council president ran on the plank of establishing a Student House of Representatives to work beside the Faculty Senate. It was a good idea, and sooner or later something like it will come to be. Because it is right.

The Department of English at Loyola has a Student Affairs Committee which has equal power with the other departmental committees. It is chaired by an elected student who chose the other members, both faculty and students.[46] The chairman of this committee has considerable drag with the department chairman, and because of that fact and the spirit it engenders, the Department of English at Loyola was recently designated in an Academic Goals study by a national consulting firm as one of the university's "Superior" departments. It was the only department in

---

44   Paragraph break added.

45   In the original, this paragraph is part of the previous one.

46   Added an "s" to "student"; in the original, Corrington appears to have typed "t" rather than "s" and then to have covered his "t" with an "s" several times.

the Humanities to be so designated. Why are we successful? Because authority is determined by ability, and there are students, English majors, whose judgment is as good—if not better—than that of the chairman. The chairman's single advantage is that he knows it and acts accordingly. On Thursday of this week, the department will meet to ratify a constitution which sets down exhaustively the procedures which shall govern internal affairs. It outlines, among other things the procedure to impeach a chairman. The original draft was written by me. When it is ratified, my powers, on paper, will be cut to the bone.[47] Will I be able to function? Very well, thank you. Will I still have authority? Yes, the only kind I should have: the personal ability to carry a majority of my colleagues and students with me on issues when I am right. And if that fails? Why, I will resign, of course. And what if a majority of English majors should vote no confidence in the administration of the department? Again, I will resign. Because power, as such, means nothing to me. When I cannot wield it any longer with the full confidence of my colleagues and students (who are also my colleagues), then it will pass to someone who can muster such confidence. That is the new style in campus politics, and I believe that it will last.

Where did I get such notions regarding my relation to students, to colleagues, to the whole manipulation of power? What pattern did I use in building the second-best English department in Louisiana? Why the pattern of the best department, of course. That of Centenary College.

Fifteen years is not so long that I have forgotten the friendship and the comradeship given me by Dr. Clark, Dr. Morgan, Dr. Willingham, Guerin, Labor and others. How was I treated? As their junior partner in a common endeavor. Our relation was not formalized; it did not need to be, but the principles were there, and that is why Centenary has sent its students on to become leaders instead of followers. That is why it is a joy to return here instead of a mechanical alumni chore.

Several years ago, when I came back briefly, the late Margaret McDonald was kind enough to write an article about me. It was built around the theme that I had been a rebel in my days here. One never knows his own Image, I guess. I had not realized that I was a rebel. In any case, my, teachers knew how to handle the type. They did not call the police to break my head; they made me a part of the whole enterprise of learning, spent hours in bull-sessions with me, and finally, by superhuman effort—and possibly corrupt practices—[48]got me into Rice University. They were not only—along with my parents—the prime architects of my personality, they were also the designers of a whole new order of relationships between teacher

---

47   Corrington was the Chairman of the Department of English at Loyola University in New Orleans from 1966-71, with a year off in 1968 when he served as a visiting professor at the University of California-Berkeley. Dr. Thomas Preston chaired the department in Corrington's absence during the 1968-69 academic year. Preston was a graduate student at Rice University while Corrington was also at Rice. Preston persuaded Corrington to join the Department of English at Loyola as part of the university's "commitment to excellence" campaign.

48   "Em dashes" added.

and learner. They created, across a distance of 300 miles and fifteen years, another good department to expand their work and their essential belief in the life of reason, the community of those who wish to know.

It is time now, I believe, to formalize this spirit in many schools. Let college administrations and governing bodies be stripped of arbitrary power. Let the faculty become devoted to teaching as its chief concern. Let students become responsible college citizens as quickly as they show the desire to do so. Let us root out George III from our colleges and begin to create real academic communities in which only wisdom, courage, honesty, and the desire to learn can confer authority. Let there be checks and balances between administration, faculty, and students. Let each portion of the community have a voice, and let each segment listen carefully to the others. Learning, as any good teacher knows, cuts both ways.

All this, beyond the rhetoric, the occasions of senseless violence, the sit-ins, and the lock-outs, is what the campus revolution is about. Is it radical? Precisely. It is radical as the teaching of Calvin and Luther was radical. Is it an attack on the seats of power? Without a doubt. It is such an attack as was Cromwell's revolt or that of Washington and Jefferson—or that of Davis and Lee. A US Senator, speaking of economic matters, once put it this way:

(There are two ways to handle our problem) One is to let it alone, to let the people starve and let them cry, let them fight and let them lie. That is one way—the old laissez faire doctrine. is the ultraconservative way. (But there is a better way) the way by which a man considers himself a part of the family of all humanity; by which one nation's problems become the problems of all its people and of all other nations. . .[49]

---

49   Here is the full passage:

> There are only two ways to go. One is the old laissez faire route; let things go as they will; let them alone. That is one way to go. That way means rolling over people. It means crushing their bones and their muscles. It means spilling blood. It means, in the final wind-up, the ordinary policy of human carnage that finally works itself out to a point where those who live—"the survival of the fittest," it is called—own the earth, and are supplied.

After a paragraph break, Long continues: "That is one way. That way will work, and it will work the way it always has worked, and no other." After another paragraph break, Long continues:

> There is another way, and that is to work according to the law that is given here in this book. There are only two ways to work. There are only two ways in which we can make this thing work at all. One is to let it alone, to let people starve and let them cry, let them fight and let them die. That is one way—the ultraconservative way. The other way, Mr. President, is the way that is laid down by the Supreme Lawmaker of all time to regulate the conduct of one human being toward another among nations and among peoples.

After another paragraph break, Long continues:

> There is the way that leaves people alone to suffer and to starve and to die. There is the way by which man considers himself a part of the family of all humanity; by which one nation's problems become the problems of all its people and of all other nations. That is the way of the law of the Gospel and the law of the Supreme Lawgiver, who says that the nation which observes it shall be a people living in a land of plenty, eating their fill, with no misery and starvation among them.

Corrington misidentifies the date of this speech as June 14, 1934. The actual date was May 3, 1934. See pp. 8001-8003, *Congressional Record: Proceedings and Debates of the Second Session of the Seventy-Third Congress of the United States of America, Volume 78, Part 8, May 3, 1934 – May 20, 1934* (Washington, D.C.: United States Government Printing Office, 1934).

That radical plea for community was delivered in the US Senate on 14 June, 1934. By Senator Huey Pierce Long, of Louisiana. I agree with the senator, and the principle he spoke of surely must apply to any college or university.

There was a day, not so long ago, when Southerners were proud to bear the name "rebel." It was the mark of manhood to stand up and speak out for change, to find ways of doing things better. This generation of students speaks in many voices, but their rebellion's theme, what they mean to say, is clear enough:

> If you can't lend a hand,
> Then get out of the road,
> For the times, they are a'changing.[50]

It seems to me that American institutions of higher learning might be at least as bold as those cardinals of the Roman church who are challenging the absolutism of the papacy. When the concept of collegiality has won, as win it must, the Church will be returned to the Church. If we in the colleges persist in our own reformation, our colleges too will become collegial, the universities universal.

There are risks to be run, and we will have to run them, because, as I said in the beginning, we are only a frame in the film of man's history. The movement of that history goes on, flood tide toward destinies we cannot imagine. A society which refuses to allow its institutions, itself, to grow, not only dies but is impacted forever in history as a failure, an abortion—like the Ottoman Empire or the Austria-Hungary of Franz Joseph, like the France of Louis XVI—or the Russia of Nicholas II.

So, this is our work in progress. To make all things new, to seek new truths that will make us free and make our lives the kind of adventures that every life should be. One day, I would like to see Centenary and Loyola become what Richard Wright called "organs of knowing." I would like to see the college and the university as the very well-spring and center of American life—places students hate to leave; places they return to time and again to continue what here they began. I think that if such a day should come, we might be able to answer the plea of the Youngbloods, who ask of us,

> Come on, people now,
> Smile on your brother,
> Everybody get together,
> Try to love one another right now.[51]

---

50   These lyrics appear to be from Bob Dylan's "The Times They Are A-Changin'" (1963), but Dylan's lyrics are slightly different:

> Your old road is rapidly agin'
> Please get out of the new one if you can't lend your hand
> For the times they are a-changin'

51   The Youngbloods, "Get Together."

The Recovery of the Humanities I

1984

This chapter originated as a lecture for the Southern Humanities Conference in Chattanooga, Tennessee, in 1984. Corrington sets out to define the "humanities" and to explain why he believes they need recovering. Corrington argues that symbolism is essential to the humanities and that symbolism has been under assault since the Enlightenment. Corrington believes that the Enlightenment ushered in an era of scientism and materialism that led to the rise of Nazism, Marxist-Leninism, secular humanism, and logical positivism, all of which contributed to the "decerebration" of the humanities. The task of recovering the humanities, according to Corrington, involves "the need to reexamine the fundamental experiences and symbols upon which any serious notion of the Humanities must be grounded, and to question our present understanding and application of those symbols." Corrington undertakes this task through the paradigms of Eric Voegelin, who frames his analysis in terms of the mythopoetic thought of certain peoples and places, the role of the human psyche, and the nature of divinity and the infinite. Corrington examines the difference between psyche and physis; the former formulates mythopoetic meaning out of the data of the phenomenal world and provides the basis for our understanding of political order. By way of consciousness, the psyche comprehends and organizes logos and thereby structures our understanding of reality, including what it means to be human.

Drawing from various Greek philosophers, Corrington suggests that all humans, as part of our very humanness, share an understanding of consciousness from which we derive the symbols that characterize and shape our laws and institutions. Corrington analyzes the shift in mythopoetic thinking from knowledge to faith after Christianity reframed the search for truth in terms of spirit rather than mind, thus altering the way we perceive consciousness and its attendant symbols that order us politically. Corrington traces the development of Christian symbolism and its political implications, namely how Christian communities transitioned from spiritual groups to imperial powers in the form of Roman rule. Christian rule manifested its symbolic order throughout Roman civilization, incorporating what Hellenistic philosophy could be put to Christian use and discarding what hindered Christian authority. Corrington maps the changes that Romanized Christianity underwent in the face of Islamic and Mongol threats of both physical and symbolical dimensions. The clash of cultures and traditions was also the clash of symbolic order and its conception of humanitas. Corrington considers modern scholarship on ancient civilizations to speculate about how those civilizations sought, in a parallel manner, to answer questions about the nature of the human within the cosmos and in relation to the divine. Each civilization has in common a cosmological mode of thought expressed as myth. Corrington concludes that Western culture and civilization cannot lay sole claim to the humanities as a field of study and as a philosophical tradition for understanding human purpose. The humanities, so termed, has been derailed, Corrington suggests, by "contraction," "mutilation," and "distortion," concepts that he carefully defines. Studying the humanities can help us to recover the experiential and symbolic understanding of human purpose over time and in disparate places and bear witness, he says, to the different claims to truth about our human place in the cosmos.

I

I take it all of us will agree that a title like "The Recovery of the Humanities" might be considered somewhat provocative. Such a title causes questions to arise: What is the situation from which the Humanities must recover? Or, alternatively, how is it that the Humanities have been lost, that they must be recovered?[52]

At last, a more vexing question may present itself: what, precisely, is this *Humanities*, which must recover or be recovered, and what is the meaning of recovery in either case?

None of the questions is frivolous, and I put them now in order that they may recommend themselves to your contemplation while I dispose quickly of another problem which you might legitimately expect to stand at the center of this discourse but which, except in passing and in order to eliminate it from the field of enquiry,[53] I shall not discuss.

Whatever our analysis of that collective symbolism we refer to as the Humanities, and whatever we may discover regarding its development from the engendering symbols in pre-classical and classical time, there must be noted the radical assault upon the symbolism itself during the past three hundred years.

The rise of ideologies from the Enlightenment *egophasnie* of the philosophes through the scientism and materialism of the nineteenth century to the political mass-movements and pseudo-therapeutics of the twentieth, including, but not limited to, National Socialism, Marxist-Leninism, secular humanism, and logical positivism has resulted in a virtual *decerebration* of the Humanities.[54] The shattering of humane learning into disciplines, fields, departments, specialties, and areas, aping the pragmatic divisions of the natural sciences—despite Lord Acton's dictum that we should study problems, not periods—has been damaging enough. The prohibition of questioning the field of reality as it is experienced by concrete human beings in concrete existential situations in a concrete world has been much worse.

We have been adjured by pseudoscientists and dictators, intellectual, political, or otherwise, that questions regarding such symbols as humanity, the soul, human nature, the eschatological goal of that "thing" called man—all these are false questions. We are warned against the disreputable practice of asking questions

---

52   This is an edited, corrected, and expanded version of the essay, published in *Politics, Society, and the Humanities*, ed.

53   Maintained the British spelling.

54   Corrington's note: "Cf. Eric Voegelin, *From Enlightenment to Revolution* (Durham, NC: Duke University Press, 1975); also *Science, Politics and Gnosticism* (Chicago: Henry Regnery, 1968)."

which have no answers in terms of the ideologies. True, the cost of asking differs from one ideological deformation to another: in the Nazi case, unseemly questions were cut off abruptly and finally. In the Marxist case, one may end up in the Gulag— or, perhaps more appropriately, in a lunatic asylum. In the case of the academy, or in psychiatric circles, or for that matter, among the churches, things are on the whole less stringent. One loses face or tenure, or the esteem of one's well-adjusted colleagues, or is expelled from the congregation of believers—all of whom agree that a particular kind of questioning, or, conversely, the failure to hold certain incontrovertible and exclusivist doctrines, constitutes a fall from that peculiar kind of humanity, which distinguishes itself by race, class, or dogma.

It would be hard to overstate the damage done to the understanding of what it means to be human in recent centuries, but a host of scholars has given its attention to the problems in the last several decades, and the results are cheering.[55] It would appear that the ideologues may be running out of intellectual steam, and the sleepwalkers awakening. To the extent that this is so, the Humanities may already be in the process of recovering from the shattering events of the past three hundred years.

But the recovery of which I wish to speak has to do with what one might call "old business," with the need to reexamine the fundamental experiences and symbols upon which any serious notion of the Humanities must be grounded, and to question our present understanding and application of those symbols.

The task must begin with some intellectual archeology because the Humanities as they have come to exist in our time, and the complex of thought and sentiment which informs them, stand as no more than a temporal point in a continuum of meaning, not as finished or accomplished things.

"What is man, that thou art mindful of him?" the psalmist asks, and that question, together with its innumerable historical responses, constitutes the initial experience from which the Humanities arise. The question of the psalmist is elevated by Professor Eric Voegelin to the status of a fundamental structure in the field of reality:

> The Question capitalized is not a question concerning the nature of this or that object in the external world but a structure inherent to the experience of reality. . . The meaning of the Question can be ascertained, therefore, only by tracing the modes from the setting in the primary experience of the cosmos, through transitional forms, to their setting in the context of noetic and pneumatic differentiations.[56]

---

55   Corrington's note: "Cf., for example, Robert Tucker, *Philosophy and Myth in Karl Marx* (Cambridge: Cambridge University Press, 1972); also Henri de Lubac, *The Drama of Atheist Humanism* (New York: World Publishing, 1963), and Eric Voegelin, *The New Science of Politics* (Chicago: University of Chicago Press, 1953)."

56   Corrington's note: "Eric Voegelin, *The Ecumenic Age*, vol. 4 of *Order and History* (Baton Rouge, LA: Louisiana State University Press, 1975), 317." This quotation has been corrected; some words were missing in the original.

This Question is evoked by the tension in man toward the limits of his existence, of the apparent lastingness of the universe together with his realization that he has come into existence from somewhere (or nowhere), and that he shall depart once more. The Question is present compactly within *mythopoetic* speculation arising in every culture in response to the contemplation of the order of the universe and the continuity of humanity—and to the inescapable relation between the two. The Question reaches to the depth of the array of "things," including the inwardness of the psyche of the observer and the outwardness of *physis*, the burgeoning, lasting, self-renewing order of the cosmos, seeking the ground of that which stands illuminated by being in the mode of existence.

There seems to be some general scholarly agreement that the Western "break with the myth," as it is called—the movement from mythopoetic to *noetic* experience of the field of reality—is represented by a famous fragment of Anaximander of Miletus, as reported by Simplicius:

> And he said that the *arche* (the principle and origin [of] existing things) was the *Aperion* (the boundless, the illimitable) . . . and the source of coming to be for existing things is that into which destruction, too, happens according to *Anake* (necessity), for they pay penalty and retribution to one another for their injustice according to the ordinance of time.[57]

Clearly, Anaximander's formulation, if it parts from its mythopoetic precedent—in this case the Homeric-Hesiodic symbol *Okeanos*,[58] the backward-flowing *River-Ocean*—hardly amounts to a metaphysical or doctrinal proposition. Its level of abstract generality is more apparent in hindsight than real, for in its compactness it refers to the substance not only of cosmology, of physics, of philosophy and theology, but of the entire spectrum of what will come to be called humane studies—including a psychology (in the Aristotelian sense) as well.

The *Boundless* of Anaximander has managed to produce violent controversy from earliest times. Is this Apeiron an undifferentiated physical substance from which the pairs of opposites emerge? Was Anaximander himself one of the *physicoi*[59] who supposed the cosmos to be the uncaused outflow of a material *arche*? Or was the Apeiron something more? Aristotle's interpretation is clear on the point:

---

57   Corrington's note: "G. S. Kirk and J. E. Raven, eds., *The Presocratic Philosophers* (Cambridge: Cambridge University Press, 1957), 105–107. Some translations from the Greek may be modified or rephrased by the present author." Corrington made several changes to the original quotation.

58   Corrington's note: "Cf. Paul Seligman, *The Apeiron of Anaximander* (London: University of London, 1962), especially 130–149."

59   Natural philosophers.

Of the infinite there is not beginning, but rather this apeiron seems to be the beginning of other things, and to surround all things and to steer all . . . and this is the Divine; for it is immortal and indestructible, as Anaximander says.[60]

The distance of this divine arche from the myth is not great. In Anaximander's articulation, shaped as it is on the mythopoetic figure of the river-ocean which, from Mesopotamian times is, at once, the surrounding waters enclosing earth and the heavenly waters perceived in the stream of the Milky Way, one discovers the cosmos as process, flowing from the darkness of the depth of non-existence into the light of existence, then receding back into darkness again.

The ambiguity of the symbolism must not be taken as an example of misplaced concreteness, as a proposition about a literal object or place in existence. The apeirontic[61] process in its enfolding mystery does not constitute anything but is itself the source of all. In Heidegger's phrase, from it flows "the presencing of the present," *alethia*,[62] the uncoveredness, the re-collectedness of what stands forth in the light of being in the mode of existence.[63]

This characterization of the Infinite as process, as the lastingness against which all passingness of things and man and the cosmos itself should be measured, cannot, obviously, be taken as the result of astronomical or physical observation, for if the fact of change and ephemerality in the field of existence is obvious, the structure of Anaximander's aperion, its process and its lastingness is not, has never been, and cannot be an object of any sort of observation at all.

Thus, the initiating fragment of Western philosophical thought appears divided into an observational component regarding the relative duration of things, and a speculative component postulating an arche of all things, a principal nonexistent, boundless, steering, and divine.

But from whence arises the speculative component which plays off against the empirical observation of physis?[64] The speculation arises within the psyche of the concrete individual named Anaximander who poses the question as to the origin of things—including himself.

The psyche and its depth becomes, experientially, the other, the opposition to external physis. It is the arche of speculation, the apeiron from which arise the

---

60   Corrington's note: "Aristotle, *Physica*, 203b7–14." Corrington cites Aristotle, but this language is similar to Kirk's quotation of Aristotle in *Presocratic Philosophers*, p. 114, passage 110.

61   Derived from the Greek *apeiron*, a "thing without limits."

62   Greek (ἀλήθεια) philosophical term for "truth."

63   Corrington's note: "The issue of the Greek imagery of analytical consciousness and its engendering from mythopoetic consciousness is an intriguing question. For some particularly telling insights, cf. Eric Voegelin, *The World of the Polis*, vol. 2 of *Order and History* (Baton Rouge, LA: Louisiana State University Press, 1957), especially chap. 5–9; Martin Heidegger, *An Introduction to Metaphysics* (New Haven: Yale University Press, 1959), especially chapters 2 and 4; Henri Frankfort, et al., *The Intellectual Adventure of Ancient Man* (Chicago: University of Chicago press, 1946), chapters 1 and 12."

64   *Physis* is a Greek (φύσις) philosophical term for "nature."

explicating mythopoetic images and later the extracting propositional structures dealing both with physis and with psyche as well, projected and treated as if both were objects standing empirical reality outside this speculator himself. The discovery of physis—nature—as a *cosmos*, an elaborate and ordered universe, is paralleled by the simultaneous realization of the psyche as a *cosmion*,[65] the cosmos, writ small— even as the cosmos will come to be understood as the human cosmion writ large.

The symbolism of the Boundless is thus more than the initial speculation upon physis; it represents the dyad unconsciousness/consciousness as well as that of non-existence/existence. The parallel is reinforced by reference back to the mythopoetic predecessor of Anaximander's symbol. Okeanos, the river-ocean, runs beneath the world as well as above it and issues forth its waters into the thousand known to the archaic Greeks. It symbolizes the horizon of reality both external and internal in their complimentary[66] characters as cosmos-cosmion. Okeanos, from whence the gods (considered as the conscious articulations of the powers of both physis and psyche) are sprung, River Okeanos which is the begetter of all.[67]

Metaphorically, physis is perceived to arise in its *alethia*[68] (uncoveredness, presence) from Lethe, one of Okeanos's tributary rivers—the darkness of apeirontic being in the mode of non-existence; one of the "things" standing in physis is psyche, which in concrete human beings arises from the lethe of *amneotic* unconsciousness into the light of consciousness. In psyche, there is evoked recognition of the burgeoning, growing parallel constants, cosmos-cosmion. This interplay of physis and psyche, in which each can be said to "arise" from the other, constitutes the fundamental structure of the field of existential reality.

The differentiation of philosophy from mythopoesis is, then, an even[69] in the soul of a questioner named Anaximander in seventh century Greece whose symbolism serves to represent compactly the process in which the interdependent opposites non-existence/existence, physis/psyche, lethe/alethia,[70] are experienced as polarities of a divine infinite now distinguished from mythic unity, yet retaining the allusive sense of mystery lying beyond the mythic-noetic horizon established by the apeirontic symbol.

The questioning regarding the apeirontic depth (the ground) continues within the psyche of Heraclitus of Ephesus who says:

---

65   Eric Voegelin explained that the "expression *cosmion* seems to me to be particularly suitable for the designation of the political realm of meaning. Because we deal empirically, in factually happening constitutions [in order] with the creation of meaning in analogy to cosmic order." Quoted in Jürgen Gebhardt's "Editor's Introduction," in *The Collected Works of Eric Voegelin, Vol. 25*, History of Political Ideas, Volume VII: The New Order and Last Orientation (University of Missouri Press, 1999), p. 15.

66   Probably intended "complementary."

67   Corrington's note: "*Iliad*, 14: 201, 246, 302; Plato, *Theaetetus*, 180, D4." The *Theaetetus* citation is not noted correctly. The passage Corrington is referring to is known as 180d.

68   Probably intended "*aletheia*."

69   Probably intended "event."

70   Probably intended "*aletheia*."

Therefore, it is necessary to follow the common (*xynon*); but although the fundamental order (*logos*) is common to all, the many live[71] as though they possessed a private understanding.[72]

And again:

Those who speak with the mind (*nous*) must strengthen themselves with that which is common (*xynon*) to all, as a polis must rely on its law, and more strongly so, for all the laws of men are nourished by the one divine law which prevails as it will, and suffices for all things and more than suffices.[73]

Heraclitus' evocation of the nous, consciousness, as the process in the psyche which discovers and elucidates the logos, reveals the common (xynon) character of order in psyche and physis, and the organ of self-consciousness in which the realization takes place. But it reveals as well the possibility of the rejection of fundamental order by men who remain dreaming even when they are awake—as if they lived in a world of their own rather than in the one cosmos common to all.

The Heraclitean search of the psyche constitutes a response to the Question in elemental form. The universe of existing things is found to possess an inherent order: it is a cosmos, and the fundamental order is identical in physis and psyche, the two modes of its expression in existence. Through the process of consciousness (nous), the structure of the uniquely human is revealed in self-reflection by way of insights that arise as the philosopher presses his inquiry toward the horizon of psyche. But, according to Heraclitus, the searching of self which constitutes the philosopher's noetic inquiry cannot exhaust the truth of the psyche. It can only approach the horizon in the manner of a Zenotic[74] paradox:

You would not find out the limits of the psyche even by travelling along every path, so deep is its logos.[75]

At the level of ideas, Heraclitus' formulation of the problem has not been improved upon in some 2,500 years. He had, as revealed in the slender stock of fragments left us, unearthed, on the one hand the insights that would lead over

---

71   Corrected from "lives."

72   Corrington's note: "Kirk and Raven, 188: Fr. 2."

73   Corrington's note: "Voegelin, *The World of the Polis*, 232 (Fr. 114)." This is similar to Voegelin's quotation, but Corrington appears to have tweaked the translation.

74   Zeno of Elea (490 – 430 B.C.E.) was a Greek philosopher known for the dialectic and for his paradoxes.

75   Corrington's note: "Kirk and Raven, 205, Fr. 45." This is not the same translation that appears in Kirk and Raven. As Corrington noted, he made some changes in the translations. The original reads: "You would not find out the boundaries of soul, even by travelling along every path: so deep a measure does it have."

time to the symbol of humanities—"being human," "those things which constitute the human." On the other hand, he had indicated the chilling reality that men are capable of resisting the logos, of denying their own necessary human participation in the common by turning to a second reality exclusive to themselves.

The insight expressed by Heraclitus grew both in meaning and significance in the form developed by Plato and Aristotle and used by Alexander of Macedon as he welded together the scattered and fractious cosmologically oriented peoples of the *ecumene*. The Aristotelian symbol *homonois*, translated variously[76] as "human thinking," or "like-mindedness"—that harmony of thought we are capable of experiencing by virtue of our common humanity centered in the identity of consciousness (nous) expressly abolished at the level of *theoria* distinctions of Greek and barbarian, Persian and Mede, worshipper of the Olympians and devotee of Mithra.

By the first century B.C., Heraclitus' insight had been virtually institutionalized in the office of the Roman Praetor Peregrine who oversaw the use of foreign laws among aliens in Rome, and stood as final authority in the conflict of laws. The Praetor sought the logos underlying the bewildering multitude of laws extant in the ecumene and applied it to cases between Egyptians and Parthians, Greeks and Gauls. The theoretical concept arising from the symbol received its fully elaborated expression in Cicero's compelling construction of a universal law for a universal humanity in the famous formula of the *De Re Publica*: *Est quidem vera lex recta ratio naturae congruens* . . .

> True law is right reason in agreement with nature; it is of universal application, unchanging and everlasting; it summons to duty by its commands and averts from wrongdoing by its prohibitions. And it does not lay its commands or its prohibitions upon good men in vain, though neither have any effect upon the wicked. It is a sin to try to alter this law, nor is it allowable to attempt to repeal any part of it, and it is impossible to abolish it entirely. We cannot be freed from its obligations by senate or people, and we need not look outside ourselves for an expounder or interpreter of it. And there will not be different laws at Rome and at Athens, or different laws now and in the future, but one eternal and unchangeable law will be valid for all nations and all times, and there will be one master and one ruler, that is, God, over us all, for he is the author of this law, its promulgator, and its enforcing judge. Whoever is disobedient is fleeing from himself and denying his human nature, and by reason of this very fact, he will suffer the worst penalties, even if he escapes what is commonly considered punishment.[77]

---

76   The original stated "various."

77   Corrington's note: "Cicero, *De Re Publica*, bk. 3, pp. 22 et seq. Loeb Classical Library (London: Heinemann, Ltd., 1922). 211."

Cicero's creation of the symbol of a *vera lex* styled after the logos for a universal humanity evokes the Heraclitean comparison of Logos and law, noting that the wicked—Heraclitus' sleepwalkers—ignore the *vera lex* at their peril and that a good man requires no interpreter of this law: he searches himself in order to understand it.

By the beginning of the Christian era, the symbolism of a universal humanity and of the humanities which characterized it had been differentiated and established as a theoretical norm in the power-centers of the ecumene and was understood as a matter of course among such leaders as the Stoic emperors, Antoninus Pius and Marcus Aurelius. As Werner Jaeger expresses it:

> [*Humanitas*] meant the process of educating man into his true form, the real and genuine human nature. . . It starts from the ideal, not from the individual. Above man as a member of the horde, and man as a supposedly independent personality, stands man as an ideal; and that ideal was the pattern towards which Greek educators as well as Greek poets, artists, and philosophers always looked. But what is the ideal man? It is the universally valid model of humanity, which all individuals are bound to imitate.[78]

Humanitas as the process of searching out and achieving the ideal form of man defines the field of study we term the Humanities as it was understood in Classical times. That complex of meanings arising from the philosopher's insight into the unity of human consciousness variously described as logos or vera lex, serves as the noetic constitution of the questioning that continues the search initiated in the West by Anaximander and Heraclitus into the common character of a human nature grounded on invariant law—the ideal, in Jaeger's phrase, which itself resonates to the order of the cosmos.

The sudden irruption of Christianity into the late Classical *ecumene* caused two extraordinary changes in sensibility. On the one hand, it claimed the truth of the Crucified and Resurrected to be unique and exclusive. Unique in that Christianity did not acknowledge itself to stand as one among the multiplicity of parallel truths acknowledged by the nations; exclusive in that it denied to its contemporaries any portion of theological truth whatsoever. The gods of the ecumene, one and all, were false.

On the other hand, and quite possibly more devastating to humanitas, Christianity, in the work of St. John and St. Paul, displaced the *situs* of truth from the nous to the *pneuma*—from mind to spirit.[79] The search for alethia of the Heraclitian One which is common to all was replaced by uncommon faith (*pistis*) in the

---

78   Corrington's note: "Werner Jaeger, *Paideia: The Ideals of Greek Culture*. Book 1 (New York: Oxford University Press, 1945), xxiii–xxiv."

79   Italics added for terms like *situs*, *pneuma*, and *pistis*.

Johannine Logos made flesh in the person of Christ. The rightly famed formalism of faith as "the substance of things hoped for, the evidence of things unseen" in Hebrews partook of Hellenistic-philosophic language, yet simultaneously vaulted beyond the process of questioning, replacing the noetic search (*zetesis*) of the philosopher with the faith (*pistis*) of the servants of Christ.[80]

The pneumatic experience, like its mythopoetic and noetic predecessors, constitutes at once the presencing[81] of a new style of truth in the psyche and the recognition that what has been perceived as truth before is, in the aftermath of the Christian theophany, *pseudos*, only an appearance, or *doxa*, mere opinion.

The Johannine insight that the logos has been incarnated in a man and the Pauline theophanic experience of the Resurrected must be understood to constitute an epoch in the history of human consciousness. The new situs of truth in the spirit rather than in the consciousness of human beings cannot be seen as simply one more event in the continuing differentiation of consciousness from the compact myth. The unified Christian symbolism, in its break from the world and from the law as expressed in the work of St. Paul, together with its intense expectation of the *Parousia*,[82] the return of the Resurrected, establishes a before-and-after structure in the psyches of those who participate.

As a result, the revelational style of truth which forms the Hebraic tradition and which is central in the experiences of St. John and St. Paul brings with it both the burden of a certainty which blesses and focuses the soul, and an eschatological rigor which devalues continuation of the Classical search (*zetesis*) for the logos of psyche and physis. When God has spoken, once and for all, what question remains?

Such an interpretation is not incorrect—so long as we carefully establish the limits of the "substance" and "evidence" of Hebrews within their experiential context and acknowledge that the meaning of the Christian symbols arises from and is dependent upon the theophany which engendered them.

The Pauline and Johannine expressions of the vision of the Resurrected must not be denied their propagandistic dimension, nor should the clear grounds upon which they invite literalist deformation from movements in the souls of those who experienced the Christian symbols as full of meaning into purported events within the field of empirical reality be ignored. Millennial expectation, a restless tension in opposition to the cosmos as it is, a contempt for the philosopher's search through questioning (now perceived as irrelevant), a minimizing of the value of other spiritualties however deeply held—all these are characteristic of the epochal change.

---

80   Corrington's note: "Cf. Jaroslav Pelikan, *The Emergence of the Catholic Tradition (100–600)*, vol. 1 of *The Christian Tradition* (Chicago: University of Chicago Press, 1971), 41–49." In the original manuscript, this is footnote 13a (p. 14). The endnotes then list a note 14, but there is no reference number for endnote 14 in the text. The book cited in the endnotes is "Alan Watts, *Beyond Theology* (New York: World Publishing Company, 1966), 204 et seq. et passim."

81   Sensing + presence = "presencing."

82   Ancient Greek philosophical term for "presence" or "arrival."

There is no purpose in laboring the point. The limits of the pneumatic symbols announce themselves. Displacement of the experiential center of the psyche from nous to *pneuma* is the shift from knowledge to faith—from noesis to pistis. The intellectual compulsion that compels men to agree upon the truths of mathematics or, assuming that they are mature enough to engage in the *bios theoretikos*, the reflective life, to agree upon the logos which moves in both physis and psyche becomes, if not untruth, at best a secondary truth. The Question insofar as it is directed at the cosmos loses both its intensity and its significance, and will regain neither for some 1,300 years. Even the questioning designed to probe and clarify the noetic depth of the psyche will tend to derail over time into spiritual examination, a search for sin and the conditions that occasion sin.

The expansion of the range of application of the Pauline and Johannine experiences is dramatic. What began as a movement of profound meaning in individual souls had become, within a century or so, a series of declarations regarding the nature of reality itself. The pneumatic revelation has, according to the claim, "made all things new." The search of the philosophers is replaced by belief in a growing body of metastatic doctrinal symbols arising among secondary post-Apostolic figures, symbols designed to preserve and to render permanent the insights of those who originally underwent the theophanic experiences. The spiritual distance between the original experiences of the Incarnation, Transfiguration, Crucifixion, and Resurrection, and the literalist dogma grafted onto them as time passed is the distance between a life lived and a life reported upon.

For all their evocative power and pragmatic historical success, the Christian symbols remain representative of movements in the soul transferred to other souls who experience like movements. The symbols do not exhaust the potential or the rationale of mankind to continue the philosopher's search, nor do they annul the primary experience of the cosmos and the symbolisms arising from that experience. The truth of the myth and the truth of the nous cannot be cancelled by the pneumatic theophany of the Resurrected. As St. Paul himself acknowledged, there would remain Jews to whom the Pauline and Johannine insights are scandal, Greeks to whom they are foolishness.

Moreover, the concrete reality of the cosmos and the mystery of physis and psyche, remain, outside the circle of Christian enthusiasts, as they were before. The lastingness of the cosmos, the spiritual discoveries of seers, prophets, and thinkers, and the reality of the Whole, embracing physis, psyche, and cosmos must be understood as an unceasing process containing, in the mode of existence, everything that has been or will be—including the spiritual movements themselves along with their encompassing claims.

By the fifth century of the present era, the classical symbolism of humanities, literally debased, had become effectively a different thing, *Christianitas*. The fundamental Christian symbols had been torn from their experiential context as purely pneumatic differentiations opening the believing soul to a new level of insight. The symbols had been literalized into, among other things, blocks of political meaning joined to Roman power. The fateful transformation of Christianity from a spiritual community into a counter of imperial power politics amounted to something more than the elevation of a sect and a doctrine among dozens of others to an authoritative position. In the crumbling cultural substance of the ecumene, the bewildering complexities of sectarian combat pitted a variety of mystery religions, Gnostic illuminati, heretical dissenters and soldier-followers of Mithra against one another. The lengthy and bloody struggle of Arian versus Athanasian reached to the imperial palace for its uncertain resolution. At last, nothing proved capable of offering a moderating resistance to the orthodox variant of the new enthusiasm and its hardening dogmatic structure.

Perhaps to its own astonishment, the Christian community found itself the substance of a new cultural and political order, its literalized and deformed symbols taken as the spiritual basis of Roman society.

The destruction of paganism was symbolized by the closing of the schools of philosophy at Athens in 529 under Justinian. Even before that, St. Jerome could not conceal his glee in contemplating the new order:

> How few are there who now read Aristotle? How many are there who know the books, or even the name of Plato? You may find, here and there, a few old men who have nothing else to do, who study them in a corner. However, the whole world speaks the language of our Christian peasants and anglers, the whole world re-echoes their words.[83]

And again:

> Even in Rome itself paganism is left in solitude. The old temples are inhabited only by the owls, and the very standards of the soldiers are emblazoned with the sign of the cross.[84]

Even St. Augustine was prepared to prohibit philosophical questioning in the name of the Faith. Speaking of the old cosmological idea of eternal recurrence—a notion prominent in Aristotle—he wrote,

---

83   Corrington's note: "St. Jerome, Preface to the translation of Galatians, in *The Principle Works*, trans. W. H. Fremantle, quoted in Herschel Baker, *The Image of Man* (New York: Harper Torchbooks, 1961), 138."

84   Corrington's note: "St. Jerome, *Letter CVII*, quoted in Baker 138."

Who, I say, can listen to such things? Who can accept or suffer them to be spoken? Were they true, it were only more prudent to keep silence regarding them, but . . . it were the part of wisdom not even to know them.[85]

The language of a common humanity was not abolished. Christ's command to go and teach all nations appeared on its face to stand parallel to the vision of Alexander and Cicero in its recognition of a common source of order within all human beings. But the In-Between (*metaxy*) symbolism of Plato had been transposed from the philosopher's psyche in equipoise between apeirontic depth and noetic height to the awful and inscrutable tension of Everyman's soul suspended between time and eternity, ringed around by lethal, intracosmic enemies—world, flesh, and devil with heaven above and hell below. In the *Civitas Dei*, the human enterprise itself was contracted to the scope of a mystery play with intelligence brought into the service of doctrine.

Wisdom no longer consisted in the loving search for the divine ground through the questioning of physis and psyche. On the contrary, the Questioning had been officially terminated with the acceptance of the orthodox Christian doctrinal symbols, and humanity, properly so-called, had become the Mystical Body of Christ.

II

In the centuries that followed, the Christian venture flourished, producing extraordinary minds of its own, combating, co-opting, or ingesting its internal dissent, whether tribal or heretical. Aside from the sudden eruption of Islam, the emerging fabric of Christendom was able, with no more than a forgivable myopia, to see itself as the carrier of the cultural of ecumenical humanitas in its new guise as Christianitas. The vastness of the Christianized realms was such that, for centuries, only at the Eastern peripheries was there sustained contact with peoples who did not, in one way or another, fit within the Judeo-Christian-Roman vision of the world.

The history of Christendom is not our topic and we must pass over immense stretches of time to contemplate the situation of humanitas as we approach our own age. But we must make one brief pause because, in the centuries following the destruction of classical civilization, there is at least one extraordinary document that speaks for those who encountered the West from outside and announced to it in chilling terms that humanity and Christianity were not one and the same.

In the thirteenth century, pressure from the Mongol expansion in the East marked a sudden and astonishing penetration into the field of Christian religious and political order. It appears that emissaries of Pope Innocent IV and Louis IX of France went to Kuyuk Khan to inform him of the immorality of his attacks upon Christendom, adjuring him to accept baptism and submit to the authority of the

85 Corrington's note: "St. Augustine, *De Civitas Dei*, bk. 22.20."

Pope. I quote the Khan's answer at length in order that you, like Innocent and Louis, may experience the shock of a voice from beyond the bounds of what represented itself as the carrier of the single definitive human truth:

> You have said it would be good if I received baptism;
> You have informed me of it, and you have sent me the request.
> This your request, we do not understand it.

Another point: You have sent me these words "You have taken all the realms of the Magyars and the Christians altogether; I am surprised at that. Tell us what has been the fault of these?"

These your words we did not understand them.

(In order to avoid, however, any appearance that we pass over this point in silence, we speak in answer to you thus:)

> The Order of God, both Genghis Khan and the Kha Khan have sent it to
>   make it known,
> But the order of God they did not believe.
> Those of whom you speak did even meet in a great council,
> They showed themselves arrogant and have killed our envoy-ambassadors.
> The eternal God has killed and destroyed the men in those realms.
> Save by order of God, anybody by his own force, how could he kill, how
>   could he take?
> And if you say: "I am a Christian; I adore God; I despise the others,"
> How shall you know whom God forgives and to whom He grants His mercy?
> How do you know that you speak such words?
> By the virtue of God,
> From the rising of the sun to its setting,
> All realms have been granted to us.
> Without the order of God
> How could anyone do anything?
> Now you ought to say from a sincere heart:
> "We shall be your subjects;
> We shall give unto you our strength."
> You in person at the head of the kings, all together, without exception, come
>   and offer us service and homage;
> Then shall we recognize your submission.
> And if you do not observe the Order of God,
> And disobey our orders,

We shall know you to be our enemies.
That is what we make known to you.
If you disobey,
What shall we know then?
God will know it.[86]

The clash of two exclusive truths is by no means unique. One chooses the Mongol Orders of Submission as illustration rather than Koranic exemplars simply to avoid comparison of two strains of the same tradition. The implications of the meeting are clarified by quoting from the edict of Kuyuk Khan:

By order of the living God
Genghis Khan, the sweet and venerable Son of God, says:
God is high above all, He Himself, the only immortal God,
And on earth, Genghis Khan is the only Lord.[87]

In the compact language of the Edicts, the Khan holds all power, spiritual and political, under the Mandate of Heaven. Those lands held by Christians belong to him and the Christians are his subjects whenever he chooses to exercise the sovereignty over them he holds of right.

This contention of opposing symbolizations of truth, of two differently organized humanities, each conceiving itself as the pre-eminent carrier of an exclusive and unchallengeable divine order foreshadowed later encounters of Christian European nation-states which, in their imperial expansiveness, would remain no wiser or more ready than before to hear the claims of others to represent humanity through their ordering symbolisms.

On the contrary, Western polity had soon made much of the world a zany patchwork of colonial entities held together by troops and trade, roamed by missionaries of various Christian sects eager to supplant ancient and virtually unknown structures of order with their own doctrinal variants of the theophany of the Apostles. At first, the encounter of Westerners with extensive and elaborate civilizations in India, Southeast Asia, China, and Japan did not cause the Christian rulers to contemplate once more the question of the Khan: "How shall you know whom God forgives and to whom he grants his mercy?"

But the very number of these alternate humanities, these other mankinds, together with the discovery of the vast territories inhabited by them and the correspondingly great spans of time over which they had existed—not to mention

---

86   Corrington's note: "Quoted in Voegelin, *The New Science of Politics: An Introduction* (Chicago: University of Chicago Press, 1953), 56–59."

87   Corrington's note: "Voegelin, *New Science*, 58."

Western sectarian wars and the rise of mutant secular ideologies alienated not only from the Christian symbols but from any spirituality at all—assured that the dominance of the West would, even as it expanded into new areas by virtue of its extraordinary technology and its consequent mastery of power politics, begin to lose its millennial assurance, and in the spiritual ebb following, the alternative human orders would at last be heard.

By the latter decades of the eighteenth century, even as secular ideologues and revolutionary activists began the task of hacking apart the spiritual remains of Christendom in Europe left over from the religious wars, the empirical and theoretical groundwork for a new humanitas had begun to form.

The horizons of mankind were widened and deepened by the work of archeologists, ethnologists, philologists, and a host of other scientists in a variety of fields.

The sudden exposure of the scope of Egyptian civilization by French, British, and German scholars had hardly been digested when Sir William Jones demonstrated the unity of the Indo-European languages through his Sanskrit studies. Within a few decades, in the hands of H. H. Wilson, Max Mueller, and others, the Vedas, Brahmanas, Aranyakas, and Upanishads[88] began to be edited and translated, revealing the presence of a line of spiritual literature extending back in time perhaps eight hundred years before Homer, and almost a millennium prior to the actual writing of the Old Testament.

Within a hundred years or so of its beginnings, the impulse of the new human sciences had unearthed Mycenae and Troy, had pushed back the cultural origins of the human species by thousands of years, and had opened up vistas for future study that would have been inconceivable, even proscribed, prior to the seventeenth century.

At the same time, the work of Schlegel and Max Mueller began the study of comparative mythology, demonstrating the astonishing similarity of mythopoetic patterns extending over continents and millennia. Some of the work was hasty, some misguided—some ended in one or another cul-de-sac. But whatever the faults of the theorization, the materials themselves, recovered from a past hardly more than legend even to those whose ancestors had participated in it, remained as empirical evidence of the duration and intensity of the human search, of the unbroken line of questioning in mythopoetic form which had existed recognizably long before the discovery of writing and which only disappears from view in the mists of the Paeleolithicum.[89]

The nature of the Vedic search for the ground will serve as a brief illustration of the contours of the Question outside the Western ecumene. Archaeological

---

88   Corrected from "Upanisads."

89   More commonly spelled "Paleolithicum."

and cryptographic research have not yet broken through the mystery of writing of the Indus Valley culture discovered by Sir John Marshall and others in the 1920s. It is certain, however, that the civilization compares in age with those of Sumer and Egypt, and its geographical extent was almost twice again as great as either. The civilization was already past its prime when Indo-Iranian invaders, calling themselves Aryan, began to move into what is present day Pakistan and Northwest[90] India. The interrelationship between Indus and Aryan culture has not been worked out, but there is good reason to suppose that, over centuries, the barbarian cosmological ideas of the Aryans were diluted by the thinking of the autochthonic peoples who had composed the Indus culture, and it may be that the later hymns of the Rg Veda[91] reflect that change. Vedic thinking illustrates the character of its questioning in book 10 of Rg Veda[92] (RV 10.129):

There was neither non-existence nor existence then;
There was neither the realm of space nor the sky which is beyond.
What stirred? Where? In whose protection?
Was there water bottomlessly deep?
There was neither death nor immortality then.
There was no distinguishing sign of night nor of day.
That One breathed breathless, by its own impulse.
Other than that, there was nothing beyond.
*

Desire came upon That One in the beginning; that was the first seed of Mind.
Poets seeking in their hearts with wisdom found the bond of existence in
     non-existence.
*

Who really knows? Who will here proclaim it?[93]. . .
Whence is this creation?
The gods came afterwards with the creation of this universe.
Who then knows whence it has arisen?[94]
Whence this creation has arisen—perhaps it formed itself, or perhaps it
     did not.
That One who looks down on it, in the highest heaven, only he knows—
Or perhaps he does not know.[95]

---

90   Changed from "North west."

91   "Rigveda," a collection of sacred Sanskrit hymns in the Old Indo-Aryan language.

92   "Rigveda."

93   Question-mark added to match that which appears in the quoted source.

94   Question-mark added to match that which appears in the quoted source.

95   Corrington's note: "Rg Veda 10.129, in Wendy Doniger O'Flaherty, *The Rig Veda* (New York: Finland books, 1981), 25. Translations from the Sanskrit are in some cases modified by the present author."

Already, in the second millennium B.C., the Vedic penetration of the Question has equaled that of Xenophanes. The intracosmic gods are brushed off as possible creators in favor of That One (Tad Ekam) and the symbolic equivalents of *eros* and *nous* have been differentiated. The polarities of non-existence and existence have been distinguished by seers who have discerned the process through which existent things emerge from non-existence. Finally, there is the poet who, amidst his questioning, has distanced himself so far from the things standing in the field of existence and from his own speculative experience of creation that he is able to raise the Question to the level of quiet *skepsis* with regard to That One. Does even he know the origin of what is?

The core of Vedic cosmogonic speculation centers upon the sacrifice as the source of creation and renewal. Purusha, a figure of primal man, is partner-victim along with the original Vedic gods and seers in the sacrifice, which is simultaneously the creation of the cosmos and its ordering:

> The sacrifice that is spread out with threads on all sides, drawn tight with a
>   hundred and one divine acts, is woven by its fathers as they come near:
> Weave forward, weave backward, they say as they sit by the loom that is
>   stretched tight.
> The Man stretches the warp and draws the weft;
> The Man has spread it out upon this dome of the sky.
> These are the pegs that are fastened in place;
> They made the melodies into the shuttles for weaving.
> What was the original model, and what was the copy, and what was the
>   connection between them?
> What was the butter and what was the enclosing wood?
> What was the meter, and what was the invocation, and the chant, when all
>   the gods sacrificed the God?
> *
> That was the model for the human sages, our fathers, when the primeval
>   sacrifice was born.
> With the eye that is mind, in thought, I see those who were first to offer this
>   sacrifice.[96]

Cosmos and sacrifice merge into a single primordial act of creation in which men, gods, and the God beyond the gods are partners in establishing *Rta*, the Vedic equivalent of logos, cosmic order, truth, reality—the concepts are virtually interchangeable in Vedic Sanskrit. The poet, through the mind's eye, participates in the eternal sacrifice, questioning the unity between the cosmos and some pre-

96   Corrington's note: "Rg Veda 10.130, in O'Flaherty, *Rig Veda*, 33."

existing ideal paradigm, and goes on to say that the order of reality is maintained by sacrificial repetition carried forward by the generations of seers in unbroken line: "When the wise men looked back along the path of those who went before, they took up the reins like charioteers."[97]

The level of discourse in the Brahmanas and Aranyakas, sacrificial manuals almost Talmudic in style, continues the line of Vedic meaning in what appears to Westerners as an extraordinarily convoluted manner simply because, contrary to Greek noetic differentiation, the manipulation and development of symbols continues within the original mythopoetic mode.

Gods rise and fall in importance; old gods drop from the devotions and new ones—or transformation of old ones—enter. Within the five volumes of the Satapatha Brahmana, dozens of seemingly contradictory myths stand side by side, in what Eric Voegelin has referred to as the "insouciance" of cosmological thinking.[98] Sacrificial implements become deified, the power of speech changes sex from the goddess Vac to the priestly Brahmanaspati—who at last becomes that portentous Vedic spiritual discovery, the Holy Power of the Word, Brahman. The term, according to one etymology, arises from the Indo-European root *brh*—denoting the burgeoning thrusting force of growth and expansion—making it closely parallel to Greek physis.[99]

In the archaic Upanishads, originally esoteric annexes to the Brahmanas for the use of certain spiritual virtuosi, it is discerned that the Tad Ekam of late Rg Vedic speculation is Brahman, at first considered the power substance that both produces and is the cosmos—unqualified, undifferentiated, subject only to negative description.

In the same early stratum of Upanishadic materials as well—although almost certainly a later development than Brahman—is the differentiation of Atman, originally the vital breath, thus etymologically similar to psyche.

The great insight of Vedic thinking then takes place: the essence of *physis-Brahman* and the essence of *psyche-Atman* are experienced to be one and the same. That which is the substrate of the intelligible universe is also the substrate of the human soul. In the *Taittiriya Upanishad* we find the lyric rejoicing of one who has penetrated past the appearances of the world and discovered the unity of his deepest self with the substrate of all that is, the supreme reality:

> I am the first-born of Rta [order, truth, reality],
> Earlier than the gods in the navel of immortality.
> Who gives me away, he indeed has aided me.

---

97   Corrington's note: "Ibid."

98   Corrington's note: "Cf. Julius Eggeling, trans., *The Satapatha Brahmana*, vols. 12, 26, 41, 43, and 44 of *The Sacred Books of the East*, edited by F. Max Müller (Oxford: Clarendon Press, 1882)."

99   Corrington's note: "Cf. Jan Gonda, *Notes on Brahman* (Utrecht: J. L. Beyers, 1950)."

I who am food eat the eater of food.[100]
I have vanquished the universe.[101]

It is difficult not to notice the parallels in this singular passage between Vedic thought and image and that of Christianity—which lies some six or seven hundred years in the future. "Who gives me away, he indeed has aided me." "Whosoever shall seek to save his life shall lose it, and whosoever shall lose his life shall preserve it" (Luke 17:33). "I, who am food, eat the eater of food,"[102] "Take and eat, for this is my body" (Mark 14:22). Finally there is the exact verbal parallel between the one who has realized his true nature and the words of Christ as reported in John 16:33: "Be of good cheer, for I have overcome the cosmos."

Similarly, a passage closely resembling the epochal work of Anaximander is set out in the Mundaka Upanishad:

This is the truth:
As from a blazing fire identical sparks eddy forth by the thousands.
Even so, O beloved, all manner of beings arise from the imperishable
And return to it once again.[103]

Brahman is equivalent to the *apeirontic* depth, unqualified, unknowable, the processive *arche* of existing things, itself nothing—even as *Atman* is equivalent not precisely to the psyche of Heraclitus, but to the *logos* of the *psyche*, deep beyond knowing. The parallels of experience and symbolization between Vedic and pre-Socratic thought are such that they have produced a fairly extensive—though singularly uninformative—technical literature attempting to demonstrate the influence of India or early Greek thought or, more rarely, the reverse. Needless to say, there is no hard evidence to support any substantial interaction between the two cultures prior to the Alexandrian penetration of India in 326 B.C. The parallels—far more extensive and detailed than I have had time to point out—reveal little or nothing about "cultural diffusion," but may well be pregnant with meaning for those who subscribe to one or another archetypal theory of human consciousness.

One must limit claims made for the Vedic work. Even the most careful translations of the Creation Hymns and the Upanishads cannot be kept free of cultural contamination, and it would be wrong to suppose that the Ṛg Veda is,

---

100   Missing punctuation here: "I, who am food, eat the eater of food."

101   Corrington's note: "*Taittiriya Upanishad*, III.10.6, in S. Radhakrishanan, *The Principal Upanishads* (London: George Allen and Unwin, 1953), 562."

102   Commas added to quotation.

103   Corrington's note: "*Mundaka Upanishad*, II.1.1., in Radhakrishnan, *Upanishads*, 680."

as it were, a precise Vedic equivalent of pre-Socratic speculation, only achieved hundreds of years earlier. That is by no means so.

However, one evaluates the "break with the myth," which in the West is supposed to portend the beginning of philosophy, no such break takes place clearly within Vedic or even later classical Hindu thought. The experiences referred to by the symbols Brahman and Atman are not differentiated from their mythopoetic context, as are such symbols as physis and psyche in Greek thinking. The Indian equivalents of Platonic *philosophia* or Ciceronian *religio* never emerge as distinct units of meaning.

The bewildering truth is that the myth becomes, in India, an intricate and sophisticated style of thinking, blending almost imperceptibly into later Nyaya logic, Vaisheshika atomism, Vedantic monism, the amazing atheistic ritualism of Karma-Mimamsa, and complex scholastic argumentation by the time of the great commentaries on the Brahmasutra by Sankaracarya, Ramanuja, and Madhva.[104]

What should not be limited is our realization that from 2400 B.C. or earlier, until the present, there has existed in unbroken continuity an Eastern spiritual and intellectual ecumene as vigorous, as productive, as intensely self-representative as the Western. For over four thousand years, the experience of the Questioning in compact form has not ceased. From Vedic and Brahmanic thinking arose Buddhism, which flowed East into China, across to Japan, down into Southeast Asia and the islands of Indonesia. Buddhism existed for some seven hundred years in India, struggling peacefully with Hinduism for precedence. Then it ebbed away. The culture of India withstood a millennium of Islamic domination—thought by some scholars to be the most brutal and bloodthirsty occupation in human history—and two hundred years of British rule thereafter.

Then, in 1910, one William Archer, chiefly known for his shabby but ubiquitous translations of Ibsen, sat down and wrote a book entitled *Is India Civilized?*[105] Western *humanitas* had come to that.

III

If our analysis is correct on principle, we find that fields of human study exclusively Western in orientation have no claim to be called Humanities. An exclusivist study of Western literature is inconclusive; an exclusivist study of Western history is impossible; an exclusivist study of Western philosophy deforms the meaning of *philosophia*, and the continuance of such mischief stunts the

---

104 Corrington's note: "Arthur A. MacDonell, *A History of Sanskrit Literature* (New York: Haskell House Publishers, Ltd., 1968), 421–424. MacDonell insists upon a line of influence running from India through the Pythagoreans into early Greek thinking, noting a number of ideational parallels whose priority with the Indians cannot be reasonably doubted, and which appear nowhere else. His points, which are generally recognized, are sufficient to keep the controversy alive; his case is not made."

105 *Is India Civilized?* is actually by Sir John Woodroffe (who also wrote under the name of Arthur Avalon). The book came out in 1918. William Archer did, however, write a book titled *India and the Future* (1917).

recovery of humanitas in its original sense—the study of that which is common to all, that in which our humanity is made luminous to itself.

The Humanities, for all their topical divisions, are discovered to be fragments of that *paideia*[106]—formation, education—that leads to a renewed evocation of humanitas. The validity of the Humanities depends upon their intelligibility as components of the continuing process of the Questioning toward the divine ground as the essence of human existence in all its multiplicity of cultural forms.

The Humanities are not the truth; they bear witness to the truth insofar as they penetrate noetically to the common experiential symbols of human beings, to the experiences of love and death, growth and decline, transformation and liberation. The scholar of the Humanities does not create the experiential symbols; he discovers and explicates their appearance in culture. The scholar of the Humanities is not an artist, a scientist, a mystic, or a philosopher. His task is to recognize, interpret, and preserve the essential unity of symbolic variation across human space and time.

Derailment of the Humanities takes place in three ways:

1. By *Contraction* of the field of experiences and symbolisms to be studied to a range religiously, topically, politically, racially, geographically, or temporally conformable to the "climate of opinion" in which the scholar works.

2. By *Mutilation* of the field through departmentalization, periodization, or nationalization of the phenomena, cutting away or ignoring embarrassing or troublesome questions that arise during research by claiming that they are irrelevant—or that, since they fall outside one's "area of study," they do not require pursuit.

3. By *Distortion* of the field through the prohibition of questions, or diversion of the search by the supplying of ersatz "final solutions" and phantasmagoric second realities provided by the ideologies.

The purpose of the Humanities is *anamnetic*:[107] the Humanities remember; the Humanities re-collect. Even in their present fragmented situation, the Humanities should force upon us the memory of humanitas in all its experiential and symbolic variety. Properly, the Humanities bear witness to the Question regarding the logos common to all, and which, called Ma'at, or Me, Rta, Dharma or Tao—or Grand Unified Theory, for that matter, stands as the unifying substratum beneath all symbolizations of human experience.

In their anamnetic role, the Humanities constitute a reflection upon the symbolic expressions of the Question as they are revealed in the psychic activities of concrete human beings in the context of their concrete situations; the Humanities do not claim dogmatic truth for their assertions, for the assertions are not theirs. Rather

---

106 Ancient Greek term referring to the training of the youth to become members of the *polis*.

107 This term derives from Voegelin and is a variation of the word *anamnesis*.

they bear witness to what had been thought and said by human beings about the search in tension toward the divine ground—in Heidegger's phrase, "How does it stand with Being?"

The Humanities are not the truth, but in their striving to record the Question in all its variety, its breakthroughs, its derailments, its sudden insights, its barren and heartbreaking deformations and exultant recoveries—in its pressing toward the human limit at the horizon of the Illimitable, the presence of truth is known.

The recovery of the Humanities takes place on principle each time a scholar breaks with the limitations pressed upon him by convention, by time and place, by ideology, and follows the Question where it leads him—because mere reiteration of the Question continues the loving search for truth, and the truth shall make you free.

The Recovery of the Humanities II

1986

This chapter originated as a lecture at Kansas State University in 1986. It builds on the ideas in the previous chapter regarding the derailment of the humanities in light of the gradual loss of noetic homonoia or sense of like-mindedness among disparate cultures with similar understandings of symbolic order. Corrington seeks to substantiate the arguments from the previous chapter by consulting T. S. Eliot's notion of order as experienced through literary texts. Corrington suggests that Eliot's notion of order:

> exists initially in the psyche of the poet-critic who represents his experience of truth by way of the symbolism of simultaneous order; it exists secondarily in the collective psyches of those who are capable of reenacting Eliot's experience theoretically, and who find themselves, as if in Platonic dialogue with the poet, bound to admit the truth of what he says about the order—even as his work continues and extends the order.

Applying Eliot's notion of order to classical texts, Corrington demonstrates that symbolized experience has a temporal element whereas the psyche, existing independently of any one person, is timeless.

Corrington references the National Socialist German Worker's Party (otherwise known as the Nazi Party), various Marxist-Leninist operations, the French Academy, and the Index Libororum of the Holy Office as examples of practices and institutions that attempted to break down the ideal order that is represented in the continuity of certain canonical texts. Corrington challenges Eliot's apparent assumption that art and literature are the proper lenses for examining symbolic order. He considers what qualities of a work make it literary as opposed to philosophical—or something else entirely. His point is not to discredit Eliot but to suggest that Eliot's notion of order in literature is nuanced and complex.

Corrington argues that what drives human culture is "the human psyche in search of itself in the multiplicity of its forms, dimensions, and possibilities—and the loving and fearing tension within that psyche toward the divine ground." Corrington returns to the idea that studying symbolic orders in different times and places reveals the commonalities between disparate peoples and cultures:

> Whether we probe the roots of high civilizations or purportedly "primitive" cultures, the result is the same: the foundations of human order are invariant: The society in question either represents itself as mirroring the order of the cosmos, the society of the gods, or expresses itself as that existential ground upon which gods and men interact with one another, the business of men and gods inextricably fused.

Understood this way, the political order of any given society can be explained as a reflection of metaxy, that state between the human and the divine whereby humans attempt to organize themselves in keeping with their beliefs about the nature of the divine and its order.

The understanding of human place in the world in relation to the divine is, according to Corrington, the humanities. Corrington critiques Eliot's notion of an ideal order but credits Eliot for what Eliot's theory discloses, to wit, the organizing possibility of symbols to convey experiential realities: "Eliot's earlier critical expression of an ideal order is thus discovered to be an inadequate but evocative symbolism which has, even as a poem might, invited us to probe the experience symbolized and rectify, through analysis of the symbolisms, the precise character of the experience." Corrington again calls for the recovery of the humanities, not for the sake of any divisive telos or ideological goal, but instead for the unifying potential of an experiential and symbolic understanding of human purpose over time and in disparate places.

The opening to this essay began with Roman numeral I. However, the following section of the essay also begins with Roman numeral I. Therefore, the Roman numeral that opens this essay has been removed so that the remainder of the essay does not require renumbering.

Some months ago in another forum I dealt with the origin and meaning of that group of activities we call the Humanities, and with the problems surrounding their recovery. This evening, I would like to extend my analysis and speculation.

In that earlier talk, I discussed the experiential origins of the symbolism *humanitas* and some of its more important classical expressions. Terms such as Paedeia-formation, education in its broadest human sense (the German *bildung,* perhaps); *homonoia,* like-mindedness, human thinking—the Aristotelian-Alexandrian symbolism under which the explosion of Greek culture, of the noetic enterprise, set out to serve as the *paedeia* not only of Hellenistic Mediterranean culture, but ultimately of western civilization.

I suggested that the foundations of classical noetic culture had been undermined by the upsurgence of spiritual fideism[108] that eventuated in the destruction of the underlying values of Greco-Roman civilization by a triumphant Christianity which replaced humanitas by Christianitas, and reduced the noetic enterprise to the status of a servant of dogmatic theology.

I believe my audience realized then that my remarks were not to be taken as an assault upon Christian religion—much less upon spiritual values in general. Quite the opposite. I proposed that the loss of a noetic *homonoia,* a like-mindedness among human beings, a common reality independent of dogma or claims of religious uniqueness and exclusivity, was in large part responsible for the fractionated condition of those areas of study and scholarship we call the Humanities.

I closed by arguing that a study of *Western* philosophy is meaningless; that a study of *Western* history is inconclusive; that a study of *Western* literature or *Western* theology is, at best, parochial. One studies philosophy, history, literature

108   Corrected from "fidism."

and theology in their wholeness as symbolic orders pertaining to the human in all its variety—or one had just as well not study them at all. *Humanitas* is indivisible— and a *paedeia* founded on principle upon truncated and divided fields of study has no business being called the Humanities.

This evening, I would like to carry the argument forward, using as my proof text a citation from one of the most distinguished poets and critics of the twentieth century.

I

There is a haunting passage in one of T. S. Eliot's earliest essays that any English-speaking champion of the Humanities might do well to memorize:

> . . . the whole of the literature of Europe from Homer and within it the whole of the literature of [one's] own country has a simultaneous existence and composes a simultaneous order. This historical sense, which is a sense of the timeless as well as of the temporal, and of the temporal and of[109] the timeless together, is what makes a writer traditional. . . .
>
> No poet, no artist of any art, has his complete meaning alone.. . . The existing monuments form an ideal order among themselves, which is modified by the introduction of the new (the really new) work of art among them. The existing order is complete before the new work arrives; for order to persist after the supervention of novelty, the *whole*[110] existing order must be, if ever so slightly, altered.. . . Whoever has approved this idea of order, of the form of European, of English literature,[111] will not find it preposterous that the past should be altered by the present as much as the present is directed by the past.[112]

Given the canons of a contemporary positivistic criticism, one might suppose that Eliot's ideal order amounts to little more than a catalogue of approved works in accepted styles stretching out over the past 2800 years. But Eliot's ideal order is not such a catalogue—nor is it a dogmatic idealist construction in the manner of Hegel or Husserl. Despite the propositional form of his statements, the "ideal order" he describes undoubtedly symbolizes Eliot's own experience of the "existing monuments" of European literature. The order exists concretely in the psyche of the poet who invites us to participate theoretically[113] in his experience of the "simultaneous existence" and "simultaneous order" of a body of symbolisms which,

---

109   Corrington did not include the word "of" in his draft, but the word appears in the source he is quoting.

110   Corrington did not italicize the word *whole* in his draft, but the word is italicized in the source he is quoting.

111   Corrington did not include the comma in his draft, but the comma appears in the source he is quoting

112   Corrington included a footnote but left out the source: "Eliot, T. S. *The Secret Wood: Essays on Poetry and Criticism* (New York: Alfred A. Knopf, 1921)." This lecture contains endnote reference numbers but no endnotes.

113   Corrington's endnotes are missing.

taken together, represent, in some measure, not only the foundations of Western culture but the intelligible order of human reality itself insofar as it is experienced through texts which we refer to as "literature."

As an aside, one might note that Eliot's rhetoric almost conceals the stratum of empirical truth in his insight: the "simultaneous order" extending from the earliest human documents (cited by Eliot as beginning with Homer) to the present is evoked concretely by a trip to any decent bookshop where one might find Homer, Hölderlin, Heidegger, and Hemingway ranged side by side by a nodding clerk whose *padeia* begins and ends with the alphabet.

Of course, analysis of simultaneous existence the attentive psyche of the larger sense of the symbol and order discovers its *situs* in [the] concrete reader who stands in intellectual and spiritual relationship to Homer and to Hemingway as to a pair of contemporaries in the equally concrete quest of human meaning, whether evoked by the *pathos* of King Priam's petition for the body of his vanquished son, or Frederic Henry's leaving behind the body of his love, walking back to the hotel in the rain.

The question of the originary *situs* of Eliot's ideal order answers itself: the order exists initially in the *psyche* of the poet-critic who represents his experience of truth by way of the symbolism of simultaneous order; it exists secondarily in the collective psyches of those who are capable of reenacting[114] Eliot's experience theoretically, and who find themselves, as if in Platonic dialogue with the poet, bound to admit the truth of what he says about the order—even as his work continues and extends the order.

But even assuming our intuitive agreement with the truth of the poet's insight, the analysis must proceed from recognition of the compact symbolisms of simultaneous existence and simultaneous order to a penetration of the symbols themselves.

This simultaneity of order and existence presupposes an element of temporality as its concrete dimension. The battle-ravaged plain before Troy, the bloody retreat from Caporetto, are not incidental to the texts in which they appear. The details of weaponry and ships, the anger of Achilles, the cynicism of Paris, the courage and horror of Hector comprise the empirical structure of the *Iliad*, as, for example, the journey of Frederic Henry in the canvas-covered railroad car past military police executing deserters is fundamental to the empirical structure of *A Farewell to Arms*.

But there is in such writings a more profound dimension as well. The details which structure the works in their temporality fall away like scaffolding within the responding *psyche* of a sensitive reader to reveal the Heraclitean *xynon*, "that which is common to all," in which time is lost in the fathomless reaches of that *psyche* whose limit, Heraclitus tells us, cannot be plumbed, so deep is its *Logos*.

Immersed in the tension of this temporal-atemporal order, the reader becomes a seer—one who remembers the future, foretells the past in the

114 Corrected from "reinacting."

imaginative reenactment of the works playing out their truth within his *psyche*. In such *metalepsis,* participation, the truth of the tale arises in the temporality of symbolized experience to found itself in the timelessness of the *psyche*. In his participative enthusiasm, the reader discovers within himself the Platonic *metaxy*, the "in-between," in which the *psyche* stands between the poles of empirical reality and the realm of meaning described by Albert Camus when he spoke of the novel as that form in which "final words are spoken."

But the arrangement of components into Eliot's ideal order obscures the fact that the force of the order depends, paradoxically, both on what the poet-critic calls its completeness—and upon its openness. The single works which comprise the order cannot stand alone, autonomous; their significance depends upon the meaning they express in relation to one another in the attentive, well-attuned *psyche* of the reader.

Moreover, from both philological and philosophical points of view, later works refer back to those which proceeded them—not because all artists are, by nature, respectful servants of that overarching past to which, like it or not, they are beholden, but because they have no alternative.

The languages, the concepts, the images later artists use are empirically what they are because of the precedent moments which shaped them; the language-symbolisms by which we express our contemporary experience not only are not uniquely ours, but bear upon them the marks of millennial usage. Such changes in or additions to the language or artistic forms which one or two generations may make are rarely in themselves epochal.

It is true and not true to say that the ideal order does not require our contribution, that it would be no less an order and no less ideal were Joyce and Proust, Hermann Brach, Robert Musil, and William Gaddis to be dropped from it somehow. It would still exist in its timelessness, but not in its temporality or its simultaneity. Such contraction and closure would cut off the order from its paradoxical roots in the present and the future and quickly render it a concern for antiquarians rather than for creators. Such mutilations of the order have occurred on a minor regional scale both through the loss of actual works in civilizational upheavals, or through the efforts of such notable institutions as the National Socialist German Worker's Party, various Marxist-Leninist operations, the French Academy, or the *Index Libororum* of the Holy Office.

Even in its purported completeness, in order to maintain its simultaneity, the ideal order must remain open to the temporal flux of creative encounter with new work—which eventuates in additions to its canon, new insights into the experiential reality both mirrored and, in Wordsworth's phrase, "half-created" by the order itself.

It follows that, as the ancient work is the precondition for the more recent, so the more recent work constitutes *de facto* a commentary on the ancient, thereby shifting our perception of it. In Eliot's phrase, "the past is altered by the present as much as the present is directed by the past."

II

The analysis of Eliot's insight as it stands in the original essay is now complete. There stands open the question of whether or not the treatment of a vast collection of concrete texts as constituting an "ideal order" of "simultaneous existence" represents an adequate expression in the form Eliot gave it.

The problems inherent in that question are not without substance.

To begin, there is the serious problem of the ontological status and analytical usefulness of the symbolisms "Literature" and "Art." If the mere raising of such a question seems shocking to literary scholars, that is probably because the present condition of the Humanities is such that an English major, an art major, a history major—even a classics major—may very well have managed to avoid the kind of philosophical discipline that asks founding questions. But once the question is asked, the status of such symbolisms as "literature" and "art" become increasingly problematic. This is not the place to work through the question in detail, but a few observations may suggest the extent of the confusion.

How are we to distinguish those texts (taken in the broadest sense) which are "literary" from those which are something else? How are we to assure ourselves that our distinctions in this regard touch the root of the matter and are not arbitrary and subjective? Is our distinction based on rhetorical characteristics—ornament, style, imagery? Or is there some substantial difference between "literature" and theological, philosophical, scientific, historical, or psychological texts? Is the work of Plato "literature?" What of Theophrastus? Nietzsche? Erwin Schroedinger?[115] Is *The Future of an Illusion* a literary work? What of Aristotle's *Poetics,* or Prescott's *The Conquest of Mexico and Peru*?[116] I would put it to you that I am unaware of any work, historical or critical, that can make a clean sweep of the above questions to the satisfaction of even a minority of scholars who propose to teach "literature."

As Eliot avers that "no artist of any art has his complete meaning alone," he might more trenchantly have said that art itself has no meaning withdrawn from the broader human context in which it arises, to which it refers, and toward which it tends.

The symbolisms "art" and "artist" like "literature" possess cognitive significance only as secondary reflective symbols originally aimed toward emphasizing not the substance of the work, but a certain superior measure of craft and style which may

---

115   Corrected from "Schroedinger."

116   These are two different books: A History of the Conquest of Mexico (1843) and A History of the Conquest of Peru (1847).

accrue to any human endeavor in the sense of classical Greek *techne.* Thus such denominations as the "art" of war, the "art" of love, Zen and the "art" of archery—or as we say today, the Chemical Engineering "literature," the computer programming "literature," etc.

As an expression of superior craft or style, the symbolisms of "art" or "literature" have little to do with substance. A cup by an anonymous potter is as much a cup as one executed by Benvenuto Cellini or Fabergé. The question of artfulness— or of "literary" quality seems accidental, secondary, and equivocal—remnant terminology of an unrealized aesthetics.

Thus we must suppose that the ideal order of texts Eliot describes must possess its ontological integrity at a more fundamental level than that of craft or style. The ancient texts stand in their integrity beyond matters of aesthetics. I do not know that any expert in the cuneiform languages can speak with assurance of the "literary" values of the *Gilgamesh* or the *Enûma Eliŝ.*[117]

We must probe deeper. At this point in our analysis, the objection might properly be raised that we are attempting to supplant an aesthetic ideal order with an antiquarian one—placing age before beauty as it were.

If that were so, the analysis would have derailed. That the character of craft or style perceived in an object cannot be primary may have been shown. But what precisely is there more fundamental than "art," "literary quality," and so on?

Presuming that we might derive somehow an adequate analytic of "literature" as something other than that which is taught in Literature classes, are we prepared to state unequivocally that Eliot's description of an "ideal order" is, in fact, about something called "literature" at all? Is it possible that we might find there is indeed an ideal order precisely as Eliot evokes it—but that it has to do with "literature" or even "art" only in a secondary and relatively unimportant sense?

Again, how is it that the ideal order must begin with Homer? And why should that order be European literature and art in despite of a world order?

Seven hundred years before Homer, the Indo-Aryan poets of *Rg Veda*[118] created a thousand hymns, some of which were not to be rivaled[119] in philosophical depth until the time of the pre-Socratics, or in strength and sweetness for 35 centuries. What of the *Mahabharata,* an epic eight times as long as the *Iliad* and *Odyssey* combined, filled with tales of love and magic and war—of which one small section is called *Baghavad*[120] *Gita,* said by some to be the most sublime spiritual text ever created by human beings? Shall we simply put aside the *Brihadaranyaka Upanishad* in favor of the *Book of Job*? Is it prudent to ignore the *Satapatha Brahmana,* the

---

117 Accents added.

118 Rig Veda.

119 Corrected from "rivalled."

120 More common spelling: "Bhagavad."

Dhammapitaka,[121] Sankaracharya's[122] penetrating and epoch-making commentary on Badarayana's[123] *Bhrama*[124] *Sutras?*

The substance of the ideal, simultaneously existing order of which Eliot spoke cannot be as he expressed it. It does not begin with Homer, and Europe, England, and America are the merest of provinces in its estimable territories.

Despite heroic attempts to cross borders so long closed that they were scarcely even recalled in 1919, Eliot's enunciation of the tradition reveals that his world was half a hemisphere. It was a world in which Homer and the Prophets of Israel marked the *arche*, the beginning and the principle of human thought—in the name of which over half of humanity could be ignored in the evocation of an ideal simultaneous order.

It is not accidental or arbitrary that the majority of modern differentiations of human experience either derive directly from or are influenced by a single impulse. As uncomfortable as positivistic thinking may be rendered by the knowledge, the great driving force at the foundation of human culture wherever and whenever it is found is not military or economic, political or even artistic in any ordinary sense.

Rather it is the human *psyche* in search of itself in the multiplicity of its forms, dimensions, and possibilities—and the loving and fearing tension within that *psyche* toward the divine ground. The force which makes us human, which has arrayed the monuments of Eliot's ideal order in its temporality and timelessness like grain broadcast from the sower's hand, is the spiritual quest in concrete human beings—that which we express in the battered, inadequate, and contemporarily impoverished symbolism invented by Cicero, "religion." There can be no doubt that drama, poetry, even narrative forms leading toward fiction have their origin in the acting out and telling of the tales of gods and men.

There is no doubt that archaic science, chiefly astronomy, began in quest of an exact scale of time upon which to establish ritual, festivals—those moments in which the divine and human orders interpenetrate.

It is now possible to demonstrate in considerable detail the compact and complex symbolisms of Mortals-immortals which interplayed in Sumeria and Babylon to shape the political order of what we assume to be the first city-states. Indeed, the archeological and philological work of the past several centuries has recovered the universal structure of the human *psyche* in its existential mode as participative in the community of men and gods, society and cosmos.

Whether we probe the roots of high civilizations or purportedly "primitive" cultures, the result is the same: the foundations of human order are invariant: The

---

121 Probably intended to write *Dhammapada.*

122 Corrected from "Sancaracaya's."

123 Corrected from "Baudarayana's."

124 More common spelling: *Brahma.*

society in question either represents itself as mirroring the order of the cosmos, the society of the gods, or expresses itself as that existential ground upon which gods and men interact with one another, the business of men and gods inextricably fused. Seventy years ago, Emile Durkheim observed that "Men owe to (religion) not only a good part of the substance of their knowledge, but also the form in which this knowledge has been elaborated."

The "ideal order" possessing "simultaneous existence" is not, therefore, primarily an array of "literary" or "artistic" objects—or any other kind of objects— as such. Rather it is the manifold of moments of spiritual insight through which the *psyche* has discovered and rediscovered itself in the *metaxy,* the "in between" of past and future, mortal-immortal, temporal and timeless, genetic and environmental, changing and changeless, cosmos and cosmion. Such moments in their interrelation within the collective of human *psyches*, we call culture. The "ideal order" of culture in its timelessness and undivided completeness, as the engendering structure of human consciousness, we call the Humanities.

As a matter of scholarly fact, the "ideal order" of a European literature as Eliot proposes it collapses under analysis simply because we now know far too much about our own past to suppose that Homer, like Athena, sprang into existence full-grown and unmediated. Nilsson's work has given us some notion of the Minoan and Mycenian precedents of Homer's archaic Greece. Through the work of Georges Dumézil,[125] we have insight into the triadic schema of Indo-European social organization as it existed in one variety or another in Greece, Persia, India, Rome, and the Slavic and Teutonic habitations. Archeological and philological advances in just the past century have woven tighter and tighter the connections between those cultures which produced and became the common human substance of Europe and South Asia.

In addition, there is of course the Semitic side of the "ideal order" to be considered. Here again, the sources for structural forms and fundamental imagery that play into early western texts have been unearthed. Ugaritic, Phoenician, Harrappan, Egyptian, Mesopotamian—all mix and interplay inextricably well back into the second millennium before Christ. Prayer, Epic, Drama, Dialogue— all are found among the earliest documents we possess. The manifold of human experiences and their symbolisms are equally present—not only in written texts, but in the ethnographic reproductions and ideogrammatic constructions of oral narratives from a wide range of cultures which disappear in time and place only as our capacity to recognize and to interpret them diminishes at the vanishing point.

Considering all this, we find ourselves turning back to Eliot's text in dismay. We do not deny the experiential validity of his ideal order even if it properly entails the whole of the Humanities rather than merely "literature" or "art." but how can such an order be reduced to the provincial and arbitrary dimensions of Europe?

125 Corrected from "Dumeizil."

It is evident now as it was when Eliot's essay was written that the components of such an order, if it is to be intelligible and authentic, derive from a welter of sources outside the Judeo-Christian Greco-Roman civilizational vector. Why then did Eliot choose to represent 'half a hemisphere' and call it an ideal order? The full answer to that complicated question has been suggested in Raymond Schwab's exhaustive treatise *The Oriental Renaissance*[126] which tells in detail of the failed rebirth of Eastern learning that took place in the West between the seventeenth and nineteenth centuries. It is hardly too much to say that the cultural situation between East and West was more propitious in 1830 than in 1919. But, as Schwab tells us, "The first idea the Occident had while gathering information on India was to bring those who did not think in Christian terms to their senses."[127]

Schwab's tact is to be admired. He might have observed with characteristic French irony that the same idea had dominated in the early centuries of our era during which the Church, as it wended its way toward ecstatic union with the Roman principate, struggled to convert, absorb, or destroy classical thinking—most particularly that kind of thinking we call 'philosophy.' Still, Schwab does not fail to reach the fundamental issue:

> In the process of considering humanity, the whole expanse of time had to be traversed, all inhabited space had to be covered, the whole world of speech sounded. Ideas on poetry, revealed religion, and architecture wavered, for neither Homer nor the Bible nor the basilicas were, now, historically unique.[128]

All this becomes immediately relevant to our case, because one suspects that we now know the answer to Schwab's chilling, culminating question: "In the vast autobiography that the nineteenth century West had begun to entitle 'Civilization,' would there really remain nothing more of itself than a brief chapter called "Local History?"[129]

III

We are not done with Mr. Eliot just yet. Our analysis and critique of his ideal order, however substantial, would amount to little more than a counter-essay if we could not return to the work of Eliot himself and see what we discover there by way of an empirical control.

---

126 Raymond Schwab, *The Oriental Renaissance* (New York: Columbia University Press, 1983).

127 Ibid., 453.

128 Ibid., 473. This footnote appeared in the original as an in-text citation.

129 Ibid., 476. This footnote appeared in the original as an in-text citation.

What we discover is illuminating. We find that the collapse of the "European literary" paradigm as exemplifying Eliot's ideal order can be documented from his own poetry.

Beginning with "Gerontion" in 1920, and continuing through "The Waste Land," which is to say, until his conversion to Anglo-Catholicism, Eliot's poetry rises from the level of Establishment verse characteristic of late nineteenth century England and America, and takes on the character of continuing multicultural insight. The human problems Eliot chooses to embody and work through in this poetry are such that a "literary" description of them (in the manner of, say, the Browning Society) is not only inadequate but absurd.

Consider the significance of the infamous "footnotes" at the conclusion of "The Waste Land." In 1956, Eliot publically repudiated them—yet even a journeyman critic might be expected to realize that the fifty-one glosses to the text constitute a vital portion of the meaning of the poem as its creator experienced it. The decision to include such notes, as well as the choice of what to annotate and what to let pass, stands as part of the reality of the work itself.

What could be the motive for such an odd academizing epilogue to a great poem—an epilogue which the poet himself would later characterize as "bogus scholarship"? The critical answers have been numerous and uniformly opaque. It seems probable that Eliot himself was unaware of the spring from which his impulse to annotate the poem arose.

The answer to the problem of motive is complex, but not complicated. Eliot the creator, as yet unsettled in a Western epigonic faith, still in the midst of a crucial *zetesis* (search), searching himself as Heraclitus of Ephesus had done some 25 centuries before, knew that the poem was done with the final Sanskrit words, *Shantih, Shantih, Shantih*. The expression of a failed quest for unity, for rediscovery of the human self in tension toward the ground of its existence by way of the Grail myth was complete. But Eliot was not solely a creator in, say, the style of a Mallarmé. He was a man of reason as well as a man of myth, a philosopher who had written a doctoral dissertation on the work of the distinguished English idealist F. H. Bradley as well as a mythosopher, to use Aristotle's term.

Eliot realized that the range of materials essential to a poem like "The Waste Land" extended far beyond the "literary"; that the human problems dealt with in the poem represented modern experience on the one hand, but, on the other, referred back to what he spoke of elsewhere as "a revelation of that vanished mind of which our mind is a continuation."[130]

Eliot the thinker realized that his text as it stood would more nearly constitute a conundrum than a poem to most readers. The expanse and intensity of culture

---

130   Corrington's note: "Smith, 71." In the original, this appeared as an in-text citation; changed to footnote. No book title given.

necessary to read "The Waste Land"—as opposed to solving it line by line in the manner of a differential equation—if it had ever existed, existed no longer. As would prove to be the case with Pound's *Cantos,* Joyce's *Finnegans Wake,* or, more recently, William Gaddis's *The Recognitions,* the demands of the work would stand in no realistic relationship to the cultural skills and knowledge of those to whom the poem was perforce addressed. The *humanitas* required to respond spontaneously to the poem was no longer extant.

The notes to "The Waste Land" thus serve theoretically as an index to modern cultural and spiritual poverty. They serve empirically as an ineffectual prosthetic for the *anamnesis,* the re-collection, which should inform our *psyches* in encounter with a work such as "The Waste Land." As readers, as human beings, we should not require the notes to "The Waste Land." But in fact we do. In our collective failure to remember, we emulate the Fisher King, Tiresias, the broken prophet. We have lost our *humanitas,* the "ideal order" of the psyche which, Eliot proposes, once shaped our lives and our doings.

The notes, then, become a symbolic tribute to the "ideal order" of past human experience, and an accusation evoking that terrible prophecy implicit in "Gerontion," drawn from the Gospel of Matthew: "An evil and adulterous generation shall seek after a sign, and no sign shall be given unto it except the sign of Jonah."

The character of the notes themselves suggests the true locus and extent of Eliot's "ideal order." The notes range from anthropological and historical treatises, Biblical quotations and paraphrases, through bits and pieces of Elizabethan and Jacobean drama and nineteenth century Symbolist poetry, to Dante, Ovid, Augustine, the Buddha, and at last, the *Brhadaranyaka,*[131] the Great Forest Upanishad. Moreover, two of the five sections of the poem, "The Fire Sermon," and "What the Thunder Said," expressly refer to Eastern thinking, and, taken as a whole, poem and notes explode the idea of an ideal order comprised exclusively of European literary monuments.

Eliot's poetry belies Eliot's criticism in this instance. The poet, like every poet worth reading, took his materials where he found them, realizing instinctively what the critic could not fully comprehend: a major work of art such as "The Waste Land," written in the twentieth century, must necessarily constitute an essay in the Humanities, an act of *Anamnesis,* re-collection.

"The Waste Land" and its notes conclusively demolishes the fiction of a European literary ideal order and replaces it with the true order of a comprehensive humanity, bringing together the range of human experiences and their symbolisms from the Paleolithic through the Indus Valley, Mesopotamian, Semitic, Sinaitic, Egyptian, and Indo-European cultures. In "The Waste Land," even if in a negative sense, and if only for a moment, the Humanities is recovered.

---

131   Also written as *Brihadaranyaka.*

IV

Eliot's earlier critical expression of an ideal order is thus discovered to be an inadequate but evocative symbolism which has, even as a poem might, invited us to probe the experience symbolized and rectify, through analysis of the symbolisms, the precise character of the experience.

The analysis had to penetrate through the opacity of secondary reflective symbols like "European literature" in order to discover that an order of the kind evoked by Eliot necessarily had to encompass all symbolisms expressing the common experience of "being human," whether, in fact, the symbols should turn out to be prehistoric, Asian, Mesopotamian, or whatever else—whether they might generally be referred to as mythopoetic, philosophical, historical, anthropological, theological or otherwise. The materials experienced as constituting the order would be what they turned out to be.

If the ideal order was to be intelligible (in the Platonic sense), it could not be less than inclusive. For if we acknowledged genuinely independent regional fields such as "monuments of European literature," and claimed for them ontological status and analytical significance, we would, by implication, find ourselves in the dubious business of arbitrarily setting up a multitude of unrelated and competing humanities above which no supervening "ideal order" could intelligibly exist.

The problem resolved itself by our turning from Eliot the critic's impressive but faulty construction of his own noetic experience of order to Eliot the poet's encyclopedic vision of humanity in all its stunning array of symbolisms. There we found the essence of the poet's *alethia*, truth, as opposed to the critic's *doxa*, opinion.

John Webster, Ovid, the Buddha, Augustine, and the Upanishadic writers stand side by side, evoked in truth for the sake of their truth, by an American poet residing in London in the early twentieth century. Dramatist, fabulist, Father of the Church, reformer of Brahminism,[132] and discoverers of Brahministic truth are re-collected as representatives of an ideal order of truth without bounds of time or space—much less of "disciplines" or "fields" such as "literature" or "art."

The ideal order of which Eliot wrote in his essay, and to which he contributed with his great poem is revealed to be that of the Humanities—which remains to be re-collected by the rest of us as T. S. Eliot did.

The task of *anamnesis*, re-collection, recovery, is not one with a *telos*, a goal, an ending. Since it partakes of the essence of human nature, its conclusion is no more determinate than that of humanity. But in our own time, this *anamnesis*, this recovery is yet hardly begun.

One of the concluding lines of "The Waste Land" indicates the state of insight achieved by the poet: "These fragments I have shored against my ruins."

Eliot has advanced the work of Heraclitus, Parmenides, and Plato; of Yajnavalkya, Buddha, and Sankaracharya, but the Humanities remains fragmented, ruinous, so

---

132   The letter "h" added here and in the adjectival form later in the sentence.

long as our arbitrary division of the rich multiplicity of things human is reckoned to be anything more than a methodological convenience, like Wittgenstein's ladder or scaffold to be climbed—then thrown away.

There is one Humanities, not several, and its recovery, its reinstatement—beyond ideology, beyond compartmentalization, beyond regional or religious parochialism—may well serve one day as an index of the recovery of our own humanity.

Part III

HISTORY

A Rebirth of Philosophical Thought

1984

This piece appeared as a review essay in *The Southern Review* in 1984. It opens by discussing the connection between Louisiana State University and Eric Voegelin and addresses the efforts of Voegelin and Ellis Sandoz to bring about a "rebirth" in philosophical thought, namely in premodern, mythopoetic forms of philosophizing. Corrington calls Voegelin's thought

> an argument directed to the reader as *spoudaios*, the mature human being who, if he is capable of *theoria*, self-reflection, will be able to reconstitute in his own *psyche* the substance of what Voegelin has experienced in recollection from a past rendered opaque for most of us by some five hundred years of cultural destruction.

For both Voegelin and Corrington, Nazism, Marxism, fascism, communism, and other totalizing ideologies of the twentieth century were the result of disordered philosophy and the divorce of modern thinking from its premodern antecedents for which humans had an innate longing, but from which they were alienated by modernity. The essay provides helpful summaries of Voegelin's most definitive theories, including his belief that modern disorder reveals symptoms of latent Gnosticism that has undergone dramatic but gradual change in light of the rise of Pauline Christianity with its various Greek influences.

The connection between Louisiana State University and the life work of Professor Eric Voegelin is a long and honorable one. Voegelin was a faculty member of LSU and appointed a Boyd Professor of Government in his latter years there. The university press[1] has published his unparalleled treatise, *Order and History*, and dozens of his former students continue to develop the insights received from him either in his classes or through his written work.

It seems fitting then for a professor of political science at LSU, Ellis Sandoz, to initiate the task of explicating what may one day be judged as the rebirth of serious philosophical thought in the twentieth century.

It is not an enterprise to be undertaken lightly. Even though conventional notions of the difficulty and impenetrability of Voegelin's work chiefly arise as a

---

1   "University Press" capitalized in original.

result of the paucity of classical and biblical education among those who purport to scholarship in the social sciences, there is no gainsaying the fact that the demands made by Voegelin upon the reader are considerable. In order to grasp the full significance of Voegelin's achievement, one must bring to his work something more than a decent education and full attention. In Keats's phrase, the arguments must be "proven on the pulses." Time and again, Voegelin's work calls upon us to evoke the deepest spring of our own experience, our own most disciplined imagining, in order to grasp his meaning.

For Voegelin's work does not constitute a "history" of anything; nor is it "scholarship" in any sense that might preclude the work of Plato, St. Paul, Origen, or St. Augustine. The whole of Voegelin's considerable output constitutes a philosophy—his own reflection upon the field of existence, its structures, and its content as he encountered them. The work is an argument directed to the reader as *spoudaios*, the mature human being who, if he is capable of *theoria*, self-reflection, will be able to reconstitute in his own *psyche* the substance of what Voegelin has experienced in re-collection from a past rendered opaque for most of us by some five hundred years of cultural destruction. In Heidegger's phrase, Voegelin's thought is, for us, *mathesis*—teaching us what we already know; it is *anamnesis*—helping us to remember, call back to *alethia* what has been lost.

Ellis Sandoz comes to the workplace fully equipped. A former student of Voegelin and a well-known scholar of political thought, he is an effective writer as well. The structure of *The Voegelinian Revolution* parallels that of an intellectual biography with its own special kind of interest through the careful use of an autobiographical memoir provoked by questions from Sandoz, passages from the early sections of the English version of *Anamnesis*, and observations made by William Havard and Gregor Sebba in a number of places.[2]

There are thinkers whose personalities seem absent from their writing. One thinks of Heidegger or Kant. There are others whose presence dominates and shapes the movement of the work. One thinks of Eckhart or Kierkegaard, and of Voegelin. Sandoz's evocation of the Viennese past, the extraordinary mixture of brilliant clashing intellectual cultures, and the dark political and historical circumstances which lie behind Voegelin's work provides for readers what has been lacking before: the sense of a concrete human being engaged in a search for the roots of a monstrous historical and spiritual predicament in which he and other men find themselves trapped. Once the biographical structure is set forth in chapters 2 and 3 this sense carries over into the exposition of Voegelin's thinking in the chapters following.

Again, Sandoz's arrangement of the materials serves to clarify the growth and changing emphasis of Voegelin's thought over some fifty years. Of particular interest

---

2   Corrington's note: "Ellis Sandoz, *The Voegelinian Revolution: A Biographical Introduction* (Baton Rouge, LA: Louisiana State University Press, 1981)."

is the shift from a diagnosis of contemporary intellectual and political disorder as modern Gnosticism (a diagnosis with which I agreed for a number of years) to a more probing analysis of consciousness. The Gnostic diagnosis, while not discarded, had to be altered (and not a great deal is gained by the addition of Hermeticism and alchemy to the equation) as it became clear that the very founding insights of Christianity contained both the experiential and the symbolic components of Gnosis. For an example not dealt with in Voegelin's work, the Pauline vision of a "fallen" cosmos—as opposed to simply the "fallen" nature of man—suggested the Christian appropriation of *physis* to the perceived situation of the human *pneuma*. It is not simply men in the world who require soteriological renovation, but the very order of the cosmos as well. It seems that Voegelin's idea of the "Balance of Consciousness" found in Plato (and, I would suggest, implicitly, in many of his predecessors as well) must stand against the vision which taints the universe with a sense of ill-being perceived by Paul—or which, in an alternative interpretation, would seem to recompact into cosmological form and to render a negative judgment upon the undifferentiated strata of existence known as "man" and "nature."

Most useful of all, Sandoz carefully relates the important recent articles published since *The Ecumenic Age* to the earlier work. I must admit that the treatment does not resolve the question of what Sandoz calls the "complementarity" of the Hellenic and Judeo-Christian visions. His explanation in regard to the "superior degree of differentiation" attributed to Pauline Christianity as opposed to the Platonic vision of the *Agathon* seems unclear. The fault, however, if indeed it is one, seems to lie with a recent refinement of Voegelin's thinking. As William Havard has noted in his contribution to *Eric Voegelin's Thought: a Critical Appraisal*, "some of [Voegelin's] closest readers have been puzzled by the way in which the concentration on the philosophy of consciousness has been accompanied by an apparent shift of emphasis to philosophical symbolization as the unique form for expressing the order of reality."[3]

A careful reading of certain statements in *The Ecumenic Age* would, at first glance, seem to provide an explanation for the shift:

> The new truth pertains to man's consciousness of his humanity in participatory tension toward the divine ground and to no reality beyond this restricted area . . . The human carriers of the spiritual outbursts do not always realize the narrow limits of the area directly affected by the differentiating process. For the differentiation of consciousness indirectly affects the image of reality as a whole . . . Still, while these consequences testify to the centrality of consciousness in man's experience and symbolization of

---

3   Corrington's note: "Ellis Sandoz, *Eric Voegelin's Thought: A Critical Appraisal* (Durham, NC: Duke University Press, 1982)."

reality, they must not obscure the fact that the differentiation of existential truth does not abolish the cosmos in which the event occurs.[4]

It would seem that this formulation must apply to the Pauline Vision of the Resurrected, and that the logic of Voegelin's equation of Classical and Christian symbolisms turns on the denial of exclusivity for any symbolism—perhaps especially one which, in certain forms, implicitly makes of the *cosmos* and of *physis* a war zone, an alien ground in which the spirit is tried. But I take it that in the field of the *psyche* as in the field of the cosmos, there is no such thing as a privileged observer. Of course, there is a large segment of Voegelin's most devoted readers who would have it otherwise. Gerhart Niemeyer has complained that Voegelin has treated Christianity as less than unique—though I cannot be sure upon which temporal or ideological or geographical stratum of Christian experience he wishes Voegelin to confer such a title.

More fundamentally, one must raise the issue of whether Voegelin has ever suggested that the symbols Incarnation-Transfiguration-Resurrection provide a definitive and final Answer to the Question, thereby terminating the philosopher's *zetesis*. In empirical fact, they have not done so, and there are those who would ask in what way and under what circumstances the pneumatic core of a theophanic experience, personal or mediated, should be allowed to override its noetic periphery and annihilate the stream of continuing self-conscious reflection upon the movement in the soul toward the divine ground. Or, since in pragmatic fact such attempted destruction is never complete, and the reflection in one form or another *does* continue, what is the purpose of such a claim?

One may be tempted to ask whether it is Voegelin's delicacy which has prevented him from stating flatly that the indisputable uniqueness of the engendering Christian experiences does not constitute a brief for its ensuing exclusivist dogmatic presentation as a "stop history" movement of the Hegelian sort, or for a culmination to the flux of divine presence in the Metaxy outside approved doctrinal channels. One must, it seems, hold in precarious balance an uncertain but loving *pistis*, which, in its exuberance, may claim to "vanquish the *cosmos*" (which remains precisely as it has always been, the background of existential reality), and an equally uncertain and no less erotic *noesis*, which, even in its affection for the *cosmos*, may tend toward its own loss of balance as it strains toward the immortalizing vanishing point of its structure at the horizon of mystery.

Sandoz deals with these problems as well as they can be dealt with by one who is, after all, carefully explicating another's thought, not setting forth his own.

---

4   No footnote in the original. The source is Eric Voegelin, *The Collected Works of Eric Voegelin*, vol. 17, *Order and History*, vol. 4, *The Ecumenic Age* (Columbia, MO: University of Missouri Press, 2000), 53. In light of the publication date, Corrington could not have used this volume. He would have used Eric Voegelin, *The Ecumenic Age*, vol. 4 of *Order and History* (Baton Rouge, LA: Louisiana State University Press, 1975).

Chapter 8, "The Vision of the Whole," is particularly satisfying for those familiar with Voegelin's work since it serves as both a summation and a promise, sharpening one's appetite for Volume 5 of *Order and History,* and for further work on specific topics by Sandoz.

The collection of essays dealing with Voegelin's work is well chosen, including previously published writing from *The Southern Review* by scholars who have known Voegelin for many years. Both Gregor Sebba and William C. Havard Jr. are represented, as is Jurgen Gebhardt, a noted German scholar. Eugene Webb's essay, "Eric Voegelin's Theory of Revelation," especially as relating to the problems I have raised above, is excellent, and in its careful phrasing (see especially pp. 176–77) may well drive to the center of the issue of Christian exclusivism.

If I have any reservation regarding the collection, it would be with regard to the inclusion of T. J. J. Altizer's review of *The Ecumenic Age* from the *Journal of the American Academy of Religion.* There were more apposite reviews, including that of Niemeyer in *Modern Age.* I rather suspect that Altizer's review is reprinted for the sake of Voegelin's response which, in its punctilious courtesy, its extraordinary erudition—"fiendish" is the word Sebba has used for it in another place—and its demolition of Altizer's spirited defense of Hegel, to be expected from the author of *The Gospel of Christian Atheism,* amounts to a *kenosis.* The cautionary lesson to be learned, I think, is that if one wishes to debate Voegelin on his own ground, one had best, as the old southern phrase has it, bring his lunch.

All in all, *The Voegelinian Revolution* and *Eric Voegelin's Thought* are welcome additions to a growing literature on the thought of a man Sandoz has described elsewhere as "great-hearted." Those like myself who owe the better part of their intellectual life to Eric Voegelin's work can only nod assent. Sandoz has found a measure.

Philosophies of History:
An Interview with Eric Voegelin

1973

This piece comprises an interview that Corrington and Peter Cangelosi conducted with Eric Voegelin for *The New Orleans Review.* Corrington and Voegelin discuss the purpose of history, the structure of reality, the nature of consciousness as it pertains to an understanding of history; symbolism in Christianity and modern culture; Gnosticism; Marxism (a substitute for or displacement of God); the recovery of Christian consciousness as it existed prior to its distortions in recent centuries; Hegel; Jung; Freud; and the inadequacy of the political signifiers "liberal" and "conservative." During the interview, Voegelin refers to Marxism as "a third-rate epilogue afterlife, of no particular intellectual interest." Voegelin concludes the interview by admonishing that "[o]ne shouldn't envision futures. That is an idle pastime. We have quite enough to do in the present."

Dr. Eric Voegelin, often rated with Spengler and Toynbee as one of the great scholars of the world, was interviewed by Peter Cangelosi, associate editor of the *New Orleans Review* (NOR), and by John William Corrington, novelist, critic, poet, and former editor-at-large of the NOR. Although Dr. Voegelin's field is primarily political science, he is widely respected as a philosopher of history.

NOR: Dr. Voegelin, what would you consider to be your major contribution to human knowledge?

VOEGELIN: Well, I have my doubts about the use of the term *contribution.* It smacks a bit of the progressivist conception that there is an advance in the history of mankind, and that everybody makes his contribution to it. Not that I doubt that there is any such continuity. But I doubt very much that my work can be categorized as a kind of contribution to anything.

The original meaning of science and of philosophy, of course, is that each has a purpose in itself and is not a contribution to anything at all. Purposes which are ultimate have no further purpose. They fall into the quite purposeless activity of exploring the structure of reality. And in that connection, I would make no difference between political science and the philosophy of history, because as Aristotle already formulated it, what the philosopher has to deal with are human affairs. Philosophy is really a *philanthropia*. And there are always three dimensions in human affairs: personal existence, the social dimension, and man as a *zoön politicon*[5]—the third part of which Aristotle never fully developed. He treated the first dimension, personal existence, in *Ethics*; social existence in *Politics*; and the third part was existence in history. Aristotle never wrote a "Histories." All three (Ethics, Politics, and Histories) are an inseparable unity in the existence of man.

And if I am, perhaps, more interested at present in the field of history than in the field of society, then the reason is that the dimension of history in man's existence has been perverted almost beyond recognition through ideologized constructions of history ever since the eighteenth century. And one has to recapture today what history means in the classical sense. History in the classical sense means that one is engaged in advancing the luminosity of consciousness by which one participates in reality, knows about reality; and in advancing the analysis of consciousness. That, you might say, is the real subject matter. And since advances of consciousness can be conducted only in personal existence, and Aristotle already recognized that if you achieve any advances, they are at the same time historical advances, because such an advance is an event in history and draws a line of meaning within history.

NOR: Would you say that is so because of what you have called in your *New Science of Politics* "representation"—because one has an advance within of consciousness, therefore there is an advance of consciousness for humankind?

VOEGELIN: Yes, in a sense yes. But that requires a little precision. Every true analysis of consciousness—that is, of one's own structural participation in reality—is an analysis in the concrete. One must concretely analyze the concrete participation processes.

But underlying that analysis is the assumption—usually glossed over or left unmentioned—that all men have the same type of consciousness, and so that what you find concretely in your advance of consciousness is valid for everybody. It cannot, of course, be proven, but it is a general philosophical assumption which attaches, to any advances of consciousness in history, a representative character.

But such advances in consciousness can be true or deformed, and the representative character can also be deformed. Because whatever a man does by way of consciousness, he wants to do something representatively for that mankind in whose existence he trusts—all human beings, just like himself.

A good example would be Turgot, who considered his work on the three stages (theological, metaphysical, and scientific) as a representative advance. Not that

5   More common spelling: "*zoön politikon*."

every human being actually participated in the advance, or was fully aware of it. Turgot coined the concept of mankind as a *masse totale*. His idea, then, was taken up by Condorcet, by Saint Simon, by Comte, by Hegel, and by Marx, and came to mean that all mankind had to follow the lead of the new type of intellectuals represented by Turgot as the men just enumerated.

So the representative claim is there. But that is, you might say, already the reunification or hypothesis of the real problem of representation—that real advances are supposedly representative of mankind. But personal opinions cannot claim to be representative of mankind. Representativeness is deformed insofar as it is claimed deliberately by people who are not representative of anything in particular except the deformation of existence which they enact.

NOR: So you would leave the category of representation for what is truly representative of man?

VOEGELIN: One cannot do that, you see, because the category of representation is fundamental in every advance of consciousness. It belongs to the nature of man to assume that one is representative in what one does. And so, representativeness must be claimed by those who, in fact, are deforming consciousness, and then claim leadership for the mass of mankind, the *masse totale*, to follow them into that deformation. So what one finds after Turgot—in Condorcet especially, and then loudly claimed by Comte, Hegel, and Marx—is that everyone has followed them into their particular prison of existence. So that even if one deforms existence into a prison, one does not cease to claim representativeness.

One has to distinguish, therefore, between true advances in the luminosity of consciousness and new deformations, which fall into Plato's category of *scotosis*— the darkening of consciousness.

NOR: Would you use the category of Gnostic for those people who would lead the *masse totale* into the prison of their own consciousness?

VOEGELIN: One can do it. But Gnosticism is one factor in a very complex set of factors to which it also belongs: apocalypse, Neo-platonic immanentist speculation, magic, Hermeticism and so on.

NOR: In the contemporary world, the category of consciousness is being rather widely used. One finds it especially in Charles Reich's *The Greening of America*. Would you say that you use the term *consciousness* in the same sense that Professor Reich uses it?

VOEGELIN: The term *consciousness* has, in fact, come into wide vogue, in the wake of Hegel. His philosophy of consciousness understood it as nobody's consciousness but an imaginary consciousness which has no subject. This is a very convenient hypothesis from which you can then hang any imaginary construction. Reich, for instance, gives the Third World a consciousness. And the Third Reich paved the way for National Socialism in Germany.

There is, of course, in Western history a long established tradition of such third salvation-realm speculations, especially in Hegel and Comte and Marx.

NOR: I wonder about the Trinitarian symbolism developed by Jung, and about the peculiar repetition of the number three in this sort of symbolism in the fifteenth century, and in Reich in the twentieth. Could the repetition of three be a factor that needs to be analyzed psychologically?

VOEGELIN: When you come to the historical materials, the three has no exclusive importance. There are all sorts of number symbolisms. The number four is important too. We have a Trinity, especially in Christianity; but trinities were known before that in the Vedas.[6] The Trinity in Christianity is due to the fact that the historical exposition of Christianity came through the events recorded in the Gospel. First, there is a God, an unknown God, who is not related to the pagan gods, the polytheistic gods; then, an Incarnation problem which gives you the second God, Christ; and then a continuation of that in history, the time dimension. So you get three manifestations of divinity: originally, the divine presence in consciousness, then the mythological element that some human being has experienced this in the son of god—which goes back to the Egyptians who saw the Pharaoh as the son of god . . .

NOR: As a sun-god?

VOEGELIN: No, as the son of god. There is a correlation in the rituals, where the priest says: "You are my son, the first one in whom I have my pleasure." It is a formula we still find in the New Testament, though we have changed the meaning of it, of course. But that is the problem, you see. And the presence, the continuation of that divinity in history, is then called Spirit.

NOR: Professor Voegelin, you first made a large impact on the intellectual world with your *New Science of Politics*. Now, since that time you have published other major works, especially *Order and History*, in three volumes, to which there will be at least one sequel. Would you, if you were to rewrite the *New Science of Politics* today, do anything different in it?

6   Original reads "Vegas."

VOEGELIN: No. Because it is a close group of lectures, and you can only do so much in lectures, and because, in its way, the book has a perfect correspondence between substance and form. I don't mean that it is the perfect book, or anything like that, or that one does not have to say more. But as a literary production in six lectures, there is no more one can put in it, and I would not change it.

There *are* a lot of things that need to be said today, that I didn't know at the time, and that I would say today.

NOR: More specifically, if I may: would you do anything differently with your third part on Gnosticism as the nature of modernity?

VOEGELIN: Well, yes. Because in the twenty-five years intervening since the book was published, we know so much more now about the continuous trends in Western intellectual history. Gnosticism is certainly not the only trend. One has to include, as I mentioned before, apocalyptic strands, the neoplatonic restoration at the end of the fifteenth century, and the hermetic component which resulted in the conscious operation of sorcery and in Hegel's determinology. Hegel expressed his formulation that the purpose of determinology is to find the magic words with which you can conjure up the shape of the future. He was, consummately, a sorcerer.

NOR: Not only a sorcerer, but a writer of spiritual cookbooks, because he wanted others to follow him down the same path. His purpose was not esoteric, but exoteric.

VOEGELIN: Well, I wouldn't use the term *cookbook* in that connection, because it is quite consciously a magic act by which reality is transmogrified into the perfect reality.

NOR: Are there any contemporary writers or thinkers who are similar to Hegel in this respect?

VOEGELIN: No. And you must not expect them to be. Hegel was a consummate craftsman, the perfect philosopher who knew his business even if he misused his knowledge.

He wanted to construct a speculative system that reconciled all interaction on the basis of an experience of alienation, and not leave a state of alienation.

That is a point which is rarely recognized. Because the people who read him usually try to interpret and explain what is going on in the terminology, but do not have enough parallel comparative knowledge to know what is going on, because Hegel has a habit of never quoting his sources. All the alienation categories—things like direction, division, separation, and so on—are taken from Plotinus. It is the Plotinus concept of all life, with a little variance.

NOR: What do you think of contemporary Marxism as an intellectual force?

VOEGELIN: I have not been aware that it is much of an intellectual force. It is a third-rate epilogue afterlife, of no particular intellectual interest.

NOR: Well, it has to be of some intellectual interest, because it is at least the public theology of the Soviet Union, of Eastern Europe, and of China.

VOEGELIN: I was thinking of such men in the twentieth century who still act as Marxists and write as Marxists—such writers say, as Garaudy and Bloch[7]—and of the shaky optical world they present. Now if that is their idea of the pursuit of happiness, well, they can pursue it. But I do not find it intellectually stimulating. It is rather a bore, an imposition. Since I am also teaching and students ask about it, I am forced to read them. But I would not do so unless I was forced into it.

NOR: Are you speaking of people like Marcuse?[8]

VOEGELIN: For instance, yes.

NOR: What about Mao Tse Tung?[9]

VOEGELIN: There is absolutely no reason why anyone should read Mao Tse Tung, except that three-fourths of the students ask questions about it.

NOR: What about the pragmatic concern of international politics?

VOEGELIN: Well, international politics is quite a different matter. In China, you have the problem that the older intellectual upper stratum, represented by the Mandarin culture, obviously could not come to grips with the modernization of China, with the integration of it into categories of civilization which emanate from the West. China felt the power of Western technology in aggression. And since the Mandarin nobility was unable to handle these problems, it was quite sensible that somebody who was not Mandarin contrived to overthrow the caste. The consequences will show later, because if you throw out the Confucian culture or

---

7   Roger Garaudy and Ernst Bloch.

8   Herbert Marcuse.

9   More common spelling: "Mao Tse-tung."

Taoist culture or Buddhist culture in China, there is no culture left at all. You can see that fact in the new production of Chinese operas which are simply horrible—shabby romantic revolutionary heroism, accompanied by sound tracks belonging to the Westerns of the 1930s. Because that was all Madame Mao ever heard. A fantastical debasement into elemental savagery.

NOR: Spengler believed that Marxism would sweep over Russia, have its day, and then go away, and that Russia's character would not have been much changed by its occurrence.

VOEGELIN: It's possible, Russian civilization is, of course, much closer to a Western type of civilization than it is to China. It is difficult to tell what effect the destruction of culture may ultimately have on China. One hopes that somebody survives and that the country recovers from that destruction. But you may have to wait a hundred years to see what happens.

NOR: What about Christianity? What is the meaning of Christianity now, according to your thinking?

VOEGELIN: I am not sure about its meaning, because I have my doubts as to whether Christianity exists at all. I can say what the meaning is of the gospels today, or, more specifically, of Matthew, Chapter 16—which is the perfect analysis of the existential tendency in relation to God, just as the fullness of Christ is. This is as true today as it was at the time the Gospel was written. But the analysis in Matthew 16 is so buried at present in secondary doctrine and dogma that few people are now aware how grandiose an existential analysis is there. One could reactivate it by reading it.

NOR: There is a term which you have used with some frequency in *Order and History* and which I think may apply here. The term is *re-Christianization*. You seemed to say that the Christian consciousness could be, as it were, re-Christianized.

VOEGELIN: Yes. I have dealt with that problem in *Anamnesis*,[10] an intermediate work published in Germany. *Anamnesis* is the recollection of what has been achieved, by way of extending the real of the past into the present. The real of the past has been buried by cultural destruction, and we have been victims of that destruction since the middle of the eighteenth century.

---

10   Corrected from "*Annamesis*." See Vol. 6, *The Collected Works of Eric Voegelin*, which includes "Anamnesis on the Theory of History and Politics" (University of Missouri Press, 2002).

NOR: Would you make a distinction between re-Christianization and nostalgia?

VOEGELIN: No, there is no problem of nostalgia in an absolutely realistic recovery of pieces of consciousness of existence which existed before they were destroyed after 1750.

NOR: I think my question was: isn't there a tendency towards derailment in the direction of nostalgia when one does reach back?

VOEGELIN: Oh, yes. There were people who have interpreted this vogue for historical knowledge and archeology as nostalgic romanticism. And in some cases, they were right. The people who uncover the facts are not necessarily the people who can best handle them once they are uncovered.

NOR: How would you react to a concept of a post Christian age?

VOEGELIN: Well, I would classify it together with other "beyond" literature: beyond morality, beyond ideology, beyond Christianity, beyond dignity and freedom, and so on. It's totally an apocalyptic type of literature, which is a phenomenon of our time, but otherwise of no particular interest.

NOR: What do you think about the Death of God theology?

VOEGELIN: There we have to be brutal. When Hegel developed his premise of the Death of God, it made good sense within his construction of that famous consciousness which is no consciousness, and which comes to its historic culmination in Hegel's work. God is present in Hegel, only now in His new manifestation in Hegel's work. So if you insist on the Death of God after Hegel, you should be aware, at least, that the alternative to the Death of God is to become a Hegelian. And if you would harp on Nietzsche, the murder of God makes sense if you become a Nietzschean. But if you just want to maintain the death of God or the murder of God, and then fool around as if nothing had happened, then you are a little man who doesn't know what he is talking about.

NOR: But surely, these movements have had some importance in contemporary life.

VOEGELIN: Yes. We are living in an epilogue period, a third generation run down by myriad sectarians.

NOR: From whom there is no rescue?

VOEGELIN: Oh yes, you can ignore them.

NOR: But to ignore them does not mean that they will go away.

VOEGELIN: No, they will remain. But you can do other things. You don't have to waste your time over them.

NOR: What other things, for instance?

VOEGELIN: Well, for instance, explore other things that we know every day is discovered anew about human consciousness. Last year, there was a book by the Swiss philologist Robert Orpheus, which traces the continuities of a certain type of consciousness from the classical period to the fifteenth century. So we have a millennial history of consciousness reopened to us.

NOR: Do you mean to say that the dominant intellectual force today would be depth psychology?

VOEGELIN: No. Depth psychology doesn't mean very much. You cannot explore the depths of the philosophical sciences psychologically. You can only draw something out of those depths by way of insights, but to handle this as psychology doesn't get you anywhere. An unconscious is never conscious, you see. An unconscious that can be made conscious by a psychoanalysist is no unconscious. And when you take Jung's archetype, there is nothing unconscious about that except that you accept it conditionally as fully conscious symbolizations of experiences of reality which have been placed by psychologists and their patients into their unconscious. So, if you analyze only pathological cases, you will find a lot of symbols "unconscious," which in healthy cases would be "conscious."

NOR: But these are real problems of people you are talking about.

VOEGELIN: One reason there are real problems in every society is what one might call a public unconscious, things which are forced into the unconscious as dominant opinions about public decency. But from the psychological point of view, these constitute a social problem. In every society, there are things which are pushed under the level of public discussion. And in a decultured situation such as ours, a lot is being pushed into the subconscious.

NOR: Such as?

VOEGELIN: Such as the whole problem of sex life, which has been uncovered by Freud in the lives of his patients. People were pretty conscious of these things in the sixteenth century, but the sex symbols which Freud uncovered later were not known to be sex symbols until the eighteenth century.

NOR: What you seem to be saying is that only when society is ordered can the individual find his own order—or would you think the reverse is true? Plato, in the volume on the polis, suggests that order begins with the individual and moves outward toward society. Would you say that society could not order itself, except in the sense that each man orders himself?

VOEGELIN: I'm not sure I understand the intention of your question. The Platonic symbolism of society and of man, by and large, of course, holds true. But if you pervert it to mean that man has to be society-written-small, then you get an inversion. These inversions of Platonic symbols are very widespread, only people usually don't realize it. Nietzsche inverted Plato's parable of the cave. But most people who read Nietzsche today haven't the faintest idea what either Nietzsche or Plato says.

NOR: Let me ask you a question which you may not wish to answer. Your work has always been brilliantly and objectively descriptive. Would you undertake in any way to make prescriptive suggestions to impede the traumatic deculturalization of our own times?

VOEGELIN: Well, the prescription is already contained in the description. People have to recover contact with reality, which has been lost in imaginary contacts with imaginary realities.

NOR: In your present thinking, do you still make use of the category of the opening of the soul?

VOEGELIN: Oh, yes. Only not exactly in the meaning that is sometimes attached to the term. As a symbol, it is very good, in opposition to the process of closing off existence. So it is the open soul, or the opening of the soul, that is opposite to the possibility of closing your soul into the state of alienation. And I use it today to describe the situation of contacting oneself. To contact oneself is to reopen.

NOR: Would you elaborate on that?

VOEGELIN: Well, the most famous case of the contact of oneself is Sartre. He literally contacts himself in the "what" (as he calls it) that has no sense of existence. Existence was a fact for him. To have meaning, one must project a meaning. One takes the meaning one has, with no outside advice as to what kind of meaning he should project. And Sartre expresses the despair of that situation in the symbolism of "being condemned to be free." Because freedom is indeed a damnation if you don't know what to do with it, and if you think of existence as a mere fact which has no relief.

NOR: Why should a man do what you say Sartre does?

VOEGELIN: Well, if you come down to the elementals, you already invent trouble, because the opening of the soul is, without doubt, simply the activity of some person, and yet there is the grace of God involved. Now I don't know why the grace of God doesn't extend to people like Sartre or Marx.

NOR: Can one know anything about the grace of God?

VOEGELIN: Well, the grace of God is a symbolism for the exercise of being open to a divine presence. That is called grace.

NOR: Is this transferrable into active life?

VOEGELIN: Of course, it is transferrable into active life. In the state of grace, you find, for instance, that your existence is governed by certain rules, such as the Decalogue. And number one is "I am the Lord your God, don't have other gods before my face." This means that, in the concrete, grace is transferrable. If you are a man in the state of grace, you shouldn't be a believer in Marx or Lenin, because that would be a substitution for God.

NOR: What about action towards one's neighbor?

VOEGELIN: If you are in the image of God, then the general assumption is that everybody else is too—human beings like yourself. And if the nature of man implies the grace of God and his perfection, in openness, then you act toward your neighbor as if he were also a man like that—graced toward perfection. That leads to difficulties, of course, because other men are not always like that. Take for instance the murder of Christ.

NOR: What about political theory today? What do you see as the future of it, or the contemporary status of it?

VOEGELIN: Well, I really don't know what that means—contemporary political theory. Either that means a philosophy of man's existence in society, or it doesn't.

NOR: In contemporary political thinking, two categories widely used are liberal and conservative. What is your reaction to that dichotomy?

VOEGELIN: Oh, that *pas de deux* has been going on for a long while. It has been perfectly analyzed, for all practical purposes, by Edgar Allan Poe. Before the Civil War apparently, we had some men like Edgar Allan Poe, who could handle such a problem and bring it back to certain original philosophical positions (like Aristotelian and Baconist) and poke fun at that. I don't know many American men of letters today who would be educated enough to write a satire on that liberal conservative tiff as Edgar Allan Poe did. They are too illiterate to handle such a problem.

NOR: Would you say that liberals and conservatives are both too wedded to ideology to be open to truth?

VOEGELIN: I don't know if they are not open to truth. It would take a personal psychological interview to see whether they are open or not. But, in fact, there are people who are not open to truth.

NOR: Did you say that there was no one identifiable as a liberal or conservative?

VOEGELIN: There is no man of letters living in America today who has the literacy to handle a problem of that nature.

NOR: Is that one reason why there is such a paucity in the political world of practical programs for what should be done?

VOEGELIN: Yes. In the years preceding the Civil War, there were men who understood the human situation. Until that time, the peace code was dependent on the English and European development. Then comes the Great Prairie and the great open spaces of the prairies, which is not the best ground for the rise of intellectual culture. And so today, we face the crisis that America will have to start over again becoming as cultivated as the Fathers of the Constitution were.

NOR: Are Europeans today as cultivated as Europeans were at the time of the Fathers of the Constitution?

VOEGELIN: Certainly not. The deculturalization process is everywhere. Men like Manchester[11] have done their work of destruction, and recovery is slow. Still, certain factors do favor the European situation. I learned a lot about philosophy from the revival of the Neo-Thomists in the 1920s and '30s. On the other hand, I learned a lot about American civilization from the still not-quite-broken tradition of common sense here.

NOR: Were destructive tendencies strong in Germany?

VOEGELIN: Yes. They have a worse effect in a situation like that in Germany because the antidote of common-sense culture is not there.

NOR: You refer to Nazism?

VOEGELIN: Not only that. But also the post-war world, the liberation rabble, the Frankfort people and the Berlin people. The burning of universities was destructive to a degree to which no French or American universities have yet been destroyed by revolting students.

NOR: Do you think American universities will be so destroyed?

VOEGELIN: I doubt it. There is still too much commonsense culture alive.

NOR: Would you say that the common-sense culture dominates American political activity in both the Democratic and the Republican parties?

VOEGELIN: Well, you get into very odd situations here. You see, a group of Leftists have polarized themselves out of the American arena. And the people who resist, like Mayor Daley, are not exactly to my taste either. And so you get very odd bed-fellowships. But there is a stratum of common sense represented by all sorts of people here in the Democratic Party.

NOR: What about the Republican Party?

VOEGELIN: Also. A man like Nixon is a corporation lawyer and knows at least what common sense in business relations is.

11   Probably William Manchester.

NOR: So, you don't think that ideology is a primary motivational force?

VOEGELIN: Certainly not. I doubt that Nixon knows about any ideologies at all that could influence him seriously.

NOR: Even such as anti-Communism?

VOEGELIN: Such as anything.

NOR: Dr. Voegelin, I wonder if you would say something about what you envision for the future?

VOEGELIN: No. One shouldn't envision futures. That is an idle pastime. We have quite enough to do in the present.

The Law and the Prophets

1973

This article was originally published in Tulane University School of Law *Law Forum* in October 1973. It included the following biography of the author:

> John William Corrington is from Shreveport. He was educated at Centenary College (BA), Rice University (MA), and the University of Sussex (PhD). He has written three novels, *And Wait for the Night, The Upper Hand, The Bombardier;* a collection of stories, *The Lonesome Traveller,* and five screenplays (in collaboration with Joyce H. Corrington) including *The Red Baron, The Omega Man, Boxcar Bertha,* and *The Battle for the Planet of the Apes.* He was a visiting professor in modem literature at the University of California, Berkeley, in 1968, and won a National Endowment for the Arts award in fiction in 1967. A story of his appears in the *Best American Short Stories of 1973.* He is a junior at Tulane Law School and is presently considering a non-fiction work to be called *Fear and Loathing in Torts.*

Corrington argues here that American institutions are the ongoing product of the dialogue between the law and the prophets; the former often represents the past efforts of the latter. The law, Corrington says, is at its core static, whereas prophecy, although not contrary to law, ensures the renewal of legal institutions after social and cultural change. Echoing Emerson, who was echoing Jesus Christ, Corrington calls prophecy the "new wine" that "fills old bottles." "The test of true prophetic wisdom," Corrington claims, "is its ultimate compatibility with the most profound purposes of the law it aims to change or to renew, however much prophetic language may tend to negate or belittle that final unity." The struggle between law and prophecy is always won by the law because the moment prophecy becomes widely accepted, it finds expression in the law.

A few years ago, before he died amidst love and honor, Norman Thomas, perennial Socialist candidate for president,[12] was asked by a reporter what new ideas he would like to inject into contemporary American society, if he were to hold the office for which he had run unsuccessfully so many times.

Thomas smiled and told the reporter that most of the ideas he had espoused back in the 1920s and '30s had been enacted into law over the years, and that the

12 Capitalized in original.

others likely would be. This caused consternation among younger Socialists and older reactionaries alike. The former held that all was yet to be accomplished; the latter were horrified that a radical like Thomas should find any satisfaction in the current state of American affairs.

One need not embrace Socialism or any other ideology in order to understand Norman Thomas's role as an American prophet, and to understand as well how American institutions are, existentially, the dynamic product of an ongoing dialogue-cum-passage at arms between the law and the prophets.

"Activist" advocates and courts aside, the ideal of law, embodied in numerous doctrines from *Stare Decisis to Res Judicata*, is a static one. The modal spirit of law is to reduce contingency to an absolute minimum, thereby establishing an order responsive only to stimuli from outside legal institutions themselves.

This is as it should be. The basic premises of social order include security, predictability, and coherence as sine qua non. The function of legal institutions is normatively to hold fast, to refine, to explicate, to order. There must be an element of stasis in the law in order that a man may know it, reflect on it—perhaps even come to love it as one of the polarities of his existence as a political being.

But a society possessing such legal institutions runs the risk of stagnation. As human beings grow in consciousness and differentiate their experience, for good or ill, so do societies. If the bulk of citizens in a society should outgrow the legal institutions which govern them, the resulting alienation must begin to erode the social fabric itself, with such a breakdown manifesting its presence at first in cynicism, corruption and lawlessness, and at last in revolt. Stasis as an ideal must be counterbalanced by some alternative reality.

The counterbalance is prophecy. Prophecy is *not* contrary to law, even when it imagines itself to be. Rather, when it is true prophecy, it is the frontier, the leading edge of law, the strategy of law's tactics, the new wine which, scripture aside, admirably fills old bottles. Prophecy is the soul of law's body, and is as mercurial and difficult to define concretely as law is solid and precise.

Still, prophecy is not so vague as all that. The test of true prophetic wisdom is its ultimate compatibility with the most profound purposes of the law it aims to change or to renew, however much prophetic language may tend to negate or belittle that final unity. Thus, in the 1920s and '30s, those who demanded concretely a just wage, an eight-hour day, an end to child labor, an extension of personal liberties under the Bill of Rights and the Fourteenth Amendment, were true prophets—as opposed to their opposite numbers who offered a troubled people the solutions of Fascism, National Socialism, or, a little later, Stalinism.

To speak of the ideal once more, there should be a separation, a clear tension between the law and the prophets. Which is not to say that all lawyers and judges should be immune to recognition of needed change, or that all prophets must be certified crazies. Rather the issues are perhaps best drawn when the advocates of stasis and those who speak for the new vision stand apart, each speaking his piece, owing as little as is practically possible to the opposition.

In the end, of course, the law always wins. True prophecy is always lost. Lost because even at the moment of its vindication, when its passion has won over the hearts of the people, it enters the law itself. It becomes that which it has contested, and things are never quite the same with it again.

Then, when a certain time has passed, passion spent, the unique event becomes ordinary practice. Prophecy-become-Law finds itself standing squarely on precedent, looking with suspicion at some new idea, some radical extension of itself, and the Law that was once Prophecy cautions calm, deliberation, cool heads, and wise counsel. Passion is brief; law is long. And the dialectic begins once more. "They do not understand how that which differs with itself is in agreement: harmony consists of opposing tension, like the bow, the lyre."

The Rabbis tell us that, before the universe was created, before time itself began, the Torah was with God. It is His Word, His Law, His very will and presence immanent in the world. I like to believe that, from all eternity, with God also there was one without shoes, wrinkled, a troublesome person, peering into the Torah critically, devoutly, lovingly—one named Isaiah or Ezekiel—fingering a scruffy beard, and muttering, "Ah yes, but still . . ."

Science, Symbol, and Meaning

1983

This essay is archived at Centenary College as "Houston Talk." It was the opening address at the Second Annual Space Industrialization Conference of the National Space Society in Houston, Texas. The subject of the essay is man's exploration of outer space and the potential physical instantiation of certain theories about the structure of the cosmos. Corrington sets out to "reconstruct" Western culture, first by defining and describing it and then by diagnosing what he calls its "deformity," which involves confusion regarding the differences between mythical and scientic modes of knowing. The essay uses the subject of space exploration as a starting point for recommending remedies to this so-called deformity. Corrington purports to derive his thesis about time and cosmic order from Eric Voegelin, Martin Heidegger, and Giorgio de Santillana. He critiques the "illusion" that scientific thinking displaced mythopoetic thinking in the West because, he says, theological and symbolic thinking has been used to make sense of the data that has been objectively arrived at and disinterestedly gathered. This illusion will no longer stand, Corrington suggests, as the expanse of space becomes more intimately known to us and we begin to acknowledge the role that myth plays in ordering our experience within the observable cosmos.

Rationalism and empiricism are, Corrington suggests, themselves forms of myth about our ability to know the cosmos that we occupy. Corrington emphasizes the limits of human knowledge and submits that modern science is, however useful, myth; science, he says, is not "co-extensive with the manifold of reality." Science equips us with symbols that can be manipulated to structure and explain our thinking about the phenomenal universe. The drive for the enterprise of space exploration represents a repressed desire to know and order our experience; it is in this sense a structural element of our psyche, something that is not new to modernity, but long felt and expressed. For this reason, Corrington believes the "leap into space is the heritage and destiny of Western Man." This is Corrington's prescription, in light of his comments on space exploration, for the "deformity" in Western thinking:

> We must re-learn and carry to the heart the old verities that existed before the rise of metaphysics and science, the truths that were carried on and carried down through the mythological structure of the psyche: the unity of humanity and the cosmos, the illusory and ephemeral quality of the ego, the one law common to all that penetrates and encompasses the fine structure and the gross structure of reality.

Some years ago, your conference director, Arthur Dula[13] and I, met under auspicious circumstances. We were both freshmen[14] at Tulane University School of Law—he a chemist and all-around student of the sciences who found himself becoming interested, if not intrigued, by history, philosophy, and literature. Myself a student of literature and philosophy, a novelist by choice, a screen and television writer by necessity who had become entranced by the legend of modern physics, that new journey of scientific Argonauts bent on discovering the structure of the universe.

We discovered at once that we shared a common and deeply felt[15] interest in one thing above all else: Man's coming journey into deep space. Incidentally, of course, we were both interested in the law—and Art will be glad to tell you how, between us, we reduced a Professor of Legal Philosophy to rubble one semester.

Over our years together, Art and I learned a great deal from one another, and before we parted, he observed to me, "If I ever have need of a philosopher, I'll be calling on you." We both got a laugh out of that since everyone knows that philosophers are of no use—like poets, priests, prophets, and the like.

Well, here I am, and I can only suggest that Art's call suggests that he knows something everyone doesn't know: that C. P. Snow was wrong. There are not two cultures, one based on science, another based on the arts and humanities. At present, it seems to me we hardly have culture, much less two.

What I want to talk about this evening[16] is the necessary reconstruction of a Western culture as part of any sensible enterprise aimed at placing ourselves among the stars. In order to do that, I have to describe the structure of Western thinking as I perceive it, and discuss at least one of the serious deformities which, it seems to me, hampers the present "climate of opinion" in regard to the enterprise of space exploration. Finally, I will briefly suggest a remedy for that deformity and the prospects for creation of new attitudes toward our future in space.

It is a matter of no small interest that there is a wide agreement on the text which is said to represent the beginnings of Western philosophy, hence the beginning of Western rationalism and scientific thinking. The great political thinker Eric Voegelin, the most distinguished philosopher of the twentieth century Martin Heidegger, and the philosopher of science Giorgio de Santillana of MIT,[17] all agree that these words herald the beginning of the Western intellectual tradition: "He said that the principle and element of existing things was the apeiron (the Boundless,

---

13   Dula, an attorney, practices space law and was the literary executor for the science-fiction writer Robert A. Heinlein.

14   "freshman" in original

15   "deeply-felt" in original

16   Corrington crossed out the word "morning" and replaced it with "evening."

17   Removed commas after *thinker, twentieth century,* and *science* because these phrases have restrictive appositives that don't require commas.

the Infinite) . . . and the source of coming-to-be for existing things is that into which destruction, too, happens 'according to necessity; for they pay penalty and retribution to each other for their injustice according to the assessment of Time.'"[18]

Now it is well and good that Anaximander receives such an exalted position in the history of human thought, if one considers that abstraction constitutes a great leap of thought.

At the same time, one should recognize that Anaximander did not invent the image of the Apeiron, or even its meaning. He only abstracted it and named it.

The looming forebear of Anaximander's symbol, the Apeiron, is as old as Greek thought. It is Okeanos, the river-ocean that surrounds the world, and the source of all. "Okeanos, from whom the gods are sprung," Homer calls it, deep-flowing, backward-flowing Okeanos which some scholars identify with the Milky Way, and most understand as the imagistic source of the cosmic dragon, the uroboros, the serpent with its tail in its mouth, a symbol found virtually everywhere—from Mesopotamia to Nigeria, from India to Mexico. In the Indian version, the cosmic source is Vritra, the serpent whom the god Indra fights to free the cosmic waters. According to the Satapatha Brahmana, in the beginning, Vritra contained "all this."

A documentation of the Okeanos-Apeiron symbolisms in detail could occupy a seminar for a semester, but with this initiating symbol of cosmogony, theogony, and world order, my point is made.

All rational thought arises from and continues to rest upon a substrate of mythological thought—just as the structure of consciousness arises from and is founded upon the unconscious.

These words of Anaximander of Miletus, who wrote in the sixth century BC, are said to constitute the break with the archaic cosmological tradition in which beginnings and principles are attributed to the gods. ~~or to a variety of mythologies~~.[19]

~~But~~[20] Of course the transference of causes and principles from the aegis of the gods to the working of abstract forces was by no means complete in the sixth century BC. Plato continued to use the myth to illustrate his meaning, calling such myths "likely stories." In his old age, Aristotle, the progenitor and master of analysis, acknowledged that he still enjoyed hearing those old stories of the beginnings and of the gods.

The ordering structures of the Orient, most of which find their source in the Rg Veda,[21] were mythological structures which, in most cases, transparently represented forces, either of physics or of psyche. In the Vedic versions, the gods never took on the mass of domestic and personal detail found in the Greek. It may

---

18   Corrington's paraphrase.
19   Strikethrough in original.
20   Strikethrough in original.
21   Rig Veda.

be for that reason that in the progress of Indian thinking, there was never that peculiar illusion that we call "the break with the myth."

For the notion that at some time in the archaic past, humanity turned away from mythic thinking and began the trek toward what would become scientific thinking, is an illusion, a prized and defended illusion held by the West for over a thousand years, and used as a formal distinction for the past four hundred. This distinction between scientific thinking and mythical thinking was almost certainly essential in the formative period of noetic thought, and the reasons are fairly clear.

1. No mode of thinking in the West which made use of the symbols of the gods could possibly be "free" thinking. Socrates discovered that at the cost of his life.

2. Religious and political institutions held a vested interest in insulating and isolating the symbols of the gods from manipulation by speculators who, in altering the characteristics of the gods, based on discoveries and theories in empirical reality would also—whether they meant to or not— radically alter the theological values associated with the gods. In theology as in the law, predictability is at last the highest value. People become uncomfortable when they are presented with the notion that the symbols by which they refer to the Ultimate Reality are subject to change with very little notice.

3. The symbols of spiritual reality, exoteric or esoteric, carry with them a vast amount of connotation, of emotional freight, which can only blind or seriously hamper the use of such symbols for purely intellectual purposes.

All in all, the odd notion that one changes the nature of reality by shifting the symbols by which one deals with reality was an illusion that had to be created and sustained—for as long as that was possible. The essence of science in its early days was its utter difference from the mythological and theological orders of experience, which had preceded it.

I would propose that the time of the illusion's usefulness has ended, and that speculation into the nature of reality in the future will, indeed, already is, beginning to fuse the symbols once more—so as to blur the distinctions between spiritual and physical symbols, and to view the cosmos once more as a single ordered universe in which men and superhuman forces stand together in love and strife.

Such an idea will certainly trouble those who have grown up within the rationalist-empiricist intellectual climate of the last 300 years and have never felt it necessary to question that structure. But when I suggest that it must be questioned, I ask nothing more than Galileo asked in the seventeenth century. And I expect a somewhat less violent and more thoughtful response than he received.

The nature of reality expresses itself through a series of images mediated within our central nervous systems. Thus mediated, the images are properly called symbols. The symbols stand as the means of rendering intelligible and preserving the range of what we call "human experiences."

Thus considered, as symbolic structures, the *Theogony* of Hesiod and Mendeleev's periodic table of the elements are of precisely the same value. They collect and represent, on the one hand the experience of the gods by men of the eighth-seventh centuries BC in Greece; on the other, the order and relative character of elemental structures at a certain level of magnitude to men of the twentieth century.[22]

It may be said that Hesiod's pedigree of the gods is of no use; that Mendeleev's periodic table[23] allows us to do things, to make things, to repeat, and to predict certain physical characteristics of reality. The first statement is untrue; the second is true, but limited in significance.

The imagery of the gods, understood as personified forces, some physical, some psychic, continues to be useful not only as a template for the understanding of the growth of culture and the history of the origins and development of consciousness, but as well for the analysis of the individual psychic structure.

We have become, since the seventeenth century so devoted to empiricism and rationalism as the tests of reality that we have managed to confuse ourselves as to the very meaning of reality itself. We seem to suppose that operational usefulness in the sense put forth by Bridgeman constitutes in some sense a measure of truth exceeding that of all other experience. Or, put another way, that operational usefulness may be said to cancel the claims of any other kind of experience.

Thus the peculiar reality of the myth has been assaulted both by rationalism and empiricism—when, in fact, both rationalism and empiricism constitute a later generation of myth making themselves.

Shifting of terms and the addition of mathematical sophistication to the inquisition of the process of reality does not represent a change in the nature of the search itself. Werner Heisenberg once observed: "We may remark at this point that modern physics is in some way extremely near to the doctrines of Heraclitus. If we replace the word 'fire' with the word 'energy' we can almost repeat his statements word for word from our modern point of view."[24]

Heisenberg, like Schroedinger,[25] who became deeply involved in Indian thinking late in his life, was too good a scientist to suppose that one could do good

---

22 Mendeleev's work is actually from the 1860s.

23 Uncapitalized.

24 Corrington did not provide an edition for his source, just a page number. The page number matched the 1962 edition, so the source would have been as follows: Werner Heisenberg, *Physics and Philosophy: The Revolution in Modern Science* (New York: Harper and Row, 1962), 63.

25 Corrington used "Schroedinger" here and above in this essay. Corrington's spelling is the modern one (after the German spelling reform), but the scientist probably spelled his own name *Schrödinger*.

science—that is, put the universe to the question time and time again—only within boundaries laid out by our predecessors.

If scientific thought—in the sense of *Wissenschaft*, ordered accumulation of facts and analysis of experience—means anything, that thought must acknowledge that, as Einstein notes, *there is no such thing as a privileged observer—or, for that matter, a privileged frame of observation, least of all a privileged methodology by which to conduct the inquiry.*[26] I understand that statement to mean that even the intellectual and logical structure of science itself as we know it does not constitute a kind of ultimate matrix for thinking. We deceive ourselves if we suppose that the order of science as we have it, represents in any sense a final resting place of thought. Perhaps the law of contradiction applies only within certain magnitudes and to certain specific types of problem. It may be that the rule of the excluded middle and the principle of identity are limited in application—as we discovered was the case with geometries—in which the sum of angles in a triangle on Riemannian irregular surfaces do not necessarily add up to 180 degrees.

The intellectual constitution of modern science is a myth. It is an extraordinarily useful and trenchant myth—quite possibly the most brilliant myth our species has ever constructed. It is a myth to be protected at all costs. But this science of ours is not co-extensive with the manifold of reality; there is no certain equality between the rationally intelligible, the empirically verifiable, and the real.

~~But~~[27] The myth of science—along with its numerous sub-myths regarding the nature and interchangeability of matter and energy, space and time—is not exhaustive. It is a product of the subtle and sometimes not so subtle interfacing of proximal and distal zones on either side of human central nervous systems—plus that peculiar and irreducible process of meditation by which symbols are manipulated to create new insights. We do not understand that process, what fuels it, or what it may point to. All we know is that we call the result "meaning." And without the sense of "meaning," nothing we do will be done for long.

I am suggesting that modern man has reached a point at which it is essential for him to begin the task of rejoining the diverse portions of his psyche into a unity. I think it is possible—and necessary—for him to begin a careful, honest, and humble inventory of the symbolic structures which, taken together, constitute the field of human meaning. This must be done dispassionately, holding at bay the temptations of attraction and repulsion that tend to distract us when we examine experience and attempt an analysis of it.

I think we must probe the symbolic structures of science and the symbolic structures of spirituality from the point of view cited by Aristotle in *The Metaphysics*:

---

26   Corrington has paraphrased Einstein.

27   Strikethrough in original.

"Each man by nature desires to know."[28] This drive to knowledge, if it is to be carried out seriously, and with the goal of attaining additional meaning and insight, would require the following axiomatic positions be held:

1. No form of knowledge, scientific, spiritual, mystical, or other constitutes, or ever will constitute a statement co-extensive with the manifold of reality.

2. No form of human experience carried on by vast numbers of people over vast periods of time, may be dismissed as pathological or as meaningless.

3. Forms of knowledge which produce operational results represent operational knowledge. No theoretical inference regarding such knowledge is justified *per se* beyond the operational results achieved.

4. Forms of experience which produce consistent operational results *must* be accorded status whether such results are theoretically explicable or not.

5. No philosophical proposition may be considered as other than a ground for further questioning.

6. The nature of questions and of analysis shall be consistent with the matter under analysis. (This is a restatement of Aristotle's dictum that there is a measure of exactitude proper to every science, and one may not require a greater degree of exactitude than the subject matter permits.)

You will ask what the discussion so far has to do with our movement into space. The answer is this: when we move out beyond our present brief journeys in the immediate neighborhood, we will be carrying with us one piece of equipment which remains essentially mysterious, untested, only marginally predictable: ourselves.

Not simply our bodies, not simply our psyches—but *ourselves*.

These selves of ours, these intricate intertwinings of what we call body and spirit, are, for all present uses, the ultimate black boxes. It is a commonplace to say that we know more about the cosmos than we know about the psyche. It *should* be a commonplace to say that the attitudes and methodologies which have achieved so much in the quest for physical knowledge, have proved worse than useless in the search for knowledge of the human psyche.

Yet it is some property of the unplumbed psyche which drives us to question, which urges us to prepare, and which will at last send us bursting forth into space. It is, by all means, possible to write a book full of what sounds like rational and empirical reasons for undertaking the enterprise of space. Our sense of survival cites the Military Reason; our acquisitiveness puts forth the Economic Reason; our desire to extend our operational knowledge sets out the Scientific Reason. And yet . . . and yet . . .

---

28   Corrington is either paraphrasing or quoting from memory. One translation states, "All men by nature are actuated with the desire of knowledge." Aristotle, *The Metaphysics of Aristotle*, translated by Rev. John H. M'Mahon (London: Henry G. Bohn, York Street, Covent Garden, 1857), p. 1

Below, above, behind, beyond every one of those reasons lies The Reason—The Reason which is not a reason at all, but an urge, an impulse, a drive long repressed to the status of day-dreaming and fantasy-mongering because there was nothing to be done about it. A reason so ambiguous that on the one hand it was left to shamans and yogis to turn the drive toward space inward, and on the other hand required that it be endlessly expressed in the myth and ritual of almost all peoples, in the prophecy of an Ezekiel[29] and the sketches of a Leonardo.

If you tell me that there are Military, Economic, and Scientific reasons for the enterprise of space, I will not disagree. I will simply reply that you are being less than fully conscious of your own deepest motivations. Because those reasons are secondary to that Reason that none of us can articulate in rationalist-empiricist terms, but which is rooted so deeply in our psyches that it can be considered a structural unit of the psyche itself.

This oblivion into which our deepest motives have fallen is so pervasive, so all-embracing, that a discussion of it in contemporary language is almost impossible. Our dedication to the rationalist-empiricist paradigm of classical physics has been so encompassing that it is difficult for us to penetrate past a veil of pragmatic reasons to the *Ratio*, the *Logos* for our actions which lies as substrate below the grasp of logical investigation as such.

I have heard it said that even if all this is true, it is no more than the fevered imaginings of men and women who would do well to turn their eyes from the stars and look at the shattered anguish of earth. There are problems to be solved on earth; why should we waste money on the enterprise of space?

This is a very popular argument in some quarters. I am certain I do not need to elaborate on it. It is not popular with me. I find it maudlin, misleading, and essentially dishonest. It hardly requires a detailed knowledge either of human history or human nature to realize that the problems of modern man are not going to be resolved by the expedient of gutting the space program and handing the funds over to meals on wheels. On the contrary, it is possible that those problems would, in the long term, be exacerbated by turning away from a vision so deeply rooted in our psyches.

We can, of course, respond to such arguments with the Military, the Economic, or the Scientific reasons for the enterprise. I would suggest that those who mount the argument are quite capable of ignoring all three of these reasons.

Since that is so, why should we not tell the truth? Why not search out that *Logos*,[30] that deepest-seated reason for the enterprise? Consider that even a politician, pressed hard enough, backed into a corner and threatened with utter annihilation, may tell the truth.

Let us then propose the Mythological Reason for dedicating ourselves to the enterprise of space:

---

29 Changed from "Ezikiel."

30 Capitalized to maintain consistency with Corrington's earlier usage.

The leap into space is the heritage and destiny of Western Man. It is implicit in the structure of his psyche from the Rg Veda[31] through the myth of Icarus and the startling similarity of the architecture of the Gothic cathedral and the modern space vehicle pointed outward toward the same infinity to that body of literature we call science fiction which incorporates and gives concrete form to the legend of space and our place in it. Seventy years ago, when the airplane was hardly a decade old, Oswald Spengler stated that the symbolic stance of Western man was the yearning for absolute infinite space. Spengler supposed that the West was in decline, that it had entered on its final phase—in some measure because the deepest symbolic drama of the Western psyche could not be worked out.

The question of Western decline remains open so far as I can tell, but the myth-structure of the Western mind began to be realized concretely that day in 1969 when Neil Armstrong became the first human being to call back across the void to his fellows, speaking of a giant step for Man.

Perhaps the essence of our human nature consists, beyond rationalist-empiricist ordering and reordering of phenomena, in the process of acting out the supreme drama of the archetypal structures programmed into us. This is what Mircea Eliade, professor of religion at the University of Chicago has said:

> Today we are on the way to an understanding of one thing of which the nineteenth century had not even a presentiment—that the symbol, the myth and the image are of the very substance of the spiritual life, that they may become disguised, mutilated or degraded, but are never extirpated . . .
>
> Images, symbols and myths are not irresponsible creations of the psyche; they respond to a need and fulfill a function—that of bringing to light the most hidden modalities of being. Consequently the study of them enables us to reach a better understanding of man, of man "as he is," before he has come to terms with the conditions of History. Every historical man carries on, within himself, a great deal of prehistoric humanity.[32]

I will not spend time setting out the various patterns of myth which point like fingers into the great void that we call space. Using the Nietzschean dichotomy of Apollonian-Dionysian world views would point out that all our knowing, all our

---

31   Rig Veda.

32   Made minor changes based on pp. 11–12 of Eliade's *Images and Symbols*. Corrington's original read as follows:

Today we are on the way to an understanding of one thing of which the 19th century had not even a presentiment—that the symbol, the myth, and the image are of the very substance of the spiritual life, that they may become disguised, mutilated or degraded, but are never extirpated . . .

Images, symbols, and myths are not irresponsible creations of the psyche; they respond to a need and fulfill a function—that of bringing to light the most hidden modalities of being. Consequently, the study of them enables us to reach a better understanding of man, of man as he is before he has come to terms with the conditions of. Every historical man carries within himself a great deal of prehistoric humanity.

great spiritual journeys, are journeys into deep space. "The way up and the way down are one and the same," Heraclitus said. "One and the same is the path of the streams when they flow into the sea," says the Rg Veda.[33] I think that the path outward into the cosmos and the path inward to the psyche, are also one and the same, employing different techniques.

Preparation for the journey into the stars thus, is not simply a matter of technological mastery and engineering skill. It is much more complex and much more demanding.

We must maintain all that we have accomplished as scientists, as rationalists and empiricists. The enterprise of science is not negotiable nor can we lessen its rigor. But we have to acknowledge simultaneously that we are not solely creatures of reason, and that indeed our deepest motives and profoundest concerns have nothing to do with reason at all.

What makes us human and drives us on, whether we call it love or patriotism, a sense of excellence or the desire to achieve—all those abstract words upon which our morale depends—is an inchoate force within that demands we fulfill a vision which hardly any of us can see clearly. It is a vision for which rationalist-empiricist language is inadequate. It is not my private vision nor yours, and its meaning extends infinitely beyond mere egoistic accomplishment.

And if the vision stands beyond reductionist scientism, beyond egoism, it stands equally beyond any institutional statement. The structures of the unconscious which fuel our activities, are neither symbolically possessed nor symbolically exhausted by religion, taken in the sense of Cicero, who invented the term and first used it. Whatever we say of it, it is not enough; however we attempt to express the vision, it extends beyond the horizon as a permanent fixture of reality toward which our psyches tend, whether the technology employed is spiritual contemplation or rocketry.

We are, in terms of the enterprise of space, not individual human beings, but a vector with an eschatological component. We cannot state our purpose, because we cannot yet know a purpose that we have not rationally defined, but which rises in us from the depths of the psyche without our willing it—able only to will that it be effected. We take certain things for granted, and that seems justified:

1. We are children of the universe, hence we belong in it.

2. We are developing the capacity to move out from our home planet, hence such movement seems not to be at variance with our natures or with the order of the universe.

3. Many of us are deeply programmed for such voyages, hence it is reasonable to suspect they constitute a structure of meaning.

---

33   *Rig Veda.*

But even if these postulates are true, even the least imaginative of us must realize in advance that the voyage into space is going to confront us sooner or later with the unimaginable. It does not require science fiction to picture situations and conditions that challenge and defeat our present abilities to process data and render it meaningful. Whether the situation be one involving inconceivable new physical anomalies or the encounter with alien life-forms, we are going to find ourselves, sooner or later, confronted with circumstances for which our present philosophical resources are not only not sufficient, but possibly self-destructive.

Thus the need for the preparation I speak of: a form of spiritual preparation by which we come to learn again what it has been necessary for us to forget. We must re-learn and carry to the heart the old verities that existed before the rise of metaphysics and science, the truths that were carried on and carried down through the mythological structure of the psyche: the unity of humanity and the cosmos, the illusory and ephemeral quality of the ego, the one law common to all that penetrates and encompasses the fine structure and the gross structure of reality.

I think the voyagers who first venture into deep space had better be the best we can send—which is to say human beings who have learned everything and forgotten nothing, most especially the spiritual and mythic heritage of humanity.

Whenever I consider that my sons and daughters generations removed will stand on other planets, under strange suns, and the shape of their lives will be so very different from our own—and yet moved, driven by the same eternal singularity that brings us together to speak for a while and drives us apart to do our work—I remember the last words of the last novel by a great American novelist, Thomas Wolfe:

> To lose the earth you know, for greater knowing; to lose the life you have, for greater life; to leave the friends you loved, for greater loving; to find a land more kind than home, more large than earth—
>
> Whereon the pillars of this world are founded, towards which the conscience of the world is tending—a wind is rising, and the rivers flow.[34]

---

34   Based on Wolfe's original, minor errors in Corrington's quotation have been corrected: two commas were added and "toward" was changed to "towards."

Part IV

GNOSTICISM

The Structure of
Gnostic Consciousness

Approx. 1976-1978

Corrington wrote this essay around the time he delivered his paper titled "Gnosticism and Modern Thought: A Way You'll Never Be" at a conference titled "Gnosticism and Modernity" held at Vanderbilt University on April 27-29, 1978. Corrington's paper "Gnosticism and Modern Thought" appears in the following chapter. "The Structure of Gnostic Consciousness" developed out of "Gnosticism and Modern Thought" as a contribution that Corrington prepared for an edition that he and Richard Bishirjian were planning to publish after the Vanderbilt conference. The edition was never published because, according to Bishirjian, some of the contributors did not want to be associated with Mel Bradford, who was contributing a chapter to the book.

Corrington was involved in organizing the 1978 conference with Bishirjian and Voegelin. Bishirjian would later relate that Voegelin considered Corrington's paper to be the best that weekend. Reproduced at the end of this essay are copies of the conference program, along with correspondence between Bishirjian and Corrington regarding planning the conference. Ellis Sandoz and Mel Bradford were also in attendance at the conferrence; Sandoz moderated a panel, and Bradford delivered a paper.

This chapter and the following three chapters can be taken as a unit and in many ways as a summary of Corrington's philosophical interpretations of Gnosticism, political order, consciousness, myth, symbolism, the psyche, and knowledge. Corrington criticizes Gnosticism for failing to deal with reality as it is constituted in consciousness. The collapse of the Gnostic understanding of reality leads to disorder, confusion, and the embrace of such things as magic that are at odds with a symbolic order emanating from a sound understanding of reality apprehended through consciousness. The Gnostic failure to comprehend reality generates delusional, ahistorical assumptions about the divinity of man and the ability of man to bring about a heaven on earth within history. Marxism is an example of a type of modern thinking that displays Gnostic elements.

The Gnostics feel alienated by, and disenchanted with, the cosmos as it exists in reality; they hate the real cosmos and remake it in the image of distorted mythopoetic concepts whose symbology of disorder is mistaken for order. To achieve gnosis, or knowledge, is actually to accept a wrong and archaic mode of mythopoetic thought, whereby magic is possible rather than beyond the realm of reality. This form of gnosis is attributable to Simon the Sorcerer or Simon the Magician, the Gnostic leader who is recounted briefly in the canonical Book of Acts of the Apostles in the New Testament. Corrington discusses the work of the twelfth century mystic Joachim of Fiore, who exposited a millenarian view of history that influenced modern symbolic systems and consciousness which, according to Corrington, represent a divorce from earlier types of mythopoetic thinking. Joachim rearticulated a Gnostic vision of earth and the cosmos, projecting eschatological salvation onto the concrete activities in which we are immersed and seeking to realize a heaven on earth within history. His notion of consciousness rendered a conceptual end to history, a fantasy in which the real is lost to a deformed system of symbolism whereby the natural desires of the psyche are satisfied by a false eschatology.

We must not act and speak like men asleep.

—Heraclitus

I

Eric Voegelin has pointed out that "the noetic field of consciousness in which the philosophers' debate about reality moves was constituted by Anaximander through the . . . dictum: 'The origin of things is the Apeiron . . . It is necessary for things to perish into that from which they were born; for they pay one another penalty for their injustice according to the ordinance of Time.'"[1]

Professor Voegelin has noted that this fragment is "the earliest extant pronouncement by a philosopher on the process of reality and its structure."[2]

But the noetic field originally differentiated by Anaximander is not the only field within the process of consciousness. There is, in addition, the *mythopoetic* field, which Professor Voegelin described so well at the beginning of *Israel & Revelation*: "We move in a charmed community where everything that meets us has force and will and feelings, where animals and plants can be men and gods, where men can be divine and gods are kings, where the feathery morning sky is the falcon Horus and the Sun and the Moon are his eyes, where the underground sameness of being is a conductor for magic currents of good or evil force that will subterraneously reach the superficially unreachable partner, where things are the same and not the same, and can change into each other."[3]

I would propose that the mythopoetic field, antecedent to the noetic, possesses a structure quite similar to it, and that the two fields are parallel in a number of ways. I would propose further that there is a central symbol, which stands in the mythopoetic field of consciousness almost precisely where the Apeirontic symbol stands in the noetic.

The symbol to which I refer is the Uroboros, the cosmic serpent or dragon, often represented with its tail touching its head or in its mouth, or tightly coiled in a circle. The Uroborotic symbol is widespread in space and time and can be found in

---

1   Corrington's note: "Eric Voegelin, *Order and History*, vol. 4, *The Ecumenic Age* (Baton Rouge, LA: Louisiana State University Press, 1975), 215." Changed a colon to a semi-colon and capitalized "Time" in Corrington's quotation to match Voegelin's original.

2   Corrington's note: "Voegelin, *Order and History*, 4:174."

3   Corrington's note: "Eric Voegelin, *Order and History*, vol. 1, *Israel and Revelation* (Baton Rouge, LA: Louisiana State University Press, 1956), 3."

pre-history, in early historical, pre-Christian and gnostic times,[4] on into Medieval and Renaissance pictorial art and literature, from Nigeria to India to Mexico.[5]

The mythopoetic symbol of the Uroboros is both precursor of the Apeirontic symbolism and complementary to it. As I have noted in another place: "This Apeiron, which is the *arche*, is, as well, the *teleote*,[6] or end, toward which all that arises into existence tends toward once more." Further,

> the Apeirontic symbol becomes luminous not simply as a mechanism for description of the cosmos, but as a symbolism that simultaneously describes a region of the psyche. The Boundless arche, from which all things arise, is the place from which consciousness and its insights arise as well. . . . The process of reality inherent in the cosmos, arising from the Apeirontic depth of the substrate of the Whole, has, arising and unfolding in it, the process of consciousness which illuminates reality both by its experiences and by the symbolizing act of differentiation from original compactness.[7]

Both Uroboros and Apeiron represent the *arche* and *teleote* of the process of reality as they were perceived by human beings at distinct moments in the growth and differentiation of consciousness in a phylogenetic sense. Moreover, both are symbols of the process of consciousness itself in an ontogenetic sense; hence, to adopt the geological terminology used by Professor Voegelin, the symbols stand in relation to one another as identical symbolisms in the separate but parallel strata within which they function. The Uroboros is representative of the ground-state of mythopoetic consciousness as the Apeiron is ground-state in the field of noetic consciousness: "The Psyche becomes the site of conscious participation in reality; the Depth [Apeiron] becomes the dimension of the Psyche from which new insights are drawn up."[8]

Stratigraphically speaking, the Uroboros lies "below" the Apeiron, like the earlier writing on a palimpsest. It is the origin and the place of return, the place where all things, both of *physis* and *psyche*, arise. Unlike the Apeiron, however, the Uroboros does not, in terms of its historical location, evolve as a result of questioning analysis, because analysis itself is a noetic methodology, and the

---

4   Unlike in his other essays on gnosticism, where he lowercases the term throughout, in the original manuscript of this essay Corrington capitalized *Gnostic* and *Gnosticism*. In order to keep the style consistent across essays, the term has been lowercased here as well.

5   In the original manuscript, Corrington had a long footnote on the Uroboros or Cosmic Serpent. To read this footnote, see Appendix A.

6   Italics added (to be parallel to *arche*).

7   Corrington's note: "John William Corrington, "Order and Consciousness/Consciousness and History: The New Program of Eric Voegelin," in *Voegelin's Search for Order in History*, ed. Stephen McKnight (Baton Rouge, LA: Louisiana State University Press, 1977), 172–73."

8   Corrington's note: "Voegelin, *Order and History*, 4:177."

exfoliation of mythopoetic symbols does not take place in that mode. Rather, one myth is critiqued only by another:

> Paraphrastic interpretations would obscure the historical stratification in the meaning of symbols. For experiences and their symbolizations are not self-contained units, carrying the whole of their meaning in themselves; they are events in the process of reality and as such related to past and future events. A paraphrase would destroy that part of meaning that accrues to symbols through their position in the history of consciousness.[9]

If we wish to compare the growth and movement of the Uroborotic derivative symbols to those which develop from the Apeirontic symbol without resorting to such "interpretation," we must speak of certain second-order symbols which refer to the separation of the Uroboros, of its rending from original undifferentiated unity and monistic wholeness into the dichotomies of male-female, dark-light, good-evil, space-time, and so on.[10] Creation itself is an act of differentiation, or establishing the fundamental bi-polarity of existence. The great symbols of the division of the Uroboros are the pair of the Great Mother and the Heavenly Father, products of the Separation of the World Parents.[11] It should be noted that this primal act of creation is perceived in some speculations as an act of violent alienation, whereby the separation destroys the original monistic unity, and the paradisiacal, surrounded and protected by the Uroboros, is breached and perfection tainted.

Creation is frequently depicted as an act of violence. In the well-known Babylonian myth of creation, the hero Marduk slays the serpent Tiamat, and creates the cosmos out of the bloody fragments of the creature. As Mircea Eliade tells us, the Babylonian New Year, or the *Akitu*, represented the epic of creation in which Tiamat, a sea-monster, hence a symbol of the Uroboros as Okeanos, is defeated by Marduk, "and the Creation took place at that very moment."[12] The creation refers both to the framing of the cosmos and to the arising of the process of consciousness, which perceives it. The

---

9   Corrington's note: "Voegelin, *Order and History*, 4:175."

10   Corrington's note (including block quotation): F. M Cornford, *From Religion to Philosophy: A Study in the Origins of Western Speculation* (New York: Harper and Row, 1957), 65–66.

> If we look more closely into this conception of pairs of contraries, we find that Anaximander is more purely rational than many of his succesors. In later systems—notably those of Parmenides and Empedocles—mythical associations and implications, which he has expurgated, emerge again. In particular, we can discern that the prototype of all opposition or contrariety is the contrariety of sex. . . . The cosmogonies open, not with the marriage, but with the separation, of earth and sky.

11   Corrington's note: "Erich Neumann, *The Origins and History of Consciousness* (Princeton, NJ: Princeton University Press, 1954), 9ff." In the original manuscript, Corrington capitalized "The" in "The Great Mother," "The Heavenly Father," and "The Separation" in this sentence. Because elsewhere in this essay Corrington did not capitalize "The" in these names, the lowercase form appears here for consistency.

12   Corrington's note: "Mircea Eliade, *The Myth of the Eternal Return* (Princeton, NJ: Princeton University Press, 1971), 56."

making of the cosmos is reflected phylogenetically in the mythopoetic creation which describes it, and ontogenetically in the process of consciousness, which both creates the cosmological myth and contemplates it. The role of hero is, in the process of mythopoetic creation, apportioned to the consciousness, which has freed itself from the encircling Uroboros, and to the Maker or poet whose consciousness "remembers" the struggle and memorializes it in poesis.

Both ontogenetically and phylogenetically, the struggle of the hero symbolizes the foundation of conscious order. If the process of reality is independent and prior to the arising of consciousness, it is nonetheless dependent upon the field of consciousness for its recognition as a component of being. The break with the monistic womb-garden of unconsciousness through the fight with the Uroborotic dragon is the mythopoetic equivalent of the noetic break with the myth which takes place definitively in the establishment of the noetic field through the differentiation of the Apeirontic symbolism and its development and elaboration. The slaying of the dragon establishes the mythopoetic field within which, by way of more and more elaborated myths, the growth of mythopoetic consciousness takes place. It should be understood that the truth of the myth is no more static than is noetic truth. The distinction is that mythopoetic truth does not differentiate conceptually as does noetic truth. It differentiates rather, by the generation of incremental myths which, in response to various kinds of turbulence in the field, elaborate and advance the complexity of the field as a whole.

This elaboration does not cease with the initial break from the Uroborotic womb-pleroma. The tension of mythopoetic existence is no less than that encountered in the noetic field. As a result, there is the mythopoetic equivalent of the Platonic Metaxy expressed in the precarious balance of the hero between the symbols of the Great Mother and the Spiritual Father.

On the one hand, the human being living in the field of mythopoetic consciousness continues to feel the temptation to relax, to fall back from the rigor of mythopoetic consciousness into the Uroborotic womb of the Great Mother, to end the clash of contraries, to find once more the monistic unconsciousness of the Pleroma. Myths of the type of Osiris, Adonis, and Tammuz figures represent this pole of the mythopoetic tension.[13]

On the other hand, there is the opposite temptation to identify wholly with the Spiritual Father component of the divided Uroboros, with exclusive consciousness. The myths presenting this polarity include those of Phaeton and Icarus, both sons of masterful, godlike fathers, both of whom were destroyed attempting to dominate their father's elements.

To lose balance within the mythopoetic equivalent of the Metaxy, then, is to either plunge back into the pre-conscious Garden which lies behind the Uroboros,

13   Corrington's note: "Neumann, *Origins and History of Consciousness*, 46."

or to attempt to dominate cosmos and consciousness, to try to go "beyond" and render existence itself no more than an appendage of consciousness, with the risk of the resultant fall back into the water of the Uroboros.

The hero of the mythos is, positively, that one who lives "in fear of the god," and whose daimon is attuned to the new insights which, in mythic form, occur in prophecy or oracular expressions. Negatively, the hero is aware of the Limit (*Horos*) of his own consciousness and rejects the sirens' offer of a dreamlike passage back to the Pleroma "below," and the crystalline challenge to become "son of the sun," like unto a god, which offers the illusion of replacing the order of *physis* with the order of an inflated psyche reigning from "above."

The mythopoetic hero who subsists in the balance knows from whence he has come and to where he shall return. He knows that the meaning of his life is to avoid the pitfalls of collapse and expansion, both of which are unsuited to the *Arete* of a mortal who recognizes the proper relationship between his psyche and the cosmos.

The differentiation of the Apeirontic symbolism, both in its psychic and physical dimensions, constitutes a fresh beginning in which the movement of consciousness breaks finally with the myth precisely as the mythopoetic consciousness had previously broken with the Uroborotic pre-consciousness. The Apeiron, like the Uroboros, is a threshold symbol; it stands as *arche* and tends to stand as an epochal structure in the history of consciousness. The "stripped" quality of the Apeiron, as Cornford describes it,[14] suggests its unique implications. The concrete imagery of the Uroboros is tossed aside in place of language, which requires a new type of mind to make anything of it. The threshing Uroboros-Okeanos-Leviathan-Chronos becomes the Apeiron, the abstract symbol of cosmic and psychic process, and the archaic symbol becomes *pseudos*, simply a "myth" in the pejorative sense, its meaning at first blurred and finally lost to noetic questioning.

But the noetic break with the myth is neither total nor unqualified. All men do not share in noetic consciousness even today, nor do those who share in it constitute in any sense an annulment of the "lower" strata. The "lower" strata remain in place not only phylogenetically in the sense that they are ineradicably part of the history of consciousness as objects of noetic contemplation, but as living and functioning components of the ontogenetic process of consciousness as it occurs in concrete human beings.

II

The fundamental gnostic experience can be described ontogenetically as an incapacity to deal with the process of reality as it is reflected in consciousness. The

---

14   Corrington's note: "C. F. Cornford, 'Mysticism and Science in the Pythagorean Tradition,' *Classical Quarterly* 16 (1922), 137–50."

gnostic personality is defective in the sense that it is unable to maintain the balance in tension between the events and circumstances emergent in empirical reality and its own consciousness. Existence in the Metaxy, the luminous interface between the process of reality and the process of consciousness, is experienced as unbearable, and the balance is lost.

The imbalancing factors, whatever they may be concretely, cause the defective personality to seek release from the disorder and confusion it experiences. The result is a speculative return from the noetic field of representation to the mythopoetic field. The reason for this is that the noetic field of consciousness will not sustain the illusions required to satisfy the needs of the gnostic personality. Obviously, no interpretation of the Apeirontic symbolism and those differentiated from it can be used to maintain the fiction that the process of reality is amenable to alteration or change by acts of magic. Metastatic transformation of reality is not a possibility within the noetic field of consciousness.

Such is not the case with the mythopoetic field. On principle, the creation of Second Realities consists in the gnostic's tendency to fall back upon that field of symbolisms in which the "logic" of magic—or, for that matter, of day-dreaming—is acceptable. In that zone of consciousness still dominated by the Uroboros and its incremental symbols, such transformations of the process of reality are perceived as possible. The Apeiron, an abstract symbol descriptive of the process of existence and non-existence, cannot be manipulated; but the dragon can be pacified, the serpent monster can be slain. It is possible to re-enter the Garden by perilous journey between the head and tail of the dragon. It is equally possible to destroy the dragon and create from its fragments a new cosmos. In that zone of consciousness, as Professor Voegelin has written, "men can be divine and gods are kings." The fact that such fantasies do not square with physical, social, or political experience is of no account, since the "laws" by which noetic consciousness determines these to be governed cannot apply to the mythopoetic field. A typical gnostic response to critiques launched against such imaginative constructions is the Marxist contempt for "Bourgeoisie objectivity."

While the noetic capability and potential are not destroyed in the gnostic conversion, they are rendered subsidiary in the sense of the term as it is employed by Michael Polanyi, and the focus of attention is turned upon the new synthetic myth, which the gnostic experiences as having relieved him of the awful tension of noetic existence. When the balance is lost between the properly subsidiary creativity of the mythopoetic field and the focal analytic power of the noetic field, the result is either collapse into the Uroborotic symbolism of exodus back to the Great Mother, or inflation "upward" into the Uroborotic mythology of conquest under the aegis of the Spiritual Father. Either the imbalanced psyche seeks to break free from the disorder of reality when, as in the phrase of Joyce's Stephen Dedalus, "history is a nightmare from which I am trying to escape," or the psyche attempts to slay the Uroboros definitively. Both possibilities are ahistorical. In the first case, history is vacated as the psyche re-establishes the "peaceable kingdom" of the Pleromatic-womb experience. In the second case, history comes to be dominated, reduced to a function controllable by the magical gnosis in the hands of the adept. It should be noted that in both cases, that of exodus or of conquest, the result is what Professor Voegelin has termed a "stop-history" movement.

To return to the Uroboros or to attempt to slay it means equally, in mythopoetic terms, to conclude the historical process simply by an imaginative return to the paradigmatic mythical structure, leaving the noetic field behind, and to make of the cosmos and consciousness one vast womb in which all is one once more, in which existence and *egophany* are one, and the one is the ego of the gnostic magician.

The spiritual pain and nausea, the awful ambiguity of existence in the Metaxy calls for a noetic heroism no less dramatic and rigorous than the mythopoetic heroism call to live among dragons. Indeed, for many, the vector of differentiating consciousness, which, at least phylogenetically, has sublimated the mythopoetic field of consciousness, has created a perception of existence which is intolerable, and which they cannot bear.

Such people choose, in Professor Voegelin's phrase, to live in a certain *untruth*[15] rather than in an uncertain truth. The twin fantasies of exodus back to Pleromatic unconsciousness or conquestion[16] of the cosmos to set up the Pleroma within it, to escape history or to dominate it, are compelling to those who cannot or will not cope with the tension associated with *the bios theoretikos*, with life in a historical present under God, or the life of loving faith aimed like an arrow toward the eschatological horizon and its mystery.

It was Heraclitus, at the dawning of noesis as a differentiated field of consciousness, who characterized the gnostic personality long before it came into being as such: "To those who are awake, there is one ordered universe held in common by all, whereas in sleep each man turns from this cosmos to one of his own."[17]

III

We must now penetrate more deeply into that class of gnostic symbols we have referred to as "classical" or "escape" symbols. The classification has a certain convenience, but possesses no ultimate significance. Other terminology might be used, for example, *Magian* gnosticism.[18]

---

15   Italics added for emphasis.

16   Possibly "conquest."

17   Corrington's note: "Kathleen Freeman, fragment 89 in *Ancilla to the Pre-Socratic Philosophers* (Oxford: Blackwell, 1962), 30." The proper quotation should read, "To those who are awake, there is one ordered universe common (to all), whereas in sleep each man turns away (from this world) to one of his own."

18   Corrington's note: "The term *magian* does not here refer to the classification of civilizations in the work of

Gnostic experiences begin with a dread or hatred of the cosmos manifested either as space or time, or both, and a corollary experience of not belonging in the cosmos or age in which one finds oneself. Whether the term *alienation* arises with Plotinus, or if we credit it to Hegel, the fact is that the primary experience of being over[19] against existence in the cosmos can be traced well back of Clement of Alexandria, who gave it its classic expression,[20] to mythopoetic structures as early as the Genesis story of the fall from the Pleromatic Garden into a world of sin and death, confusion and disorder. Obviously, every expression of alienation is not gnostic.[21] The symbols of alienation which appear in a gnostic context represent what T. S. Eliot called in another context symbols which lack an "objective correlative." The term refers to a response which is out of all portion to the stimulus which caused it to arise. The gnostic world-hatred in its context is of such kind. When we are confronted with it, we are forced to conclude that something more than the stated experience is involved.

Perhaps the clue to the distinction between those symbols of alienation which simply express the anguish to be expected as part of the *condition*[22] *humana* and those which are gnostic, rests with the gnostic conception that the cosmos itself is defective, that it is, in fact, *acosmos*, in the sense that it is a realm of total disorder created by a demiurge, himself an "abortion," the perverted offspring of the fault of Sofia (or Sophia-Prunikos) whose fall from the Pleroma signified both the breach of Pleromatic splendor and the initiation of cosmic creation. The mythos of an intracosmic Golden Age along the lines of compact mythopoetic forms is wholly absent from classical gnosticism, and, as we will see, reappears only in the "historical mythos" or "narrative philosophy" of modern gnosticism where Rousseau's noble savages and Marx's primal communards frolic in an earthly Pleroma.

Thus classical gnostic symbols of alienation are not, as in the case of earlier compact insights, circumstantial. Rather they are absolute, and are couched in purely mythopoetic terms. In the gnostic expression of alienation, no specific thing has occurred to trigger the sentiment; it is the fact of creation and existence as such which demonstrates the universality of defect and evil. It is not circumstance which is the source of the gnostic experience of alienation, but the very creation—and its Creator.

The second symbol common to gnostic fabrications is that of the hidden, nameless, or even "non-existent" god. Curiously, in some variants, this god is

---

Oswald Spengler. Rather it refers to Hans Jonas's observation that Simon Magus, in Roman surroundings, was referred to as 'Faustus,' the favored one. The division of gnostic paradigms into 'Magian' and 'Faustian' would carry with it considerable literary weight, yet I suspect that the distinction would be a defensible one."

19   Probably "overly."

20   Corrington's essay: "Cf. Eric Voegelin, *Science, Politics, and Gnosticism* (Chicago: Henry Regnery, 1968), 10."

21   Corrington's note: "Eric Voegelin, "Immortality: Experience and Symbol," *Harvard Theological Review* 60, no. 3 (1967), 236ff."

22   Should read *conditio*.

named Adamas or Protos Anthropos.[23] This First Man stands beyond the cosmos altogether, within the Uroborotic circle. He is guiltless of creation, though no explanation is ever given as to why he cannot control the demiurge. The result is an accidental cosmos created by a defective god who is ignorant of the true God beyond, and creates a tomb for those sparks of Protos Anthropos, which somehow fall into space and time.

The third symbol is the gnosis itself. This knowledge, given by an adept or brought by a savior, is, in all cases, the key to the final escape from the charnelhouse[24] of the cosmos. It is that unique insight not available to the hylic or psychic man, but only to the pneumatic illuminati who sleeps in flesh unaware of his true nature. The gnosis may be a formula for conduct, an insight into the truth of being, or a combination of both.

The fourth symbol is that of the Escape from the cosmos. Whether couched in terms of a savior who comes bearing the gnosis, or simply of an elite of spirituals who pass it on, the Escape is from the doom of intracosmic existence. The variants are too numerous to catalogue, but they include, for example, both ascetic and libertine varieties, those who are freed virtually while still in the flesh, and those promised freedom at death. There is little chiliastic or messianic symbolism in the major gnostic literature.

The fifth symbol circles back to the first and is implied by it. The symbol of the Pleroma encircled by the serpent is that place from which the gnostic has been flung, and to which he yearns to return. In certain gnostic constructions, the Pleroma is, like its god, "unnamable." In others it takes on the characteristics of a concrete "great good place" along the lines of contemporary socialist fantasies. In all cases, it is the Uroborotic "treasure" which is sought. The image of the Garden or *paradiseos* is often used. The threshold symbol of the Uroboros who protects what lies within stands as *Horos* or *Peri*, boundary or Limit.

The Pleromatic Garden, guarded by the Uroboros, is the place where the increate cosmos and undifferentiated consciousness float as one. The Pleroma is one, and that one is all. But the Pleromatic Garden has its physical counterpart, set out not in contemporary gestalt psychology, but in a somewhat more surprising place. In Hippolytus's *Refutation of All Heresies*, we are supplied with a text ascribed to Simon of Gitta, the Magus, supposedly from his magnum opus, the *Megale Apophasis*, or *Great Announcement*: "How then and in what manner does God mould men? In the Garden, he maintains. The Garden, he says, must be the womb; and the scripture will teach us that this is true when it says 'I am He that moulded

---

23   Corrington's note: "Werner Foerster, *Gnosis: A Selection of Gnostic Texts*, ed. R. McLachlan Wilson, vol. 1, *Patristic Evidence* (Oxford: Clarendon Press, 1972). See *Apocryphon of John*, 28.1., in Foerster, 1:108; Irenaeus's *Adversus Haereses*, 1.1, in Foerster, 1:127; *Adversus Haereses*, 1.2.5 in Foerster, 1:196; *Adversus Haereses*, 1.14, in Foerster, 1:203. See also *Adversus Haereses*, 1.3.7."

24   Perhaps "channel house."

thee in thy mother's womb,' (Isa. 44:2) for this is how he makes the text run. The Garden, he says, is Moses' allegorical term for the womb, if one is to believe the text. But if God moulds man in his mother's womb, that is, in the Garden, as I said, the Garden must be the womb, and Eden the placenta, and the river which come out of Eden to water the Garden the navel."[25]

We see that quite early in the Christian period, about 220 AD, there had arisen a gnosis which related the phylogenetic mythos of the Pleromatic Garden to the ontogenetic reality of the womb. The Naassenes incremented the mythos, as Hippolytus tells us. These Naassenes "had the effrontery to praise the serpent," and to claim that the serpent is "liquid substance," and nothing which exists can exist without it. They said, moreover, that "Eden is the brain, being, as it were 'bounden' and enfolded in the membranes which surround it, like the heavens; and paradise is man, to the extent of his head alone."[26] The effrontery of the Naassenes seems to have consisted primarily in rehabilitating an archaic myth of creation, and in linking together, through it, the process of reality and the process of consciousness.[27]

Womb and brain become analogues for the dual physicalpsychic site of the Garden, from which all things arise in the mythopoesis of the Uroboros. The process of reality and the process of consciousness are symbolized in their rising from enfolding womb and brain, and both are recognized as paradisical sites related to the manifold of the cosmos itself, as in the Ophian construction, "Leviathan," the serpent who surrounds the great sea of the universe, is called "the soul of the cosmos," and is said to protect the Origin, and all that arises from it.[28]

I would propose that these five symbols form the foundation of all classical gnostic speculation, and that they show "escape" or "exodus" gnostic thought to be a regression to an archaic mythopoetic mode of thinking in which gnostic manipulative magic is perceived as possible. I would propose, moreover, that any system in which these symbols appear and are similarly used is a gnostic system.

IV

It is only with the work of Joachim that we begin to see arise a consistent pattern of thought which we have referred to as "modern" or "conquest" gnosticism. We should note the incipient presence of the modern version of the symbols in the work of gnostic mythographers in the classical period. The work attributed to Simon has the Magus describing himself as "He who stands, who has stood, and who will always stand," which, in context, is hardly a symbol of exodus. Again,

---

25   Corrington's note: "In Foerster, *Gnosis*, 1:256, et. seq. Another translation is available in *The Ante-Nicene Fathers: Translations of the Writings of the Fathers down to AD 325*, ed. Alexander Roberts and James Donaldson (Grand Rapids, MI: W. B. Eerdmans, 1967) 5:77, et. seq."

26   Minor changes in punctuation and capitalization made here to match Foerster's text.

27   Corrington's note: "Hippolytus, *Refutatio*, 5.6.3–11, in Foerster, *Gnosis*, 1:263 and 280."

28   Corrington's note: "Origen, *Contra Celsum*, 6.25, in Foerster, *Gnosis*, 1:95."

in the tradition ascribed to Montanus, there is the symbol of the savior or leader, Montanus himself, as the living embodiment of the Holy Spirit, or the God-head as a whole, and the symbol of a coming eschatological Kingdom on earth to be presided over by those who share *pneuma*[29] with the embodied Spirit.[30]

Although these symbols maintain themselves in the interim between the decline of classical gnosticism and the rise of Joachitic speculation through the ideas of the Adoptionists and the Messalians,[31] they do not become of major importance until the *debut* of Joachim.

An initial question which may arise is whether there are not vast differences between the symbolisms of classical gnosticism and that of modern gnosticism as typified by the work of Joachim and his followers. The answer must be negative, but negative in the sense that we have already seen exhaustively how the distinct symbolisms of Uroboros and Apeiron serve the same function of representation in different fields of consciousness. There are numerous distinctions between classical and modern gnostic symbols—as there are between Uroborotic and Apeirontic symbols—but I see little in the way of substantive difference. The symbolisms of classical gnosticism appear to be exclusively mythopoetic in form as well as in substance. They constitute what Schelling called a "narrative philosophy." But that is a literary term. There is no such thing as a philosophy which does not consist in a pattern of question and answer. Again, while classical gnosticism does not prohibit questioning as does its modern equivalent, it simply does not admit such noetic penetration. As we have said, the differentiation of mythopoetic constructions moves by the interplay of one myth with another, not by way of dialogue or questioning.

The work of Joachim, despite its dependence upon the underlying pattern of classical gnostic symbols, constitutes a real epoch in the history of consciousness. Although we find the old symbols once more in his writings and those of his followers, they are no longer couched in purely mythopoetic terms, since the millennium intervening has widened the human field of noetic consciousness, and since the Christian drama of tension between the mundane order and the order of transcendence has been clearly differentiated as the process of history in the work of St. Augustine.

The evolution of the classical gnostic symbols into their modern equivalents is relatively easy to account for. Initially, the experiences of human beings do not substantively alter across time and space. The experiences of Joachim and his followers, as the symbols demonstrate, were fundamentally the same as those of their ancient gnostic predecessors.

---

29   Italics added.

30   Corrington's note: "See Adolph von Harnack, *History of Dogma* (New York: Russell & Russell, 1958), 2:97–100. Also J. H. Milman, *History of Latin Christianity* (London: John Murray, 1854), 1:38f. Also Robert Rainy, *The Ancient Catholic Church* (New York: Scribner, 1902), passim."

31   Corrington's note: "Steven Runciman, *The Medieval Maniche: A Study of the Christian Dualist Heresy* (Cambridge: Cambridge University Press, 1955), see 18–25."

Thus when the experience of alienation becomes, as in the case of Joachim and his followers, too intense to manage within the spectrum of orthodox symbols, the old symbols arise once more to be relocated or reallocated within the now clearly differentiated field of noetic consciousness which we call history.

First, Joachim himself reallocates the symbol of the evil of the cosmos as the evil of the *Saeclorum*, "the ruin and dismay of the century," he calls it. The evil attributed to matter and to the enclosing cosmos by the classical gnostics, becomes primarily associated with time in the gnosticism of Joachim and those following him.[32] It is a question of emphasis, since, as Henri-Charles Puech has shown, the gnostic hatred of the eon was a portion of classical loathing of the cosmos.[33] But it is a significant emphasis, in that the gnosticism of the twelfth century could no longer easily manage to attribute defect to the cosmos because of the intervening theological fixity of a good creation corrupted by the sin of man. Rather, the *situs* of evil is a temporal one: the age leading to the manifestation of Anti-Christ, the Joachitic analogue for the classical demiurge.

Second, the symbol of the unknown god of the Pleroma is transformed into the Holy Spirit of the monastic orders, especially of the Spirituals. Which is to say into a God,[34] if not opposed to that of the Schoolmen, at least a God revealing very different aspects. This God is a Holy Spirit of continuing revelation unmediated by the Roman See.

The third symbol, that of the gnosis, is icily controlled and bereft of exuberance in the work of Joachim: "When I awoke at dawn, I took to the Revelation of St. John. There, suddenly, the eyes of my spirit were struck with the lucidity of insight, and it was revealed to me the fulfillment of this book, and the concordance of the Old and New Testaments."[35]

The revelation through Revelation does not arouse in Joachim the impulse characteristic of mythopoetic consciousness. Joachim does not critique the mythos of Revelation with a myth of his own. Rather he transfers the meaning of scripture, its "hidden" meaning, into the process of history, which itself had been opened by the breakthrough into the noetic field of consciousness. Scripture, properly understood, becomes a commentary on and the key to the process of history. This gnosis is not available to all, and those who will not understand its expounding by monastic "interpreters" show themselves beyond salvation.[36]

---

32   Corrington's note: "Joachim of Fiore, *Liber Concordie*, quoted in Karl Löwith, *Meaning in History: The Theological Implications of the Philosophy of History* (Chicago: University of Chicago Press, 1949), 147."

33   Corrington's note: "Henri-Charles Puech, 'Gnosis and Time,' in *Man and Time*, ed. Joseph Campbell (Princeton, NJ: Princeton University Press, 1957), 38ff."

34   Corrington capitalizes the term "God" when referring to a generic god.

35   Corrington's note: "Löwith, *Meaning in History*, 147."

36   Corrington's note: "Joachim of Fiore, *Tractatus Super Quartuor Evangelia*, trans. James Counahan (unpublished manuscript), 7."

The fourth reallocated symbol is that of the classical Gnostic Escape. Literarily, the symbol perishes, since exodus is now along the vector of the historical process. But the triumph of what Joachim refers to as the monastic "Church" constitutes the new symbol of "conquest" within intramundane history.[37] In reference to the "new order of spiritual sons" which will arise from the body of the old Church, Joachim quotes John 20:21,[38] "He who overcomes, I will permit him to sit with me upon my throne; as I also have overcome and have sat with my Father on his throne."[39]

Fifth, the immediate result of this reallocation by Joachim of the classical gnostic symbols of defiency,[40] Holy Spirit as hidden god, gnosis, and escape from the mythopoetic field of consciousness into the noetically structured process of history was to transfer as well the Pleromatic goal of classical gnosticism into the order of mundane existence, thereby transforming mythical extracosmic salvation into a project to be realized concretely in historical reality. The classical gnostic dream of escape from the cosmos is replaced by a vision of empirical transformation of the process of reality, to be achieved by various means, into the "heaven on earth" of the innumerable post-Joachitic systems.

The crucial and decisive portion of the complex of Joachitic symbols is the relocation of the Pleromatic within history, and its identification as a "place" set in empirical reality. Since the Garden obviously did not exist as a geographical location, even "East of Eden" in the twelfth century, the "place" in question had to be a temporal location. According to Joachim, the "place" was on the far side of the year 1260 AD, when the Third Status, designated later as the time of "The Eternal Gospel" would be reached. St. Augustine had, characteristically, rejected as "ridiculous fables" the early Christian millennial speculation dealing with a Kingdom to be established on earth. This literalism, borrowed directly from Jewish apocalyptic and messianic hopes, was replaced in Augustine's work with the parallel histories of the *Civitas Dei* and the *Civitas Mundi*, which construed the tension of existence in the Metaxy as a fundamental structural unit of the Christian interpretation of existence. The Kingdom had come insofar as it would ever enter into existence, in the person of Jesus Christ, and it persisted in time and over space as the Church, the *corpus mysticum*, the community of faith. St. Augustine's work had indicated in detail the stratification of the fields of consciousness as well as those of history, claiming that the tension of existence is, after all, not simply a matter of body versus soul (later to be vulgarized into Schopenhauer's "World Knot" of matter and mind), but of the internal tensions between strat[41] and regions of the soul itself.

---

37   Corrington's note: "Fiore, *Tractatus*, 27."

38   This is actually Revelation 3:21, not John 20:21.

39   Corrington's note: "Fiore, *Tractatus*, 64."

40   Probably intended "deification."

41   Probably intended "strata."

Joachim, who had reason to know better, hypostatized the structure of consciousness by attempting to expand the process of history to fill the plenum of reality, and to substitute the tension of historical existence yearning for the Third Status for the tensions within the soul in its eschatological movement amidst the fields of consciousness. More precisely, he substituted an eschatology of history conceived as an empirical presence for that eschatology which lies at the root of consciousness, and which had been differentiated by Plato and St. Paul in their parallel breaks from the Uroboros-Apeiron symbolisms into those of the *Agathon* and the *Eschaton*.

The eschatological vector of history exists, not because history is an empirical and annalistic chronology of events, but because history is a dimension and a process within the noetic field of consciousness.

The radical reallocation of the classical gnostic symbols into the field of historical ~~field of~~[42] speculation retains certain surprising elements of the original mythopoesis we have traced—more than enough to show the continuity of the underlying initial gnostic experience, and the recurrence of that experience in recognizable symbolic transfers. In the *Super Hieremiam*, a work attributed to Joachim but dating from about the middle of the thirteenth century, we discover the Uroborotic symbol and its Pleromatic center once more:

> Tribulation, of course, still looms large. The *ecclesia contemplativa* of the [T]hird [S]tatus lies between the two tribulations of Anti-[C]hrist and Gog at the close of history, or, to use the common metaphor, between the seventh head of the [d]ragon and its tail. To reach it (changing the metaphor) the hazardous crossing of the first gulf must be made: the ark must be carried over Jordan and the *passio vel tribulatio futura ecclesie generalis* must be suffered.[43]

The dragon, also expressed in Joachitic interpretation as the Johannine Beast rising from the sea, represents the old Okeanos now personified, quite understandably, as Anti-Christ, the coiled serpent which must be conquered in order to regain entry into the Pleromatic Garden from which man has been cast into the "dismay and ruin" of history.[44] The journey past the Uroboros, from the misery of dualistic disorder back into the Garden of the Holy Spirit in the Third Status, lies within history. The

---

42   Strikethrough added to reveal accidental repetition.

43   Corrington's note: "*Super Hieremiam*, fragment 18, quoted in Marjorie Reeves, *The Influence of Prophecy in the Later Middle Ages* (Oxford: Clarendon Press, 1969), 306." Small changes made based on the 2000 reprint of 1969 edition of Reeves. Added brackets to "Third Status," "Anti-Christ," and "dragon" because this is how Corrington writes those names throughout the text, but Reeves writes, instead, "third *status*," "Antichrist," and "Dragon."

44   Corrington's note: "The dragon represents, also, according to Marjorie Reeves, the Johannine Beast rising from the Sea, and Joachim so denominated it. The dragon symbolizes Anti-Christ in whatever manifestation it is found, according to Joachim. See Marjorie Reeves and Beatrice Hirsch-Reich, *The Figurae of Joachim of Fiore* (Oxford: Clarendon Press, 1972), 146 et. seq."

reallocation of symbols establishes the Pleromatic monistic goal as lying "ahead," not "above," to be negotiated by the monastic orders who will form both the model and the spiritual elite of the Third Realm.[45] There will be a "withering away" of the institutional Church and of the sacramental system. The spiritual community will have no use for such things, and this "society of autonomous persons," as Professor Voegelin has called it, will survive until the end of history.

This renovated Church of the monks will constitute a merging of the *Civitas Dei* and the *Civitas Mundi*. History, understood as that dimension of consciousness in which the tension of the Augustinian dichotomy is recognized and balanced, thus rendering luminous the process of consciousness itself as the eschatological vector of the process of reality, will cease to exist. There can be no continuation of history if the mystery from which reality and consciousness alike arise is emptied into the earthly realm of existence and rendered wholly under the domination of a spiritual elite whose logos becomes their own personalities as existent in the world-immanent Kingdom of Grace.

The ontology underlying Joachim's flattening of the Augustinian paradigm of history into a single speculative future structure in the process of reality recalls the peculiar symbolism of St. Ambrose:

> Luna is diminished that she may fill the elements. Therefore is this a great mystery. To her it was given by Him who confers grace upon all things. He emptied her that He might fill her, as He also emptied Himself that He might fill all things. He emptied Himself that He might come down to us. He came down to us that He might rise again for all. . . . Thus Luna has proclaimed the mystery of Christ.[46]

The passage, rife with astrological and probably alchemical overtones, is gnostic. It suggests not simply a metastatic transformation of the cosmos and human reality, but an emptying of the ground of being into the cosmos and history. This flattening of the process of reality into a single dimension which then becomes a non-mysterious stasis containing and expressing the manifold of all being which has been "emptied" into it constitutes what Professor Voegelin has called a *gigantomachia*, a fantasy of such titanic dimensions that it is, on its own terms, unanswerable. In the annals of the subsequent creation of Second Realities, none, save perhaps that of Hegel, has the scope of the fabrication of Joachim and his successors.

---

45   Corrington's note: "One notes that there is a vertical pattern in the symbolisms of classical gnosticism, and a horizontal pattern in those of modern gnosticism. A monograph is needed to clarify the history of apocalyptic and messianic elements which, by the way, virtually always possessed 'conquest' and horizontal forms."

46   Corrington's note: "St. Ambrose, *Hexameron*, 4.8.32. This concept appears again in an even more bizarre form in 1965 in T. J. J. Altizer's *The Gospel of Christian Atheism* (Philadelphia: Westminster Press, 1966)." Here Corrington mentions 1965 for a book published in 1966.

On principle, the work of reallocating the classical gnostic extramundane symbols of exodus into the historical field in the form of symbols of conquest is complete with Joachim and his immediate followers like Gerard of Borgo San Donnino. The uncertain and tension-ridden process of history has been abolished and the process of reality has been filled with the *Status* of the Third Realm of the Holy Spirit. In the phrase of Steven Runciman, the new community of Joachitic gnostics is to live "one long Pentecost." The cosmos itself is conquered, and the drama of existence in the Metaxy is compressed into an utter reversal of classical gnosticism: the entrapped sparks of light do not now make exodus, returning to the hidden god, Protos Anthropos, in the extracosmic Pleroma. On the contrary, the sparks are united into a community, and the hidden god is emptied into the Pleroma of the Third Realm. Anthropos is again one—on earth is the Saeclorum of the "Eternal Gospel" where man himself will, in later versions of the fantasy, like that of Feuerbach, become God through the conquest of cosmos and history, recapturing those divine "projections" that are him, Anthropos. The classical gnostic *libido asconditus* has become the *libido dominandi*, and there shall be no other after it.

The breadth of the reversal constitutes fantasy-construction of the first order when it is viewed in the context of what precedes and follows it. Joachim has provided the speculative structure which renders earlier mythopoetic prophecy, for example that of the Christian Sibyllines, programmes for chiliastic activism rather than mere heavenly hopes:

> But the residue which have cared for justice and good deeds, yea, and godliness and righteous thoughts, shall angels bear up and carry through the flaming river unto light, and life without care, where is the immortal path of the great god;[47] and three fountains, of wine and honey and milk. And the earth, common to all, not parted out with walls or fences, shall then bring forth of her own accord much fruit, and life and wealth shall be common and undistributed. For there shall be no poor man, nor rich, nor tyrant, nor slave, none great nor small any longer, no kings, no princes; but all men shall be together in common. And no more shall any man say "night is come," nor "the morrow," nor "it was yesterday." He maketh no more of days, nor of spring, nor winter, nor summer, nor autumn, neither marriage, nor death, nor selling, nor buying, nor set of sun, nor rising. For God shall make one long day.[48]

---

47   The lowercase "god" here might have been a typographical error because in the last sentence of this quotation, Corrington capitalizes "God."

48   Corrington's note: "M. R. James, *The Apocryphal New Testament* (Oxford: Clarendon Press, 1924), 524. Another translation is available in Edgar Hennecke, *New Testament Apocrypha*, trans. R. McLachlan Wilson (London: SCM Press, 1974), 2:718."

The quotation does not come from Ranters or Levellers or some other late medieval or reformation extremist. It is ascribed to the second century, and is said to be Christian. The interweaving of pragmatic and spiritual concerns, of workaday hopes and transcendent yearnings suggests the penetration of the noetic field in which social amelioration can be achieved, by elements of the mythopoetic field where magic transformations can take place. The juxtaposition of the two in a single document illustrates chillingly the result of the merging and flattening of the process of reality into a single dimension containing in chaotic disarray symbols from the gnostically deranged fields of mythopoetic and noetic consciousness.

> Joachim . . . could not foresee that his religious intention—that of desecularizing the Church and restoring its spiritual fervor—would, in the hands of others, turn into its opposite: the secularization of the world which became increasingly worldly by the very fact that eschatological thinking about last things was introduced into penultimate matters, a fact which intensified the power of the secular drive toward a final solution of problems which cannot be solved by their own means and on their own level. . . . The revolution which had been proclaimed within the framework of an eschatological faith and with reference to a perfect monastic life was taken over, five centuries later, by a philosophical priesthood, which interpreted the process of secularization in terms of a "spiritual" realization of the kingdom of God on earth. As an attempt at realization, the spiritual pattern of Lessing, Fichte, Schelling, and Hegel could be transposed into the positivistic and materialistic schemes of Comte and Marx. The third dispensation of the Joachites reappeared as a third International and a third *Reich*, inaugurated by a *dux* or a *Führer* who was acclaimed as a savior and greeted by millions with *Heil!*[49]

Löwith's analysis is incomplete only insofar as it leaps from the twelfth century to the seventeenth century without reciting the dreary passage, unbroken in the intervening centuries, by which Joachim's modern gnostic speculation moved through Beghards, Beguines, Brethren of the Free Spirit, Fifth Monarchy Men, and so many more on its lethal progress from medieval Calabria to Nuremberg and the Finland Station.

---

49   Corrington's note: "Löwith, *Meaning in History*, 158–59." Corrected some extraneous capitalization to match the original Löwith text.

Gnosticism and Modern Thought: A Way You'll Never Be

1978-1979

As explained in the introduction to "The Structure of Gnostic Consciousness," Corrington delivered this essay at the Vanderbilt conference on Gnosticism in 1978. The original version of this essay, located in the archives at Centenary College, consists of a typed document with handwritten pages at the end. Because the handwritten pages seem topically distinct from the rest of the essay, they have been moved to Appendix B. Corrington intended this essay to be part of a volume of essays on Gnosticism.

Corrington opens the essay with a reference to Nick Adams, a character from a short story by Ernest Hemingway who has established for himself an alternate, deformed sense of reality—a Second Reality—whereby he orders his experience. Corrington likens this Second Reality to the structure of consciousness accepted and propagated by Gnosticism. Corrington argues that the Gnostic acceptance of a false reality brought about an embrace of magic and fantasy, both of which the Gnostics used to order their social and political experience. This perceived form of order is, in fact, disorder. Gnosticism is manifest in modern political movements, Corrington suggests, and it renews and reuses certain symbols to describe the nature of the world. It premises itself, moreover, on assumptions about the divine ability of man to achieve a unified, monistic, salvational telos on Earth. Gnosticism, which is part of an irrepressible drive for the divine that is common to each psyche, has a coherent ideational narrative structure that makes its symbology appealing and plausible. Gnosticism is a symptom of the desire to achieve the symbolic return to the womb, a representation of paradise in which unity, perfection, and order are attained. The Gnostic thus seeks to realize in the concrete world, by way of magic and other breaks from reality, the supposedly ultimate and eternal state in which pure, transcendent unity and monism are instantiated. Corrington sees Gnosticism in the scientism of the modern era. If metaxy represents the proper understanding of the place of man and the divine on earth, the Second Reality, which the Gnostic chooses over metaxy, is a distorted teleological worldview. Corrington submits that more would be known about modern Gnostic tendencies in the form of ideology if there were not a breakdown of the disciplines into such compartments as history, science, political science, theology, psychology, and so on.

"Let's not talk about how I am," Nick said. "It's a subject I know too much about to want to think about it any more."

—Hemingway, "A Way You'll Never Be"

I

In Ernest Hemingway's famous short story dealing with combat on the Italian front in World War I, his hero, Nick Adams, has been seriously wounded at Fossalta. He is now "certified nutty," and his thoughts, his words, his responses are frighteningly inappropriate. He no longer exists within the frame of reference common to his Italian soldier-comrades who have not been injured. His wound, nearly fatal, combined with the horror of general death, destruction, and disintegration of values, has driven him to create a Second Reality of his own, a mode of dealing with his experiences which bears no relation to that reality within which ordinary men live out their lives. It is this Second Reality of Nick's to which the title of the story, and the subtitle[50] of this article, refers, and it is to that deformation of the reality of human experience that I refer in speaking of "a way you'll never be."

In the pages following, I will attempt to show something of the origins and history of that peculiar type of human thought and response to experience, which has come to be called "gnosticism." I will set out its origins from a historical perspective, and will distinguish between the "classical" gnosticism of the early centuries of the Christian era, and the "modern" gnosticism, which appears first in the twelfth century of the Christian era, and continues unabated down to the present time.

Moreover, I will attempt to show, albeit in a cursory fashion because of the limitations of space available, the intimate and well-documented interrelation between "the gnosis," both classical and modern, and the phenomena of magic, Hermeticism, astrology, alchemy, and Kabbalism. I will suggest that gnosticism, which refers not to a single sect or even a rigorously defined point of view, is best understood as a generic term, and that the classical and modern gnostic sects include definitionally and analytically the other phenomena noted, as well as a host of more recent spiritual and intellectual aberrations. More significantly, I would hope to suggest the fundamental *pneumopathological*[51] disorder, which lies at the root of gnosticism, whatever form it may take, and the experiential reasons that it has flourished through the centuries.

Finally, I would hope that the analytical narrative would evoke a certain pattern of recurrent symbols and patterns of thought which distinguish gnosticism sufficiently for purposes of identification, no matter what nomenclature it happens to take on in a given place and time.

It should be noted at the onset that gnosticism as a modality of response to experience has not been invariably so called even when it has been minutely described. For example, in recent times, it has been referred to by one distinguished scholar as "ideological thinking."

---

50 Hyphenated in the original.

51 This term was popularized by Voegelin and coined by Friedrich Schelling.

Ideologies always assume that one idea is sufficient to explain everything in the development from the premise, and that no experience can teach anything because everything is comprehended in this consistent process of logical deduction.[52]

Nor is gnosticism, in its role of producing Second Realities, limited to any specific area of human experience. Theologies, sciences, politics, economics, philosophies—indeed, the entire spectrum of human thought, may be marked by symbols which reveal the gnostic caste of experiences and sentiments. It is a cardinal error to suppose that humanity possesses a divisible consciousness, neatly compartmented in such a manner that certain areas of experience tend to be treated from one perspective, others from another. If gnosticism were, after all, no more than a term descriptive of any *idée fixe*, or the occasional extreme eccentricity of the sort found, say, in the novels of Robert Smith Surtees, the subject would hardly be worth discussion, much less the present volume.

But gnostic consciousness, whatever its subject, is not, as it were, simply mad for the hunt as was Surtees's[53] Jorrocks.[54] On the contrary, gnosticism, whatever its form or the period in which it appears, proposes itself as a unique and exclusive knowledge of the very meaning of existence itself. Whether it makes its appearance in the guise of religious doctrine or historical theory, scientific paradigm or political creed, its pretensions are invariably ultimate. It purports to replace every other view of experience and every other kind of knowing. Gnosticism, more or less explicitly, sets itself up as the long-sought single mode of truth which, when grasped and accepted by a believer, has the power to reduce and obliterate the obvious and apparent variety of existence to a single principle. It proposes to annihilate the contradictions of existence and to cancel the intolerable dualism of human experience. Unity, oneness, monism as a view of reality always lies at the root of gnostic phenomena.[55]

Thus gnosticism, in whatever context it may appear, is a salvific structure in consciousness. It presumes a certain world condition, a certain means by which that condition may either be rectified, escaped, or dominated. And it proposes

---

52 Corrington's note: "Hannah Arendt, *The Origins of Totalitarianism* (New York: Harcourt, Brace, Jovanovich, 1973), 470."

53 Robert Smith Surtees.

54 Cockney grocer in Surtees's fiction.

55 Corrington's note: "I am hardly unaware of the apparent paradox of this view. Rather than repeat myself here, I would direct the reader to John William Corrington, "Order and Consciousness/Consciousness and History: The New Program of Eric Voegelin," in Stephen McKnight, ed., *Voegelin's Search for Order in History* (Baton Rouge, LA: Louisiana State University Press, 1977). Briefly, the universal definition of gnosticism as a system of thought characterized by its radical dualism is a definition established by viewing gnosticism's evaluation of things as they are. But, it seems to me, a far more significant determinant of the system is to look at its *ideal* situation, the state of things it seeks to achieve. Such an examination quickly reveals that the end state desired by every gnostic system without exception is that of a monism as radical as the dualism, which it claims to discern within the process of reality."

a set of symbolisms purportedly adequate to describe and delimit the whole of experiential reality.

Some of the gnostic symbols most universally found among the sects and dispersed in the culture of the period immediately preceding and following the time of Christ seem to be these:

1. The Cosmos is inherently evil and defective. It is the creation of a demiurge or demonic spirit ignorant of, jealous of, or otherwise at odds with the True God.

2. Human beings, or at least some of them, are in fact sparks or emanations (*aporroia*) from the True God trapped or imprisoned in matter and flesh.

3. Those who are sparks or *sperma* from the True God, here imprisoned in matter, alienated from our true source, can find salvation or the means of return through gnosis, an anoetic coming to know from whence we come, where we are, and whence[56] we are destined to go.

4. This gnosis is available only to those who are "spiritual" beings, as opposed to mere psychic or hylic beings. The spirituals form a "third realm" of elite beings.

5. Those who accept the creator-god of the cosmos—frequently identified with the God of Israel—are in utter opposition to the True God to whom possessors of the gnosis return.

6. The *teleos* or desired final state of the gnostic is reunion with the Pleroma, the high Heaven of the True God, ultimate unity and oneness—as opposed to the created cosmos and its dualism or pluralism.

7. This *Pleromatic*[57] unity or monism wholly undifferentiated, represents the proper and original state of "spiritual" men.

8. The mode through which gnosticism expresses itself is specifically mythopoetic. It is ahistorical and nonphilosophical.

I would propose that these eight fundamental symbolisms are common to virtually every Gnostic sect in one form or another, and appear with endless variations in the documents of related ideational structures of the classical period such as Hermeticism, astrology, magic, late Neo-Platonism, and alchemy. There are, of course, other symbols widely dispersed among these structures. The concept of a Soter, a redeemer, who descends from the True God to bring gnosis is fairly common, but not nearly universal. The conversion experience, the sacraments (both sublime and obscene), the community of spirituals—all these have considerable representation amongst the sects. But all these symbolisms are also present in

---

56   Probably intended "whither" or "where."

57   Italics added.

ideational structures, which lack any trace of gnostic inclination. For that reason, I will limit my analysis to the eight symbols listed above.

I will attempt to show that there is an underlying substrate of empirically discernible thought or sentiment which is common to all gnostic mythopoesis whether it appears as Valentinianism, Simonianism, Hermeticism, magic, alchemy, or Kabbalism, or some similar convention. I will further suggest that the symbols we have listed above are characteristic of that substrate, even beyond its classical appearance, and on into the Medieval and Modern periods.

Obviously, the analysis must reach past a surface of apparently divergent symbols and penetrate the original experiences, sentiments, and expressions from which the divergences arose through the process of differentiation. It may be that such an analysis, to the degree it is successful, will reveal that the bewildering variety of symbols and ideational structures we are accustomed to dealing with refer more realistically to an equally divergent and bewildering variety of human personality types than to genuinely distinct and distinguishable views of the process of reality itself.

Needless to say, the application of Ockham's razor, before the present company, is an incredibly hazardous task. It is rendered more so by the fact that each of the areas I must touch upon in order to suggest my conclusions would require a monograph written from the point of view I am setting forth. But if it can be shown to a reasonable degree of probability that a single substrate underlies all the phenomena we are discussing, we may have put an end to that most vexing type of problem, which we lawyers are accustomed to call "distinctions without differences."

I do not mean to suggest that the differentiation of a substrate common to gnostic movements, magic, alchemy, Hermeticism, and the innumerable variety of modern movements would somehow obviate study of these subgenres. On the contrary, should a single such substrate be plausibly shown, the detailed study of each concrete and apparently disparate version would seem to become more necessary than before. Indeed, one would suppose that the detailed study of comparative forms of gnosticism would become a central concern for those of us who, with whatever misgivings, find ourselves presently in the position of pathologists working upon tissue-samples of a world-wide social structure *in extremis*, with no reliable taxonomy or histological paradigm at hand.

Let me then attempt a first approximation in language which we all understand and share. I wish to suggest that every variety of gnosticism, including the specific varieties already mentioned and a number which, unmentioned, are easily identified, contains a fundamental element that Voegelin has characterized as the belief in "a metastatic[58] transformation of reality through an act of faith."[59]

---

58   Corrington uses this term several times. The word in common usage typically refers to cancer. However, Corrington, following Voegelin, used the word to refer to change, reformation, and revolution.

59   Corrington's note: "Eric Voegelin, 'Autobiographical Sketch' (unpublished manuscript)."

This capacity to believe that the constituents of the Cosmos, of existence itself, are actually open to radical alteration by way of commitment to a gnosis, to a creed, to an idea, a form of knowledge peculiar to those who have accepted it and dedicated themselves to it, is a presupposition so deeply and consistently buried in gnostic thought that it cannot be called one of the principal[60] gnostic symbols. At the same time, it is the presumption upon which the eight symbols set out above the rest. Moreover, it is the structural constituent of gnostic thought, which explains the vitality and irrepressible nature of gnosticism.

The capacity—or the need—to ignore empirical and noetic experience, and to substitute in its place a doctrine at odds with both is, after all, not the most common property of humanity. If it were, there should soon be no humanity. While it is indisputable that "metastatic visions" or Second Realities, if they are not too extreme, can support existence for a time, it is equally clear that the pressure of primary reality invariably reasserts itself, whether in the nature of physical or psychological law.

But is gnosticism, then, simply a form of lunacy? Are the gnostic enthusiasts *Furiosi*, as the insane were called in the time of Torquato Tasso? Are the inmates of madhouses simply cousins-german of Simon Magus and Marcion, Joachim of Fiore and Jakob Boehme, Nietzsche and Marx, B. F. Skinner and Charles Reich? Obviously not. Even given that Simon died calling himself "the Standing One," and Nietzsche succumbed in an asylum at Jena, that Skinner cast himself as an unhappy deity at the conclusion of *Walden II*,[61] and Charles Reich has recently come out of the closet to acknowledge a personal reason for his hatred of reality, still things are not so simple.

The distinction between gnostic thought and madness is, I think, the difference between a degree of control and utter instability. Madness in the Middle Ages was not simply a matter of one's deciding to live in a Second Reality or "acting inappropriately," as present day alienists, perhaps inappropriately, call it. Rather it was their unwillingness or incapacity to negotiate or hold commerce between their vision and primary reality, which resulted in their commitment to one Bedlam or another.

Historically, the gnostic thinkers have managed as a rule to avoid such problems. One must note that gnostic thought has even been marked by its capacity to deal with and even to invade primary reality to make converts of those marginal personalities who are neither aggressive nor imaginative enough to create real alternatives to forms of life they find insufferable, but who, at the same time, are unstable enough to become enmeshed in the schemes of stronger personalities when they are presented with the opportunity. This very fact, revealed in detail by the history of ideological movements in the twentieth century, suggests that, as there are heresiarchs and heretics, so there are, and have always been, gnostic leaders and originators and followers. Simple madness, as I understand it, is more

---

60   Corrected from *principle*.

61   Skinner's book was titled *Walden Two*, but commentary about the book often uses "*Walden II*."

original. No one follows another into lunacy. Whatever strain of lunacy may possess one, it is his own; he owes neither its origination nor its development to another.

Thus one comes to suspect that gnosticism, unlike ordinary madness, must possess a structure, a logic, and a common source in human consciousness which is not properly attributable simply to mental or emotional defect. But what theory of consciousness can be set out which will account for both normative reality by which most human beings are governed, and for the multitude of gnostic speculations which we find divergent from it?

An analysis of the question, given the presently available materials, must, it appears, carry us into the realm of psychology despite the danger of derailment in that most labile of contemporary "universes of discourse." But before we must run that risk, we may initiate our analysis by citing a remarkable but rarely quoted passage from Hippolytus's *Refutation of All Heresies*.[62] Hippolytus offers the text as an example of the teaching of Simon of Gitta, Simon Magus,[63] of whom the Fathers report that he was the Great Father of gnostic thought. However that may be, the opinion seems to have been general, and thus one encounters *ab initio* the classical linkage of magic and gnosis. According to Hippolytus, Simon taught, in the *Megale Apophasis*, or *Great Announcement*,[64] thus:

> How then and in what manner does God mould men? In the Garden, he maintains. The Garden, he says, must be the womb; and scripture will teach us that this is true when it says "I am he that moulded thee in thy mother's womb" (Isa. 44:2) for this is how he makes the text run. The Garden, he says, is Moses's allegorical term for the womb, if one is to believe the text. But if God moulds man in his mother's womb, that is, in the Garden, as I said, the Garden must be the womb, and Eden the placenta, and the river which comes out of Eden to water the Garden (Gen. 2:10) the navel.[65]

It may seem strange to find in this passage, and in its detailed continuation in Hippolytus, a basic gnostic text. But if I understand the text aright, Simon is here establishing the fundamental or ground-state of the gnostic view of reality. The womb and the Garden (*paradesios*) are a single monistic and undifferentiated unit, and to

---

62   Starting here, this chapter overlaps with Corrington's "Brief History of Gnosticism" (BHG) 1&2.

63   Simon of Gitta and Simon Magus are the same person: a Samaritan convert to Christianity known for sorcery. See Acts 8:9-24.

64   This text is usually known as the *Apophasis Megale* and is also translated as *Great Declaration*.

65   Corrington's note: "Werner Foerster, ed., *Gnosis: A Selection of Gnostic Texts*, trans. R. McLachlan Wilson (Oxford: Clarendon Press, 1972), 1:256, et seq. Another translation is available for comparison in Alexander Roberts and James Donaldson, eds., *The Ante-Nicene Fathers: Translations of the Writings of the Fathers down to AD 325*. (Grand Rapids, MI: W. B. Eerdmans, 1967), 5:77, et seq." Foerster's book is actually in 2 volumes. This passage is from vol. 1, *Patristic Evidence*; therefore, vol. 1 added to Corrington's citation. In BHG, Corrington also cites this passage, noting volume 1, but gives a different page number: in BHG he indicates "p. 266." Corrected *The Ante-Nicene Church Fathers* to *The Ante-Nicene Fathers: Translations of the Writings of the Fathers down to AD 325*.

speak of the one is to express the other. In some sense they are, in Simon's view, one. In Hippolytus, the correspondences between womb and Garden are set out at considerable length in an attempt, it appears, to bind together physical and psychic reality.

The womb, then, becomes at least the physical analogue for the Pleroma, the original state from which, in a host of gnostic systems, the "sparks of divinity" which constitute "spiritual men" have rained down and been captured in matter to form the essence of human beings.

To the Simon of the *Megale Apophasis*, the pleromatic state is "the dwelling place where the root of all things has its foundation."[66] This "unnamed highest heaven," as Severus calls it, is a heaven of complete and undifferentiated unity with the Unknown God and his Aeons, variously named and numbered in different gnostic mythopoetic versions.[67] The Great God can, in most gnostic myths, only be described negatively, but the Aeons and sometimes even the Great God or Protos Anthropos, as he is sometimes called, are described as an ultimate and unspeakable unity, bisexual, male, and female in one.[68]

Virtually all of the gnostic mythologies establish the initial act of creation as an act of differentiation, some act whereby other entities arise from The Unnamed, the Hidden, The Great God of the pleromatic heaven. The act of creation is identifiable with the beginning of differentiation.[69] Whether the quotation in question from Hippolytus establishes a necessary Sophia-female figure as inherent in the creation mythopoesis and as the initial break with primal unity, it is nonetheless true that almost every version of the early gnostic mythopoesis reaches a point where an "abortion" or defective being is produced from the process of differentiation. This defective being is variously called Self-Willed, Aldaoboath, Sabaoth, or Achemoth, and is frequently identified with the God of Israel.[70]

If we assume that the passage quoted from the *Megale Apophasis* is representative of early gnostic thought (without regard to the textual question of whether Simon of Gitta was or was not its author), we must recognize that by 236 AD at the latest, there was extant the notion that womb and paradise were identical.

It is here that we find it useful to move from Hippolytus to ~~that of~~[71] Erich Neumann, whose classic study, *The Origins and History of Consciousness*, offers a crucial insight into

---

66   Corrington's note: "Foerster, *Gnosis*, 1:252–253."

67   Corrington's note: "Ibid, 1:46."

68   Corrington's note: "Apocryphon of John 28:1, in Foerster, *Gnosis*, 108; Irenaeus, *Adversus Haereses*, bk. 1, ch. 1, in Foerster, *Gnosis*, 127; Irenaeus, *Adversus Haereses*, bk. 1, ch. 2, pt. 5, in Foerster, *Gnosis*, 196; Irenaeus, *Adversus Haereses*, bk. 1, ch. 14, pt. 1, in Foerster, *Gnosis*, 203. It would take up much time and space to document completely all the passages in patristic and gnostic literature alluding to androgynous or bisexual characteristics of the Hidden God in gnostic myths, and hence the undifferentiated character of the pleroma."

69   Corrington's note: "See the *Letter of Eugnostus*, in Foerster, *Gnosis*, 25–34; *The Hypostasis of the Archons*, in Foerster, *Gnosis*, 40–52; and Foerster, *Gnosis*, passim."

70   Corrington's note: "Irenaeus, *Adversus Haereses*, ch. 29, pt. 2, in Foerster, *Gnosis*; Apocryphon of John 30:1–35:51."

71   Strikethrough added.

the process of consciousness by which humanity has come to awareness.[72] Neumann,[73] a student of Carl Jung, describes the nature of human consciousness in terms of an evolutionary development, which is to say a growth in terms of differentiation: "The evolution of [western][74] consciousness as a form of creative evolution is the peculiar achievement of western man. Creative evolution of ego consciousness means that through a process stretching over thousands of years, the conscious system has absorbed more and more unconscious contents and progressively extended its frontiers."[75]

This evolution of consciousness, moving from the compact material which Neumann characterizes as "unconscious contents" using Henri Bergson's notion of "creative evolution"—what Neumann calls "transpersonal"—is simultaneously a personal and a societal process: "The evolution of consciousness by stages is as much a collective human phenomenon as a particular individual phenomenon. Ontogenetic development may therefore be regarded as a modified recapitulation of phylogenetic development."[76]

One must be careful to avoid the limitations of the biological implications which Neumann's positivistic heritage required of him. But the analogy is not without merit. The interplay between the proximal and distal aspects of the individual transformation boundary, between the "inside" and the "outside" of the human nervous system, constitutes the matrix of human culture in which consciousness arises and exfoliates: "a substantial part of mythology is seen as the unconscious self-delineation of the growth of consciousness in man."[77]

Neumann makes use of the mythological stages in the evolution of human development of consciousness, beginning with the stage in which "the ego is contained in the unconscious, and [leads] up to a situation in which the ego not only becomes aware of its own position and defends it heroically, but also becomes capable of broadening and relativizing its experiences through the changes effected by its own activity."[78]

Neumann describes the initial state from which human consciousness erupts, both within the individual and within the cultural matrix: He sets out the symbols

---

72 Corrington's note: "Erich Neumann, *The Origins and History of Consciousness*, trans. R. F. C. Hull. Bollingen Series, no. 42 (Princeton: Princeton University Press, 1954)." Translator added to citation.

73 In his notes, Corrington misspelled Neumann's first name as "Eric." It is "Erich" and has been corrected accordingly in the notes and bibliography.

74 "Western" is in brackets because it does not appear in Neumann's text. Corrington might have added it because the previous sentence refers specifically to Western orientation.

75 Corrington's note: "Neumann, *Origins and History*, xviii."

76 Corrington's note: "Neumann, *Origins and History*, xx."

77 Corrington's note: "Neumann, *Origins and History*, xxiv." Following Chicago Style, the ellipses opening this quotation have been removed, even though they indicate that the beginning of the sentence was not quoted. In order to keep that lowercase "a" (to show that this quotation is not the complete sentence), the punctuation at the end of the previous paragraph has been changed from a period to a colon so that the quotation doesn't need to be a full sentence with the initial word capitalized.

78 Corrington's note: "Neumann, *Origins and History*, 5."

of "original perfection"—the circle, the sphere, the egg, and the rotundum, the round of alchemy.[79] These are symbols of "the perfect state in which the opposites are united—the perfect beginning because the opposites have not yet flown apart and the world has not yet begun, the perfect end because in it the opposites have come together again in a synthesis and the world is once more at rest."[80]

This primal unity, comparable to the stage of compact consciousness described by Voegelin, is that in which "the world parents, heaven and earth, lie one on top of the other in the round, spacelessly and timelessly united, for as yet nothing has come between them to create duality out of the original unity. The container of the masculine and feminine opposites is the great hermaphrodite, the primal creative element."[81]

This image, Neumann suggests, brings to mind Plato's original man, where too the androgynous round stands beginning.[82]

But the ultimate symbol selected by Neumann for the Beginning, is that of the Uroboros, the primal dragon which bites its own tail, self-begotten and eternal. The choice is an apt one, in that few symbols can be traced so widely. This particular symbol of the round is the "symbolic self-representation" of the dawn-state "showing the infancy both of mankind and of the child."[83]

> Since the ego has and can have no experiences of its own in the embryonic state, not even psychic experiences—for its experiencing consciousness still slumbers in the germ—the later ego will describe this earlier state, of which it has an indefinite but symbolically graspable knowledge, as a "pre-natal" time. It is the time of existence in Paradise where the psyche has her pre-worldly abode, the time before the birth of the ego, the time of unconscious envelopment, of swimming in the ocean of the unborn.[84]

The question of origin is always answered by "womb," whatever symbol be chosen to express it. But the answer refers, obviously, to more than a concrete aspect of female creatures. Rather, it is an image, a cosmic region where origins are veiled. "In the pleromatic phase of life, when the ego swims about in the round like

---

79   Corrington's note: "Neumann, Origins and History, 8; also cf. Carl Jung, Psychology and Alchemy, vol. 12 of The Collected Works of C. G. Jung (London: Routledge & Kegan Paul, 1953–1979), s.v. 'rotundum.'"

80   Corrington's note: "Neumann, Origins and History, 8."

81   Corrington's note: "Neumann, Origins and History, 9."

82   Corrington's note: "F. M. Cornford, Plato's Cosmology: The Timaeus of Plato, 34." Corrington did not give edition information for Cornford's book, although it is probably the 1937 edition (London: Routledge & Kegan Paul, 1937).

83   Corrington's note: "Neumann, Origins and History, 11. For the provenance of the Uroboros symbolism, see Neumann, Origins and History, 9–10. Cf. also Carl Jung, Aion, vol. 9, pt. 2 of The Collected Works of C. G. Jung (London: Routledge & Kegan Paul, 1968), passim." Spelling correction in footnote: "provinence" to "provenance." Also, Corrington did not give all the publication information for Jung, so that information has been added to Corrington's note.

84   Corrington's note: "Neumann, Origins and History, 11–12."

a tadpole, there is nothing but the uroboros[85] in existence. Humanity does not yet exist, there is only divinity; only the world has being . . . The world is experienced as all-embracing."[86]

The infantile ego and the ego of early humanity are[87] seen as the same by Neumann, "feebly developed, easily tired." The individual ego, like the collective ego rises like a small island out of the ocean of unconsciousness, "then sinks back again . . . he swims about in his instincts like an animal." This is the maternal side of the Uroborotic state in its positive manifestation, "the refuge for[88] all suffering, the goal of all desire." "The dawn state of perfect containment and contentment was never an historical state (Rousseau was still projecting this psychic phase into the historical past, as the 'natural state' of the savage). It is rather the image of a psychic state of humanity, just discernible as borderline image."[89]

Neumann describes what he calls the "ascent to consciousness" as "unnatural." "The desire to remain unconscious, is a fundamental human trait," or rather "fixation in the unconsciousness"—what we would call the compact stage of consciousness—appears to be the "natural" thing, if only in statistical terms. Thus, it is the "struggle between the specifically human and the universally natural"—or unconscious—which constitutes "the history of man's conscious development."[90]

The symbolism of the Uroboros as the rotundum, the great primeval round of pre-consciousness thus not only describes the infantile individual consciousness, but the collective cultural consciousness of humanity as well, according to Neumann. This participation in a world without differentiation and ego-structure has been described by Voegelin at the beginning of *Israel and Revelation*:

> Whatever man may be, he knows himself a part of being. The great stream of being, in which he flows while it flows through him, is the same stream to which belongs everything else that drifts into his perspective. The community of being is experienced with such intimacy that the consubstantiality of the partners will override the separateness of substances. We move in a charmed community where everything that meets us has force and will and feelings, where animals and plants can be men and gods, where men can be divine and gods are kings, where the feathery morning sky is the falcon Horus and the Sun and Moon are his eyes, where the underground sameness of being is a conductor for magic currents of good or evil force

---

85 Corrington capitalized this word, but Neumann (or his translator) did not in the original.

86 Corrington's note: "Neumann, *Origins and History*, 14–15."

87 Changed "is" to "are" to match Neumann.

88 Changed "of" to "for" to match Neumann.

89 Corrington's note: "Neumann, *Origins and History*, 16."

90 Corrington's note: "Neumann, *Origins and History*, 16."

that will subterraneously reach the superficially unreachable partner, where things are the same and not the same, and can change into each other.[91]

It is the original tension, the tension from which every other tension must be understood to arise, this breaking from the round to become a "self" with autonomous meaning. To experience the parting or destruction of the Uroboros—otherwise symbolized as the parting of the World Parents, the two sides of the round which are male and female sexually and yet sexlessly one in the serpent-form, is to experience a break from the ground-state of living being, to reach for an "unnatural" state, an excited state, which is "specifically human."[92]

It seems evident that the pleromatic state Neumann describes as a "borderline image," describing human consciousness at its earliest discernible stage, is virtually identical with the symbolism of the pleroma set out in gnostic systems. Neumann's choice of the term *pleromatic* to describe the "dawn-state" is not simply a fortuitous metaphor. It is accurate. The quotation given from *The Great Announcement* ascribed to Simon Magus in Hippolytus has, in this connection, only the added virtue of a certain literalness. Its implications cannot be avoided. From the gnostic point of view, Paradise is, existentially speaking, the womb. It is the place from whence the sparks of pneuma which form "spiritual" men come, or are flung. It is the place to which they yearn to return. In certain sects, Neumann's symbolism is evident in a surprisingly specific manner. Worship of the serpent, the Uroboros, is commonly attributed to the Ophians, who characterize the Great Circle of the cosmos, the eternal sea of space as "Leviathan," or the "Soul of the Universe."[93] To the Naassenes who, according to Hippolytus, "had the effrontery to praise the serpent," the serpent is "liquid substance" and nothing which exists can exist without it. It has "the goodness of everything else within it, as in the horn of the unicorn."[94] They say that "Eden is the brain, being, as it were, bounden and enfolded in the membranes which surround it, like the heavens; and Paradise, they think, is man, to the extent of his head alone."[95] The Naassenes describe the Great God as Adamas, bisexual, both Father and Mother, "Man of the Mighty Name." According to the summary of Ophitic thought in Irenaeus,[96] the Great Mother, Prunikos-Sophia,[97] attempting to counteract the works of her son, the creator-god Ialdabaoth, sends the serpent

---

91   Corrington's note: "Neumann, *Origins and History*, 3."

92   Corrington's note: "See Mircea Eliade, *The Myth of the Eternal Return* (Princeton, NJ: Princeton University Press, 1971), 37–42, esp. p. 40, n. 70. Also pp. 55–60."

93   Corrington's note: "Origen, *Contra Celsum*, bk. 6, ch. 25, in Foerster, *Gnosis*, 1:95."

94   Corrington's note: "Hippolytus, *Refutation*, bk. 5, ch. 6, pts. 3–11.1, in Foerster, *Gnosis*, 1:263."

95   Corrington's note: "Hippolytus, *Refutation*, Foerster, *Gnosis*, 280."

96   Corrington's note: "Irenaeus, *Adversus Haereses*, bk. 1, ch. 30, pt. 7, in Foerster, *Gnosis*."

97   According to Hans Jonas (among others) this should be Sophia-Prunikos. See also same passage in "Brief History of Gnosticism 1 & 2."

to seduce Adam and Even[98] into breaking Ialdabaoth's commandment, knowing that if they should eat of the fruit of the forbidden tree, they would come to realize that the creator was not the Great God of the Beyond, but the True God was the Primal Inutterable Man of the pleroma. "It is the first success of the transcendental principle against the principle of the world, which is vitally interested in preventing knowledge in man as the inner-worldly hostage of Light: the serpent's action marks the beginning of all gnosis on earth which thus, by its very origin is stamped as opposed to the world and its God, and indeed as a form of rebellion."[99]

The Uroboros is thus a "threshold" symbol, and as such, it must be seen from at least two perspectives. From the proximal side, that is, the interior side, the Uroboros is guardian and Great Mother, symbol of the Universal Soul of all things which are one.[100] It is the "liquid substance," the amniotic fluid, without which nothing can exist.

From[101] the exterior, worldly, or distal side, the Uroboros appears variously as the Angel with the flaming sword guarding paradise from those outcasts who have the knowledge of good and evil, which is to say the consciousness which flows from differentiation, or as the bridge between worldly existence and the transcendental pleroma. The serpent or dragon, who surrounds the pleromatic state by taking its tail in its teeth in many versions, guards "primal blessed formless substance, which is the cause of all forms in the things that are formed."[102] The significance placed upon androgyny by the ophitic and Naassene gnostics fits into the pleromatic compactness set out by Neumann, as does the tail-in-mouth image of the cosmic serpent which is wholly self-sufficient and independent of the needs of existential creatures who must depend upon interaction with one another for their fullness. To be castrated in the existential world, for example, as were Attis and Osiris, was to have the "earthly parts" cut off, and thus to have "gone over to the eternal substance above, where ... there is neither male nor female, but a new creature, a new man (St. Paul, Eph. 2:15; 4:24; 2 Cor. 5:17) who is bisexual."[103]

Neumann points out the extreme tension involved in the formation of individual and cultural consciousness. It is "unnatural" in that it represents a break from "the great whirling wheel of life, where everything not yet individual is submerged in the union of opposites, passing away and willing to pass away."[104] Existence, after

---

98   "Even" is in BHG1&2 as well, but Corrington must mean Eve.

99   Corrington's note: "Hans Jonas, The Gnostic Religion: The Message of the Alien God and the Beginnings of Christianity (Boston: Beacon Press, 1963), 93."

100   Overlaps with BHG1&2 seem to pause here (BHG has some text not included here, between this paragraph and what follows).

101   Overlap with BHG picks up again.

102   Corrington's note: "Hippolytus, bk. 5, ch. 6, pt. 18, in Foerster, *Gnosis*, 266."

103   Corrington's note: "Hippolytus, bk. 5, ch. 6, pt. 15, in Foerster, *Gnosis*, 266."

104   Corrington's note: "Neumann, *Origins and History*, 16. But to see a more abstract, more developed version of the Uroborotic symbolism, see Eric Voegelin, *The Ecumenic Age*, vol. 4 of *Order and History* (Baton Rouge, LA: Louisiana State University Press, 1956), passim, on the symbolism of the *Apeiron* of Anaximander. See also Corrington, 'Order and Consciousness.' The Apeiron as a symbol of the ground of being is both *arche* and *telos* of the process of reality,

all, in the fullness of differentiation, is a painful and desperate experience. To be "oneself" is, specifically, not to be The One, the All, not to be "at one with the universe" as the cliché quite properly goes. There is, then, as a substrate of even the most powerful personality or cultural _____[105] structure of the pre-egoistic which desires to return, to plunge past the barrier of the Uroboros from the distal side, back into that fullness, that wholeness and unity, which it guards. This is what Neumann calls "Uroborotic incest." The term, apparently synonymous with Freud's death-wish,[106] is not felicitous, since it has nothing to do with sexuality, but rather with an aspect of consciousness.

> Uroboric incest is a form of entry into the mother, of union with her, and it stands in sharp contrast to other and later forms of incest. . . . it is more a desire to be dissolved and absorbed; passively one lets oneself be taken, sinks into the pleroma, melts away in the ocean of pleasure—a *liebestod*. The Great Mother takes the little child back into herself, and always over uroboric incest there stand the insignia of death.[107]

I suggest that the pleroma of the gnostics, the high heaven with its serpentine boundary and its androgynous True God is, in fact, an infantile mythopoetic reconstruction of the pre-conscious state, both as to the individual and the collective.[108] The gnostic pleroma and the dawn-state described by Neumann both represent conditions in which the elements we consider fundamental to a developed consciousness are lacking. I would suggest further that the gnostic symbolisms we have set out above can all be traced back to an emotional incapability to sever one's own personality from the vision of the pleromatic state as Neumann describes it. In other words, that peculiar capacity to create Second Realities, to suppose the process of reality itself can somehow be altered by an act of metastatic faith, some trick of spiritual magic, is at root an infantile regression, an attempt to escape the terrible burden of participation in a cosmos which is not a "sea of pleasure" or a primordial state of nondifferentiation. The essence of the gnostic dream is an eternal monism. The gnostic *Gospel of Thomas* sets out a purported *logion* of Christ which sums up the gnostic conception of the final state, the coming of the Kingdom.

---

thus 'tail-in-mouth.' Things arise from it and pass away into it. It thus stands as a non-imagistic symbolism, but one which still contains the sense of the cycle, or the circles so basic to later Gnostic thought which never achieves the level of differentiating consciousness reached by Plato, whose work 'straightens out' the Uroboros and the Apeiron, to show the movement from depth both Uroborotic and Apeirontic to a height signified by the One (hen)."

105   A blank appears in Corrington's text, although this sentence seems complete. In BGN this sentence is the same and there is no word between "cultural" and "structure."

106   More commonly known as the "death drive."

107   Corrington's note: "Neumann, Origins and History, 17."

108   Overlap with BHG more intermittent starting here.

Jesus said to them: "When[109] you make the two one, and when you make the inner as the outer, and the outer as the inner and the above as the below, and when you make the male and the female into a single one, so that the male will not be male, and the female [not] be female, when you make the eyes in the place of an eye and a hand in the place of a hand, and a foot in the place of a foot, [and] an image in the place of an image, then shall you enter the Kingdom."[110]

Let me make clear that I am no psychologist, nor am I overly concerned with that discipline. When I use such terms as "infantile regression," I wish them to be understood "in the common and popular sense of the words," as the Civil Code of Louisiana directs us to interpret the language of the law. I specifically do not wish to imply a dogma or freight, such terms with the ideation of any school. Rather I wish to follow the evidence to its logical conclusion, and I propose that this blurring of dichotomy, this insistence on the proper unity of all things in their ideal state which appears as a fundamental proposition in classical gnosticism and, as we shall see, in modern gnostic thought as well, must, of necessity, point to the infantile character of gnosticism. As I have noted in another place, following Professor Voegelin's view, the balance of consciousness is not easily maintained, nor are its tensions mere irritants. The temptation to derail, to lose the balance, to fall backward into the unproblematical state of unconsciousness—or, for that matter, to leap toward infinity, into the doom of what Neumann calls "inflation" of the ego, is constant and immense. Voegelin described it many years ago:

> The life of the soul in openness toward God, the waiting,[111] the periods of aridity and dullness, guilt and despondency, contrition and repentance, forsakenness and hope against hope, the silent stirrings of[112] love and grace, trembling on the verge of a certainty which if gained is lost[113] — the very lightness of this fabric may prove too heavy a burden for men who lust for massively possessive experience.[114]

What is unbearable about the world is not flesh as flesh, or matter as matter. It is the ineradicable duality of existence. It is that there are other things than

---

109 Light correction here (punctuation and capitalization). Originally stated: "Jesus said to them, when you make…"

110 Corrington's note: "Logion 22 in Edgar Hennecke, ed., and trans. R. McLachlan Wilson, *Gospels and Related Writings*, vol. 1 of *New Testament Apocrypha* (London: Lutterworth Press, 1963), 298."

111 Corrington repeated this phrase twice. Because doing so was probably accidental, the repeated phrase has been deleted.

112 Corrington wrote "or."

113 In Voegelin, this is not "lost" but "loss." However, the use of "lost" for "loss" seems to abound in other sources when this passage is quoted. The difference between the two words changes the meaning.

114 Corrington's note: "Eric Voegelin, *The New Science of Politics: An Introduction* (Chicago: University of Chicago Press, 1952), 122."

oneself. The core of gnostic thought in every form is finally almost pathetically, terrifyingly simple: it is the overpowering childish wish that all things should be oneself, that one should be the cosmos and all beyond it. What more profound "lust for massively possessive experience" is there, after all, than that of an infant? The very act of differentiation and its realization is a cleaving away from the individual consciousness all else to be placed in the dualistic or multifarious perspective of the process of reality. Jung points out that the image at the center of the mandala figure, whether it arises in dream or in art, is indistinguishably the Self or God.[115] Thus the gnostic, for all his noted horror of dualistic reality, is not in fact so much against flesh or matter as such, but passionately desirous that all polarities should collapse, all dichotomy vanish into one—and that the one should be himself.[116]

But the experience of the gnostic, oriented as he is toward womb-life and Uroboratic unity, is not exhausted by a description which would attempt to characterize him as a case of arrested development, one who constructs elaborate if absurd systems in order to escape the ambivalence and ambiguity of life in existence. There is more.

The breakthrough of individual and cultural consciousness from the circle of the Uroboros, according to Neumann, includes, later on, the manifestation of the hero-stage which, as mythology makes clear, must include the fight against the dragon. Now the Uroboros which represents, in the alternate symbol of the joined World Parents, both father and mother, requires that the hero fight a double-battle.

> Since in the mystery religions the fight with the dragon is conceived only as the fight with the mother dragon, representing the unconscious chthonic aspect, the inevitable result is identification with the spiritual father, so far as the dragon-fight situation is reached at all in the mystery religions.[117] The failure of the fight with the father-dragon, the overwhelming force of spirit, leads to patriarchal castration, inflation, loss of the body in the ecstasy of ascension, and so to a world-negating mysticism. This phenomenon is particularly evident in Gnosticism and Gnostic Christianity.[118]

"Inflation" represents that break with the world symbolized by the myth of Icarus, son of Daedalus, the great artificer, who ignores his father's warning and flies too near the sun. Even beyond the Uroboros symbolism, the ego which comes to fill the whole horizon of the self must fall. "The infiltration of Iranian and Manichean influences strengthens the martial component in the hero, but because he is still a Gnostic at heart,

---

115 Corrington's note: "Carl Jung, *The Archetypes and the Collective Unconscious*, vol. 9, pt. 1 of *The Collected Works of C. G. Jung* (London: Routledge & Kegan Paul, 1958), 389. See also Jung, *Aion*, 40."

116 End of overlap with BHG1&2.

117 Punctuation and capitalization changed and added to match original text.

118 Corrington's note: "Neumann, *Origins and History*, 254."

he remains hostile to the world, the body, materiality, and woman. Although there are certain elements in Gnosis that strive for a synthesis of opposites, these always fly apart in the end; the heavenly side of man triumphs and the earthly is sacrificed."[119]

In this phase of psychic derailment, the gnostic, rather than attempting or desiring a reunion with the original pleromatic state, creates, from the materials of his own ego a surrogate for the pleroma. In the "illimitable expansion of the ego," as Neumann describes it: one finds "intensified associations . . .[120] paroxysms of will and action, senseless optimism, and so forth."[121] "Just as mania and melancholia are merely two forms of madness, of the devouring uroboric state which destroys all ego consciousness, so regression to the unconscious, i.e., being devoured by the Great Mother, and the flight to "nothing but" consciousness, i.e., being devoured by the spiritual father, are two forms in which any truly compensated consciousness, and the striving for wholeness, are lost."[122]

The symbol of the serpent with its tail in its mouth is indeed an "insignia of death" to the personality, which cannot bear the tensions which draw it toward the equally false unities of ego-loss and ego-mania.

Spiritual inflation, a perfect example of which is the frenziedness of Nietzsche's *Zarathustra*, is a typical western development carried to extremes. Behind the overaccentuation of consciousness, ego, and reason—sensible enough in themselves as the guiding aims of psychic development—there stands the overwhelming might of "heaven" as the danger which goes beyond the heroic struggle with the earthly side of the dragon and culminates in a spirituality that has lost touch with reality and the instincts.[123]

Neumann describes still one more form of spiritual derailment, maintaining that it is distinguishable from inflation:

> The form which this kind of degeneration usually takes in the West is not spiritual inflation, but sclerosis of consciousness, where the ego identifies with consciousness as a kind of spirit. In most cases, this means identifying spirit with intellect, and consciousness with thinking. Such a limit is utterly unjustified, but the patriarchal trend of development "away from the unconscious" and towards consciousness and thinking makes the identification understandable.[124]

While it is not difficult to identify cases of the "sclerosis" Neumann describes, most clearly in the line of thought, which extends from Descartes through modern

---

119 Corrington's note: "Ibid."

120 Ellipses added.

121 Corrington's note: "Neumann, *Origins and History*, 384."

122 Corrington's note: "Neumann, *Origins and History*, 385–386."

123 Corrington's note: "Neumann, *Origins and History*, 386."

124 Corrington's note: "Neumann, *Origins and History*, 386."

scientism, I am not sure that there is any fundamental difference between inflation and sclerosis. On the contrary, the sclerotic state Neumann describes probably represents a metastable inflationary state momentarily stabilized because of propitious conditions in a specific existential situation. Clearly, both inflation and sclerosis, like collapse of ego, eventuate in a pneumopathological shattering of the balance of consciousness, a derailment into fantasies, Second Realities, which take leave of the process of reality and mutilate the process of consciousness in its relation to reality. Neumann himself recognizes the meaning of such loss of balance with its resultant contraction of the personality and the personality's perception of the context of reality around it:

> The individual who lacks the support of a compensatory movement inside himself drops out of the ordered fabric of civilization. For him this means the breakdown of transpersonal experience, a shrinking of world horizons, and the loss of all certainty and meaning in life.
>
> Two general reactions are to be observed in this situation. The first is regression to the Great Mother, into unconsciousness, a readiness to herd together in masses, and so, as a collective atom with new transpersonal experiences, to gain a new certainty and a new point of vantage: the second is flight to the Great Father, into the isolation of individualism.[125]

I must acknowledge that, unlike Neumann, I see both of these models of spiritual and psychological derailment as infantile. The vector of a mature spiritual growth, after all, is not one side of a coin: rather it is a passage between two forms of destruction. A clearer and more substantial expression of a similar view appears in Voegelin's *The Ecumenic Age*, where he characterizes the two principal forms of gnostic thought. Voegelin speaks of pragmatic conquest and spiritual exodus. The endless outthrusts of the Ecumenic empires on the one hand, and the almost equally numerous attempts to break with the process of reality on the part of sects are, in their effects and meaning, difficult to distinguish one from the other. The process[126] of reality, and the concomitant process of consciousness, can, in themselves, neither be dominated nor escaped. Interestingly, Voegelin chooses Anaximander's symbolism of the *Apeiron*, the great circle of existence itself, from which things rise and to which they return, as the motif to describe the necessity (*Ananke*) which is inherent in reality—and, if Neumann's model is correct, in the process of consciousness as well:

> If reality is understood in the comprehensive sense of Anaximander's dictum, obviously man can neither conquer reality nor walk out of it, for

---

125 Corrington's note: "Neumann, *Origins and History*, 390–91."
126 Capitalized in the original.

the Apeiron, the origin of things, is not a thing that could be appropriated or left behind through movements in the realm of things. No imperial[127] expansion can reach the receding horizon; no exodus from bondage is an exodus from the *conditio*[128] *humana*; no turning away from the Apeiron, or turning against it, can prevent the return to it through death. Any and every gigantomachia ends with the defeat of the giants. Conquest and exodus, thus, are movements *within* reality.[129]

The connexity between Neumann's regression and Voegelin's exodus, between Neumann's inflation and Voegelin's conquest seems reasonably clear, and becomes clearer upon reading both volumes. Loss of the balance of consciousness—a term used by both Neumann and Voegelin[130]—results in personal and civilizational destruction, in an incapacity to play the role of a mature person (*spoudaios*) or a mature society.

> Not only power, money, and lust, but religion, art, and politics as exclusive determinants in the form of parties, nations, sects, movements, and "isms" of every description take possession of the masses and destroy the individual . . . The disintegration of personality caused by an idea is no less dangerous than the disintegration caused by empty, personalistic power-strivings. The results of both can be seen in the disastrous massing together and recollectivization of modern man.[131]

It is necessary to note at this point that, so far, we have dealt primarily in our references to the texts with that form of gnosticism called regressive by Neumann, exodus by Voegelin. That is because ancient, or classical, gnosticism is chiefly of that sort. It goes without saying that there is a quite real system of reciprocity between the facts of ancient conquest and the texts of ancient exodus, but it is equally true that the texts which reveal inflational or conquest gnosticism are, for the most part, a later development as are the acts which constitute modern exodus.[132] In the second part of this essay, we will turn our attention to the modern expression of gnosticism of the conquest or inflational type.

---

127 Changed "Imperial" to "imperial."

128 Probably *condicio*.

129 Corrington's note: "Voegelin, *Ecumenic Age*, 215. See also Corrington, 'Order and Consciousness.'" Corrington just noted O & C for this quotation. It is actually from vol. 4 of *Order and History*, which is called *Ecumenic Age*. Citation fixed to match volume.

130 Corrington's note: "Neumann, *Origins and History*, 360, et seq.; Voegelin, *Ecumenic Age*, 227, et seq."

131 Corrington's note: "Neumann, *Origins and History*, 392."

132 Corrington's note: "It is true that both Herodotus and Thucydides cite living examples of the inflational variety of gnostic thought. Histories, I, 207; and in what Voegelin characterizes as 'the icily controlled account of the Melain dialogue' of Thucydides (*Ecumenic Age*, 183), but these examples are, at most peripheral, matters of the appetites, and in no case constitute 'systems' in the sense of extended symbolic structures designed to achieve metastatic purposes." Corrected spelling of Herodotus in footnote.

Presently, however, we must complete our discussion of the forces which balance consciousness in opposition to these powerful forces toward imbalance. Professor Voegelin suggests that it is the task of the philosopher to preserve the balance between the experienced lastingness and qualified rigidity of the cosmos on the one hand, and the theophanic events which penetrate the process of consciousness on the other, and to do so "in such a manner that the paradox becomes intelligible as the very structure of existence itself."[133]

Taking into account the positivistic language which burdens Neumann's thought, I would suggest that what he proposes as the experience of the archetypes, following Jung, parallels Voegelin's concept of the theophanic events.

> All symbols and archetypes are projections of the formative side of human nature that creates order and assigns meaning. . . . The collective re-enactment of the determining archetypes in religious festivities and the arts associated with them gives meaning to life and saturates it in the emotions set free by transpersonal psychic forces in the background.[134]

Translating "psychological" language into ontological language, Neumann appears to be describing as a fundamental part of the balance of consciousness the occurrence of theophanic events, the irruption into consciousness of elements which both resolve and enlarge the meaning of the process of reality for those who experience them, but which, at the same time, invite by their very power pathological regression or pathological inflation. What Neumann refers to as *centroversion*, the balancing factor in the process of consciousness is, in the language of Plato, the *metalepsis*, the consuming certainty of participation in the human-divine drama of the process of reality, a participation which is utterly lost by succumbing to the temptations of regression or inflation. Neither the infant nor the alien participates in the manifold of reality and discovers the luminosity of his own consciousness as it lovingly interplays with its partners in being. The most subtle terror in losing the balance of consciousness, as far as the individual human being is concerned, is that he loses with it any sense of the actual meaning of the very process of which he is an inextricable part.

But maintenance of the balance of consciousness is not simply a matter of avoiding identifiable pathologies. There is, in the very structure of consciousness itself, in that aspect of consciousness which we call *history*, a pattern of drift, a tendency to lose the balance almost imperceptibly. Neumann describes it in this way:

---

133 Corrington's note: "Voegelin, *Ecumenic Age*, 228." Standardized all citations from *Order and History* vol. 4 to *Ecumenic Age* (Corrington cited the book differently throughout the manuscript).

134 Corrington's note: "Neumann, *Origins and History*, 371."

At first everything is under the unconscious emotional compulsion of the symbols which appear in the ritual, whose aim it is to represent and "enact" them. . . . Later the ritual takes the form of a sacred action which is "played" by the collective for the collective, though it is still invested with all the force of magic and ritual efficacy.

Gradually, the *meaning* of the symbol is crystallized out, detaches itself from the action, and becomes a cultural content capable of conscious realization and interpretation. Although the ritual is acted as before, it is something of a game with a meaning . . . and the interpretation of the symbols therein represented and enacted becomes an essential part of the initiation. The accent, then, has already fallen on conscious assimilation and the strengthening of the ego.[135]

If we read this passage as a description of the movement of consciousness from compact to differentiated form, moving from *cultus* to religio to *ars*, and if we read also the classical meaning for the psychological phrase "strengthening of the ego," that is to say, the growth of the *amor sui* of St. Augustine, in contrast to the *amor dei* from which the process must inevitably commence, we realize that Neumann's final state, that in which the symbols originally numinous have become "objects" to be "interpreted" parallels closely Voegelin's description of the work of Cicero and the later Stoics. "For the Stoic dogmatism, like the later Christian theology, has the civilizational purpose and effect of protecting a historically achieved state of insight against the disintegrative pressures to which the differentiated truth of existence is exposed in the spiritual and intellectual turmoil of the ecumenic situation."[136]

The value of such a system is obvious, as Neumann points out: "The organization of life inside this framework precludes—in the normal person—any dangerous invasions from the unconscious and guarantees him a relatively high degree of inner security, enabling him to lead an ordered existence in a world-system where the human and the cosmic, the personal and the transpersonal, are all articulated with one another."[137]

The corresponding problem with this drift toward spiritual *stasis*, called by Neumann "the cultural canon," is that it is metastable. It does not correspond to the movement of the process of consciousness. The more substantially the secondary symbolisms of religion and doctrine are established as the all-absorbing channels through which the process of consciousness must articulate itself, the more certainly are the pressures created that produce the spiritual imbalances eventuating variously in new breakthroughs which will, in their theophanic character, perceive

---

135 Corrington's note: "Neumann, *Origins and History*, 372."

136 Corrington's note: "Voegelin, *Ecumenic Age*, 43–44."

137 Corrington's note: "Neumann, *Origins and History*, 375."

the dogmachies as untruths to be struggled against and destroyed. Moreover, almost in the manner of a centrifuge, the theophanic irruptions will throw out not only insights which relate to the process of reality, but others which will bear no such relationship at all, but which will attempt either to escape and deny the meaning of reality, or attempt to consume it totally in egophanies and fantasies which identify themselves as co-extensive with the process of reality itself. While the variants must occupy and interest us, it is clear that both regressive and inflationary gnostic forms represent psychic systems incapable of participation in the process of reality, and that the empirical results of both variants must be civilizationally destructive.

Precisely how do these irruptions, these theophanic events arise? They arise in concrete human beings. The challenge to an extant doctrine or dogma[138] are those who are "invaded" and who come to experience the cultural canon as *pseudos*:

> The exceptions to this rule—exceptions, however, upon which the community depends—are the "outsiders," those who fall within an enlarged category of the type known in myth as the hero, the Great Individual. . . . The hero or Great Individual is always and pre-eminently the man with immediate inner experience who, as seer, artist, prophet, or revolutionary, sees, formulates, sets forth, and realizes the new values, the "new images." His orientation comes from the "voice," from the unique, inner utterance of the self . . . The canon [is] always "founded," so far as we can judge, in accordance with the revelations enunciated by the voice.[139]

It would be unfair to suppose that Neumann realized the implications of what he says here. He was far less prepared than Jung to acknowledge the presence of a ground beyond both individual and community from which, logically, the "voice" must arise. Far more significantly, his admission that the foundation of the cultural canon was invariably revelational matches precisely Voegelin's contention that "the life of reason, thus, is firmly rooted in a revelation."[140]

The question arises immediately, however, as to how it is possible to determine which, if any, components of an individual theophanic insight constitute potential additions to the cultural canon, and which represent gnostic derailments? In the present context, it is an inadequate response to suggest that "By their fruits shall ye know them." Fortunately, the analysis does not depend utterly on hindsight. On the contrary, the correct response is, hopefully, implicit in what has gone before. There is the criterion of the participatory nature of the insight and its unfolding. Moreover, there remains, always, the backdrop of the cosmos, the process of reality

---

138   "Doga" changed to "dogma."

139   Corrington's note: "Neumann, *Origins and History*, 375–76."

140   Corrington's note: "Voegelin, *Ecumenic Age*, 228."

itself, from which consciousness arose, to which it returns in the Apeirontic sense. Pragmatically, the question is resolved by reference to its metaleptic character and to its validity in terms of its relationship to the empirically determinable nature of elemental reality. No insight cancels these two aspects of reality, nor can any insight, however tempting, pretend to transform them. The process of reality and the fundamental realization of human beings on the whole in regard to their participation in it does not yield either to collapse into regressional fantasies of the weak psyche, nor to the inflationary surge of the psyche which purports to consume reality and replace it with its own ego. The very significance of the term "compensation," as Neumann uses it, suggests a stratum of mystery, which must be realized, minimally as an indefinably but empirically determinable human capacity to avoid both collapse and inflation.

Further, there is the insight that the participatory nature of the psyche's presence in the flux of the process of reality is governed by limitations which are neither debatable nor escapable. Those limits (*peri*) are physical, biological, and psychic (a word chosen as a poor compromise between "spiritual" and "psychological," in the absence of a rigorous demarcation between the two zones of experience).

The problem is reduced, to some degree, by the fact that any "voice" which announces a purported theophanic insight in total disregard of the limits placed upon human beings by biological and physical laws is a "voice" rapidly silenced. Those whose daimon forbids reproduction, like the Shakers, are not problems—at least, not for long. Those insights which, on the other hand, deal primarily with the process of consciousness and must, in some fashion, be distributed between the "psychological" and the "spiritual" aspects of human personality are far more problematical. It would be pleasant to suppose that the balance of consciousness could be, as to these aspects of the spectra of reality, described in such a fashion as to render it amenable to contemporary standards of "psychological" determination. That is not the case. While it is quite possible to set out philosophically what constitutes the balance, and to point it out existentially, it is not possible to express the nature of the balance or to predict its constituents before the fact. The balance of consciousness is not a "scientific" determination. It is experiential. It is experiential both in the primary sense of personal knowledge and secondarily in the sense of experience which can be transmitted not by "science" but by the exchange of "knowledge carried to the heart," in the phrase of Allen Tate, knowledge which is widespread among normal human beings, but which does not admit repetitive experiment and concrete measurability.

We thus find ourselves in the midst of an apparent paradox—not in relation to gnosticism, but in relation to its opposite: normative human consciousness. It is not gnosticism, which possesses as a substantive constituent a certain indefinable horizon of mystery. On the contrary, gnosticism possesses a unique definitiveness. Whatever variant of it we may confront, there is, invariably, a central monistic "truth" involved. That truth may not be obvious, and it may not be simple, but it is always describable in terms of the peculiar "gnosis" in question. To possess gnosis of that certain truth—whatever it may be—is always perceived as the singular necessity which guarantees salvation. To know that Simon Magus is "The Standing One" is enough; to understand the awful fall caused by Sophia and her son Sabaoth is enough. Because, as we have seen, the essence of gnosticism is its monistic character, its fear and hatred of the complexities of the structure of reality as ordinary human beings experience it, and its determination to annihilate those distinctions, to push them aside as illusions, evil emanations, without relation to true reality.

Thus maintenance of the balance of consciousness is, theoretically at least, a more complex problem than succumbing to one or another variant of gnostic derailment. The fact is, in purely empirical terms, it is easier to drift into a gnostic variant than to maintain the balance.

> Certain problems that became acute in gnosticism were latently present even in Plato's work, as for instance the identity of the God who is radically "Beyond." The Gnostics recognized in the hitherto unknown God of the abyss a divine being different from the creator-god, in particular from the Yahweh of the Old Testament. In their conception of reality, an evil daimon had devised the prison of this world for the purpose of holding captive in it the spark of the divine *pneuma* in man. As distinguished from this daimon, the true God is so absolutely beyond the world that he has nothing to do with its creation; and still less would he care to incarnate himself in it. The Gnostic imbalance of consciousness, thus, causes a split to run through divine reality, separating the daimonic powers of the world from the pneumatic divinity Beyond.[141]

The essence of gnosticism was, then, to destroy the concept of an evolution of consciousness, and to replace its growth with a *stasis* in which the whole of reality could be explained through the simplistic description of a daimonic world-creator and an unknown god Beyond to whom those possessing the gnosis might reach. In this *schema*, there was no growth of consciousness—hence no history, hence no eschatological vector in time. Rather there was simply an indeterminate tension between prison-world and pleromatic freedom, between the abortive creator-god and the true god of the Beyond, which tension could be resolved only through that gnosis which freed souls from the world, that they might return whence they had

141 Corrington's note: "Voegelin, *Ecumenic Age*, 234."

come. The process of reality, hence, ceased to have meaning in any sense; it was no more than a way-station for those imprisoned to break free. The concrete experience of concrete human beings in the world was without meaning; only the gnosis and the power it conferred had meaning. One's suffering, one's triumphs in the cosmos were without meaning. Only the gnosis and the escape it offered had significance.

Seen from this perspective, it is possible to describe gnostic systems, whether regressive or inflationary, as failures of the balance of consciousness occasioned by incapacity of one kind or another to maintain the admittedly severe tension of life lived in what Voegelin has called the Metaxy, the "in-between" which, by its very failure to resolve experience, to choose one polarity over another, participates in the mystery of movement of reality beyond its own determinable ontological structure. At a less elevated level, the mystery inherent in the process of reality and its movement is experienced as ambiguity. The sharpness and anxiety of such experience is a central motivation of gnostic desire. To embrace the gnosis is to escape, at least imaginatively and speculatively, the frequently awesome tensions of a life lived "in-between." Whether the fantasy is that of the infantile return to the pleroma, or of demiurgic dominance of a pleromatic state, the motivation for choosing the Second Reality over the Metaxy is the spiritual or psychic incapacity of individual human beings to withstand the gnostic promise of unity amidst the numbing ambiguity of endless variety and multiplicity. The self-centeredness of the infant or the megalomaniac is horrified by the plethos of the cosmos. Its richness and abundance defeats the concupiscence of the illimitable ego, necessitating some form of gnostic derailment in order to avoid a more immediately obvious psychosis. The gnostic break with reality, given the fragmented nature of its premises, is always a reasoned break, in what Neumann has called a "natural" direction—that is, escape from the process of consciousness as a balanced function. It is precisely because the gnostic derailment moves toward one or the other polarities which are inherent in every human being that gnosticism has had such large success. The religious symbol of temptation is itself a block of meaning which compactly expresses the reality that every person is pulled toward a resolution of the tensions experienced in the Metaxy, and that the balance is only maintained by an intricate and elaborate structure of countervailing experiences and symbolisms which nonetheless hover always at the edge of a false resolution by choosing a "One" that offers unconsciousness as against a "Many" that offers confusion.

II

We must move now to an examination of the resurgence of gnostic thought in that form which rises in the Middle Ages and continues thereafter virtually without abatement. The link which connects "classical" gnosticism with medieval gnosticism is the teaching of Montanus, that formidable heresiarch of the fourth century. His doctrines are as difficult to fix as are those of Simon, given the thinness and occasional inconsistency of the earliest accounts.[142] Still, enough of the outlines are preserved for us to understand that Montanus was something less than the heretic he was made out to be—to a point. It appears that he and the two women who accompanied him and also claimed the status of prophets taught the doctrines of The Great Church as they were then understood. But Montanus went well beyond that doctrinal base, identifying himself with the Holy Spirit, maintaining that he was, in fact, Father, Son, and Holy Spirit incarnate on earth. He was the incarnation even as Christ had been. Moreover, Montanus taught the coming of an eschatological kingdom[143] on earth for his followers, the literal descent of the Heavenly Jerusalem from above.[144] This millennial enthusiasm gathered much force in Phrygia and appears to have maintained its chiliastic character long after Montanus himself vanished. From time to time, as Harnack notes, the Montanist churches would gather their people together, sell all their goods, and go into the desert to await the imminent coming of the Lord.[145] Noted for extreme asceticism, and considered by some authorities to represent a reaction against the Church's accommodation with the empire, the Montanists bridge the gnosticism which flourished in the second and third centuries, and that which came to flower in the twelfth century. Milman specifically connects Montanism with the ideas of the movement surrounding Joachim of Fiore, as does Paul Tillich.[146]

The most significant feature of Montanus's thought seems to have been his insistence upon an earthly millennium, presaged by the prophecy of Montanus:[147] a new dispensation of the Holy Spirit as promised by Christ when he proclaimed to the apostles the coming of the Paraclete.[148] Obviously, this feature alone presages the Joachitic "Third Status" or "Third Realm," the central symbolism of his work. It is quite possible that other characteristics of Joachitic symbolism were also present in the teaching of Montanus and his successors.[149]

---

142   Corrington's note: "See Adolph von Harnack, *History of Dogma* (repr., New York: Russell & Russell, 1958), 2:97–100. See also Henry H. Milman, *History of Latin Christianity* (London: John Murray, 1854), 1:38–39." Corrected J. H. Milman to Henry H. Milman.

143   Capitalized in original.

144   Corrington's note: "Harnack, *History*, 2:96."

145   Corrington's note: "Harnack, *History*, 2:95n2."

146   Corrington's note: "Milman, *History*, 1:38; Paul Tillich, *Systematic Theology* (Chicago: University of Chicago Press, 1963), 3:345."

147   Corrington used a semi-colon here. The passage in Rainy that he was referring to suggests that what is after the semi-colon is actually explaining the prophecy; therefore, a colon seems more appropriate and has replaced the semi-colon.

148   Corrington's note: "Robert Rainy, *The Ancient Catholic Church* (New York: Scribner, 1902)."

149   Corrington's note: "Rainy notes that Montanist communities, claiming to be orthodox, nonetheless chose to establish separate communities, leading to the possibility that the Montanists conceived themselves to be a 'community of autonomous persons,' already living in a Third Age through the illumination of the *Novus Dux* or Holy Father, Montanus. This view, it goes without saying, cannot be confirmed on the slender evidence available. But see Norman Cohn, *The Pursuit of the Millennium*, rev. ed. (New York: Oxford University Press, 1970), 25, et. seq., and Marjorie

When we begin to discuss the work of Joachim and his followers, the question at once arises as to whether the Joachitic symbols suggest the same fundamental types of experience which produced "classical" gnosticism.

The answer is affirmative, but it must be a qualified affirmation. There is no evidence that Joachim was influenced in any historical sense by the work of the Montanists, though it would be foolish to rule out the possibility.[150] At the same time, it should be understood from our lengthy reading of Neumann's work, that no direct historical connection is required in order for similar experiences to eventuate in identifiably similar symbolisms. It is quite reasonable to say that the experience which gives rise to the gnosticism of the Middle Ages is the same as that which gives rise to classical gnosticism, if we recognize that the experience has been filtered through almost a millennium of Christian symbols. The classical gnostic symbols of a hidden god beyond the Israelitic demiurge have long vanished, as have the indefinite and vague redeemer and Anthropos symbolisms found in the old gnosis. Further, through the work of Montanus, and quite possibly others, there has been a fusion of gnostic tendencies and prophecy. The Great Church, in its institutional power, has long been done not only with the mythopoetic gnosis, but with prophecy as well. The work of the Medieval Church, for the most part, has done with Jewish apocalyptic, with Revelations, and even with the insights set out in the Johannine Gospel and the Pauline Epistles. In its great good time, the Church has chosen philosophy as the vehicle of its intellectual development, and not only philosophy but Greek philosophy; and not only Greek philosophy, but Aristotelian philosophy. As Montanism appears to have been essentially a counterforce to that Christian Church, which became both Roman and Catholic, so the new gnosticism must be understood to be a counterforce to the superbly crafted Christian rationalism of the high middle ages. Methodologically, the new gnosticism consists in the view that there resides in Holy Scripture a hidden meaning, and that knowledge of this hidden meaning is to be revealed through a combination of profound study and divine revelation, or, more properly, inspiration. Certainly, the idea that scripture contained a hidden meaning or meanings is hardly original with Joachim.[151] Still, it was a renewal within the tradition of the Church in opposition to the *religio* of the Roman Saeclorum,[152] which had long before encapsulated original spiritual

---

Reeves, *The Influence of Prophecy in the Later Middle Ages* (Oxford: Clarendon Press, 1969), 295, 298."

150   Corrington's note: "The 'godded' prophet who, in the phrase of Runciman, lives 'one long pentecost' passes on his world-feeling through Adoptionists like Paul of Samosota, and the Messalians who held to gnostic dualism, repudiation of the Old Testament, and conceived their adepts as 'pneumatics,' and, after a novitiate, as literally part of God. This sect, arising in the fourth century, can be traced as existing in the eleventh century in Thrace, still vital and attempting to convert its neighbors. Stephen Runciman, *The Medieval Manichee: A Study of the Christian Dualist Heresy* (Cambridge: Cambridge University Press, 1955), 18–25."

151   Corrington's note: "Cf. Gershom G. Scholem, *On the Kabbalah and Its Symbolism* (New York: Schocken Books, 1969), 37, et seq. Also Cohn, *Pursuit of the Millenium*, 108, et seq."

152   Corrington's note: "On this, see Voegelin, *Ecumenic Age*, 40, et seq."

experience and transmuted it into a basis for social order, in order to protect a "historically achieved state of insight against the disintegrative pressures to which the differentiated truth of experience is exposed in the spiritual and intellectual turmoil of the ecumenic situation."[153] When Joachim of Fiore came upon the medieval scene, the Church was singularly sensitive to irruptions of what by then appeared to be a new spiritual type, claiming both the works of scholarship and the faith of inspiration, and directed toward a new gnosis in relation to the divine books—already thoroughly explicated—upon which the institution itself is based.

Nonetheless, at Pentecost, between 1190 and 1195, Joachim received an inspiration, which transformed his understanding of scripture: "When I awoke at dawn, I took to the Revelation of St. John. There, suddenly, the eyes of my spirit were struck with the lucidity of insight, and it was revealed to me the fulfillment of this book, and the concordance of the Old and New Testaments."[154]

This gnosis of the Abbot Joachim had as its subject scripture, but its object, fatefully, was history. The inspired reading of scripture by Joachim revealed to him that history was divided into three ages, that of the Father, set out in the Old Testament; that of the Son, comprehended in the New Testament; and that *status* yet to come, the age of the Holy Spirit. Each age unfolded its beginning within the *status* prior to it, and the third and final age, that which would produce the "Third Gospel," the "Eternal Testament," would comprise the rest of history, according to one of Joachim's most notable followers, Gerard of Bargo San Donnino.

The details of Joachim's prophetic view of history are set out in a number of places.[155] What concerns us more is his attitude toward the world, and the nature of his experience as it is revealed in his work. Are his sentiments, and the symbols through which he expresses them, compatible with those of the classical gnostics, when we have taken into account the intervening differentiations which have taken place between the time of the Patristic writers and the founders of monasticism?

> The signs as described in the gospel show clearly the dismay and ruin of the century which is now running down and must perish. Hence I believe that it will not be in vain to submit to the vigilance of the believers, through this work, those matters which divine economy has made known to my unworthy person in order to awaken the torpid hearts from their slumber by a violent noise and to induce them, if possible, by a new kind of exegesis to the contempt of the world.[156]

---

153 Corrington's note: "Voegelin, *Ecumenic Age*, 43–44."

154 Corrington's note: "Karl Löwith, *Meaning in History: The Theological Implications of the Philosophy of History* (Chicago: University of Chicago Press, 1949), 147."

155 Corrington's note: "See particularly Reeves, Influence of Prophecy; Löwith, Meaning In History; Cohn, Pursuit of the Millennium; Voegelin, New Science of Politics."

156 Corrington's note: "Joachim of Fiore, preface to *Liber Concordie* (Venice: Simon de Luere, 1519), quoted in

The *contemptu mundi* Joachim espouses appears more nearly gnostic than Christian, in that it is excited by the "dismay and ruin of the century which is now running down." Joachim's Third *status* was to be an age of monastic perfection in which the Holy Spirit would move directly among men, and neither preaching nor the sacraments would be any longer required. The degenerating world-age would be rescued by the rise of a class of Spiritual men. Joachim's metastatic speculations break radically with the Pauline "one for all" theology of Christ's salvific mission:

> The existing church, though founded on Christ, will have to yield to the coming church of the Spirit, when the history of salvation has reached its plenitude. This ultimate transition also implies the liquidation of preaching and sacraments, the mediating power of which becomes obsolete when the spiritual order is realized which possesses knowledge of God by direct vision and contemplation.[157]

In Joachim's view, the clerical church would wither away, and the "spirituals" would become one in the now fully realized Mystical Body of Christ.

The manner in which Joachim's alienation, now manifested as a problem of the *seclorum* rather than a problem of the *mundus*, was picked up by the Franciscan Spirituals who saw in their own founder the *Novus Dux* prophesied by Joachim, and in the works of certain of Joachim's followers, for example Gerard of Bargo San Donnino. The symbolism of an Eternal Gospel, which abrogated wholly the Old and New Testament, became the initiating point for what must be called an ideology and which invited the overthrow of "all previous institutions and authorities in a third and final Dispensation."[158] The previously impossible task set by gnosticism, an escape from or a denial of the world, a yearning for the pleromatic state, is converted in the work of the Joachitic writers into an enterprise which will take place in the world, and which requires for its successful completion only time, activism, and the gnosis. If the pleroma cannot be re-entered by a magical act which obliterates matter and space, it can be created in the world through time and energy. This is by no means to suggest that the work of the Joachitic speculators in some way rehabilitated matter or the flesh. On the contrary, the old suspicions, which, in their gnostic forms, had touched both Johannine and Pauline Christianity, remained. But the original gnostic symbolisms had been expanded and sophisticated.

To summarize the new gnostic symbolisms set out by Joachim and those who followed him:

Löwith, *Meaning in History*, 147–48."

157   Corrington's note: "Löwith, *Meaning in History*, 151."

158   Corrington's note: "Reeves, *Influence of Prophecy*, 59–60."

1. The world and time are in decline. Spirit is posed against flesh, illumination against matter. The text of St. John is central in its literal truth, "It is the Spirit which gives life; the flesh profits nothing" (John 6:64).

2. There is, however, a doctrine and a gnosis through which souls can escape the alienation of these latter days. That way is through a "double spiritual understanding" of scripture as set out in the work of Joachim:

   > Sacred scripture, as some of the saints say, would become worthless if it were naked to all. On this, you ought to consider, O Man, who it is who speaks in the gospel and knows that the Spirit of the Lord is in it. Learn to respect in the Sacred scriptures a spiritual understanding.[159]

3. Through this gnosis, the spirituals shall be transformed. "We shall not be what we have been, but we shall begin to be other."[160]

   > For we, called in these latest times to follow the spirit[161] rather than the letter, ought to obey, going from illumination to illumination, from the first heaven to the second, and from the second to the third, from the place of darkness into the light of the moon, that at last we may come out of the moonlight into the glory of the full Sun.[162] [163]

4. This gnosis, at least in the beginning, will belong to a certain core of the spiritual elite, as in the teaching of a number of classical gnostic sects. This "pneumatic" elite will be the monastic society of autonomous persons which both signifies and represents the meaning of the Third Age in which the previously hidden, sacred meaning of worldly history will be manifested. The Third Age will render meaningful the "new earth" of Revelation, in which past things will have passed away.

   Through the persons of the faithful, prophecy will transform hitherto refractory reality; there will be, at last, a *renovatio mundi*, a metastatic transformation within history itself. That transformation will at last embrace all humanity, creating[164] a "kingdom of the saints." The evil forces must, of

---

159 Corrington's note: "*Tractatus Super Quatuor Evangelia*, trans. from the text of E. Buonaiuti by James Counahan, PhD., sec. 4."

160 Corrington's note: "Joachim of Fiore, *Psalterium decem cordarum abbatis Joachim* (Venice: 1527), quoted in Frank Manuel, *Shapes of Philosophical History* (Stanford, CA: Stanford University Press, 1965), 40." Reworked this citation based on Chicago Style and on Manuel's note. Removed chapter title "Augustine and Joachim."

161 Corrington capitalized "Spirit," but in the original it is "spirit," and he lowercased "sun" (at the end of the sentence), which is capitalized in the original.

162 Corrington's note: "Joachim of Fiore, *Liber Concordie*, quoted in Reeves, *Influence of Prophecy*, 292."

163 Corrington's note: "See Foerster, *Gnosis*, 1:172, a fragment from Heracleon in relation to Valentinianism, which shows the antiquity of 'spiritual' interpretation among the Gnostics, and the distinction between those who worshipped in flesh, and those who worshipped in spirit and in truth. Fleshly worship, to Heracleon, represents those who 'worshipped the creation, and not the true creation.' In *Megale Apophasis*, it is said that the nature of fire is 'double,' part apparent, part hidden, as is the meaning of scripture to Joachim." In the original, this note interrupts another footnote, and in the margin there is a handwritten note that states, "note refers to previous #." Because of the awkwardness of a footnote within a footnote, these two footnotes have been combined as one.

164 Corrington wrote "created" in the original.

course, be resisted and destroyed in a series of awful apocalyptic encounters, and the vanguard of the spiritual movement will be the contemplative orders.

5. The final *status* within history would then become a situation of "peace and beatitude," a final consummation. The followers of Joachim made clear that this final *status* would be political:

> The future in the third status belongs chiefly to a rejuvenated Roman church. At the sound of the seventh trumpet the mystery of labor will be completed, the partial life of action will pass away and the perfect life of contemplation will appear, resuscitating the sevenfold spiritual intelligence. The Greek church will return to the true fold, the Jews will be converted, and the day of liberty for the church will dawn. When the third status dawns,—'quem et in ianius iam tenemus'—the only authority remaining will be the ecclesia contemplantium.[165]

The acosmic pleromatic state of the classical gnostics is transformed in the Joachitic speculation into a future earthly situation, but it remains pleromatic nonetheless, and has become, obviously, the model for the host of messianic and chiliastic eschatological enterprises, which followed from the work of Joachim and his immediate successors. The "vertical" gnosis of classical gnosticism becomes, at the hands of Joachim and his followers, conscious or otherwise, a "horizontal" gnosis. That which was "high" is now "yet to come." But whether the symbolisms are spatial or temporal, the experiences are identifiably the same. For example, in the *Super Hieremiam*, a spurious work attributed to Joachim dating from the middle of the thirteenth century, it is made clear that the third age stands beyond the catastrophe of the battle with Antichrist:

> Tribulation, of course, still looms large. The *ecclesia contemplativa* of the third *status* lies between the two tribulations of Antichrist and Gog at the close of history, or, to use the common metaphor, between the seventh head of the Dragon and its tail. To reach it (changing the metaphor) the hazardous crossing of the first gulf must be made: the ark must be carried over Jordan and the "passio vel tribulatio futura ecclesie generalis" must be suffered.[166]

The symbol of the dragon and the need to find a passage between head and tail shows the remarkable continuity of certain structures across time and space, and their recurrence in comparable cultural situations. Re-entry into the gleromatic state, the third age beyond the dualistic reality of the world as we experience it, is indeed a heroic and dangerous enterprise, "ferox et dura."[167]

---

165 Corrington's notes: "Reeves, *Influence and Prophecy*, 307."

166 Corrington's note: "Reeves, *Influence and Prophecy*, 306."

167 Corrington's note: "The dragon represents, also, according to Reeves and Hirsch-Reich, the Johanine Beast rising from the sea, and Joachim so denominated it. The dragon symbolizes antichrist in whatever manifestation it is

I would contend moreover that the symbolism of the Trinity as it is used in Joachim's work partakes of the Uroboratic and pleromatic structure as well. Godhead is susceptible to two types of interpretation in Joachim's work:

> Joachim, then, founded his interpretation of history upon a belief that it reflected the nature of the Godhead, sometimes in the two-fold relationship of Father and Son, sometimes in the three-fold relationship of Father, Son, and Holy Spirit. . . . it is important to realize that Joachim's spiritual longing to approach the mystery of the Triune God was part and parcel of his scriptural and historical studies.[168]

The Father-Son dichotomy in Joachim's writing is the description of a field of spiritual order in an incomplete and unsatisfactory state: two ages, two testaments, the age of the law and the age of the gospel. But perfection demands the triune structure, procession of Father, Son, and Holy Spirit, as seen from the vantage point of the prophet of the third *status,* whose own speculations, indeed, have been inspired by that Spirit which is not yet truly represented in the world. There is, in a manuscript attributed to Joachim, a *figura* of the Trinity, in which the Divine Persons are shown in intertwined serpentine ascending nodes, framed by leafy branches, with the Holy Spirit at the apex, turning and flowing back down again to cross with the Son and the Father once more. The figure appears to represent the primacy of the Spirit and the Uroborotic[169] unity of the Divine Persons.[170] Indeed the coiled serpent, or dragon-figure, is a major symbolism for the *Mysterium Ecclesiae* in the work of Joachim and his followers, embodying the sweep of history itself in the figure of a single-headed coiled serpent.[171] The passage between the dragon's head and its tail is the way back from the misery of dualism, of a reality in which Old and New Testament offer no relief to the Spiritual who finds himself in an eon of conflict between Church and Empire, amidst general corruption and demoralization.

In terms of the structure of consciousness, the central meaning of the symbolism of the Third Age is the reconciliation of opposites which have come to plague history once again, as in the ecumenic age. The tensions, temporarily either driven underground or held in *stasis* by the fervor of institutional and doctrinal creation in the *Sacrum Imperium,* have become unbearable once more. As in the time of the breakup of the old cosmological empires, the experience of those who speculate

---

found, according to Joachim. See Marjorie Reeves and Beatrice Hirsch-Reich, *The Figurae of Joachim of Fiore* (Oxford: Clarendon Press, 1972), 146, et. seq."

168   Corrington's note: "Reeves and Hirsch-Reich, *Figurae,* 20."

169   Should read "uroboric."

170   Corrington's note: "Graphics collection, Zurich Central Library, Bx606, reprinted in C. G. Jung, *Aion,* opposite 254."

171   Corrington's note: "See Reeves and Hirsch-Reich, *Figurae,* plates 34, 36, 44."

upon and yearn for the Third Age is the experience of living amidst *pseudos,* amidst a species of untruth, which cannot simply be corrected by reformist zeal.

The exodus from reality which typified classical gnosticism was a vertical structure, which was produced by the recurrent concupiscent power-drives of the Persian, Macedonian, and Roman orders. The response to these radically secular orders was the attempt to create a Second Reality which, however warped and partial, countered the malevolence and meaninglessness of the power-orders with equally radical pneumatic orders. These constituted civilizational structures of the kind Neumann refers to as compensatory spiritual and cultural structures.

The situation in the late twelfth century was, in terms of historical detail, vastly different. Yet the archetypal response of horror at the apparent disintegration of spiritual meaning in the field of reality dominated by the Church was much the same. The millennium just past had not seen the return of Him for whom all creation awaited, groaning in travail.

> Man's original dependence on a pneumatic sphere, to which he clung like a child to its mother, was threatened by the kingdom of Satan. From him the pneumatic man was delivered by the Redeemer, who broke the gates of hell and deceived the archons: but he was bound to the kingdom of heaven in exactly the same degree. He was separated from evil by an abyss. This attitude was powerfully reinforced by the immediate expectation of the Second Coming. But when Christ did not reappear, a regression was only to be expected. When such a great hope is dashed and such great expectations are not fulfilled, then the libido perforce flows back into man and heightens his consciousness of himself by accentuating his personal psychic processes; in other words he gradually moves into the centre of his field of consciousness. This leads to separation from the pneumatic sphere, and an approach to the realm of the shadow. Accordingly, man's moral consciousness is sharpened, and, as a parallel to this, his feeling of redemption becomes relativized. The Church has to exalt the significance and power of her ritual in order to put limits to the inrush of reality. In this way she inevitably becomes a "kingdom of this world."[172]

The rescue of the field of consciousness from the vast array of classical gnostic speculations between the second and fourth centuries turns out not to have been a definitive victory. On the contrary, the Christian synthesis, for all its passion and profundity, depended psychically upon the promise of a final eschatological event which, because it would conclude and consummate history, made history bearable. But every promise given *sine die* is interpreted somehow, and the non-scriptural, but popular notion that Christ would

---

172　Corrington's note: "Jung, *Aion,* 256."

return in a "great year," a millennium, may well have undergirded the stability of the Church such as it was, in a doctrinal sense from the time of Augustine until the twelfth century.

Jung apparently supposes that the whole success of the Christian endeavor was founded in part at least upon the promise of the imminent return of Christ and the chiliastic new order to follow. The wearing thin of the spiritual expectation manifested itself at first in the late medieval orgy of Millennialism recorded in Norman Cohn's *Pursuit of the Millennium*, and afterward in the clearly seen shift from a vertical to a horizontal vision: from an eschatology of the Beyond to an eschatology of the Future. The loss of faith in a Christian millennium brought the "libido" flowing back into man once more from its proper Christian positionality outside man. At this point, one must notice that the psychological jargon-term echoes the use of the term by Augustine. The *libido Christi* is contracted to a *libido dominandi*; the fragility of faith is shattered by the false speculation of knowledge in the gnostic sense. The loss of faith not only relativizes the redemptive aspect of the church, but, over time, relativizes even the valuation of the structure of consciousness and the meaning of its participation in the process of reality. "Objective" thought, rigorously perceived, as in the philosophes and the Newtonian type of scientist, is only possible when the possessor of "objectivity" views himself as an object among objects—to the exclusion of any other stratum of meaning. The result of such a mutilation of consciousness is not only to render the Church as a "kingdom of this world," but to condemn the "objective" observer who holds such sentiments to the bitter consistency of construing himself as a creature of this world as well.

It must be obvious by now that there is a radical antithesis between *pistis* and gnosis, between faith and knowledge in the gnostic sense. Faith, as Paul explained it, is "the substance of things hoped for, the evidence of things unseen" (Heb. 11:1).[173] It is the concrete belief in what cannot be known within history. It is substance and evidence in the field of differentiated Christian consciousness in the sense that through *pistis* the structure of human consciousness moves beyond itself, becoming a vector rather than a reversible process, and by so doing reveals to man the luminous and transcosmic implications of his consciousness. The symbolism of the Resurrected as it appears in the work of Paul, despite its gnostic overtones and vocabulary, is an anti-gnosis. It knows "nothing but Christ, and Him crucified ( )."[174] [175] Christ has "conquered the cosmos" not by escaping it or nullifying its

---

173   The KJV reads, "Now faith is the substance of things hoped for, the evidence of things not seen."

174   The empty parenthetical is in the original. Corrington probably intended to add something here.

175   Corrington's note: "Charles Guignebert, *The Jewish World in the Time of Jesus* (New Hyde Park, NY: University Books, 1954), 245–46, et seq."

meaning, but by entering it and establishing the center of the structure of human consciousness as its openness toward the Father. But of equal importance is the insight that the new ordering of the soul through faith does not carry with it either the need or the possibility of the abolition of the cosmos through an act of gnostic magic. The nature of the cosmos and its duration, albeit groaning and filled with travail, remains. Added to it, however, is the *amor dei* of Augustine, in sharp and permanent distinction to the *amor sui*. The question is then formulated in terms of Pauline Christianity not as a battle between the love of God and an *amor mundi,* as it is falsely formulated by the gnostics, but between the love of God and the love of self. The evil in the world is not an inherent characteristic of creation as the gnostics would have it, but an inherent characteristic of the defective human structure of consciousness which allows its libidinous elements to turn back upon itself, thus mutilating the structure itself. The loss of faith is the symbolism which underlines this turning-around by which the eschatological vector of human consciousness toward the divine ground becomes what Neumann calls the "incestuous" return to the threadbare pleroma of radical self-love. This perversion, triggered by interior and exterior events, and absorbing the entire field of reality, moves the libido of the spiritual adept to the center of the field, displacing any sense of the source of its own existence or of the context in which it exists. Voegelin has called this operation variously *egophany*, or *gigantimachia*.[176] Whatever it is called, it is "a system divorced from reality."[177]

What Jung refers to as a heightening of consciousness in man, with the resultant gradual separation of consciousness from the "pneumatic sphere" can be described in more traditional language as a loss of the *amor dei* and the concomitant internalization of the libido, thus leaving the field of consciousness wholly to the *amor sui*. The process is not so obvious in the work of Joachim and his followers from a literary point of view. The speculative construction of a Third Realm in which the Spirit will dominate seems, literarily, a yearning for the Future Vision of a promised state of worldly perfection. But the immanentization of eschatological meaning renders that meaning subject to the manipulations of those who announce it. And that manipulation is virtually announced when we note further that the Third Age will be defined and shaped by the monastic orders of Spirituals who, it so happens, include Joachim and his followers, both Franciscan and Dominican. The renovated Church will not be a Mystery, an institutionalized probing of the meaning of the process of reality and the structure of consciousness. Rather it will be a merging of the divergent *civitas mundi* and the *civitas dei*. History as that zone of consciousness, which both recognizes and attempts to reconcile the existentially

---

176   *Egophany* and *gigantimachia* were in quotation marks; changed to italics because they are terms being mentioned and explained.

177   Corrington's note: "Guignebert, *Jewish World*, 244."

distinct realms will cease to exist, because the dimension in which it is, on principle, incomplete, will have ceased to be a mystery and will, at most, be a problem.

What occurs in the Joachitic speculation is that the meaning of the intramundane Third Age becomes the single focus for the whole of being itself. Augustine's skillfully maintained differentiation between sacred history and mundane history is blurred or destroyed and the famous remark of Clemenceau, "Ah yes, Padre, but everything belongs to Caesar" is foreshadowed. The flattening of history to a non-mysterious chain of future events, however pietistic that future and those events may be, constitutes a destruction of the manifold of experienced reality, and, predictably, hands the meaning of being over to the power-forces which, even in Joachim's day, had perfected their concupiscent[178] appetites into a series of pragmatically successful partial orders, each striving to oust all the others.[179]

Underlying Joachim's flattening of the process of history to a single dimension is the peculiar doctrine of St. Ambrose symbolized as *kenosis:*

> Luna is diminished that she may fill the elements. Therefore is this a great mystery. To her it was given by Him who confers grace upon all things. He emptied her that he might fill her, as He also emptied Himself that He might fill all things. He emptied Himself that he might come down to us. He came down to us that He might rise again for all. . . . Thus has Luna proclaimed the mystery of Christ.[180]

The concept, rife with astrological elements and perhaps a touch of alchemy, even in its Ambrosian form, is gnostic. It suggests, not simply, a metastatic transformation of the cosmos and human reality, but an emptying of the Ground of Being into the cosmos, into history, so that existence in an intramundane sense becomes the sole field of being. This flattening of reality into a single field, aside from its ontological absurdities, illustrates the severe derailment of consciousness pushing itself into an exclusive position in the center of the field, purporting that the kenosis of the Ground has at once ended the separation of divine and mundane history, and rendered the zone of mundane history divine. The demonic act of constricting the whole field of reality into the meagre[181] confines of an egophanic Third Age in which all of being is kenotically exhausted, poured out into history,

---

178 Corrington had "concupiscential."

179 Corrington's note: "See Werner Heisenburg, "Positivism, Metaphysics and Religion," in *Physics and Beyond* (New York: Harper & Row, 1972)."

180 Corrington's note: "Ambrose, *Hexameron*, bk. 4, ch. 8, pt. 32. This concept appears again in an even more bizarre form in 1965 in Thomas J. J. Altizer, *The Gospel of Christian Atheism* (Philadelphia: Westminster Press, 1966)." There is no edition listed for Ambrose. The passage, because of its ellipses (used by Jung), appears to have been quoted from Jung's *Mysterium conjuntionis* (vol. 14 of his Collected Works). Added the 1966 publication date for Altizer's work, even though it conflicts with the 1965 date provided by Corrington.

181 More common spelling: "meager."

adumbrates the narrowed and pneumopathological structure of consciousness which follows upon the Joachitic derailment. When self-interpretation places the power-complex of the ego as the centerpiece of the interpretation, the spiritual catastrophe is complete.

The transference from a gnosis, which denies the world to one which denies everything but the world in effect, establishes a pattern so appealing to human appetites that it is virtually irreversible. Classical gnosticism with its theme of exodus from the world and hatred of the prison of the body stood in radical opposition to the empirical reality experienced by humanity at large and in absolute antagonism to human appetites (except in its libertine manifestations), but the "new" gnosticism triggered by Joachim's speculations pandered to the worst and most powerful tendencies in human nature. The exodus motif, dominant from Simon through Montanus, becomes now a theme of conquest and self-will. What is sought in the renovated gnosticism is not an extracosmic unity with a mythological and unknown Creator, but the utter domination and control of mundane history, and of the process of reality itself through gnosis, knowledge of the secrets through which the world can be transformed into no more than an expression of the will of the pneumopathic speculator.

It is superfluous to say that such a concept had no place in the thought of the Abbot or in that of his followers. Rather their motive was to revive the "eschatological passion" which had shaped primitive Christianity and stood as the originating symbol of the Church. The coming of the Kingdom of God, the Second Coming of Christ, repentance, rebirth, and resurrection—all had been crusted over in the Great Church by "a vast mass of vested interests and secular concerns."[182] The result, as Jung observes, had been the dominance of the Faith by the machinery of the Church, and a profound distrust on the part of Church officials of those who sought, by whatever means, to penetrate back through the encrustation to the initiating experiences upon which the Church had been built.

But Joachim's speculation transferred eschatological expectation from its original transhistorical position into the field of history itself by rendering it the proper subject not only of generalized prophecy, but of a kind of *roman à clef* treatment in which dates could be given and roles assigned to groups and individual players.

> Joachim, like Luther after him, could not foresee that his religious intention—
> that of desecularizing the Church and restoring its spiritual fervor—would,
> in the hands of others, turn into its opposite: the secularization of the world
> which became increasingly worldly by the very fact that eschatological
> thinking about last things was introduced into penultimate matters, a fact
> which intensified the power of the secular drive toward a final solution of

182   Corrington's note: "Löwith, *Meaning in History*, 157."

problems which cannot be solved by their own means and on their own level. . . . The revolution which had been proclaimed within the framework of an eschatological faith and with reference to a perfect monastic life was taken over, five centuries later, by a philosophical priesthood, which interpreted the process of secularization in terms of a "spiritual" realization of the Kingdom of God on earth. As an attempt at realization, the spiritual pattern of Lessing, Fichte, Schelling, and Hegel could be transposed into the positivistic and materialistic schemes of Comte and Marx. The third dispensation of the Joachites reappeared as a third International and a third *Reich*, inaugurated by a *dux* or a *Führer* who was acclaimed as a savior and greeted by millions with *Heil!*[183]

Löwith's analysis is incomplete only insofar as it fails to take into account the dreary procession of Joachitic gnosis prior to the philosophes of the seventeenth and eighteenth centuries. For the sake of dramatic presentation, he moves from Joachim and his followers through the epigones of the *Aufklärung* to the great and awesome horrors of the nineteenth and twentieth centuries. Such a treatment, quite correct on principle, neglects to show the pattern of transformation through which the symbols of Joachitic gnosis passed on their way from Calabria to Nuremburg and the Finland Station.

III

It is surprising that none of the scholars who deal with gnosticism either in its classical, medieval, or modern phases has seen fit to account for those works containing elements of Hermetic, magical, astrological, alchemical, or kabbalistic thought contemporary with the unquestionably gnostic works. The interpenetration of these subgenres together with the almost indiscernible blending of elements between them and what is specified as "gnostic" raises the question of whether, in fact, these subgenres, more or less, are not themselves simply special cases of gnostic thought. In this section, I will attempt to show that the named genres amount to no more than less generalized gnostic phenomena, that the same fundamental ideas and sentiments which underlie gnosticism form their bases, and that this great common theme has been noted and commented upon by various authorities previously. Finally, I will try to show that the common theme we discover in these various genres can be related to the monistic drive we have noted before, which has been described in psychological language by Erich Neumann.

The extant documents upon which we base our knowledge of Simon of Gitta, the Magus, "Father of all Heresies," invariably make much of the fact that, above and beyond his doctrinal claims, Simon was an accomplished magician, and he

183 Corrington's note: "Löwith, *Meaning in History*, 158–59."

attempted to purchase from the apostles the secret of their power (Acts),[184] obviously supposing them to be adepts like himself. Again both Foerster and Jonas include in their works on gnosticism the *Poimandres* attributed to Hermes Trismegistus. Jonas quotes portions of the document along with commentaries from Arnobius and Servius, which add to the gnostic elements obviously present and certain cosmogonic ideas dependent upon astrological concepts for their meaning.[185]

It appears that there is, perhaps, a *prima facie* case for an interrelation of the concepts which may be worth pursuing. What of alchemy?

Let us begin by suggesting once more the common theme which can be seen as uniting the apparently heterogeneous structures we are discussing: it is the speculation concerning a transformation or *renovatio* of the field of empirical reality through the metastatic power of a doctrine unknown to the ordinary run of human beings, and which is held by a certain company of adepts. Each of the structures mentioned above sets up a class of illuminati, magi, perfect masters, or whatever title the specific sect may use. These elite may, by way of the particular gnosis in question, alter or manipulate the process of reality, either spiritual, physical, or both, depending upon whether the *telos* of the speculator be salvation from the material world or transmutation of the elements.

Now we know from the texts that the doctrine of Simon Magus and his magic were one.[186] Even ignoring the lurid account of Simon in the *Pseudo-Clementines,* all accounts agree that he worked wonders and proposed a fairly primitive gnostic doctrine. Both Simon's theory and his practice proposed that belief in "The Standing One" allowed the believer, like Simon himself, to actually affect the process of reality, both spiritual and physical. This type of belief is found also, less exuberantly presented, in the work of Joachim's successors, as well as in Joachim's work itself. The *Novus Dux* would make the way straight, and "lead all mankind away from the love of earthly things and towards the love of things of the spirit."[187] The activist element in gnosticism is thus specifically contained in its relation to magic, astrology, and prophecy. Simon's magic, no less than Joachim's *Novus Dux* and monastic elite as agents of change, suggests the determination to alter reality by use of the tools available to the gnostic.

But no aspect of gnosticism contains a larger and more obvious commitment to active manipulation of reality than does the science of alchemy. The success or failure of spiritual *renovatio* is always debatable; the transmutation of physical reality presents to potential debaters a concrete and empirical construct which must be dealt with in concrete terms.

---

184 Corrington didn't finish the citation. Simon Magus appears in Acts 8:9–24.

185 Corrington's note: "Jonas, *Gnostic Religion*, 157."

186 Scholars seem to know little about Simon Magus; there is an ongoing debate regarding whether the Simon Magus mentioned in gnostic texts is real. Simon Magus also appears in apocryphal works.

187 Corrington's note: "Cohn, *Pursuit of the Millenium*, 110."

The transcendental theology of Christendom deals wholly with the evolution of man's spiritual potencies in the direction of perfect life in Christ. But the physical perfection of humanity is forgotten or ignored therein. Side by side, however, with transcendental theology, there flourished the Hermetic school of science in the West, nominally deriving its arcana from the theurgic philosophical traditions of the Graeco-Alexandrian period. The disciples of this college present themselves before us under two aspects—as Magi and Alchemists.[188]

Waite goes on to suggest that both Magus and Alchemists "operated in the region of phenomena, and the magicians represent the connecting link between transcendental evolutionary mysticism and what may be called the physical mysticism of the transmutory process."[189] Waite quite rightly sees in the fantasies of the alchemist a "double understanding" of the process which is at least as old as the great cosmological myths: the "upper-lower" and "inner-outer" correspondences upon which, as we have seen, the gnostic Gospel of St. Thomas rests—even as the pharaonic "Son of the Sun" symbolism of incarnation depends upon it.

The alchemical symbolism possessed, according to Waite, "a dual field of application—in man and in the mineral world. This application was not arbitrary, and it was not forced. There is a parity and parallel between all mystical processes, because all are evolutionary. The transcendental illumination of the illuminated Christian Mystic is the application of the evolutionary law to the soul of man. The physical Mysticism of the alchemists applied the same principle in the metallic kingdom, while the magician was concerned with the creation of an environment which acted as a species of forcing-house for the external eduction of the transcendental faculties of the inner man."[190]

The experimental foundation of alchemy had its philosophical basis, according to Waite, in "the Great Dogma of Hermes." The connection is also made by Waite between Hermetic literature and the tradition of freemasonry.[191] Thus the interconnections between all these speculative structures aiming at the transformation of spiritual or physical reality have been made with some frequency before. Waite also notes, for what it may be worth, that

[t]he rise of alchemical literature is coincident with the collapse of Theurgic Neo-Platonism, the downfall of Gnosticism, the proscription of the pagan cultus, when the extinction, or loss, of all knowledge of the inner meaning

---

188   Corrington's note: "Arthur E. Waite, *Azoth; or, The Star in the East* (repr., Secaucus, NY: University Books, 1973), 52."
189   Corrington's note: "Waite, *Azoth*, 52–53."
190   Corrington's note: "Waite, *Azoth*, 53."
191   Corrington's note: "Waite, *Azoth*, 52."

of Greek and Latin mythology—a knowledge vested in the priests of the cultus—was very likely to ensue, and, indeed, might seem almost inevitable. It was coincident also with degradation of the Mysteries, and with the materialization of the Christian Church.[192]

Jung describes the "mystical science" as

rather like an undercurrent to the Christianity that ruled on the surface. It is to this surface as the dream is to consciousness, and just as the dream compensates the conflicts of the conscious mind, so alchemy endeavors to fill in the gaps left open by the Christian tension of opposites.[193]

Jung goes on to elaborate his own highly technical description of the mythopoetic archetypal substrate upon which alchemy is based. Then, far more significantly, from our point of view, he says, "I hope the reader will not be offended if my exposition sounds like a Gnostic myth. We are moving in those psychological regions where, as a matter of fact, Gnosis is rooted. The message of the Christian symbol is Gnosis, and the compensation effected by the unconscious is Gnosis in even higher degree."[194]

One need not agree with Jung as to the "gnosis" of Christian symbolisms—though the interrelation of gnosis and certain Christian symbols is obvious. What is of central importance is his identification of alchemical with gnostic thought.

Lynn Thorndike notes that the earliest appearance of alchemy in classical literature dates from about the third century AD, which is virtually to agree with Waite in respect to alchemy's rise paralleling the decline of gnostic sects which flourished in the second and third centuries. Zosimus[195] of Panopolis, writing apparently in the third century, "says that the fallen angels instructed men in alchemy as well as in the other arts, and that it was the divine and sacred art of the priests and kings of Egypt, who kept it secret."[196] Once more, the connection between alchemy and Hermes is made, and even Democritus is cited by Pliny and Seneca as devoted to magic and a practitioner of alchemical transformations. Thorndike sees magic and alchemy as closely related:

Indeed, the papyri in which the works of alchemy occur are primarily magic papyri, so that alchemy may be said to spring from the brow of magic . . . There are also [in manuscripts] frequent bits of astrology and suggestions

---

192   Corrington's note: "Waite, *Azoth*, 54."

193   Corrington's note: "C. G. Jung, *Psychology and Alchemy*, 23."

194   Corrington's note: "Jung, *Psychology and Alchemy*, 25."

195   Alternative spelling: "Zosimos."

196   Corrington's note: "Lynn Thorndike, *During the First Thirteen Centuries of Our Era*, vol. 1 of *History of Magic and Experimental Science* (New York: Columbia University Press, 1923), 193–195."

of Gnostic influence. Often the encircling serpent, Ouroboros, who bites or swallows his tail, is referred to. . . . In a tract concerning the serpent Ouroboros we read, "A serpent is stretched out guarding the temple. Let his conqueror begin by sacrifice, then skin him, and after having removed his flesh to the very bones, make a stepping-stone of it to enter the temple. Mount upon it and you will find the object sought. For the Priest, at first a man of copper, has changed his color and nature, and become a man of silver; a few days later, if you wish, you will find him changed into a man of gold."[197]

There is little use in laboring the interrelations between gnosticism, magic, hermeticism, and alchemy. That the connections are real and present is attested to by various commentators, ancient and modern. It is equally clear that a lengthy monograph is required to trace the precise nature of the interrelations.

I would suggest that the reason this has not been done previously is that, until relatively recent times, scholarship in English has been rigidly compartmentalized. The conventional division of learning into "disciplines" has tended to require a separation between studies purportedly "theological," "history of ideas," "history of science," "psychology," "political science," and so on. The data-collecting and methodological advantages of "disciplines" is thus often outweighed by the inability of the specialist to penetrate—or indeed, even to recognize—the theoretical problem presented directly to him because its solution would require that he pass beyond the range of his specialist skills. Of course, unfortunate as it may be, problems in reality do not necessarily conform to the arbitrary divisions devised in the flush of rationalistic fervor. The shape of the problems takes its character from elements somewhat less flexible than course divisions in a school of arts and sciences.

In the quotation cited from Thorndike above, for example, the passage dealing with the Ouroboros[198] is richly illuminating if one is familiar with gnostic and cosmological mythopoesis, and with the analytical psychology of Jung and Neumann. From the standpoint of alchemy, the World Serpent known in some gnostic myths as Horos, the Limit, must be bypassed or re-entered or conquered in order to accomplish The Great Transformation. The Priest—or hero—is, by his act of sacrifice and conquest of the Ouroboros, able to enter the temple of the Pleroma, where he is changed by stages from base copper to gold—as the gnostic catechumen may, in the mythos of certain gnostic sects, move from hylic or chthonic to psychic and finally to pneumatic being. The myth of transformation from the base to the perfect is, as Waite tells us, parallel in the soul and in the physical world, according to all the sub-genres of gnosticism. More than that, the transformation of metals is only symbolic of the deepest meaning of the art: "Even as all magical power is in the inward man, so is the *Magnum Opus* defined to

---

197 Corrington's note: "Thorndike, *During the First Thirteen Centuries*, 197."
198 In the handwritten pages (and in BHG) Corrington wrote "Uroboros."

be before all things the creation of man by himself, and that perfect emancipation of his will which ensures his universal dominion over Azoth and the domain of Magnesia."[199]

The theme of transformation of physical reality thus merges into that of spiritual reality, and at last reveals itself as the metastatic fantasy of self-creation, a theme fundamental to the work of Feuerbach and Marx, alchemists less forthright than Waite. It is in Man that one must seek the First Matter of the philosophers, and his "self-creation" is the *magnum opus* of all such gnostic magic. While, inevitably, the language of all post-Joachitic gnostics, whether pseudo-alchemists or political activists, is laced with fulsome tributes to Christ, the angels, and the Faith, the drive to conquer the process of reality itself through gnostic transformation is in no significant way distinct from the same appetite as it appeared in Simon Magus when he sought to increment his magic by purchasing the power of the apostles. Exodus toward or conquest of the pleromatic state symbolized by the Ouroboros is the primary informing myth which lies behind all the gnostic sciences, magic, alchemy, hermeticism, astrology—or certain areas of contemporary science, social science, and paradoxically, the anti-science movements.

The case for a similar relationship between gnosticism and kabbalistic materials requires somewhat more detailed discussion and virtually a new beginning, since, while the Kabbalah is a product of the same archetypal mythopoesis discussed by Erich Neumann, its tangential connections with other gnostic forms arise and are mediated from within the structure of Talmudic Judaism—a basis quite different from that provided by Hellenized cosmological mythos and Iranian deposits laid down in a Christian context. Yet even so, the certainty of the connection can be briefly suggested. Gershom G. Scholem, who calls classical gnosticism "gnostic nihilism" describes what he considers the primary world experience of the gnostic mystic:

> In his mystical experience the mystic encounters Life. This "Life," however, is not the harmonious Life of all things in bond with God, a world ordered by divine law and submissive to His authority, but something very different. Utterly free, fettered by no law or authority, this 'Life' never ceases to produce forms and to destroy what it has produced. It is the anarchic promiscuity of all living things. Into this bubbling cauldron, this continuum of destruction, the mystic plunges.[200]

This plunge into anarchic destruction, which produces the "Luciferian radiance," is represented most notably in gnosticism by the libertine sects, capable of incredible acts of debasement.[201]

---

199 Corrington's note: "Waite, *Azoth*, 59."

200 Corrington's note: "Scholem, *On the Kabbalah*, 28–29."

201 Corrington's note: "See Foerster, *Gnosis*, 313–325, especially the passage quoted from Epiphanius, *Panarion*, 25–26."

The relationship between gnosticism and the Kabbalah[202] is far more general, however, according to Scholem. "Suffice it to say that tenuous as the threads connecting the oldest Kabbalistic tradition with gnostic tradition may be, I am convinced that they existed."[203]

But, he notes wisely, that the connection may not be one of historical or literary influence, but rather

> a parallelism of psychological and structural development . . . for gnosticism itself, or at least certain of its basic impulses, was a revolt, partly perhaps of Jewish origin, against anti-mythical Judaism, a late eruption of subterranean forces, which were all the more pregnant with myth for being cloaked in philosophy.
>
> In the second century of our era, Classical Rabbinical Judaism banished this form of heresy, seemingly for good; but in the Kabbalah this gnostic view of the world not only re-emerged as a theosophical interpretation of Jewish monotheism—and this at the height of the medieval Jewish rationalism—but was able to assert itself at the center of Judaism as its most secret mystery. In the Zohar and in Isaac Luria gnostic and quasi-gnostic symbols became for orthodox Kabbalists the profoundest expression of their Jewish faith.[204]

The parallels between classical gnosticism and its medieval eruption in Joachitic Christianity, and those between early Jewish apocalyptic gnosis and its reappearance in medieval Kabbalistic writing, is awesome. Scholem's erudition, moreover, draws the parallels sharply.

> The beliefs held by the radical wing of the Sabbatian movement—that great outburst of spiritualist Messianism—disclose striking parallels to the development which the teachings of Joachim of Floris[205] underwent in the middle of the thirteenth century at the hands of the radical "spirituals" of the Franciscan order. What Joachim meant by the "Eternal Gospel" is essentially the same as what the Kaballists meant by *Torah de 'atsiluth*. Joachim believed that in this Evangelium Aeternum the mystical meaning of the Book would be revealed in a new Spiritual Age and would take the place of the literal meaning. That is exactly what, *mutatis mutandi,* the *Torah* de 'atsiluth meant to the Kaballists before the Sabbatian movement. But some of the

---

202 Corrington spelled "Kabbalah" as "Kaballah" several times. Spelling corrected.

203 Corrington's note: "Scholem, *On the Kabbalah*, 97."

204 Corrington's note: "Scholem, *On the Kabbalah*, 97–98."

205 Fiore.

Franciscan followers of Joachim identified their masters with the "Eternal Gospel," which they regarded as a new revelation of the Holy Ghost. This is very much what happened to the *Torah de 'atsiluth* among the Sabbatians . . . The fulfillment of the new spiritual Torah implied the abrogation of the *Torah de-beri'ah*, which was taken to represent a lower state of being and identified purely and simply with Rabbinical Judaism. Antinomianism led to a mystical nihilism which preached the transvaluation of all hitherto existing values and adopted the slogan: *bittulah shel Torah zehu kiyumak*, "The annulment of the Torah is its fulfillment."[206]

For present purposes, it is not necessary to expand in detail the intimate ideational and experiential relationships between gnosticism and Kabbalah. The issue at hand is rather whether Kabbalah may reasonably and profitably be considered a subgenre of gnosticism.

A preliminary answer must be, as in the case of Hermeticism, that, pretermitting accidental distinctions attributable to the vastly different cultural and intellectual context in which Kabbalism arose, there seems little reason to suppose that the underlying spiritual experiences of the gnostic and the Kabbalist are sufficiently distinct to establish them as wholly separate categories of thought.[207]

As Scholem demonstrates, Kabbalism and the medieval gnosticism of Joachim of Fiore are flowers which spring from the same roots. In fact, the Jewish version persists in its original spiritual form much longer than does its Christian equivalent. In "The Gates of Paradise,"[208] written by Jacob Koppel Lifschitz in the eighteenth century, the language is amazingly like that of Joachim and his followers.

> In the *Shemittah* in which we live, the commandments of the Torah are a divine necessity . . . this Torah is called *Torah de beri'ah* and not *Torah de 'atsiluth*. For in this *shemittah* all creation, beri'ah, stems from a sphere, from which they [its works] develop and combine in a manner appropriate to the law of this *shemittah*. Consequently, we speak of a Torah of Creation, *Torah de beri'ah*. But in the preceeding[209] *shemittah*, which was one of grace

---

206 Corrington's note: "Scholem, *On the Kabbalah*, 83–84."

207 Corrington's note: "See A. E. Waite, The Holy Kabbalah: A Study of the Secret Tradition in Israel as Unfolded by Sons of the Doctrine for the Benefit and Consolation of the Elect Dispersed through the Lands and Ages of the Greater Exile (New Hyde Park, NY: University Books, 1960), especially p. 69: 'Yet Gnosticism is not Kabbalism, though there are occasional analogies between them, and something of a common source may be attributable to both.' See also Guignebert, Jewish World, esp. bk. 3, ch. 3, sec. 4, 'Judaism as a Syncretic Religion,' and bk. 4, ch. 2, sec. 3, 'The Syncretic Gnosis.' See also Adolphe Franck, The Kabbalah: The Religious Philosophy of the Hebrews (New Hyde Park, NY: University Books, 1967), 194–198, et passim. Israel Efros, in Studies in Medieval Jewish Philosophy (New York: Columbia University Press, 1974) points out Saadia Gaon's struggle against those Jewish scholars whose speculations lead toward the gnostic doctrine that an angel or demiurgus created the world and mankind. For the texts, see Saadia Gaon, The Book of Beliefs and Opinions, trans. Samuel Rosenblatt (New Haven: Yale University Press, 1948)."

208 Quotation marks in original.

209 Preceding.

and in which there was consequently neither evil desire nor reward nor punishment, a different cosmic law [*hanhagah*] necessarily prevailed. The words of the Torah were so interwoven as to meet the requirements of this specific cosmic law, and the actions that brought the preceding *shemittah* into being came from a higher sphere, namely that of Wisdom. And so, accordingly, its Torah is called *Torah de 'atsiluth,* for the meaning of '*atsiluth* is the secret of divine wisdom ... at the end of the sixth millennium[210] the light which precedes the cosmic Sabbath will spread its rays, swallowing death and driving the unclean spirit from the world. Then many commandments will be abrogated, for example, those relating to clean and unclean. Then a new cosmic law will prevail, in keeping with the end of this *shemittah,* as it is written in the *Book Temunah.* That is the meaning of the ancient words: "A new Torah will go forth."[211]

The shemittah (-im?)[212] are cosmic cycles, in each of which certain of God's attributes are revealed. Clearly Lifschitz speculates that in the sixth and final shemittah, as in Joachim's Third Age, a society of autonomous persons, freed from the original obligations of Torah, will come to dominate existence.

But even contemporary Kabbalistic thought seems to possess certain characteristics we associate with gnosticism. Scholem tells of a friend who went to Jerusalem in 1924 to learn of Kabbalah: "Finally he found a Kabbalist, who said to him: I am willing to teach you Kabbalah. But there is one condition, and I doubt whether you can meet it. The condition, as some of my readers may not guess, was that he ask not questions."[213]

The condition set out by the Kabbalist is less surprising when one reflects upon the close relationship between Kabbalah and gnosticism. The prohibition of questioning, as Voegelin has shown, is fundamental to gnostic thought, particularly in its modern variants. Such a condition is essential in order to preserve the Gnostic— or Kabbalistic—Second Reality. Scholem's surprise suggests the distance between his own perception of reality and that of the Kabbalistic variant of gnostic thought:

A body of thought that cannot be constructed from question and answer— that is indeed a strange phenomenon among Jews, the most passionate questioners in the world, who are famous for answering questions with questions. Here perhaps we have a first oblique reference to the special

---

210   Corrected from "millenium."

211   Corrington's note: "Scholem, *On the Kabbalah,* 84–85."

212   Corrington probably was deliberating about making this word plural. According to *Merriam-Webster Unabridged,* the plural of *shemittah* is *shemittot* or *shemitoth.*

213   Corrington's note: "Scholem, *On the Kabbalah,* 87."

character, preserved even in its latest forms, of this thinking which expounds but has ceased to inquire, a thinking which, as Schelling put it, might be termed "a narrative philosophy." To the great philosopher of mythology, it may be remembered, such a "narrative philosophy" was an ideal.[214]

But a philosophy, in which the Question is not a fundamental constituent is not a philosophy at all, but rather an ideology. The ideal of Schelling is fulfilled in ideological structures, but they are not philosophies; they are syncretic myths designed to deny the movement of consciousness from compact mythopoetic form to the differentiated noetic-pneumatic form[215] of realization. The ideological myths do not represent a reversal of differentiation, which is impossible on principle. Rather, they suggest the attempt to evade noetic structure by opposing to it a synthetic myth protected by the prohibition of questioning.

The prohibition of questioning is, negatively, the denial of movement in the process of consciousness, an attempt to establish stasis at some arbitrarily fabricated point in the process of reality; positively, the prohibition maintains that the "truth" set forth in the synthetic myth constitutes a definitive position in the process of consciousness beyond which only *pseudos*, falsehood, can possibly be discovered. To prohibit questioning, then, is to attempt to freeze the symbolisms which express human experience by suggesting that any extension of or alternative to those symbols constitutes factitiousness (*stasiodes*), rather than the reality of differentiating movement in human consciousness which is itself represented by the Question.

> The history of Judaism, perhaps to a greater degree than that of any other religion, is the history of the tension between these two factors—purity and living reality—a tension which has necessarily been heightened by the special character of Jewish monotheism . . . The more the philosophers and theologians strove to formulate a unity which negates and eliminates all symbols, the greater became the danger of a counter-attack in favor of the *living* God who, like all living forces, speaks in symbols.[216]

See Appendix C for Corrington's additional notes on gnosticism and modern thought.

---

214 Corrington's note: "Scholem, *On the Kabbalah*, 87."

215 In the original, rather than a hyphen, there is an equal sign (=).

216 Corrington's note: "Scholem, *On the Kabbalah*, 89."

A Brief History of Gnosticism, Part I

Approx. 1976

The exact dates for Part I and Part II of this essay are unknown. Portions of this essay, however, overlap with "Gnosticism and Modern Thought," so Corrington wrote at least some of the text while he wrote "Gnosticism and Modern Thought." It is not clear which essay came first or whether Corrington undertook "A Brief History of Gnosticism" as part of a larger project on gnosticism, perhaps an uncompleted book.

This essay examines how our empirical knowledge of the world, or experience, is necessarily bound up in the sum of our memory and interpretation of events and hence of our comprehension of history. Our experience is also an element of consciousness insofar as consciousness is the mind's awareness of itself in relation to the phenomenal world. The structure or makeup of consciousness is an ordered pattern of symbols. The structure of Gnostic consciousness is shaped by a hatred or dissatisfaction with the concrete reality of the world and an attempt to remake the world in the image of a false reality. Gnostic thought is regressive because it seeks to unite all things in an ideal state of unification that recalls the state of the infant in the womb whose radical break from the womb resulted in alienation and a sense of disorder.

In the epilogue to his classic study, *The Gnostic Religion*, Hans Jonas pointed out the similarity between gnostic thought and the thought of contemporary nihilist and existentialist thinking.

The question of "influences" and "connections" is not raised. Rather it is obvious that the similarities relate to the constitution of human consciousness rather than some repetitive feature of empirical human history (except as history is an aspect of consciousness).

Every human experience is embodied, that is, historical. It has a set of time-space co-ordinates and is unique because of that determination. At the same time, every human experience is simultaneously happening to a subject, and the subject is, in terms of the constitution of his consciousness, something other than unique. If his experiences are embedded in history, and his immediate and empirical responses to them constitute a four-dimensional non-repeating matrix, the process of consciousness itself possesses a structure which is determinative across the time-space matrix. That is why correlations such as the one professor Jonas pointed out take place.

But what is the structure of the process of consciousness? Is it a poetic invention, or a noetically verifiable pattern? I suggest that it is the latter. I would propose to show that certain primary gnostic symbols reveal, collectively, an organization of response to certain historical conditions which is neither random nor arbitrary, but fully determined by the structure of consciousness.

That the constellation of symbols we call *gnostic* arose within and under the pressure of the attenuated breakup of the great cosmological empires is well known. These symbols reflect the loss of cultural integrity, a radical rejection of world experience as it was lived under the ecumenic Hellenistic and Roman empires, with the consequent loss of intracosmic divinities and their mythopoetic binding force. We must believe that those whose eclectic creativity constructed the gnostic systems were moved by a profound nausea, a hatred of the world, pragmatically experienced as the inadequacy of the impenal symbols of order to resolve or hold in balance the tensions between the public *power-field* and the private *Benoma*, emptiness, left in the wake of vanished cultural structures in terms of which vast numbers of human beings had found their consciousness shaped. The loss of the empirical civilizational structures carried with it the concomitant loss of the sense of reality of the cosmos itself. The former surroundingness of the world had become unintelligible, a meaningless and abortive round of conquest and defeat, birth and death, a senseless rising and falling of denatured power-structures capable of dominating empirical reality for a time, but unable to give meaning or purpose to that reality. The result was the gnostic fabrication of a second reality.

The most revealing symbols evoked by gnostic experience were those dealing with the beginning and the end. These symbols, which I shall refer to as *pleromatic* symbols, pointed, in a variety of images and aspects, toward a primal, extracosmic unity, undifferentiated, androgynous, prior to all, "non-existent," "wholly other," outside time and space, utterly disconnected from the cosmos or with its abortive creation. These symbols, both cosmogonic[217] and paradisicial,[218] unified the gnostic vision of the "true reality" from which the pneumatics had been cast, according to a variety of mythopoetic vessions,[219] and to which, by nature, he would at last return.

But what, in the phrase of Clement of Alexandria, is the true knowledge of the *pleroma*,[220] the "gnosis of who we were, what have we become, where were we, into

---

217   Having to do with cosmogony, or mythical origin accounts of the universe.

218   Possibly "paradisiacal" or "paradisical."

219   Possibly "visions" or "versions."

220   Corrington mistyped *pleroma* as *plesoma*; spelling corrected.

what place we have been flung, whither are we hastening, from what delivered? What is birth, and what rebirth?"[221]

A useful starting-point in our attempt to penetrate the gnostic sentiments, in order to analyze[222] the fundamental structure of consciousness revealed [in][223] pleromatic symbols is a certain text from Hippolytus's *Refutatio*.[224] He offers the text as an example of the teaching of Simon of Gitta, the magus "Father of All Heresies." According to Hippolytus, Simon taught, in the *Megale Apophasis*, or *Great Announcement* thus:

> How then and in what manner does God mould men? In the Garden, he maintains. The Garden, he says, must be the womb; and scripture will teach us that this is true when it says "I am he that moulded thee in thy mother's womb" (Isa. 44:2), for this is how he makes the text run. The Garden, he says, is Moses' allegorical term for the womb, if one is to believe the text. But if God moulds man in his mother's womb, that is, in the Garden, as I said, the Garden must be the womb, and Eden the placenta, and the river which come out of Eden to water the Garden (Gen. 2:10) the navel.[225]

If I understand the text aright, Simon is here establishing the fundamental or ground-state of the gnostic view of reality. The womb and the Garden (paradesios)[226] are a single monistic and undifferentiated unit, and to speak of the one is to express the other. In some sense they are, in Simon's view, one. In Hippolytus, the correspondences between womb and Garden are set out at considerable length in an attempt, it appears, to bind together physical and psychic reality.

The womb, then, becomes at least the physical analogue for the *pleroma*,[227] the original state from which, in a host of gnostic systems, the "sparks of divinity" which constitute "spiritual men" have rained down and been captured in matter to form the essence of human beings.

To the Simon of the *Megale Apophasis*, the pleromatic state is "the dwelling place where the root of all things has its foundation."[228]

---

221 A paraphrase of the definition of *gnosis* according to Theodoto, a Valentinian adherent of gnosticism.

222 Changed from British to American spelling.

223 Editor's addition.

224 Beginning here, this essay overlaps with Gnosticism and Modern Thought (GMT).

225 Corrington's note: "Werner Foerster, ed., *Gnosis: A Selection of Gnostic Texts*, trans. Robert MacLachlan Wilson (Oxford: Clarendon Press, 1972), 1: 266, et seq. Another translation is available for comparison in *The Ante-Nicene Fathers: Translations of the Writings of the Fathers down to AD 325.*, ed. Alexander Roberts and James Donaldson (repr., Grand Rapids, MI: W. B. Eerdmans, 1967), 5:77, et seq." In Corrington's note, the title *The Ante-Nicene Church Fathers* has been corrected to *The Ante-Nicene Fathers*. The date Corrington used for this work (1967) has not been changed, although Corrington probably used the 1965 edition. "Gnosticism and Modern Thought" cites this passage as page 256 (not 266).

226 Paradeisos.

227 Capitalized in original; because Corrington does not capitalize *pleroma* elsewhere, the word has been changed to lowercase.

228 Corrington's note: "Foerster, *Gnosis*, 1:252–53."

This "unnamed highest heaven," as Severus calls it, is a heaven of complete and undifferentiated unity with the Unknown God and his Aeons, variously named and numbered in different gnostic mythopoetic versions.[229] The Great God can, in most gnostic myths, only be described negatively, but the Aeons and sometimes even the Great God or Protos Anthropos, as he is sometimes called, are described as an ultimate and unspeakable unity, bisexual, male and female in one.[230]

Now the pleroma possesses "*one* desire and one purpose," according to Irenaeus.[231] All the Aeons are alike, at one.[232] The pneumatics shall enter the "bridal chamber," attain the vision of the Father, and enter into the "intelligible and eternal marriage of the [pleromatic] union."[233] In an interesting parallel to the pleromatic[234]-womb analogy of Simon, there is a brief fragment in Hippolytus (*Refutation* 6.37.6–8) which is accepted by Foerster as an authentic fragment of the teaching of Valentinus:

> From the depths come forth fruits,
> From the womb comes forth a child.[235]

Depth, *Bathos*, is, of course, one of the many names given the Unknown God[236]—who is often characterized, as we shall see, as Mother-Father united in one.

Virtually all of the gnostic mythologies establish the initial act of cosmic creation as an act of differentiation, some act whereby other entities arise from the Unnamed, the Hidden, the Great God of the pleromatic heaven. The act of creation is identifiable with the beginning of differentiation. Whether the quotation in question from Hippolytus excerptions[237] from *The Great Announcement* establishes a necessary Sophia-female figure as inherent in the creation mythopoesis and as the initial break with primal unity, it is nonetheless true that almost every version of the early gnostic mythopoesis reaches a point where an "abortion" or defective being

---

229 Corrington's note: "Foerster, *Gnosis*, 1: 46."

230 Corrington's note: "*Apocrypon of John*, 28.1., in Foerster, *Gnosis*, 1:108; Irenaeus, *Adversus Haereses*, 1.1, in Foerster, *Gnosis*, 1:127; Irenaeus, *Adversus Haereses*, 1.2.5, in Foerster, *Gnosis*, 1:196; Irenaeus, *Adversus Haereses*, 1.14.1, in Foerster, *Gnosis* 1:203. It would take up much time and space to document completely all the passages in patristic and gnostic literature alluding to androgynous or bisexual characteristics of the Hidden God in gnostic mythism and hence the undifferentiated character of the pleroma."

231 Corrington's note: "Irenaeus, *Adversus Haereses*, 1.2.6."

232 Corrington's note: "Irenaeus, *Adversus Haereses*, 1.2.5."

233 Corrington's note: "Clement, *Excerpta ex Theodoto*, 64.1."

234 Changed from *pleromatci*.

235 From Valentinus's hymn "Summer."

236 Corrington capitalized this term elsewhere, so it has been capitalized here.

237 This sentence is difficult to parse. Here is a slightly edited version:
Whether the quotation in question—from Hippolytus's excerptions from *The Great Announcement*—establishes a necessary Sophia-female figure as inherent in the creation mythopoesis and as the initial break with primal unity, it is nonetheless true that almost every version of the early gnostic mythopoesis reaches a point where an "abortion" or defective being is produced from the process of differentiation.

is produced from the process of differentiation.[238] This defective being is variously called Self-Willed, Aldaoboath, Sabaoth, or Achemoth, and is frequently identified with the God of Israel.[239]

If we assume that the passage quoted from the *Megare Apophasis* is representative of early gnostic thought (without regard to the textual question of whether Simon of Gitta was or was not its author), we must recognize that by 236 AD at the latest, there was extant the notion that womb and pleroma were analogous.

It is here that we find it useful to discuss the work of Erich[240] Neumann, whose classic study, *The Origins and History of Consciousness*, offers a crucial insight into the growth process of the consciousness. Neumann describes the nature of human consciousness in terms of an evolutionary development, which is to say a growth in terms of differentiation: "The evolution of consciousness as a form of creative evolution is the peculiar achievement of Western man. Creative evolution of ego consciousness means that, through a process stretching over thousands of years, the conscious system has absorbed more and more unconscious contents and progressively extended its frontiers."[241]

This evolution of consciousness is simultaneously a personal and a societal process: "The evolution of consciousness by stages is as much a collective human phenomenon as a particular individual phenomenon. Ontogenetic development may therefore be regarded as a modified recapitulation of phylogenetic development."[242]

One must be careful to avoid the limitations of the biological implications which Neumann's positivistic heritage required of him. But the analogy is not without merit. The interplay between the proximal and distal aspects of the individual transformation boundary, between the "inside" and the "outside" of the human nervous system constitutes the matrix of any human culture in which consciousness arises and exfoliates. Thus "a substantial part of mythology is seen as the unconscious self-delineation of the growth of consciousness in man."[243]

Neumann makes use of the mythological stages in the evolution of human development, of consciousness, beginning with the stage in which "the ego is contained in the unconscious, and [leads] up to a situation in which the ego not only becomes aware of its own position and defends it heroically, but also becomes

---

238   Corrington's note: "See the *Letter of Eugnostus*, in Foerster, *Gnosis*, 1:25–34; *The Hypostasis of the Archons*, in Foerster, *Gnosis*, 1:40–52; and Foerster 1, passim." In the original, two footnotes here were separated by a line indicating that they should be different footnotes. However, this exact passage is also in GMT, where the placement of the footnotes is much more obvious, so the format in GMT has been followed.

239   Corrington's note: "In Foerster, Irenaeus, *Adversus Haereses*, 29.2; *Apocryphon of John* 30–5; 51."

240   Throughout the manuscript, Corrington had "Eric."

241   Corrington's note: "Erich Neumann, *The Origins and History of Consciousness*, Bollingen Series, no. 42 (Princeton: Princeton University Press, 1954), xviii."

242   Corrington's note: "Neumann, *Origins and History*, xx."

243   Corrington's note: "Neumann, *Origins and History*, xxiv."

capable of broadening and relativizing its experiences through the changes effected by its own activity."[244]

Neumann describes the initial state from which human consciousness erupts, both within the individual and within the cultural matrix. He sets out the symbols of "original perfection"—the circle, the sphere, the egg, and the *rotundum*, the round of alchemy.[245] These are symbols of "the perfect state in which the opposites are united—the perfect beginning because the opposites have not yet flown apart and the world has not yet begun, the perfect end because in it the opposites have come together again in a synthesis and the world is once more at rest."[246]

This primal unity, comparable to the stage of compact consciousness described by Voegelin, is that in which "the World Parents, heaven and earth, lie one on top of the other in the round, spacelessly and timelessly united, for as yet nothing has come between them to create duality out of the original unity. The container of the masculine and feminine opposites is the great hermaphrodite, the primal creative element."[247]

This image, Neumann suggests, brings to mind Plato's Original Man, where too the androgynous round stands at the beginning.[248] Such a figure is almost a commonplace in gnostic literature dealing with the pleroma. There is "the Father who upholds all things and nourishes the things that begin and end. This is he who stands, took his stand, and will stand, being a male-and-female power like the pre-existing power which neither begins nor ends, existing in unity; for from this proceeded the conception which is in unity, and became two. Now he was one; for having this [conception] in himself he existed by himself."[249]

But the ultimate symbol selected by Neumann for the Beginning is that of the Uroboros, the primal dragon which bites its own tail, self-begotten and eternal. The choice is an apt one, in that few symbols can be traced so widely. This particular symbol of the round is the "symbolic self-representation of the dawn-state showing the infancy both of mankind and of the child."[250]

Since the ego has and can have no experiences of its own in the embryonic state, not even psychic experiences—for its experiencing consciousness still slumbers in the germ—the later ego will describe this earlier state, of which it has

244 Corrington's note: "Neumann, *Origins and History*, 5."

245 Corrington's note: "Neumann, *Origins and History*, 8. See also Carl Jung, *Psychology and Alchemy*, vol. 12 of *The Collected Works of C. G. Jung* (London: Routledge & Kegan Paul, 1953), s.v. *rotundum*." Publication information added for the Jung reference.

246 Corrington's note: "Neumann, *Origins and History*, 8." Page numbers added for this footnote and the following footnote.

247 Corrington's note: "Neumann, *Origins and History*, 9."

248 Corrington's note: "Plato, *Timaeus*, 34 (Comford translation). Cited in Neumann, *Origins and History*, 8." Added the attribution to Neumann.

249 Corrington's note: "Hippolytus, *Refutation* 6, g. 4–18.7 [18.4–5.] (From the *Great Announcement*.)"

250 Corrington's note: "Neumann, *Origins and History*, 11. For the provenance of the Uroboros symbolism, see Neumann, 9–10. See also Carl Jung, *Collected Works*, vol. 9, bk. 2, *Aion*."

an indefinite but symbolically graspable knowledge, as a "pre-natal" time. It is the time of existence in paradise where the psyche has her preworldly abode, the time before the birth of the ego, the time of unconscious envelopment, of swimming in the ocean of the unborn.[251]

The question of origin is always answered by "womb," whatever symbol be chosen to express it. But the answer refers, obviously, to more than a concrete aspect of female creatures. Rather it is an image, a cosmic region where origins are veiled. "In the pleromatic phase of life, when the ego swims about in the round like a tadpole, there is nothing but the Uroboros in existence. Humanity does not yet exist. There is only divinity; only the world has being. . . . The world is experienced as all-embracing."[252]

The infantile ego and the ego of early humanity are seen as the same by Neumann, "feebly developed, easily tired." The individual ego, like the collective ego, rises like a small island out of the ocean of unconsciousness, "then sinks back again. . . . he swims about in his instincts like an animal." This is the maternal side of the Uroborotic state in its positive manifestation, "the refuge for[253] all suffering, the goal of all desire." "The dawn state of perfect containment and contentment was never an historical state (Rousseau was still projecting this psychic phase into the historical past, as the 'natural state' of the savage). It is rather the image of a psychic state of humanity, just discernible as borderline image."[254]

Neumann describes what he calls the "ascent to consciousness" as "unnatural." "The desire to remain unconscious is a fundamental human trait." Or rather "fixation in the unconscious"—what we would call the *compact stage* of consciousness—appears to be the "natural" thing, if only in statistical terms. Thus it is "the struggle between the specifically human and the universally natural"—or unconscious—which "constitutes the history of man's conscious development."[255]

The symbolism of the Uroboros as the rotundum, the great primeval round of pre-consciousness, thus not only describes the infantile individual consciousness, but the collective cultural consciousness of humanity as well, according to Neumann. This participation in a world without differentiation and ego structure has been described by Eric Voegelin at the beginning of *Israel and Revelation*:

> Whatever man may be, he knows himself a part of being. The great stream of being, in which he flows while it flows through him, is the same stream to

---

251 Corrington's note: "Neumann, *Origins and History*, 11–12." Corrected these words based on Neumann's text: *symbolically-graspable* to *symbolically graspable*, *pre-worldly* to *preworldly*, *Paradise* to *paradise*. Placed this quotation in the text proper, but in the original it appears to be an additional footnote.

252 Corrington's note: "Neumann, *Origins and History*, 14–15."

253 Corrington had "of" in the original; corrected to match Neumann's text.

254 Corrington's note: "Neumann, *Origins and History*, 16."

255 Corrington's note: "Neumann, *Origins and History*, 16."

which belongs everything else that drifts into his perspective. The community of being is experienced with such intimacy that the consubstantiality of the partners will override the separateness of substances. We move in a charmed community where everything that meets us has force and will and feelings, where animals and plants can be men and gods, where men can be divine and gods are kings, where the feathery morning sky is the falcon Horus and the Sun and Moon are his eyes, where the underground sameness of being is a conductor for magic currents of good or evil force that will subterraneously reach the superficially unreachable partner, where things are the same and not the same, and can change into each other.[256]

It is the original tension, the tension from which every other tension must be understood to arise, this breaking from the round to become a *self*[257] with autonomous meaning. To experience the parting or destruction of the Uroboros— otherwise symbolized as the parting of the World Parents, the two sides of the round which are male and female sexually and yet sexlessly one in the serpent form—[258]is to experience a break from the ground-state of living being, to reach for an "unnatural" state, an excited state, which is "specifically human."[259]

It seems evident that the pleromatic state Neumann describes as a "borderline image" describing human consciousness at its earliest discernible stage is virtually identical with the symbolism of the pleroma set out in gnostic systems. Neumann's choice of the term *pleromatic* to describe the "dawn-state" is not simply a fortuitous metaphor. It is accurate. The quotation given from *The Great Announcement* ascribed to Simon Magus in Hippolytus has, in this connection, only the added virtue of a certain literalness. Its implications cannot be avoided. From the gnostic point of view, Paradise is, existentially speaking, the womb. It is the place from whence the sparks of pneuma,[260] which form "spiritual" men, come or are flung. It is the place to which they yearn to return. In certain sects, Neumann's symbolism is evident in a surprisingly specific manner. Worship of the serpent, the Uroboros, is commonly attributed to the Ophians, who characterize the Great Circle of the cosmos, the eternal sea of space as *Leviathan*, or the *Soul of the Universe*.[261]

To the Naassenes who, according to Hippolytus, "had the effrontery to praise the serpent," the serpent is "liquid substance" and nothing which exists can exist

---

256   Corrington's note: "Eric Voegelin, *Order and History*, vol. 1, *Israel and Revelation* (Baton Rouge, LA: Louisiana State University Press, [1956]), 3." There was no publication information for *Order and History*, but elsewhere Corrington cites the 1956 edition, so that edition has been added to Corrington's attribution to Voegelin.

257   Placed in single quotation-marks in the original.

258   Replaced comma with an "em dash."

259   Corrington's note: "Mircea Eliade, *The Myth of the Eternal Return* (Princeton: Princeton University Press, 1971), 37–42, esp. 40n70. Also 55–60."

260   Comma added for clarity.

261   Corrington's note: "Origen, *Contra Celsum*, 4:25, cited in Foerster, *Gnosis*, 1:95."

without it. It has "the goodness of everything else within it, as in the horn of the unicorn."[262] They say that "Eden is the brain, being, as it were, 'bounden' and enfolded in the membranes which surround it, like the heavens; and Paradise, they think, is man, to the extent of his head alone."[263] The Naassenes describe the Great God as Adamas, bisexual, both Father and Mother, "Man of the Mighty Name." According to the summary of Ophitic thought in Irenaeus, the Great Mother, Prunikos-Sophia,[264] attempting to counteract the works of her son, the creator-god Ialdobaoth, sends the serpent to seduce Adam and Even[265] into breaking Ialdobaoth's commandment, knowing that if they should eat of the fruit of the forbidden tree, they would come to realize that the creator was not the Great God of the Beyond, but the True God was the Primal Inutterable Man of the pleroma.[266] "It is the first success of the transcendent[267] principle against the principle of the world, which is vitally interested in preventing knowledge in man as the inner-worldly hostage of Light: the serpent's action marks the beginning of all *gnosis* on earth which thus by its very origin is stamped as opposed to the world and its God, and indeed as a form of rebellion."[268]

The Uroboros is thus a "threshold" symbol, and as such, it must be seen from at least two perspectives. From the proximal side, that is, the interior side, the Uroboros is guardian and Great Mother, symbol of the Universal Soul of all things which are one.[269] It is the "liquid substance," the amniotic fluid without which nothing can exist.

As to what this pleromatic womb contains, the gnostics are quite as literal as is Simon:

> Monoimus the Arabian utterly departed from the thought of the sublime poet when he thought that man had such a character as the poet gave to Okeanos, when he said, "Okeanos, the origin of gods, the origin of men" (Homer, Iliad 14.201).[270] He changes this to a different wording and says that man is the all, that is the beginning of all things, without origin, incorruptible, eternal . . . this man is a single unity, incomposite and

---

262 Corrington's note: "Hippolytus, *Refutation*, 5.6.3–5.11.1, cited in Foerster, *Gnosis*, 1:263."

263 Corrington's note: "Foerster, *Gnosis*, 1:280."

264 Should read *Sophia-Prunikos*. Corrington's passage here is similar to Jonas's text on p. 93 of *The Gnostic Religion*.

265 Corrington probably meant "Eve"; however, "Even" appears in both transcriptions of this passage (see also "Gnosticism and Modern Thought") and elsewhere in BHG.

266 Corrington's note: "Irenaeus, *Adversus Haereses* 1.30.7."

267 Corrington had *transcendental* in the original.

268 Corrington's note: "Hans Jonas, *The Gnostic Religion* (Boston: Beacon Press, 1963), 93."

269 The overlaps with GMT end here.

270 "For I am faring to visit the limits of the all-nurturing earth, and Oceanus, from whom the gods are sprung, and mother Tethys, even them that lovingly nursed and cherished me in their halls, when they had taken me from Rhea, what time Zeus, whose voice is borne afar, thrust Cronos down to dwell beneath earth and the unresting sea." From the Iliad, Book 14, line 201.

indivisible, composite and devisible . . . dissimilar and similar, like some musical harmony which contains within itself everything which one might name or crave unnoticed, producing all things, generating all things. This unity is mother, this is father.[271]

It appears at least possible that Hippolytus failed to see Monoimus's point: it is in the okeanos of the womb or the womb of okeanos that primal man arises, and in that state he is indeed the as yet undifferentiated all, incorruptible eternal, containing all things within himself, a womb within a womb.

From the exterior, worldly,[272] or distal side, the Uroboros appears variously as the Angel with the flaming sword guarding paradise from those outcasts who have the knowledge of good and evil, which is to say the consciousness which flows from differentiation, or as the bridge between worldly existence and the transcendental pleroma. The serpent or dragon who surrounds the pleromatic state by taking its tail in its teeth in many versions, guards "primal blessed formless substance, which is the cause of all forms in the things that are formed."[273] The significance placed upon androgyny by the ophitic and Naassene gnostics fits into the pleromatic compactness set out by Neumann, as does the tail-in-mouth image of the cosmic serpent, which is wholly self-sufficient and independent of the needs of existential creatures who must depend upon interaction with one another for their fullness. To be castrated in the existential world, for example, as were Attis and Osiris, was to have the "earthly parts" cut off, and thus to have "gone over to the eternal substance above, where . . . there is neither male nor female, but a new creature, a new man, (St. Paul, Eph. 2:15, 4:24; 2 Cor. 5:17) who is bisexual."[274]

Neumann points out the extreme tension involved in the formation of individual and cultural consciousness. It is "unnatural" in that it represents a break from "the great whirling wheel of life, where everything not yet individual is submerged in the union of opposites, passing away and willing to pass away."[275] Existence, after all, in the fullness of differentiation, is a painful and desperate experience. To be

---

271 Corrington's note: "Hippolytus, *Refutation*, 8.12.1–15.2 [12.1 –12.5]." This passage is from Foerster, p. 248. Foerster (or his translator) used "Ocean," not "Okeanos." There are also some differences in capitalization between Corrington's version and Foerster's version.

272 Overlap with GMT starts back here.

273 Corrington's note: "Hippolytus, *Refutation*, 5.6.18, in Foerster, *Gnosis*, 266."

274 Corrington's note: "Hippolytus, 5.6.15, in Foerster, 266."

275 Corrington's note: "Neumann, 16. But to see a more abstract, more developed version of the Uroborotic symbolism, see Eric Voegelin, *Order and History*, vol 4, *The Ecumenic Age*, passim on the symbolism of the Apeiron of Anaximander. See also John William Corrington, "Order and Consciousness/Consciousness and History: The New Program of Eric Voegelin," in *Voegelin's Search for Order in History*, ed. Stephen McKnight (Baton Rouge, LA: Louisiana State University Press, 1977). The Apeiron as a symbol of the ground of being is both *arche* and *telos* of the process of reality, thus 'tail-in-mouth.' Things arise from it and pass away into it. It thus stands as a non-imagistic symbolism, but one which still contains the sense of the cycle, or the circle so basic to later gnostic thought which never achieves the level of differentiating consciousness reached by Plato, whose work 'straightens out' the Uroborotic and Apeirontic to a height signified by the One (hen)."

"oneself" is, specifically, not to be The One, the All, not to be "at one with the universe" as the cliché quite properly goes. There is, then, as a substrate of even the most powerful personality or cultural structure, the pre-egoistic which desires to return, to plunge past the barrier of the Uroboros from the distal side, back into that fullness, that wholeness and unity, which it guards.

This is what Neumann calls "Uroborotic incest." The term, apparently synonymous with Freud's death-wish,[276] is not felicitous, since it has nothing to do with sexuality, but rather with an aspect of consciousness.

> Uroborotic incest is a form of entry into the Mother, of union with her, and it stands in sharp contrast to other and later forms of incest . . . it is more a desire to be dissolved and absorbed; possibly one lets oneself be taken, sinks into the pleroma, melts away in the ocean of pleasure—a *Liebestod*. The Great Mother takes the little child back into herself, and always over uroborotic incest there stand the insignia of death.[277]

I suggest that the pleroma of classical gnosticism, the high heaven with its *horos* or serpentine boundary, and its androgynous True God is, in fact, a mythopoetic[278] reconstruction of the pre-conscious state, both[279] as to individual and collective.[280] The relation between pleroma and womb is clear enough, as is the true occupant of the pleromatic womb: "And there are others who assert that the Forefather of all things himself, the Pre-beginning and the Pre-unthinkable, is called 'Man' and that this is the great and hidden mystery, namely that the power which is above all and which embraces all is termed Man."[281]

It is man who is begotten in the pleroma, and who goes on to create *aeous*[282] and limits—and gnostic systems, as well. The pleromatic symbols in their monistic simplicity represent the reaction of the gnostic personality to the severe tensions of existence in the imperial *ecumene*. Gnostic systems, like other magical structures, are the result of experiences which empty the process of reality for those who must embrace them. The gnostic capacity to create Second Realities, whether of the classical kind, or of the medieval or modern sort, is a response to the threat of a

---

276   More commonly known as "death drive."

277   Corrington's note: "Neumann, *Origins and History*, 17." Capitalized *Liebestod* and removed capitalization from "uroborotic incest" to match Neumann's text.

278   This originally said "mythe poetic." The same passage appears in GMT with the word *mythopoetic* instead of "mythe poetic."

279   Originally "boty" appeared here, but the same sentence in GMT states "both."

280   Overlap with GMT becomes more intermittent starting here.

281   Corrington's note: "Irenaeus, *Adversus Haereses* 11.12.3, in Foerster, *Gnosis*,197." This passage is from Foerster; Corrington did not credit Foerster in the original. Minor alterations made so that the passage matches Foerster's original text.

282   Probably *aeous*.

loss of relation to any sort of reality at all. To dream that an uninhabitable world-situation can somehow be transformed by an act of metastatic faith, some trick of spiritual legerdemain, is, at root, as analysis of the symbols reveal, a form of nostalgia, a regression, an attempt to escape the burden of participation in a cosmos which is not "a sea of pleasure," or a primordial state of non-differentiation. The essence of the gnostic dream is an eternal monism. The gnostic *Gospel of Thomas* sets out a purported logion of Christ which sums up the gnostic conception of the final state, the coming of the eternal Kingdom.

> Jesus said to them, when you make the two one, and when you make the inner as the outer, and the outer as the inner, and the above as the below, and when you make the male and the female into a single one, so that the male will not be male, and the female [not] be female, when you make the eyes in the place of an eye and a hand in the place of a hand, and a foot in the place of a foot, and an image in the place of an image, then shall you enter the Kingdom.[283]

I propose that this blurring of dichotomy, this insistence on the proper unity of all things in their ideal state which appears as a fundamental proposition in classical gnosticism, must, of necessity, point to the regressive character of gnostic thought. The balance of consciousness is not easily maintained, nor are its tensions mere irritants. The temptation to rerail,[284] to lose the balance, to fall backward into the unproblematical state of unconsciousness—or, for that matter, to lean toward infinity, into the doom of what Neumann calls "inflation" of the ego, is constant and immense. Voegelin described it many years ago: "The life of the soul in openness toward God, the waiting, the periods of aridity and dullness, guilt and despondency, contrition and repentance, forsakenness and hope against hope, the silent stirrings of love and grace, trembling on the verge of a certainty that if gained is loss—the very lightness of this fabric may prove too heavy a burden for men who lust for massively possessive experience."[285]

What is unbearable about the world is not flesh as flesh, or matter as matter. It is the ineradicable duality of existence. It is that there are other things than oneself. The core of gnostic thought in every form is finally almost pathetically, terrifyingly simple: it is the overpowering childish wish that all things should be oneself, that one should be the cosmos and all beyond it. What more profound "lust for massively possessive experience" is there, after all, than that of an infant? The

---

283 Corrington's note: "*Logion* 22, in Edgar Hennecke, ed., *New Testament Apocrypha*, vol. 1, *Gospels and Related Writings*, trans. R. McLachlan Wilson (London: Lutterworth Press, 1963), 298." Added bibliographic details to Corrington's citation to complete it.

284 Probably intended "derail."

285 Corrington's note: "Eric Voegelin, *The New Science of Politics* (Chicago: University of Chicago Press, 1952), 122."

very act of differentiation and its realization is a cleaving away from the individual consciousness all else to be placed in the dualistic or multifarious perspective of the process of reality. Jung points out that the image at the center of the mandala figure, whether it arises in dream or in art, is indistinguishably the Self or God.[286] Thus the gnostic, for all his noted horror of dualistic reality, is not in fact so much against flesh or matter as such, but passionately desirous that all polarities should collapse, all dichotomy vanish into one—and that the one should be himself,[287] adrift for eternity in the pleromatic womb of his own undifferentiated self.

---

286   Corrington's note: "Carl Jung, *The Collected Works*, vol. 9, bk. 1, *The Archetypes and the Collective Unconscious* (London: Routledge, 1968), 389. See also vol. 9, bk. 2, *Aion* (London: Routledge, 1968), 40."

287   Overlap with GMT ends here.

A Brief History of Gnosticism, Part II

Approx. 1976

Corrington points out that there have been many Gnostic schools and sects over time. The attempt to understand early Gnostics presupposes something innate or universal in the human condition because it necessarily involves a projection of our own experience and empirical knowledge of the world onto past figures, events, and modes of thought. The Gnostics expressed in symbols their experiential knowledge of the divine that was a source of freedom from the hated reality of the concrete world. Corrington maps different forms of Gnosticism and describes important Gnostic figures throughout various times and places. The structured symbols of Gnosticism that ordered Gnostic consciousness reified the sense of alienation that derived from the unintelligibility and disorder of the cosmos. Gnosticism considered ideal unity to be the desired end of empirical knowledge. The drive for ideal unity is evident in modern ideologies such as National Socialism, Marxist-Leninism, and other forms of totalitarianism that seek to realize an eschatological state of an eternally perfect order or ultimate reality here on earth. The Gnostic field of symbology fulfills a desire for perfect order or ultimate reality that has never been actualized concretely.

I

As Phillip Neill has pointed out, one looks for *the* gnostic mythos in vain.[288] The same is true of *the* gnostic sect. The congeries of syncretic religious groups collectively referred to as gnostic were of as many hues as the spiritual and intellectual situation of the late Hellenized near east could supply. The same is true of the doctrines and scriptures generated by these sects. Both sects and doctrines run the gamut of influence from pre-Christian Jewish and Iranian dualism, through Greek mystery-cult speculations, to Egyptian, Coptic, and Syriac religious theories.[289]

Even the question of a gnostic stratum of doctrines prior to Christianity is unsettled. Some authorities maintain that gnosticism, however wide it may cast its net for materials, is and was always dependent upon the primitive Christian

---

288 Corrington's note: "Stephen Neill, *The Interpretation of the New Testament, 1861-1961* (New York: Oxford University Press, 1966), 177."

289 Although Gnosticism is usually capitalized, Corrington chose to lowercase it in his essays. This was probably because, as he explains in this paragraph, there are many different types of gnosticism and not one single Gnosticism.

community for its vitality and for its soteriology.[290] Others insist that the common element of gnostic doctrines was the pre-Christian Jewish messianism, which had crested in its intramundane form in the centuries just prior to the birth of Christ, and which was crushed by Roman power in the first century AD.[291]

It is quite probable that no solution to these questions of origin will ever be unambiguously solved.[292] No amount of documentation will ever allow us to place ourselves in the position of those who found in the gnostic doctrines and communities an answer—or solution—to their own spiritual quests. It is only possible to examine the prime symbols evoked by the documents and ascribed to the communities, and then to analyze[293] these data within the context of the historical period in which they arose through the lens provided by our understanding of human nature.

Such an enterprise presumes the constancy of human nature. Without such a presumption, any analysis of ancient ideas is absurd on principle. It is possible to understand only by analogy, and if such understanding is judged to be false, not only the past is barred to us but even a definitive analysis of contemporary ideas becomes impossible.

Despite numerous archeological discoveries over the past century, the earliest account of gnostic ideas which has come down to us remains the classic account by the bishop of Lyons,[294] Irenaeus (120?–202). His *Adversus Haereses* is a compendium of those varieties of gnosticism extant between the time of the Apostolic fathers and his own. Among the sects he names are the Valentinians, the followers of Ptolemy and Colorbasus, the Marcosians, the Simonians, the followers of Menander, Saturninus,[295] the Basilideans, the Ebionites, the followers of Cerinthus and of [the] Nicolaitanes; of Cerdo and of Marcion, of Tatian, [the] Encratites, of Carpocrates; of the Barbeliotes, of the Ophites and Sethians, and of the Cainites.[296]

In addition, we know of others: the Messalians, who rose later, and the Montanists, who, apparently, arose in reaction to the increasing compromises of the Great Church with Roman power.[297] There is some question as to the gnostic character of

---

290 Corrington's note: "Neill, *Interpretation of the New Testament*, 180." Changed soterology to soteriology.

291 Corrington's note: "Neill, *Interpretation of the New Testament*, 180–81. See also R. M. Grant, *Gnosticism and Early Christianity* (New York: Columbia University Press, 1966), 1–38."

292 Corrington's note: "The issue of a 'pre-Christian' gnosticism, and the separate issue of the precise sources for the remarkably similar gnostic tenets, despite the proliferation of sects, may indeed, be a false issue. The entire question deserves study from the point of view of depth psychology. Cf. Carl Jung, *The Collected Works of C. G. Jung*, vol. 9, bk. 2, *Aion*, and vol. 14, *Mysterium Coniunctionis*. (London: Routledge and Kegan Paul, 1953–1979)."

293 In several places, Corrington uses the British spelling *analyse*. Changed to American spelling throughout this edition.

294 In French the city is *Lyon*, but in English there is an "s" at the end.

295 Corrected from *Saterninus* to match Jonas's text.

296 Many of the names mentioned in this sentence are not only people but also sects (e.g., Encratites, Nicolaitanes, Ophites, Sethians, and Cainites). Added "the" in brackets (e.g., the Encratites, the Nicolaitanes) to indicate the double meaning: people and sects.

297 Corrington's note: "Steven Runciman, *The Medieval Manichee* (Cambridge: Cambridge University Press, 1955), 21 et seq."

Montanism, and it is true that the sect does not reveal all the characteristics which are common to most of the others. But, as we will see, Montanism insists upon the prophetic capacity of believers, holds a millennial creed, and, most significantly, Montanus himself preached that he was the Paraclete, God Father, Son, and Holy Spirit in one.[298]

Other important commentators on gnosticism include Tertullian, who himself, after struggling against the Valentinians and other sects, succumbed to Montanism, chiefly, it appears, as a protest in reaction to the spirit of accommodation with the "powers of the world" under the auspices of the Roman See.[299] In the third century, there is the work of Hippolytus (170?–236), *Refutation of All Heresies*, who, while discussing much of the material found in both Irenaeus and Tertullian, adds much of his own.[300] In addition to the list cited above, Hippolytus mentions these gnostic groups: the Naasseni,[301] the followers of Secundus, of Epiphanes, of Prepon, of Apelles. Notably, he also adds one Monoimus, whose doctrine we will cite specifically. Finally, if the description of their doctrine is correct, it would appear that the Docetians, in addition to their generally-known heresy regarding the flesh of Christ, were Gnostic as well.[302]

While this catalogue is less than complete, the writers mentioned represent a large sample of the writings of the fathers on those sects which are recognizably gnostic.

It now becomes necessary to list those symbols which, while not common to every one of the heresies listed, are most common, and which reveal the underlying types of spiritual experience upon which the gnostic doctrines are based.

1. In most gnostic sects, we find the doctrine that the world was created not by the "high god," "the good god," or "the hidden, unknown god," but by a lesser spirit, variously identified with the Israelite God, the Demiurge, Ialdaboath, Sabaoth,[303] or certain Archons or angels, or even Satan.

2. Following from this, it is argued by most of the sects that the material world is evil, and is the botched creation of the ignorant Israelite God, who is himself often considered an accidental result of the fall of Sophia, a primary spirit from the Pleroma, the perfect dwelling-place of the unknown god and his archons.

---

298   Corrington's note: "Adolph von Harnack, *History of Dogma* (New York: Russell and Russell, 1958), 2:97–100. A similar view is held by J. H. Milman, *History of Latin Christianity* (London, 1854), 1:38–39."

299   Corrington's note: "Cf. Tertullian, *Contra Valentinus*, and his *Five Books Against Marcion*, available in various editions."

300   Corrington's note: "Hippolytus mentions numerous other sects and heretical groups, but his descriptions are too vague to include them within the characteristically gnostic spectrum."

301   Possibly "Naassenes."

302   Corrington's note: "Cf. Hippolytus, *The Refutation of All Heresies*, 8:2:3, in *The Ante-Nicene Fathers: The Writings of the Fathers down to A.D. 325*, eds. A. Roberts and J. Donaldson (Grand Rapids, Michigan: William B. Eerdmans, 1965), 5:117–21. All references to the writings of the Fathers will be cited [from] this edition unless otherwise specified."

303   Sabaoth is not necessarily the name of a god, but a word (meaning "hosts") usually attached to God's name in Hebrew.

3. This botched or evil material creation includes the flesh of humanity which is no other than a prison for the "sparks" of the true divinity which Jehovah or the Demiurge has captured.

4. Most men who possess this divine spark are ignorant of it, requiring enlightenment so that they can realize that they are of divine origin. In some of the doctrines, all men possess such a spirit; in others, only "one in a thousand, two in ten thousand" are possessed of the spark. The rest are mere earthly creatures, and will perish utterly.

5. For those possessing the spark of divinity, the world is a place of suffering and confusion, an alien place, but finally of no consequence. To the "spiritual" man, the laws and customs of the material world are of no account. The spiritual is in the world; he is not of it.

6. The pathway back to the divine light is available to men. Salvation from the prison-world lies through knowledge—the *gnosis*. This gnosis is variously described, and the way through which it is gained is described in countless ways. According to a fragment from Clement of Alexandria, himself the proponent of a "Christian" gnosis, it is

> the knowledge of who we were and what we became, of where we were and whereinto we have been flung, of whereto we are hastening and wherefrom we are redeemed, of what birth is and what rebirth.[304]

It is of the greatest importance to note that the gnostics, in radical contradistinction to Christian orthodoxy, maintain what Thomas Aquinas would call "an unequivocal knowledge" of the divine, of its nature, its purposes, and, by implication at least, of the divine plan for mankind.

7. As a consequence of the theory of Jehovah as malevolent or ignorant, the imprisoner of humanity's[305] divine sparks, there is, in many of the sects, a strong current of antisemitism. Marcion of Pontus is particularly explicit in his rejection of the Old Testament, "abolishing the law and the prophets."[306]

8. While, in almost all versions, Christ appears prominently as redeemer, messenger, or, minimally, as prophet, in no version does[307] he appear as in orthodox Christian theology, even as it existed in the first and second centuries.

---

304   Corrington's note: "From *Excerpta ex Theodoto*, in Eric Voegelin, *Science, Politics and Gnosticism* (Chicago: Regnery, 1968), 10."

305   Changed *humanty* to *humanity*.

306   Corrington's note: "Irenaeus, *Adversus Haereses*, 1:27:2, in Roberts and Donaldson, *The Ante-Nicene Fathers*, 1:352."

307   Corrington had "do" in the original.

9. In a number of versions, the theme of the hidden god as an androgyne appears. This god is either man-woman in one, or asexual. In other versions, the Proarches or Eons[308] reproduce lesser spirits asexually.

10. Associated with this theme, I think, is the commonly noted radical dualism of most gnostic sects. While this dualism is chiefly described in relation to the tension between the hidden god and the creator Demiurge, it extends to the world-spirit, and to the law-freedom dichotomies as well. The radical dualism found in most gnostic sects reveals the manner in which the gnostic experiences the world: as a series of discontinuities which are, to him, irresolvable.

11. All, or nearly all of the sects, operate from an ahistorical framework of belief. The gnostic creation-myths do not purport to set forth a pragmatic account of the world's provenance,[309] as does the Judaic revelation. Again, the mythical mode of thought common to gnostic sects precludes their being philosophically oriented.

12. Finally, and of least importance, since in fact, it is primarily a practical result of their cosmogony, the gnostic sects tended to be moral extremists. The result of their indifference and contempt for the world and the flesh produced ascetic and libertine strands of gnosticism.

These, then, are the predominant symbols through which the Gnostic experience was expressed in the first four centuries of the Christian era. An analysis of such a rich array of symbols must penetrate the symbols themselves and attempt to recreate the experiences and sentiments which underlie them. The task is perhaps less formidable than it might have been a hundred years or so ago, because, if the gnostic symbols appear to be alien to us, they are, upon examination, transparent inasmuch as the typical experiences which they evoke bear close resemblance to experiences common today.[310] Again, in addition to the methodologies and techniques of historical and philosophical analysis, we have available the gestalt analytical tools, by which a constellation of symbols may be shown to correspond to states of the developing individual psyche as it gains in consciousness.[311] The amalgam of viewpoints thus available enables us to classify gnostic experiences in such a way as to recognize them when they irrupt much later into the field of medieval thought in the work of Joachim of Fiore and his successors.

---

308 Possibly "Aeons."

309 Changed "provenance" to "provenance."

310 Corrington's note: "Cf. Hans Jonas, *The Gnostic Religion* (Boston: Beacon Press, 1963), 320–40."

311 Corrington's note: "Cf. Erich Neumann, *The Origins and History of Consciousness* (Princeton: Princeton University Press, 1954), 5–127. Also, Carl Jung, *The Archetypes and the Collective Unconscious*, vol. 9, bk. 1 of *The Collected Works of C. G. Jung.*"

II

We have referred to the "gnostic experience" as if it were a datum in history. Of course it is not. Rather, it is a series of experiences extended in time and space, conditioned by the circumstances, both civilizational and personal, within which the various experiences took place. The unity of the experiences and the sentiments evoked by them is predicated upon the constancy of human nature; the diversity of images through which the symbols are expressed is predicated upon the individuation of that human nature as it occurs concretely in specific persons.

The situation in which gnosticism arose was one of attenuated civilizational breakdown. Asia Minor and North Africa were strewn with the wreckage of the old cosmological empires; Greece was a ruin, its power passed to the barbarians of the north, its intellect dissipated and diffused by *skepsis*. The city-state, which had been not only the civilizational unit of the Greeks but the spiritual focus as well, was as fully ravished as the remnants of the Egyptian empire, now ruled by the Ptolemies, itself a mummy, still the reputed place of ancient learning where a Solon or a Plato might have looked for *sophia* four hundred years earlier, but now more nearly a museum of sterile forms.[312] "She lived on her artificial life for a time under the Persians and the Ptolemies, ever sinking, till she became . . . a land of ancient marvels to be visited by wealthy Greeks and Romans, who have left their names scratched here and there upon her hoary monuments."[313]

But the Greeks, however wealthy, were no better off, nor were the Persians or the shattered remnants of Babylon. In the wake of the ephemeral conquests of Alexander came the new power-complex of Rome to gather the scattered pieces of the empires into a new structure based not on religion, commerce, or culture, but upon raw military power and a concept of politics so simple and direct that the aged and effete near eastern cultures had no response to it.

If the Mediterranean area was a graveyard of cultures and civilizational structures, it was equally a charnel house of spiritual symbolizations. With the destruction and decay of the societies which had embodied them, the ancient religious formulations had come crashing down. The "uprootedness" of the old orders produced an equal rootlessness in those people who had ordered their lives around them. Syrians, Persians, Greeks, Jews, Phrygians, Egyptians, and a hundred other nationalities wandered about in the shell of Alexander's Hellenized *ecumene,* tracking Roman conquests or Greek traders, going as far as India or Nubia for enlightenment.[314]

---

312 Possible rewording of this sentence for the purpose of clarity:
The city-state, which had been not only the civilizational unit of the Greeks but the spiritual focus as well, was as fully ravished as the remnants of the Egyptian empire, now ruled by the Ptolemies, [and] itself a mummy, [and although] still the reputed place of ancient learning—where a Solon or a Plato might have looked for *sophia* four hundred years earlier—[it was] now more nearly a museum of sterile forms.

313 Corrington's note: "J. H. Breasted, *A History of Egypt* (New York: Scribner's Sons, 1909), 595."

314 Corrington's note: "Cf. R. M. Grant, *Gnosticism and Early Christianity* (New York: Columbia University Press, 1966); also see R. M. Grant, *Augustus to Constantine* (New York: Harper and Row, 1970) for discussion of the Graeco-

The confusion of peoples and sects was matched by a confusion of purposes. Without cultural or spiritual roots, desperation had become a considerable element throughout the civilizational field of the former Alexandrian conquests, and the Romans had nothing to offer but law, administration, and the worship of their city's power. In this deracinated welter of spiritual cripples, only a handful of sects had managed to establish themselves. For a certain time, and to a certain class of cosmopolites, Epicureanism and Stoicism served; for others, the obscurantism of Greek and Egyptian mysteries. For the Jews, the age-old strand of Messianism, almost broken by the unending series of disasters from the time of the Persian conquest through the Macedonians and Romans, still managed to make intelligible a national life which had become one long punishment for crimes unspecified since the demise of the Prophets.

Above all, the term *alienation*—first used by Plotinus—describes the spiritual situation among the masses of peoples herded into a species of unity by Rome. They were a population, but not a people. The reality of their existence had been brought into question by the civilizational destruction which had made them orphans, even in their own nominal countries. The Stoic response to this condition was the symbolization of the *ecumene* as a single homeland for all men. This position was easy enough for a Cicero or an Aurelius who, whatever their trials, lived in the city of their birth and partook of her unparalleled power and the sweeping drama of her contemporary history. For Cicero to say that "there is one law at Rome and at Athens" as a metaphysical statement was less than a transcendent insight; in fact, Roman power made it immanently true.

But the *mass man*[315] of the empire found himself in quite another condition. His life was determined. For the most part, he was unlikely to be a citizen of the only place where citizenship counted for anything: the single surviving city-state of Rome. His politics, outside the minor quarrels and diversions of towns and provinces, was under the *potestas* of Rome. The languages with which he might converse generally were either Latin or, more probably, *koine* Greek. The Roman gods, little more than symbols of power even among cultivated Romans who had worshipped only their city and their image of their own *dominum* since the time of the Twelve Tables, must needs be honored. Even the law, in matters of moment, was that of the Praetor, the *ius gentium*—no one's law, yet everyone's law.

Existence for the bulk of the empire's subjects had become monadic. The world was a field of frenzied power-politics in which ancient customs, beliefs, culture all had been homogenized or reduced to the status of commodities or antiques. It was in this context that Christianity was born, and parallel with it, those religious inventions we call *gnostic*.

Roman world in the first century."

315   Removed hyphen and italicized to emphasize that this is a name for a certain type of person.

If the essence of Christianity as a world-religion resides in its continuity with Judaism in the early phases, gnosticism immediately departs from it by its consistent rejection of the Old Testament. The world is created by a demiurge, the gross product of Sophia's fall from the Pleroma.[316] Crudeness, a taste for self-congratulation, violence, and cruelty are the characteristics of this lower power. The world is fundamentally evil, and the source of that evil arises from the creator, and from the fact that creation itself is utterly sealed off from the Pleromatic virtue of the "hidden god."[317] Evil, darkness, matter, ignorance, these are the characteristics of empirical reality as much of the ecumenic population experienced it between the time of Alexander and the Christianization of Rome.

The problem was one of intelligibility. The death of the old empires, as we have noted, coupled with the almost ceaseless violence and military action of the period caused a profound disorientation among people who had lived within long-established societal orders founded either upon cosmological mythos, or upon the historical revelation of Israel. In either case, life in existence was rendered meaningful by a parallelism with a luminous and understandable order of cosmos or of Torah.

The end of the old empires shattered this mythos of order, as well as that nascent symbolization of the Hellenic type, philosophy. All was swept away into the maelstrom of confusion and invalidation which characterizes the early ecumene. The blocks of meaning, smashed along with the political structures which embodied them, did not vanish, because the cosmological form of ordering primal experience cannot vanish. The experience of the cosmos, its rhythms, its returns, its lastingness never alters. This cosmic ongoingness is the ground bass, the continuo, of human existence. But the symbols by which it was evoked by the old empires were rendered unintelligible insofar as they related—or, more properly, attempted to relate—the meaning of the cosmos to survivors of a concrete society which no longer existed.

Thus the early ecumene was a disordered field of elemental power-relations amidst which lay the dismembered fragments of cosmological truth which no longer related to the experiences of human beings flung forth from the extinct societal orders, and who were not members of any other society which had mastered the problem of expressing the meaning of existence through generally intelligible symbols.

The gnostic tendency to see in the Creator-god a source of evil suggests that R. M. Grant's insistence upon Jewish apocalypticism[318] and its frustration as a

---

316   Corrington's note: "Irenaeus, *Adversus Haereses*, 1.2.3, in Roberts and Donaldson, *The Ante-Nicene Fathers*, 1:319. Also 1.4.1."

317   Corrington's note: "Irenaeus, *Adversus Haereses*, 1.1.1, in Roberts and Donaldson, *The Ante-Nicene Fathers*, 1:316. An interesting note on this concept of a 'hidden' or 'incomprehensible' god is mentioned in Arnold Toynbee, *A Study of History* (London: 1934), 1:144, where he notes that the god of the Hyksos was an 'unknown god,' identified by the Egyptians with their god Set." Corrected the date on volume 1 of Toynbee's book.

318   Changed from "apocalyptic."

prime source for gnosticism may well be correct. Only those immediately aware of the Jewish symbols would be likely to choose Yahweh as the cause of evil, the defective creator of the world. In any case, the disorientation which plagued the ecumene—*alienation*, as we have come to call it in its contemporary form—came to be effectively a kind of cosmological aphasia, a breakdown between vague memories of order, and the ability to symbolize them effectively. It is a species of *ignorantia*: what is the meaning of life; singly or collectively? From whence do we come? Where do we go? Why does the cosmos last, while we are born only to die? What does the idea of society, of the city, the state, or the empire mean? How is it that I am a part of all this, and what must I know or do in order for the shattered fragments of my living to coalesce into a pattern of meaning?

In modern parlance, the result of this alienation or identity crisis among the socially and spiritually displaced persons left in the wake of Macedonian and Roman conquest was the production of *mass men*, or "superfluous people."[319] Human beings, stripped of the old values inherent in family, tribe, village, city and empire, governed by representations of cosmological mythos, now lived in an ionized state. On the one hand, they were mere social atoms, related to existence primarily through patterns of military and administrative order. Taxation, trade, even law and religion existed and were shaped by the new power-political order, and no aspect of life was untouched by the *kulturkampf* of Alexander and his companions, and by their Roman successors.

It was through a turning away from this meaningless field of power-politics, and from a cosmos perceived as parallel in meaninglessness in its domination by elemental power, that the fundamental symbols of gnostic thought were created. The unintelligibility of the cosmos was accounted for by the Demiurge, as was the "prison" character of matter and flesh. All that was subject to physical coercion became evil, and the source of evil.

But the meaninglessness of the cosmos did not do away with the inner feeling of everyone. For those who still maintained the interiorized sense of meaning, the new gnostic symbols evoked a "hidden god," an inexpressible one, far beyond the brutal mechanism of the cosmos, from which certain spirits had come forth, to which they would return. The Valentinian Proarche, who presided in the transcendent peace and perfection of the Pleroma, the anti-cosmos, was the source and the destiny of the divine pneumatic "sparks" contained in the souls of the elect. The gnostic Sophia, as fallen member of the pleromatic Eons,[320] had given birth to the Demiurge. The fall of Wisdom had evoked the mindless unholy counter-order of pure power. It is not difficult to see in "the powers that be," the cohorts of earthly

---

319   Corrington's note: "The most incisive discussion of the phenomenon is that of Erich Neumann, "Mass Man and the Phenomena of Recollectivization," appendix 2 of *The Origins and History*, 436. See also the final chapter of Hannah Arendt's *The Origins of Totalitarianism* (New York: Harcourt, 1973)."

320   Possibly "Æons" or "Aeons."

power which dominated the faulty cosmos without knowledge of the Hidden God, a *lex* without a *logos*.[321]

The presence in most gnostic systems of Sophia seems strong evidence for Grant's contention that the core of gnostic thought stems from apocalyptic Judaism.[322] Sophia, according to the Midrashim, is Torah, the living Word of God, by which the world was created, and the very first of his creations.[323] The gnostic mythologues simply place Sophia above the God of Israel, purporting that she is mother of the Demiurge, and one of the Eons[324] of the Pleroma, produced by the Hidden God. By so doing, the gnostic sects explain at once the inherent evil of the cosmos, and generate a new extracosmic deity whose divinity is not lessened by the act of creation. The "failed" God of Israel who did not honor what were taken to be his apocalyptic and messianic promises, becomes the demonic force which is responsible for the defects of creation, and his Sophia becomes the creative but fallen connection between the darkness of creation and the distant light of the Hidden God.

In Erich Neumann's classic study of the stages of development of individual human consciousness, he calls the original ground-state of pre-egoistic human psyche, that of the unborn and the newly-born person, the "Pleromatic" state. It is a condition of total non-differentiation, symbolized frequently by the *Uroboros*, the legendary serpent eating its tail, a sign of completeness. In this state, we are told, there are no differentiations: no light or dark, no male or female, no self and no non-self, no subject and object. The unity of the psyche in the uroborotic[325] state is complete, but unconscious. It is not aware of itself as it is not aware of otherness.[326]

It is this unity which the gnostic seeks, and which is symbolized by gnostic thought. The Hidden God of the Pleroma is, in one sense, the projection of the gnostic's own yearning for an orientation, a unity of meaning that he cannot possess within the disorder and meaninglessness of the cosmos. The androgyne symbol common to gnostic speculation, the "all in one" character of the Pleroma, as Neumann describes it as a psychic state, matches the motif as it is reported in Irenaeus: "For they maintain that sometimes the Father [the Hidden God] acts in conjunction with Sige [one of the original Eons], but that at other times he shows himself independent of both male and female."[327]

---

321 Corrington's note: "Irenaeus, *Adversus Haereses*, 1.1.1, in Roberts and Donaldson, *The Ante-Nicene Fathers*, 1:316." This footnote reference was missing; it existed in the endnotes but not in the text proper. It appears to belong here, although the names used in Irenaeus are different from those Corrington uses.

322 Corrington's note: "Grant, *Gnosticism*, 39 et passim."

323 Corrington's note: "*Midrash Rabbah: Bereshith*, ed. H. Freedman (London: Soncino Press, 1939), 1:3–4, and 6. Sophia-Wisdom is seen by R. Kahana as the first of God's creations. See also R. Oshaya, 1. The parallel between the Jewish Torah and the Christian Word as instruments of creation is obvious. Cf. John 1:1–5." Corrington mentions R. Oshaya in the footnote, but the footnote is incomplete and Oshaya is not mentioned anywhere else in his notes or bibliography.

324 Possibly "Æons" or "Aeons."

325 More common spelling: "uroboric."

326 Corrington's note: "Neumann, *The Origins and History of Consciousness*, 14–16."

327 Corrington's note: "Irenaeus, *Adversus Haereses*, 1.2.4, in Roberts and Donaldson, *The Ante-Nicene Fathers*, 1:318."

And again, "even respecting Bythus himself [a name of the Hidden God], there are among them many and discordant opinions. For some declare him to be without a consort, and neither male nor female, and in fact, nothing at all; while others affirm him to be masculo-feminine, assigning to him the nature of a hermaphrodite."[328]

Of course, for our purposes, non-sexuality and dual-sexuality are essentially the same. The Hidden God, in gnostic thought, stands against the differentiation of consciousness itself, as, for example, in the gnostic *Gospel According to St. Thomas:*[329]

> Jesus says to them: When you make the two (become) one, and when you make the inside like the outside and the outside like the inside, and the upper like the lower! And if you make the male and the female one, so that the male is no longer male and the female is no longer female, and when you put eyes in the place of an eye, and a hand in the place of a hand, and the foot in the place of a foot, and an image in the place of an image, then you will enter (the Kingdom!).[330]

The passage demands the renovation of the catechumen. He must lose the sense of differentiation in the unity of the Hidden God. All must be experienced as one. He must, finally, replace his differentiated body with a "spiritualized" body, and in the place of his old images, place that inexpressible image of the Hidden God.

There are numerous other references to this androgynous character of the Hidden God—all of which indicate, if Neumann is correct, that the gnostic paradise indeed represents the imaginative construction, under the pressure of the stark reality of the ecumene, of a "pre-ego" state, as the image of paradise. Indeed, if further proof were needed, there is an astonishing passage in Hippolytus in which he discusses the doctrine attributed to Simon Magus:

> How then, he says, and in what manner does God form man? In Paradise; for so it seems to him. Grant Paradise, he says, to be the womb; and that this is a true (assumption) the Scripture will teach, when it utters the words, "I am he who forms thee in thy mother's womb.". . . If, however, God forms man in his mother's womb—that is, in Paradise—as I have affirmed, let Paradise be the womb, and Eden the afterbirth, "a river flowing forth from Eden,[331] for the purpose of irrigating Paradise," meaning by this the navel.

---

328   Corrington's note: "Irenaeus, *Adversus Haereses*, 1.11.5, in Roberts and Donaldson, *The Ante-Nicene Fathers*, 1:332."

329   This is usually referred to as the *Gospel of Thomas* or *Gospel According to Thomas*.

330   This is cited as "note 24a," but that note does not appear in Corrington's endnotes. This passage is similar to the Lambdin translation.

331   Corrington had "Edem" instead of "Eden."

> … For the infant that was formed in Paradise neither receives nourishment through the mouth, nor breathes through the nostrils: for as it lay in the midst of moisture, at its feet was death, if it attempted to breathe.

It is this Paradise of the womb, upon which Simon Magus and Erich Neumann agree, that represents the Pleromatic Paradise toward which gnostic doctrine points.

Still another primary gnostic characteristic points in the same direction. As Grant, among others, points out, gnosticism, in severe contradistinction to Christianity (and to Judaism, for that matter), is in all cases, more or less ahistorical. It neither achieves the status of an ideation concretely unfolding in time (except, of course, insofar as the existence of gnosticism itself is a datum in history), nor does it ever grow to the maturity of Philosophy.[332] It is rather a synthetic mythos, evoking the symbols of infantile pre-consciousness, and projecting them through its speculative cosmogenesis upward and forward to the level of a transcendent "return" to Pleromatic bliss. It is thus a kind of atavistic attempt to achieve on the level of a synthetic, consciously constructed myth (as opposed to the organic myths of the old empires and primitive peoples) the unity of the ruined cosmological orders. In fact, as Neumann's work suggests, the stage of consciousness represented by the gnostic pleroma more nearly approaches a stage of consciousness-development prior to that of developed cosmological order which, after all possessed a fully articulated cosmogenesis, a set of hero-myths in most cases, and an articulated motif from pre-history called by Neumann the "division of the world-parents" in which the uroboros is initially divided, and consciousness is born. The image of the Egyptian Nut being elevated above Geb by Shu is a clear pictorialization in which sexuality, subject-object, and the entire ensemble of primary differentiations begins.[333] The Judeo-Christian parallel to this original division is, of course, the creation of Eve out of Adam's rib, though it is obvious that the Genesis story has been heavily overworked by generations of redactors, and that the form in which we have it corresponds to a very late stage of mythopoetic development.

Another primary symbol which is closely related to the basic gnostic expression of reality is the radical dualism, so often noted as to be a cliché in critique of gnostic invention. The symbol, however, seems universally misunderstood.

It is true that virtually every gnostic sect embraced the motif of the evil of the cosmos and the good of the Pleroma. What is not understood, especially in gnostic terms of "modern" gnostic thought, is that the dualistic condition of existence, which the gnostic experiences as the horror of spiritual alienation, constitutes the situation of meaninglessness from which he yearns to escape. The *desired* condition which the gnostic seeks to achieve is, after all, an equally radical monism, the

---

332 Corrington's note: "Grant, *Gnosticism*, see chapter 5, "From Myth to Philosophy?" 120–50."
333 Corrington's note: "Neumann, *The Origins and History*, 106ff."

infantile indivision and utter gratification of the Pleromatic state. It must be noted that the dualism of Christianity differs from the gnostic in that it is never resolved: the distinction between creator and creature is fundamental; the "image of God" in which man is made is not God. Even in the state of divine perfection, that of the Beatific Vision, there can be no question of man becoming "one" with God. The distinction between man and God, so carefully maintained in almost all of the early Christian Fathers, is blurred in gnostic thought, and there are certain gnostic sects in which this blurring becomes, explicitly, an avowal that man and God are one.[334]

This becomes a matter of supreme importance when, in the nineteenth and twentieth centuries, gnosticism ceases to be a mere religious antiquity, and suddenly bursts forth in spasms of activist millennialism, creating the "pleromatic" states of National Socialism, Marxist-Leninism, and the ghastly apparatus of Totalitarianism in its variants of racist or "classless" monism. It cannot be urged too strongly that, from its beginning, the peculiar nature of gnosticism affirms a dualism only in order to conquer or destroy it. The gnostic fantasy, in its transcendental forms, seeks to abolish the order of existence by a denial of the meaning of existence, and by establishing a return to the Hidden God as the *only* meaningful aspect of reality. In its modern immanentist form, gnosticism attempts to abolish the dualism it so despises by action in history, proposing to create in the future the millennial kingdom of the saints, the Classless Society, or Das Dritte Reich, a Pleromatic future order purged of the Jewish or bourgeois elements it hates. The shift from "vertical" forms of gnosticism related to an extra-historical and transcendent concept of ultimate reality to a "horizontal" form aimed at some indefinite future is a topic outside the scope of this paper, but remains, nonetheless, a part of the total history of gnostic thought.

Perhaps no symbol of gnostic fantasy is so important to an understanding of the pneumopathology it represented—and still represents—as the concept of "gnosis" itself. Irenaeus distinguishes between "gnosis" and faith in this way: "They further hold that the consummation of all things will take place when all that is spiritual has been formed and perfected by Gnosis (knowledge); and by this they mean spiritual men who have attained to the perfect knowledge of God . . . And they represent themselves to be persons."[335]

> Animal men, again, are instructed in animal things; such men, namely, as are established by their works, and by a mere faith, while they have not perfect knowledge. We, of the Church, they say, are those persons.[336]

---

334 Corrington references a "note 25b" at the end of this paragraph, but he has already referenced a different "note 26," and there is no "25b" in his endnotes.

335 Typographical corrections made to this paragraph to match the original translation of Irenaeus.

336 Corrington's note: "Irenaeus, *Adversus Haereses*, 1.6.1–2, in Roberts and Donaldson, *The Ante-Nicene Fathers*, 1:323."

Gnosis, of course, has no use for faith. Clement of Alexandria speaks of a "Christian gnosis," in contrast to that of his heretical opponents. After citing the opinions of Basilides and the followers of Valentinus, which agree with the report of Irenaeus above, Clement denies the "natural" character and the lower status of faith: "Well, Sensation is the ladder to Knowledge (gnosis); while Faith, advancing over the pathway of the objects of sense, leaves Opinion (doxa) behind, and speeds to things free of deception, and reposes in the truth. . . . Faith is something superior to knowledge, and is its criterion."[337]

To the Fathers, as later to Aquinas, a direct and total gnosis of God, while one dwelt in the flesh, was impossible, and a claim to such knowledge was blasphemy. Knowledge of God, as Thomas would later express it, was but *analogia entis,* and even Aristotle had admitted that "judgment which follows knowledge is in truth faith," and that "knowledge is founded on demonstration by a process of reasoning," but that "first principles are incapable of demonstration."[338]

Faith, then, precedes knowledge even in a purely existential sense, and there can be, according to Clement, no knowledge but one flowing from faith. It is on this fundamental ground that the "irrationalism" of gnosticism is presumed. Since it is axiomatic that every statement about reality assumes as a first principle a number of axioms which must be taken on faith (for example, the intelligibility of experience itself), a gnosis which rejects such a prior assumption must be mere doxic fantasy, a dream generated from psychic needs and insecurity of the dreamer—not from a spiritual contemplation of the cosmos, its origin in the divine ground, and the meaning of the theophany of Christ which is at once subject and object of faith. Gnosis, disclaiming faith, is thus demonstrably irrational; faith, on the other hand, is beyond, prior, to reasons whether the subject-matter be geometry or the Christian faith.

We must now attempt briefly to recapitulate the motive of gnostic rejection of faith in the sense of Paul's "Substance of things hoped for, the evidence of things not seen," and its replacement with a rationally indefensible claim to perfect knowledge. What motivates the gnostic to claim an impossible gnosis of a Hidden God instead of accepting as his guide the intellectually respectable *pistis* of the Christians?

The reason is apparent from our discussion of the meaning of the earlier primary gnostic symbols. *Pistis* (trust, faith) is the response of Aristotle's *spoudaios,* the mature man, one who has learned to acknowledge and to live at peace within the Metaxy, the "in-between," where the tensions of existence and transcendence clasp him, body and soul, "like the lyre, like the bow." The temptation to break the

---

337   Corrington's note: "Clement of Alexandria, *Stromata* 2.4, in Roberts and Donaldson, *The Ante-Nicene Fathers,* 2:350." The capitalized words were not capitalized in Corrington's text, although they are capitalized in the source Corrington quotes.

338   Corrington's note: "Clement of Alexandria, *Stromata,* in Roberts and Donaldson, *The Ante-Nicene Fathers,* 2:350."

tension, to deny either world or spirit, is especially strong among certain types of personality when faced with the kind of societal disarray represented by the ecumene. This temptation, as history has shown, may make itself known either as a rejection of transcendent truth through means either methodical or hysterical, or through a denial of the truth of existence by means of an infantile yearning for the pleromatic unity, as in the gnostic case before us. Maintenance of the totality of human experience as valuable, establishing through faith those spiritual channels through which transcendence enlightens existence even as existence bears witness to transcendence, requires a kind of exultant faith, a sense of the inexorable penetration of the orders of being, each into the other. Acceptance of the cosmos as fundamentally good in itself, and as an ikon revelatory of the divine ground is an act of such faith and simultaneously the progenitor of faith.

On the contrary, the gnostic atavism, the yearning for the androgynous condition of the pleroma, for the faceless god, and the rejection of existence as a field of meanings, requires radical remedy if the psyche is not to break down. After all, the elaborate gnostic symbols are not causative; the pneumopathology revealed by them would exist just as surely even if the gnostic, for one reason or another, did not evoke the symbols. In this regard, it is worth noting that the passage from gnostic to Christian, as in the case of Augustine, or from Christian to gnostic, as in the case of Tertulliana is an index of the condition of the soul. Where faith serves for the Christian who is capable of balancing the claims of transcendence with those of existence, the gnostic must claim—and believe—in a certain and undeviating knowledge of transcendent meaning in order to hold at bay the continuing threat of non-existence thrust upon him by the alien meaninglessness of the cosmos.

To summarize, an analysis of the original gnostic symbols—those extant from the first through the early fourth centuries—amounts to a diagnosis of profound spiritual disturbances caused by the civilizational upheaval which produced and maintained the power-fields of the ecumene. No longer able to participate in the ritual myths of the cosmos, the gnostic speculators created a wide variety of symbols which, from the point of view of depth psychology, point to a form of atavistic infantilism. Radically dualistic (as opposed to the balanced dualism— "relaxed dualism," as Paul Henry calls it—of Christianity, Plato, and Plotinus[339]), rigidly ahistorical and non-philosophical, fitfully monotheistic, insisting upon a gnosis without basis except in the fantasies of its inventors, contemptuous of the world, of social order, gnosticism resembles a well-wrought fairytale which satisfies by its images and promises, rather than fulfilling by its meaning.

By the fourth century, most of the gnostic sects had perished. They were not, as Arianism later would be, crushed by the power of the Church in its league with Rome. They had simply faded away as fantasies tend to do. Of the remaining groups,

339   Corrington's note: "Plotinus, *The Enneads*, with an introduction by Paul Henry (New York, n.d.), xxxviii."

the one which continues our history was composed of the followers of Montanus.[340]

The doctrines of Montanus are clearly inseparable from those of his followers. The reports in the Fathers are thin, sometimes inconsistent, but it is nonetheless possible to establish the main points of his doctrine. To begin, he was not precisely a heretic, in that he and the two women who accompanied him and claimed along with him the character of prophets maintained the doctrines of the Great Church as they were then understood. It was in his "going beyond" the teachings of the Church that his speculations and his claims conflicted with Christian belief. Montanus identified himself with the *Paraclete*, the Holy Spirit, and maintained that he was, in fact, Father, Son, and Holy Spirit incarnate on earth. He was, that is, the Incarnation even as Christ had been. Moreover, Montanus promised an eschatological Kingdom on earth to his followers, the literal descent of the Heavenly Jerusalem from above.[341] This millennial enthusiasm gathered much force in Phrygia and maintained its chiliastic character long after Montanus himself vanished. From time to time, as Harnack notes, the Montanist churches would gather their people together, sell all their goods, and go into the desert to await the imminent coming of the Lord.[342] Noted for extreme asceticism, and considered by some authorities to be a reaction against the Roman accommodation that had already begun, the Montanists seem to represent at once the last major sect of the "old gnosticism" and the first of the "new gnosticism."

Milman specifically connects Montanism and its concept of the presence of the Spirit with the ideas of Joachim of Fiore.[343] It seems clear that Montanus held, in compact form, the concept of a further revelation along the lines of Joachim's much later "Third Testament" and "Third Realm" speculations.

How does the "new gnosticism" differ from the old? None of the older sects had preached a specifically millennial doctrine; the pleroma and its Hidden God were extramundane. The "gnosis" had not, in the old form, had the character of prophecy. Oddly enough, both of these elements are found, vaguely expressed, in the Johannine works rather than in gnostic documents. Again, the symbol of gnostic dualism has lost its edge; the polarity is no longer found between cosmos and pleroma. Now it has been immanentized, and takes the form of a rigorous asceticism in opposition to the softening Christian mores. This asceticism, which Harnack suspects may have contained a prohibition against marriage of the Marcionite type,[344] was set forth alongside the theme of androgyny connected with

---

340 Corrington's note: "For an overview of Montanism, see Harnack, *History of Dogma*, vol. 2, chap. 3."

341 Corrington's note: "Harnack, *History of Dogma*, 2:96."

342 Corrington's note: "Harnack, *History of Dogma*, 2:95n.2."

343 Corrington has a "note 33b" here, but there is no such note in the endnotes. The next note in the endnotes (34. Ibid., 2:99) seems to refer to Harnack's *History of Dogma* and not to Milman's book.

344 Corrington's note: "Harnack, *History of Dogma*, 2:99."

Christel.[345] There is, finally, the division of humanity into "psychic" and "pneumatic" persons in the typical gnostic fashion.

Harnack maintained that it was, indeed, the Johannine writings which inspired speculation of the Montanist type, and whether Montanus represented an end or a beginning it is clear that his doctrines represent an immanentizing—or a historicizing—of elements which had possessed the quality of mythos in their old gnostic forms.[346] This new component alone would be more than reason enough to point out Montanus's importance, and to make of his speculation a benchmark in the history of gnostic thought. His work, combining as it does both past and future gnostic symbols, seems, despite the regrettable paucity of information concerning him, to be the first of those theological formalisms which, once created, refused to die as had the older gnostic ideas, and which waited like time-bombs to go off when the spiritual substance of the *Sacrum Imperium*[347] began to ebb in the twelfth century.

III

Montanism, beginning about 160 AD, according to Spengler, was depressed by the successes of the Great Church in its union with Rome.[348] But it does not die. The "godded" prophet who lives, in Runciman's phrase, "one long Pentecost,"[349] in his certainty in being one with God, and the living Paraclete, passes on his world-feeling through *Adoptionists*, like Paul of Samosata,[350] and the Messalians, who held the gnostic dualism and the repudiation of the Old Testament, conceived their adepts as "pneumatics," and, after a novitiate, quite literally part of God. This sect, beginning in the fourth century, can be traced as existing in the eleventh century in Thrace, still vital and attempting conversion of its neighbors.[351]

From the fourth century onward, however, the strain of counter-Christianity which we have described as gnostic becomes less and less important in the

---

345 Corrington's note: "Harnack, *History of Dogma*, 2:98 et passim."

346 Corrington's note: "Voegelin appears to take the view in volume 4 of *Order and History* (Baton Rouge: Louisiana State University Press, 1956–1987) that modern gnostic movements issue from the Johannine tradition rather than from the contemporaneous gnostic sectaries. Cf. 20ff. It is worth noting that Eusebius quotes Dionysius to the same effect:

> Some of them (the Montanist teachers) look on the Law and the Prophets as nothing, neglect to obey the Gospel, esteem the Epistles of the Apostles as of little worth, but, on the contrary, declare the doctrine contained in the Revelation of John to be a great and hidden mystery. (*Historia Ecclesiastica*, 7:24)

Voegelin would extend this influence to include the Johannine gospel as well as the Apocalypse. As we have noted, Grant concurs in this judgment. I am less sure. I suspect that the question of influences here are more complex. Lacking certain dates for the various gnostic documents in most cases, the interplay between gnostic sects and the 'gnosis' of the Johannine gospel remains conjectural."

347 Imperium Romanum Sacrum.

348 Corrington's note: "Oswald Spengler, *Decline of the West* (London: George Allen and Unwin, 1932), 2:227."

349 Corrington's note: "Runciman, *The Medieval Manichee*, 18."

350 Corrington's note: "Runciman, *The Medieval Manichee*, 19."

351 Corrington's note: "Runciman, *The Medieval Manichee*, 21–25." Corrington's footnotes 39–41 could be combined into one footnote so that the page numbers are simply 18–19 and 21–25; however, the footnotes remained separated here.

ensemble of leading ideas which influence cultural growth in the ecumene. Both the cosmogonic "fairy tale" tendency of the gnostics and their various doctrinal peculiarities dim in the brilliance of the new Roman Church, and amidst the forbidding tasks of rebuilding a world-order. The diminished pulse of gnosticism became, for almost 700 years, a kind of subtone, an almost invisible strand of counter thought below the apparently overpowering spiritual and intellectual structure of the Great Church, a single thread of anti-rationalism, of radical dualism, of resistance to earthly authority, of prophetism, and enthusiastic speculation. The power of the Church and her absorptive capacities easily held in check or diverted these impulses into acceptable channels within the amazing diversity of the ecclesiastical structure.

But in the twelfth century, the gnostic pulse quickened once more. The diffuse and uncentered gnostic speculations, now quiet tributaries of a once powerful stream, began to flow together once more.

In the writing and preaching of Joachim of Fiore (1131–1202) the gnosticism of Montanus, which itself had contained in more or less representative forms most of the old gnostic ideas, rose again. As in Montanus's work, the Johannine writings and the mystery of the Paraclete were central to the speculation. Joachim, a Cistercian monk, received an inspiration at Pentecost around 1190. Thereafter, he and his school, a congeries of Franciscans and Dominicans, including one Gerard of Borgo San Donnino, whose book, published in 1245, *Introduction to the Eternal Gospel,* caused a storm of controversy, took the following positions:

1. The world is experienced as radically evil and defective; the present age is one of ruin and dismay, an iron age, and certain to perish.

2. It is possible to grasp, through a revelatory gnosis, all history as an object of cognition through application of the symbol of the Trinity to the span of world-immanent events.

3. As a result of this gnosis, history is to be understood as composed of three segments: the Age of The Father—wherein the Jews were slaves to Yehweh;[352] the Age of the Son, in which a partial freedom from Jewish legalism was achieved; and the Age of the Spirit, in which perfect freedom would be obtained by pneumatic union in grace.

4. The first age was that dominated by married couples; the second that of clerics; the third—and final—age would be that of monks, a community of autonomous persons linked together by the indwelling of the Spirit, and without the necessity for laws of any kind.

---

352 It is possible that Corrington deliberately misspelled "Yahweh" to avoid offending followers of Judaism who refuse to write or say this proper name for the God of Israel. For this reason, "Yahweh" is often abbreviated YHWH.

5. This Third Age would reveal the *Dux e Babylon*, the Anti-Christ (interpreted by Joachim as Frederick II),[353] who would be conquered, and the millennium of Franciscan Spirituals would then continue until the Judgment.

6. In the Third Realm, the institutional church would "wither away," since the Spirituals would no longer require the mediation of preaching or sacraments, being by their gnosis in grace.

7. The Prophecy of Joachim is, itself, the Third Testament, the Eternal and Final Gospel, arising from the New Testament even as the New Testament had arisen from the Old. The Revelation of St. John was its key source, even as Isaiah had been that of the New Testament.[354]

As in the old gnosis, Joachim's prophecy is festooned with detailed fantasy. Rather than cosmogonic, Joachim's deals exhaustively with correspondences between the personae of the Old and that of the New Testaments, assigning the multitudinous roles available in St. John's Apocalypse to historical personages. But for all this surplusage, his fundamental ideas, taken over with activist zeal by the Franciscan Spirituals,[355] are quite plain. And, by now, quite familiar.

Stripped of their intricate imagery, we find Joachim's speculations lying along a line of thought identifiable with that of Montanus, and through him, with that of the old gnostics. This identity is not based upon a similarity of images, since, after all, even among the old gnostics, it was quite possible to show a development from crude compactness to a fairly sophisticated level of differentiation. Rather the identity rests upon the similarity of experiences underlying the symbols. The corruption of the present age as an experience appears to be similar in Joachim with that experience in the old gnostics. Though the spiritual and cultural contexts differ widely, the tension to escape pragmatic history is the same. The dualism, while less stark in Joachim's work, is still operative, with the yearning toward the transcendent pleroma replaced by an immanent Third Age, equally monistic in its conception once the Anti-Christ, the new Demiurge, is conquered or avoided. Thus acosmic dualism is replaced by a systemic dualism. The corruption of the present age is not a function of the cosmos and its creator; rather it is the result of institution failure—of the Church and the Empire—which has brought things to this sorry pass. The social order replaces the cosmos as the locus of evil, but the mode of escape from this evil remains a gnosis.

Here the "secret knowledge" becomes an awareness of the coming Third Realm of the Spirit, who takes on the mystical attire of the Hidden God. Again, it

---

353 The Holy Roman Emperor (1194-1250).

354 Corrington's note: "In general, my description of Joachim's work follows that of Karl Löwith, *Meaning in History* (Chicago: University of Chicago Press, 1949), chap. 8. The analysis of Joachitic symbols in Eric Voegelin's *The New Science of Politics*, (Chicago: University of Chicago Press, 1952), 110ff, remains invaluable." Corrington has *New Science of Politics* as published in 1953. There are 1952 and 1954 editions, but there is no 1953 edition; therefore, the date in Corrington's note has been changed to 1952.

355 These are also referred to as the *Fraticelli* or *Spiritual Franciscans*.

must be noted that the Hidden God is no longer seen in the strictly cosmological formulation of a Valentinus. Rather the Spirit is of the kind evoked by Montanus, Paul of Samosata, and the Messalians who, after all, had worked up their inventions on the basis of a more developed and sophisticated Christian doctrine than had Simon or Valentinus, both of whom had lived within Apostolic times.

Joachim's prophetic method, as well as his dependency upon the single obviously "mythical" book in the New Testament, Revelation, inclines toward a "re-mythologization" of Christian history. This tendency is revealed in Joachim's conception that history as a whole is to be considered an object of cognition. If this is so, then history is not a process, but rather a finished and complete intellectual product, requiring nothing but the filling in of minor details to stand as pristine and self-contained as did the most ancient cosmological mythoi. Such an iconic history is no longer open to the flow of experience and realization; it is no longer a drama of the exchange of faith and grace, and man's part in it is reduced to that of automaton. The mystery of humanity's destiny through space and time, preserved in the Augustinian tension between an imperfect earthly city and a perfect heavenly one, both sharing meaning, is blurred and then abolished in millennial certainty and activist zeal.

As sacraments and homiletics are abolished, so is the *corso* through which man experiences the unfolding of pragmatic history as the movement of the Mystical Body in space through time. What Joachim purports to be the new age of existential freedom becomes the new age of transcendent slavery. The partner of man and God in history is dissolved, and in its place, humanity is faced with the *fait accompli* of a finished cosmos, handed from above, inexorable, total—and with no room in it whatever for the spontaneity which had characterized the making of Christian truth before.

The twelfth century begins the "Time of Troubles"[356] for Christendom. The tensions between Church and state, between regular and ordinary clergy, between Pope and Emperor have become too great to continue in equipoise. The tension tilts from that of faith in existence reaching out to grace in transcendence, into belief in the present clawing its way toward immanent realization in a future millennial eschaton. The driving out of the original gnostic demons has failed, for they have returned bearing others with them, no longer serving a hidden and utterly transcendent god in a pleromatic state to be achieved beyond existence. Now they are bolder, and their objective is to unveil the hidden, and to render that which had been transcendental as immanent, merely a matter of temporal sequence rather than one of a distinction in the very orders of being. And the case of the civilizational values concerned is worse than before.

In the work of Joachim of Fiore we see, on the one hand, the primary symbols associated with the old gnosticism. Their articulation has changed and developed,

---

356   Placed in quotation marks because *Time of Troubles* seems to refer primarily to a period of Russian history.

even as had the articulation of Christianity itself. But there remains the fundamental experience of the defectiveness of the present order, of the "gnosis" which can achieve an escape from this blighted earthly situation, and of the pleromatic state to be achieved by those "pneumatics" who master the gnosis. This deceptively simple formula, in its endless variants, has, since its irruption in the second century, become increasingly important in the understanding of western political thought. As Karl Löwith points out, "Far remote and dead as this quarrel of the thirteenth and fourteenth centuries seems to be today, there can be little doubt that it re-enacts the spiritual fervor of early Christianity and also conditions the modern irreligions of progress."[357]

If one applies the categories of Spengler's thought to the problem, the Magian consciousness in which Christianity arose was capable of dealing with the eschatological tension toward transcendence which is indisputably central in the Gospels and the Letters of Paul—and almost out of control in the Johannine combination of Jewish apocalyptic and Hellenistic categories. Within the Magian ambit, the tension was supportable. All creation groaned, but the balance between existence and transcendence was maintained. The eschaton was not an event to be achieved within history, but was to be its climax in the Beyond. The spiritual desolation of the ecumene was not to be abolished by immediate action through a messianic Soter, but rather was to be rendered intelligible by the Incarnation in history of that Personality whose presence was, albeit a mystery as it referred to the divine ground itself, nonetheless the living explanation in faith of history's meaning. Within Magian consciousness, that Presence continued as the Mystical Body which came to overlay and absorb Roman power in the Sacrum Imperium. This articulation was powerful enough to hold at bay and finally to repress the infantile urgings of early gnostic fantasy. The cosmos was not an object of human manipulation, but the spacio-temporal domed theatre in which history would unfold, awaiting its consummation at the Time of God's choosing.[358]

But the transition to the northern Faustian soul could not long sustain such tension. The profound "yearning toward infinite space and time," which Spengler says characterizes the Faustian soul, must needs actualize its yearning in concrete form.[359] But transcendence is not concrete; nor is it possible to "get hold of" history as if it were a thing. Thus, in this awful frustration, the repressed gnostic contents burst forth anew from the Christian past. This time, since Faustian consciousness

---

357 Corrington's note: "Löwith, *Meaning in History*, 145." Due to added footnotes, and, most particularly, the compiling of the documents, the footnote numbers in Corrington's original are inaccurate for this document. In the original, Corrington skipped from note 41 to 43, although there was a 42 in the endnotes. Corrington marked this passage as 43, but it is indeed 42. Portions of this quotation were corrected to match Löwith's text.

358 Corrington's note: "Cf. Spengler, *Decline of the West*, 2:238–40."

359 Corrington's note: "Spengler, *Decline of the West*, 1:183 et passim." Although Spengler talks about this idea ("yearning toward infinite space and time") at length, this exact quotation does not appear in either volume of *Decline of the West*. The previous footnote, which cites 2:238–40, designates the correct pages for this discussion, but this quotation does not match Spengler's text. Corrington may have been paraphrasing.

was ascendant, the controls upon it present in Magian consciousness had begun to weaken. Gnosticism is, in Spengler's phrase, "an arbitrary discovery" to Faustian man whose consciousness could not grasp its perils. It is given new formalisms, a new spatiotemporal orientation, and sent forth on its journey once more.

But the change from Magian consciousness to Faustian does not denote a similar alteration either in the manifold of reality or in the nature of man. In both there is a certain plasticity; hence it is possible to speak with some accuracy of modes of "consciousness." It is even possible, by an enormous input of energy, and an unparalleled ruthlessness, to deform both for a while. One can reduce mystery to the status of a problem among other problems—for a while. "It is, no doubt, always possible (logically and psychologically) to degrade a mystery so as to turn it into a problem. But this is a fundamentally vicious proceeding, whose springs might perhaps be discovered in a kind of corruption of the intelligence."[360]

Perhaps it is this desperation of the Faustian will to extend itself over and to dominate all time and space which has reared the *imago* of gnosticism once more in our time. Perhaps, though we no longer consider such things, the cycle of history has turned once more, and the rational order must give way to the irrational in the law of eternal return.[361] "History," Stephen Dedalus says in *Ulysses,* "is a nightmare from which I am trying to awaken." Perhaps we have not really ever escaped the prehistoric modes of our remote fathers. Perhaps we must, less often than they did, but no less certainly, abolish history.

> The life of the soul in openness toward God, the waiting, the periods of aridity and dullness, guilt and despondency, contrition and repentance, forsakenness and hope against hope, the silent stirrings of love and grace, trembling on the verge of a certainty which if gained is loss—the very lightness of this fabric may prove too heavy a burden for men who lust for massively possessive experience.[362]

It is the burden of history in existence which gnosticism in all its variants attempts to set aside. A bogus certainty is preferable to a certain faith. But, for the Christian, history is the cross which brings the Mystical Body to its Moment of Truth. Neither the past nor the future is Beyond. They are in us and about us. And the Moment is all time, all space, cosmos and infinity moving through existence darkly, that faith may be knowledge, and then face to face. But not yet. Not just yet.

---

360 Corrington's note: "Gabriel Marcel, *The Mystery of Being* (Chicago: Henry Regnery, 1960), 1:260."

361 Corrington's note: "Cf. Mircea Eliade, *The Myth of the Eternal Return* (Princeton: Princeton University Press, 1971)."

362 Corrington's note: "Voegelin, *The New Science of Politics,* 122."

APPENDICES

Appendix A

Reproduced here are copies of the "Gnosticism and Modernity" conference program along with correspondence between Bishirjian and Corrington regarding planning the conference.

Vanderbilt Conference on Gnosticism & Modernity
April 28-30, 1978
Draft of Schedule

Thursday
April 27, 1978

4:30-9:30 P.M.   Registration

Friday
April 28, 1978

8:30-9:00 A.M.   Late Registration   Faculty Club

8:30-9:00 A.M.   Breakfast   Faculty Club

9:00 A.M.   Welcome

9:15 A.M.   First Session:
                           Gnosticism and Recent Scholarship

                           J. W. Corrington, Author, New Orleans, Louisiana
                           "Gnosticism and Modern Thought: A Way You'll Never Be"

                           Gregg Edwards, Program Officer, National Science
                           Foundation, Washington, D.C.
                           "Gnostic Thinking--Its Uses and Abuses"

                           Stephen McKnight, Associate Professor of Humanities
                           University of Florida, Gainesville
                           "Gnosticism, Modernity, and the Fallacy of
                            Misplaced Concreteness"

                           Moderator: Professor Ellis Sandoz, Head
                                       Department of Government
                                       East Texas State University
                                       Commerce

12:30 P.M.   Lunch   Faculty Club

Friday
April 28, 1978

1:30 P.M.   Second Session:
                        Literature and the Idea of the Modern

                        Thomas Landess, Professor of Literature
                        University of Dallas, Texas
                        "The Artist as God: James Joyce and
                        Esthetic Gnosticism"

                        Eugene Webb, Professor of Comparative
                        Literature and Comparative Religion
                        University of Washington, Seattle
                        "Gnosticism, Alchemy, and Ennui: The
                        Literary Expression of the Spiritual
                        Crisis of Modernity"

                        Moderator: Stephen Tonsor, Professor of History
                                    University of Michigan, Ann Arbor

5:00 P.M.   Hospitality   Faculty Club

6:30 P.M.   Dinner

8:00 P.M.   Third Session
                        The Loss of History

                        Gerhart Niemeyer, Emeritus Professor of
                                Government
                        University of Notre Dame
                        South Bend, Indiana

Saturday
April 28, 1978

8:30-9:00 A.M.   Breakfast   Faculty Club

9:15 A.M.   Fourth Session:
                         Modern Ideology

                         Juergen Gebhardt, Professor of Politics
                         Ruhr-Universität Bochum, Germany
                         "Ideology and Reality--The Ideologue's
                         Persuasion in Modern Politics"

                         Klaus Vondung, Professor of German Literature
                         Comprehensive University of Siegen, Germany
                         "Spiritual Revolution and Magic: Patterns
                         of Speculation and Political Action in
                         National Socialism"

                         Moderator: Professor William Havard, Head
                                     Department of Political Science
                                     Vanderbilt University
                                     Nashville, Tennessee

12:30 P.M.   Lunch   Faculty Club

1:30 P.M.   Fifth Session:
                         Gnosticism and Revolution

                         Melvin E. Bradford, Professor of Literature
                         University of Dallas, Texas
                         "Dividing the House: Lincoln's Political
                          Rhetoric and Gnosticism"

                         Fr. John Counahan, Luling, Louisiana
                         "Modern Spiritual Men"

                         J. M. Porter, Professor of Political Science
                         University of Saskatchewan, Saskatoon
                         "Luther and Gnosticism: The Case of the
                          Peasant's Revolt"

                         Moderator: Dante L. Germino, Professor of
                                     Government and Foreign Affairs
                                     University of Virginia
                                     Charlottesville

Saturday
April 28, 1978

5:00 P.M.	Hospitality	Faculty Club
6:30 P.M.	Dinner	Faculty Club

8:00 P.M.   Sixth Session:
                   The Quest for Certitude

                   Richard J. Bishirjian, Assistant Professor
                   Political Science
                   College of New Rochelle, New York
                   "Carlyle's Political Religion Revisited"

                   Thomas Hollweck, Assistant Professor of
                   German Literature
                   University of Colorado
                   Boulder, Colorado
                   " *Trust in German Philosophy and Poetry at the Beginning of the 19th Century* "
                   Moderator: Fr. Francis Canavan, S.J.
                             Professor of Political Science
                             Fordham University, Bronx, N.Y.

Sunday
April 29, 1978

8:30-9:00 A.M.   Breakfast   Faculty Club

9:15 A.M.   Seventh Session:
                   Science, Politics and Gnosticism--After
                   Twenty-five Years

                   Eric Voegelin, Philosopher
                   Stanford, California

                   James Wiser, Associate Professor of Government
                   Loyola University of Chicago, Illinois
                   "From Cultural to Philosophical Anthropology:

Contributors   -   9-25-76

1. Tom Landess, New England Puritanism, *UD*
2. Mel Bradford, Lincoln's Second Inaugural, *UD*
3. Bishirjian, Carlyle and Renaissance Hermetism, *CNR*
4. Corrington, Ancient Gnosticism, *New Orleans*
5. Cleanth Brooks, Blake & Shelley, *Yale*
6. Stephen McKnight, Neo-Platonism, *Univ. Fla.*
7. Jene Porter, Luther, *Univ. Saskatchewan, ok*
8. Wasinger, English Puritanism, *Detroit*
9. Wiser, *Loyola Chicago*
10. Webb, *Univ. West. ok*
11. Gebhardt, *Ideology and Reality*

Commentators

15. Eric Voegelin
16. Niemeyer

830

Length: 20/pages; 5,000 to 7,500

15

Due: August, 1977

Essays Needed

Response to Dante Germino
Behaviorism
Magic, Alchemy
Kabbalah

Letters Out: Vree ✓
Webb ✓
Hollweck, *Univ. Colorado* ✓
Gebhardt, *Bochum*
Yates, *Univ. London*
Vondung

N. Kress Hoover

Hollweck
Murphy
Vondung

Late Abstracts

Landess ✓
Bradford ✓
Brooks
Wasinger ✓
Corrington ✓
Murphy ✓
Havard ✓
Gebhardt ✓
Landess ✓

8 October 76

Dear Dick,

Excuse the paper. I've just finished a long piece of work, & am continuing to use what comes to hand.

Still no word from Mel Bradford? I hope he will contribute. I knew & enjoyed his company years ago when I was at LSU. By the way, I think the Kabbalah idea is excellent. But we're still in need of one or more scientists — otherwise, I'm gonna have to do scientism myself — along the lines of Voegelin's 1948 article on Newton & Leibniz.

Let me say that the problem you raise in relation to my theory that Gnosticism is a genus with multiple subspecies is, possibly, a pseudo-problem. I think the core of Gnosticism is the spiritual incapacity to grasp the complimentarity of — what will you? — spirit-world, or mind-matter. I see no substantive distinction between the imbalance of Valentinian or Basilidean anti-world gnosis, & enlightenment anti-spirit gnosis. It seems to me that Gnosticism represents a breakdown in the ability to deal with the dualistic (& complimentary) nature of human experience, & the immense tension created in the soul by this dichotomy of experience. to my mind, it is of no great moment whether one comes down on the side of spirit or world, of mind or matter (or, as with the ancient gnostics & certain puritan sects, on the side of asceticism or libertinism). to come down on a side to the exclusion or devaluation of the other is to derail into a form of gnosis.

I think you will find, in Fifth Monarchy men or in radical empiricists, in Montanus & Marx, the same symbolic constellations & the uncontrollable urge to degrade, eliminate, ignore, or utterly dominate either one side or the other of the dichotomy of actual human experience. the urge is to establish a radical monism in all the cases I am aware of. It seems to me inconsequential as to what monism is chosen: the event, the spiritual condition, we call Gnosticism invariably attempts to suppress one or another sector of the whole of human experience by denying its (a) reality, (b) value, (c) intelligibility, or (d) its experienced meaning.

please consider this, & cite me a specific case which appears clearly gnostic, yet does not embody these characteristics. I think we should check out our own models of Gnosticism before we get

into editing the book because I have a gut-feeling
that if we can set out a thorough-going,
consistent, & reasonably detailed model of
Gnosticism which holds for virtually all cases
of ideological or spiritual disorders, we are in
a position to make some notable waves in
what passes for the "intellectual community."

In direct relation to this, I'm enclosing the
initial draft of my paper for Steve McKnight's
book on Voegelin for the LSU press. In it, you'll
see a long footnote (long for a footnote,
but not long enough to cover the subject,
obviously) on the fundamentally monistic
character of Gnostic "Second Realities." You will
also recall Robert Tucker's stunning book on
"Philosophy & Myth in Karl Marx" which shows the
intimate relation between "Second Realities" & personal
fantasies. The desire to obliterate capital & create
a "Classless society," beyond its fantasy character,
is also an illustration of the urge toward a monistic
order.

Let me suggest that you take a look at Jung's
theory of the "shadow" — also set out by Eric
Neumann in an otherwise ghastly book called

"Depth psychology to a New Ethic." The book is simply monstrous in its clanking positivistic ignorance to its bumptious contempt for the "old" Judeo-christian (or even classical) ethic, but it does have the merit of showing the mechanism of the "shadow" portion of man's psyche, the "other" which he attempts to suppress in order to be "good."

Now the crucial point he makes is that any suppressed contents is destructive to will manifest itself in peculiar ways. One must come to terms with that "shadow" or "other." It must become conscious to be "worked through." All the psychological baggage aside, I think he has a point: the origin of Gnosticism seems to me to be the breaking of the righteous tension between various aspects of experience which cannot be reconciled. those who simply cannot live comfortably with paradox are candidates for Gnostic fantasies.

Be that as it may, I hope you can find time to read to critique freely my enclosed essay. The final draft must go to Steve on 1 December, I I would vastly appreciate you making sure I am not committing some egregious gaffe, or misrepresenting Professor Voegelin in some awful way. I take our collective enterprise very seriously, considering it to be probably the most important involvement, intellectually, that we are likely to take part in. I am convinced that, in the near future, the return to classical models of human science will begin to score impressive gains over the tradesmen who have taken over not only political science, but psychology & philosophy as well. They are intellectually & spiritually dead. Voegelin has handed us the shovels. Let's get to burying them.

You'll be pleased to hear that I've been tentatively approached about the possibility of a professorship in the Department of Humanities at the University of Florida. It is, apparently, a department of generalists gathered from philosophy, music, law, history, literature, et al. Sounds rather like the place I always wanted to find. I'll keep you posted if any thing comes of it.

As to the Dallas job, I have no intention of either denying my caste of mind, nor of becoming an ideologue in its behalf, but your cautions really only confirmed my certainty that I want no part of a catholic institution (5 years with the Jesuits was more than enough: at one point, as chairman of their English Department, I was removed &

threatened with firing if I did not withdraw my petition to the University Rank & tenure committee for a hearing to determine whether or not one of my best faculty-members was or was not tenured. Believe it or not! I told them to go to hell, but it was rough), & would be most dubious concerning another administrative post. I prefer research.

Let's try to exchange some more ideas on the nature of Gnosticism (we'll have to sketch it out for an introduction sooner or later, anyhow), & set up a kind of prospectus for our people. We have to exercise at least a minimal degree of editorial control, so that the essays will be within some reasonably circumscribed limits.

When we're ready as between ourselves, we can send this out, along with tentative deadlines for the papers, & dates for the conference. We should also get provisional titles & subjects within the next three to five months so that we can start running some numbers on possible publishers.

I expect we'll need a fairly well-developed prospectus both for foundations & for publishers,

including a discussion of Gnosticism, or a list of
contributors & titles of papers. The sooner we
get this under way, the better.

Let me hear from you about the paper. I need
your comments.

Also: should you have a spare xerox of your
polysci primer, I'd like very much to see it.

Sincerely,

Bill

19 October 76
New Orleans

Dear Dick,

Just got in from the Court of Appeal to find your letter. I'm of the opinion that, taken together, we've got some strong contributions lined up. The Hegel piece & the Nazism & magic thing—both add some intellectual spice to the proceedings.

I await your *prunes* part three anxiously. I hope you don't regard my view of gnosticism as dogmatic. My legal training — similar to that in hard science — tends to make me sniff & delve until a hypothesis can be constructed. Then to defend it on the grounds that, if it has <u>prima facie</u> validity, that's a good place to start — wherever you end up.

I would, of course, not expect anyone to agree with the hypothesis. But it has one enormous advantage (<u>if</u> it is correct): it provides us with a generalization both broad & deep, into which

all manner of phenomena, even mutually
contradictory on the surface, can be fitted.
Yet it is not vague: the thesis that a drive toward
monism is the fundamental characteristic
of gnostic orders, whether scientistic or mystical,
ancient or modern, seems to me to be testable
empirically on the documents of the various
subspecies — or species, if gnosticism is a genus —
If the thesis should hold, it would in no way
detract from the various symbolizations &
structures which we find in hermeticism, magic,
etc. It would simply put the axe to those critics
who have maintained that the definition of
gnosticism is too vague to use as an analytical
tool. If the essays we collect show that, if
extrapolated to the highest level of generality, we
are dealing with a determined monism, two
things result: the analytical usefulness of the
term & the various complexes of symbols we
identify with it become clearer, &, I would
think, eminently defensible. Secondly, the
antithesis of Gnosticism arises from the very
analysis of gnosticism itself: right order,
metaphysically & ontologically, requires a
dualistic, complementary structure in all
circumstances, precisely as is required in physics.

I can think of nothing more useful than establishing a philosophical parameter which would suggest a first approximation of the order or disorder inherent in symbolisms which, wherever in the spectrum of thought they may occur, will certainly have political consequences.

Let me say two things about your contribution to the book, & your present situation. First, the book (& hopefully the conference) have no deadline at present, & that is the way it should remain for the present — until we can get a clear idea of when the majority of our contributors will be able to get their pieces done. Should your grant come through, you can then determine whether it is best to hold off on a deadline, or give over doing the Carlyle piece. Secondly, for my own taste, your primary part there sounds more exciting & immediately useful than the Carlyle. You will get used to my Aristotelean-Scientific temperament: I always prefer the substantial generalization to the perfectly-crafted small piece because a) the small piece can be done by any competent craftsman. b.) the generalization, when it works, marks an epoch, however small, & forces new things to happen. Now I am of the opinion that the time for things to begin going our way is now, & that a solid book that has the balls to establish testable generalizations right next to extensive particular essays could accomplish a great deal — across the board.

Amidst all this generalizing, I almost forgot to tell you that I was in Baton Rouge last week, & spoke to the Editor of the LSU press, & to Lewis Simpson of <u>the Southern Review</u>. Both found our project interesting, & I have no doubt a good solid book of essays of the kind we're trying to gather would be well-received.

Have I sent you a copy of the enclosed essay? I think it is quite important to my thesis on gnosticism. It is hard going. Be patient, & let me know what you think of it. Yes, I know Bishop Berkeley would approve.

Finally, back to your contribution: I think your
historical development from gnosticism to atheist
humanism sounds just right. Is it possible
that we might wish to combine or alter
my piece in relation to yours, so that they
either follow, one upon the other, or are
combined into a single joint-author essay?
I did that with Miller Williams for the
Introduction to Southern Writing in the Sixties, a
2-volume anthology LSU Press put out about 10
years ago. Since my piece begins at the presumptive
"beginning," & yours apparently goes beyond mine,
they might either fit together, or look good, one
after the other. One of these ways might be
the best way for you to minimize new work, &
yet have a solid contribution. When I see
your port three, it'll be easier to determine.

As for pushing my thesis, I wouldn't wish to
do so in the book unless a) the essays showed
by a clear preponderance of evidence that the
hypothesis is correct, & b) that you agreed with
it without reservation. Having set up the hypothesis,
we are at the evidentiary stage, & if it is sound,
the essays should collectively reveal it without

any foreknowledge on the part of the contributors. If radical monism is the desired end-result of a gnostic enterprise, then the "law" thus observed should reveal itself whenever proper questions are directed at the symbols & the methodologies by which they are manipulated (which methodologies consist of symbolic operations themselves). Failing this, the hypothesis is at least in doubt.

I'm looking forward to hearing your comments on "order & consciousness." I want the essay to have a maximum of authority, because that will assist our present venture.

Sincerely,
Bill—

P.S. I'm writing to Globus (article enclosed). He may be the scientist I've been looking for.

Dear Dick,

I enjoyed your letter, but most of all enjoyed receiving your primer. I've had only time to read the section on gnosticism, but it is excellent. I was struck by the similarity of our views, & even the similarity of quotes & ideas we find important in Voegelin. You'll note this when you read my consciousness piece, I think.

thanks for including the Voegelin letter. We read it differently. Voegelin advises "caution" in using gnosticism as a genus. I would concur. But he is hardly in a position to reject such a use, since he has done so over most of his career. He explains "gnosticism" in terms of the ancient gnostics, then calls Joachim a "gnostic," & then, in diversworks, so identifies the puritans, encyclopedists, scientism, positivism in all its varieties, marxism & all other Hegelian variants, National Socialism, & even psychoanalysis! As we thus span a millenium & move from Simon Magus to Adolf Hitler under the rubric of "gnosticism," but must not add Hermeticism, magic, or Alchemy?

It seems to me, caution considered, that Voegelin has swallowed eagles to gag on gnats. Thus, with respect, I cannot agree. I do see caution indicated by the phrase "all gnosis is not gnosticism," that is wholly correct, & the caution should extend, obviously, into the study of Hermeticism as well as into, say, Marxism. Marxism as economics & as political method is to be considered just as one considers capitalism. But, as Voegelin notes, these are matters outside "doctrine." The Marxist economic & political structures are to be judged, I would think, by pragmatic success; & the marxist "doctrine" does not admit of such cavalier standards. "Doctrines" are not to be put to the proof, & no questions are allowed — for the obvious reason that the answers will be devastating to the "doctrine."

My concern in all this is certainly not to preserve a term for its own sake. Rather my concern has two aspects: 1) gnosticism is, at long last, a recognized word for a determinate constellation of political & theological ideas, sentiments, & action-frames. 2.) As a generic, it might well allow us to begin establishing a recognizable morphology for all the species of "second realities" which plague us. I loath disorganization in what purports to be a science. It is well enough for poets & novelists to move my intuition, by a "logic of the emotions." that is not a useful or even healthy way to move within science. If we cannot order the symbolic structures with which we deal, we are doing no more than creating new symbols of disorder based upon _doxa_, & in my "opinion," _doxa_ & six bits will get you a pack of cigarettes in _some_ machines.

Simpson is _not_ LSA press ~~editor~~; [director] he is editor of the _Southern Review_. My contact at the press is an editor, Beverly Jarrol, ~~that~~ She edited Volume IV of O.SH. I'll talk to her when I can about the _Primer_.

I've been looking at G.R.S. Mead on Hermeticism — I've had his 3 volumes on Hermes since the 1960's — bought them in London at John Watkins in Cecil Court, but, like some Jakob Boehme, I never got a chance to read it before. Looks like the same old thing to me: sort of the "climate of opinion in matters spiritual" floating around in the two centuries before & after Christ. For my purposes, the provinance of this kind of thing is not of overriding importance, since it appears almost universally once men break beyond animism. To me, its identification, its dynamics, & its results are most important.

4

I am presently completing a film treatment for a deadline, & have some work on a case against IBM. then I'm heading home to North Louisiana for 10 days of hunting & fishing. During that period, I'm going to try to jot down some preliminary ideas about my generic gnosticism. It obviously is an attempt to destroy Vroegelius' "balance of consciousness" — i.e. the dualistic complementarity of the reality of the cosmos. But, the fault here, seen pragmatically, is the inevitable result of the gnostic attempt to render a monistic philosophy within some time-frame. Would gnosticism — even to the deification of man — be injurious if it were specifically noted to be a post-historical reality, about which nothing can be done? Gnosticism is to prevalent & too insistent to be treated as if it were a species of disease like cancer. things are not so simple. I will enlarge on this later.

Sincerely
Bill

December 2, 1976

Dr. J. W. Corrington
1724 Valence
New Orleans, La. 70115

Dear Bill,

I tried to place a call through to your office today, but you were out. Let me summarize what I wanted to discuss with you.

(1) Can I have an update on the status of those contributors you have solicited: Brooks, McKnight, Porter, Wiser? I'm particularly concerned that Wiser stay with our project since, in my judgment, he is the best political theorist (of his generation) in America today. Enclosed is a book review of a book by J. E. Bruns, The Forbidden Gospel. If one of your cohorts has not settled on a topic, perhaps he would like to analyze this work. Again, I think Wiser would be good to respond to Germino.

(2) I believe I can get Niemeyer to make an original contribution, though he has now agreed to be a commentator. What do you recommend?

(3) Tom Landess has offered to publish our book. What do you think?

(4) My own time limitations now seem to preclude a lot that I originally intended. Unofficially, I got the grant. But I think I will write an essay on Carlyle, minus the original work I wanted to do.

(5) I think it would be in order to send a letter to our potential contributors, which outlines our purpose, and lists the topics of each of our contributors. I assume that you will contribute a piece analyzing the generic uses of the term "gnosticism," and will grapple with the serious issues that implies.

(6) Once that has been penned, I would like you to consider inviting the following to be commentators on the essays: Ellis Sandoz (East Texas State); Havard; Hallowell (Duke). Any suggestions on your side?

By now, I trust you have received my comments on your "Consciousness" study. I'm open to your remarks.

Cordially,

enclosures

LAW OFFICES

STEVEN R. PLOTKIN
OWEN J. BRADLEY
JAMES C. AZCONA
JOSEPH M. SINGERMAN
JOHN WILLIAM CORRINGTON
JONATHAN M. LAKE
MARTIN L. BROUSSARD, JR.

6 December 76

Dear Dick,

I was about to write to you when your letter came. I've been out of things for two weeks in order to make up for my relative ignorance of Hermetic and Alchemical literature. I've gone through Mead's Thrice Greatest Hermes, all of Jung on Alchemy, Scholem's Kaballah, Waite's Holy Kaballah, and have re-read some of Eliade's stuff, including The Two and The One, which leads back to the androgny of Christ-Lapis, etc. In any case, I have a handle on the materials. I've orderedYates' Bruno and am passing time with Boehm and Eckhart.

All this has been useful, because I can now see the general lines along which a revision of my brief 'history' of Gnosticism should be carried out. I now see Voegelin's phrase "Second Reality" better stated as 'anti-reality.' The parallel with particle-anti-particle is, to say the least, startling. Gnosticism and Hermeticism seem to blend, with magic and Alchemy as their respective operational auxiliaries. Simon Magus, the Gnostic, was a magician; Paracelsus, the Hermetic, was an Alchemist. Obviously, I'll have to sketch out a general theory, with a minimum of illustrations, leaving details for later work, and for others.

Let me respond to the points you raise.

I think Niemeyer would make a top-flight contributor, and I would rather see him, fresh out of translating Anamnesis, in that role than as a commentator.

You say Tom Landess has offered to publish the book? What are his auspices? Does he run a press? My inclination would be to say, let's get a commitment if it's a press that can assure reasonable advertising and distribution/ However, given the list of contributors we have, I see no reason to feel that we're going to be in a bad position for a publisher, but, of course, if Tom wants to do it and has the capacity to do it, I think he should have first crack.

I agree that we should be ready now to send a letter to our probable contributors. I'm enclosing a rough draft which you should take as indicative--or alter to suit yourself. I think, however, this letter should merely state our general purpose, presumptive cut-off date, our plans to seek publication (unless you cann firm it up with Tom), and our plans to seek funds for a symposium just prior to--or possibly just after--publication.

Then, in the letter, I think we could ask for, by return-mail,

9TH FLOOR, BARONNE BUILDING NEW ORLEANS, LOUISIANA 70112 / 504 524-1393

more or less firm topics and, hopefully, provisional titles--
since I think we will need those for the purpose of approaching
a possible funding agency.

Once we have this information, I think we might get it all
together and send out a kind of provisional table of contents,
so that everyone has an idea of what is going on.

By the way, do you have a copy of the Germino article? I don't
have it, or a cite (part of the limitation of law: rare trips
to the periodical rack at Tulane), so I can read his strictures
on "gnosticism" and direct Jim Wiser to it.

Your suggestions for commentators seem fine to me. All of them
are well-known, and all write fluently and well, and are given
to sharp insights.

I am still concerned about the lack of any scientists, philosophers
or historians of science. I am well aware of the problems involved,
but I am going to put a note in my letter asking for suggestions
by our contributors as to people who might be interested, since a
vast degree of current gnostic thought is found in science--most
especially the "soft sciences."

As to your contribution, I think Carlyle is a sterling figure. I
wonder whether he had influence in the later British strands of
thought (so untypically British) which led to Oswald Moseley, et.
al. Are you going to home in on "Heroes and Hero-Worship?"

Please forgive my not acknowledging your comments on my Voegelin
paper sooner. It was kind and gracious of you to take out time to
read it. I've taken into account some of your cuts, and done some
qualifying. In general, I left the structure alone, because I
mean to do another piece linking some of Voegelin's work with
some of Jung's and Neumann's. Voegelin's excellent treatment of
the Apeiron symbolism invites similar work on the Uroboros
symbolism (the serpent with its tail in its mouth) which is
incredibly universal, and which, from India to 17th Century
England, always occupies the same orbital of meaning. The Apeiron
clearly derives from a similar experience of primal unity, and is
the differentiated philosophical abstract concept drawn from the
Uroboros symbol. What I want to do is to suggest that Voegelin has
avoided using the tools of analytic psychology because of a personal
prejudice, but that, in the case of symbols like the Uroboros, it
is useful and empirically determinable that we are dealing with
an archtype, the meaning of which is common in all its contexts.

By the way, my present undertaking, aside from a new film script,
is an essay called "Toward the Skandalon," which deals with the
work of Bultmann and that of Phillip Frankm, the physicist. Bultmann,
as you know, wants to "demythologize" scripture; Frank wants to
purge physics of "metaphysics." The two enterprises are very similar,
and reveal some symmetries that are more than interesting. I'll
send you a copy.

By all means, rewrite my letter, fill in what you think is needed
additionally, and send it back. I will then get a fair copy, have
it xeroxed, sign the copies, and send them to you for mailing.

Sincerely, Bill

LAW OFFICES

STEVEN R. PLOTKIN
OWEN J. BRADLEY
JAMES C. AZCONA
JOSEPH M. SINGERMAN
JOHN WILLIAM CORRINGTON
JONATHAN M. LAKE
MARTIN L. BROUSSARD, JR.

11 January 77

Dear Dick,

Thanks for yours of 27 December.

I don't know Cecil Crabbe at LSU, but I might be able to get to him indirectly through Bill Havard, if it seems worth the effort.

It would be great for you to get back to Dallas. That would put you in some kind of distance where we could get together when the book begins to jell.

My best shot so far is a possibility at Vanderbilt. They're looking for a super-interdisciplinary Andrew Mellon Professor with a base in English. Man, do I qualify! If they're serious, and the candidacy is really open, I can get a ton of high-powered recommendations.

By the way, may I put you down as a referee?

I didn't want to mention it until it had gotten firmed up, but I've finally conned Jim Counahan, a former Dominican, and a close friend of mine, into translating Tractatus Super Quatuor Evangelia. We got the Latin text done by Buonaiuti in the 1930's, and Jim has begun the translation. We're going to do a lengthy Introduction, beginning with Joachim's medieval reputation, make the Hermetic and Alchemical connections, and then bring it up to date, to show the Abbot's modern influence. I frankly don't think we'll have a hard time getting a publisher, and it will certainly be a boon for political theory. Joachim is frequently mentioned but rarely read. If we get a publisher, we may add the commentary on the Apocalypse, and even the Figura, if Jim can hold out, and the publishers want a big book. Jim is a philosophy PhD, and has good Latin.

God knows I take no pleasure in the present condition of the Church, but it appears she has lost her memory. Rather than hunker down and wait for a genuine new line to take, she seems to flounder in all directions. She's leftist in Latin America, and the Italians are all over her as a giant landlord in Rome. Sounds like a panic-pattern. The personal anguish is that she seems unable to produce a new insight--something she has always done in the past.

Let me hear from you.

Sincerely, Bill

9TH FLOOR, BARONNE BUILDING, NEW ORLEANS, LOUISIANA 70112 / 504 524-1393

LAW OFFICES

STEVEN R. PLOTKIN
OWEN J. BRADLEY
JAMES C. AZCONA
JOSEPH M. SINGERMAN   17 December 76
JOHN WILLIAM CORRINGTON
JONATHAN M. LAKE
MARTIN L. BROUSSARD, JR.

Dear Dick,

I enclose the letter signed. I couldn't see anything that
needed changes. I assume you have all the addresses, but
if not, let me know. I can find, amidst a pile of papers,
those of Wiser, Porter, Brooks, etc.

I have to admit I've never given much thought to being a
college president. Seems as if it would be a more lethal
undertaking than teaching, more time-consuming, more loathsome,
and, lacking a good tenured position at the school as a fall-
back, a consummate misery. At the same time, I have no aversion
to talking to people. I enjoyed my administrative role as
chairman in terms of finding and hiring good people, and then
letting them the hell alone to do what I knew they were willing
and able to do. My relations with a 15 member faculty were
outstanding (ie, elected unanimously to a second term, being
supported unanimously by faculty plus student representatives
in various clashes with administration), but everything I
attempted was a hassle with deans and presidents--the same ones
who, a little later, were chased from office by student Luddites.

Still, there is a deep pleasure in organizing and facilitating
a worthwhile enterprise, and if it were possible to actually do
that as a college president in the present "climate of opinion",
I might like it. I have the advantage of a lively interest and
real affection for the sciences--lacking in too many humanists--
plus a working and real knowledge of the operation and topology
of professional schools.

As to my religion, I hate to sound like a copy-cat, but in all
honesty, I am a "pre-Trentine Christian." My own intellectual
roots are in Augustine and Aquinas, but I grew up in a solidly
Protestant town, and went to a Methodist college, where I did
thrive. I also married a Methodist, and my daughter is a Methodist.
I would have no great difficulty in identifying myself as such,
though my own spiritual position has never found much help in
institutional strivings.

However, I would approach a Catholic institution like Dallas
only with extreme caution. I was educated by the Jesuits--twice,
and I have no intention of becoming involved once more in the
threshings of a dissolving theological system. I have no doubt
that the Catholic faith will persist--but I am quite sure that
the present institution is useless as a basis for the pursuit
either of scientia or the Agathon.   P.T.O.

9TH FLOOR, BARONNE BUILDING NEW ORLEANS, LOUISIANA 70112 / 504 524-1393

I'm enclosing a <u>Vita</u> just in case you should come across anything that might seem <u>worth</u> following up.

I'm glad to know Tom has got himself a press. My only hesitation would be in relation to distribution, as a practical matter. If he could give us reasonable assurance of plenty of reviewer's copies where they're needed, and of a decent shot at distribution, I'd be glad to go along with him. Failing that, I do think that we have a real possibility at LSU. The Press Committee there is accustomed to the language and subject-matter of our work, since they've published most of Voegelin, and are publishing Steve McKnight's book of essays on Voegelin. A book in which his theses would obviously be central should not evoke blank astonishment there.

Let me hear from you soon.

Sincerly, Bill

J. W. Corrington
1724 Valence
New Orleans, LA 70115

R. J. Bishirjian
69 Leland Avenue
New Rochelle, NY 10805

December 20, 1976

Dear Colleagues:

As you know from earlier correspondence, we are well along in the planning of a volume of essays provisionally entitled Gnosticism and Modernity. We have been gratified by your response to our project announcement, and can report to you the names of the following distinguished scholars in numerous fields who have agreed to contribute commentaries or original essays to the book. Our colleagues in this endeavor include Gerhart Niemeyer, Klaus Vondung, Eric Voegelin, William Murphy, Thomas Hollweck, Jurgen Gebhardt, Eugene Webb, Stephen Wasinger, Thomas Landess, M. E. Bradford, Jene Porter, Stephen A. McKnight, Cleanth Brooks, and James Wiser.

Because until now our communication with you has been limited to personal letters from either of the two of us, we would like to take this opportunity to mutually sketch, in broad outline, the general plan of the book, and to provide you with the procedural information necessary for its publication.

The term "Gnosticism" should be understood, we feel, in an extended rather than in a narrow sense. Generally, we take our inspiration from the work of Professor Eric Voegelin whose use of the concept in its generic sense includes those intellectual movements such as Hermeticism, Alchemy, Magic, Kabbalah, Rosicrucianism, Millennialism, and certain strands of Neoplatonism and Scientism. Concisely, we are concerned with patterns of "Second Reality," using Musil's phrase, which tend to contract consciousness of reality. Since all of you have worked in this area before, no more extensive definition should be required.

Clearly, the merit of a book such as this will be enhanced by the breadth of the essays. Thus we will begin with a fairly lengthy historical and definitional essay, written by Bill Corrington, which will, hopefully, establish the parameters within which the other essays will operate, and which will relieve the authors of the remaining essays from establishing their subject in the field of intellectual history. This does not preclude, of course, essays critical of the value of "Gnosticism" as an analytical tool, or essays which in effect incorporate the arguments and findings of recent scholarship by such persons as Frances Yates, Daniel Walker, Hans Jonas, or Dante Germino.

Turning to more procedural concerns, for receiving essays we have set the final date of September 1, 1977. We also plan, in the near future, to file proposals with the National Science Foundation and other funding agencies and institutions to the end that a Symposium on Gnosticism and Modernity might be held in conjunction with the publication of the book. In order to prepare the proposal, we request that you send us, no later than January 25, 1977, a provisional title and brief abstract of your essay. The abstract need not exceed 200 words. Shortly after receipt of these abstracts, we hope to be able to announce tentative publishing arrangements.

-3-

When we have received the titles and abstracts of the essays, we will be writing you again, including what will amount to a provisional table of contents of the book. We will keep you informed as we progress in our plans for publication and the symposium.

One final note: may we also ask that you suggest the names of further possible contributors in one specific area, the area of the physical sciences. We feel that inclusion of thought in this area would be most desirable, and will appreciate your suggestions.

With best wishes for this Christmas, we are

Sincerely yours,

Richard J. Bishirjian   J. W. Corrington

LAW OFFICES

STEVEN R. PLOTKIN
OWEN J. BRADLEY   28 January 1977
JAMES C. AZCONA
JOSEPH M. SINGERMAN
JOHN WILLIAM CORRINGTON
JONATHAN M. LAKE
MARTIN L. BROUSSARD, JR.
JOHN P. COSENTINO

Dear Dick,

I was about to send a copy of Jene's abstract to you. Glad
to get Webb's piece. His application of the principles to
a rather wide spectrum of literary work is a fine idea,
though I hope he doesn't go so wide as to thin out his
effect. I might drop him a note and suggest that keeping
Les fleurs du mal as his centerpiece, with a few jaunts
toward other writings, would solidify his project, and
give him ample foundation for a series of later papers.
Baudelaire was a figure of such central and lasting importance that any substantial gnosticism shown in his work
could, almost by reference, be suggested as having had
profound impact on most modern poetry and fiction.

As I said earlier, I'm quite ready to work with Tom Landess
on our book. Should you want to go with him rather than
give LSU a shot, we can do that. I certainly have nothing
approaching a commitment from them, though I do have good
contacts with the Press, and with the editors of the Southern
Review, etc.

Your idea about establishing a Humanities Institute is
intriguing. The only problem would be, where the hell do
we go find 2 or 3 million dollars--or more--which would be
called for to establish an endowment? Any ideas? For my
part, I would wish to make it an Institute for Advanced
Studies, bringing in political philosophers, theologians,
and scientists of the order of Polanyi, Heisenburg, and
so on. There must be young Eleiades, Polanyis, Voegelins,
and so on, in various fields. I am dedicated to the proposition that theoretical physicists and people like us have
a great deal to say to one another, and that such discourse
will found the symbolic basis for future knowledge.

If something should turn up at Dallas, I would be willing
to risk a Catholic institution, barring the Jesuits. If
you and Tom and Mel were there, I would surely feel at home.
Does Dallas have a Law School? I have good credentials in
Jurisprudence, so that I feel I could make my base in English,
Political Science, Law or, if they have it, a film department.

I've gotten no other abstracts as yet. They may all come to
you. In any case, when we hit the deadline, we'll yell like
hell, and try to draw in the rest. Then, armed with those,

9TH FLOOR, BARONNE BUILDING, NEW ORLEANS, LOUISIANA 70112 / 504 524-1393

and with a reasonably long description of what the book will do, what its audience will be, and so on, I'll go up to Baton Rouge and begin hustling the Director of the Press. The fact that he's doing Tom McKnight's book on Voegelin and that I'm in it may well help us. We'll see.

Let me hear when you start getting some more abstracts. I will write to Ronald Geballe to see if I can corner us a honest to God physicist.

I will also send a copy of my piece on Gnosticism to Webb so he can see the character of the thing before I enlarge and revise it.

Lemme hear.

Sincerely,

Bee

LAW OFFICES

STEVEN R. PLOTKIN
OWEN J. BRADLEY
JAMES C. AZCONA
JOSEPH M. SINGERMAN
JOHN WILLIAM CORRINGTON
JONATHAN M. LAKE
MARTIN L. BROUSSARD, JR.

7 March 77

Dear Dick:

Here's Steve McKnight's abstract for our book. I'm writing to tell him that he & I are somewhat at cross-purposes, since my "history" of Gnosis will treat it as a generic term, under which the others, hermeticism, magic, scientism, positivism, will all be comprehended. We'll work it out, so as not to be confusing.

Cleanth Brooks will be delayed, but he's surely worth waiting for. He's completing a new book on Faulkner just now.

I sent my vita to Tom Landess. Haven't heard from him yet. Have you gotten any new abstracts? We may have to cast our nets wider, & bring in such people as Harvard as primary contributors.

Let me hear from you.

Sincerely,
Bill

9TH FLOOR, BARONNE BUILDING, NEW ORLEANS, LOUISIANA 70112 / 504 524-1393

LAW OFFICES

STEVEN R. PLOTKIN
OWEN J. BRADLEY
JAMES C. AZCONA   13 March 77
JOSEPH M. SINGERMAN
JOHN WILLIAM CORRINGTON
JONATHAN M. LAKE
MARTIN L. BROUSSARD, JR.
JOHN P. COSENTINO

Dear Dick,

Aha, you rug-merchant, I have excellent news for you! The nose
of the camel is well entrenched within the tent of LSU Press.

One of my oldest friends there is Beverly Jarrett, one of the
senior editors. Last week I was up in Baton Rouge arguing before
the Louisiana 1st Circuit Court of Appeal, and went by LSU Press
when I got done. Bev is just begging to edit Steve McKnight's
book of essays on Voegelin, and we talked about the Bishirjian-
Corrington book. She says LSU would be extremely interested in
it. Bev, by the way, edited The Ecumenic Age for LSU, so she is
well into what we're about. In order to edit that book, she read
all Voegelin's earlier work, dealt with him at length, and fell
somewhat in love with him. She is extremely sympathetic.

She is also now dating one Thomas Szasz, who is a professor of
psychiatry in New York, and who has written some 15 books--mostly
knocking hell out of his witch-doctor colleagues. She detailed
his work, showed me some, and so I have written him, asking if
he would like to contribute. He is also knowledgeable as to
Voegelin, and will understand where we're coming from. Thus we
may add a psychiatrist to our ranks, and advance the politics
of being published. All a guy needs is a good lawyer.

By the way, she also mentioned some of the names on the publishing
committee, and I know them, and feel they would lean toward a good
book I was involved with. One is an editor of The Southern Review,
where I am frequently published. Voila!

Please send me another copy of our joint letter. I managed to lose
mine in the welter of short stories, briefs, film scripts and
philosophical mss. awash on my desk.

I will get my abstract in soonest. I am not insensitive to the
abject humiliation of one editor having to wait for the abstract
of his fellow-editor in order to get on with it.

In a month or so, I'll drop a gentle prodding line to Cleanth
Brooks. He's worth waiting for--a very large plus substantively,
reputation-wise, and at LSU Press. He started his illustrious
career at LSU back in the early 1930's. He also knows and much
admires Voegelin.

                    Lemme hear, *Bill*

Appendix A

LAW OFFICES

STEVEN R. PLOTKIN
OWEN J. BRADLEY
JAMES C. AZCONA
JOSEPH M. SINGERMAN
JOHN WILLIAM CORRINGTON
JONATHAN M. LAKE
MARTIN L. BROUSSARD, JR.

17 March 77

Dear Dick,

Here is a new abstract from Father James Counelan, PhD in philosophy, who is presently translating Joachim's *Tractatus* with me. We thus add the clergy & an active scholar on Joachim's work to our group.

Did I mention that, in addition to our book, LSU press is interested in the Joachim translation as well, aware as we are of its importance to contemporary theory.

Let me hear from you.

Bill

9TH FLOOR, BARONNE BUILDING, NEW ORLEANS, LOUISIANA 70112 / 504 524-1393

277

LAW OFFICES

STEVEN R. PLOTKIN
OWEN J. BRADLEY
JAMES C. AZCONA
JOSEPH M. SINGERMAN
JOHN WILLIAM CORRINGTON
JONATHAN M. LAKE
MARTIN L. BROUSSARD, JR.

18 April 77

Dear Dick,

Your last letter got lost before I could answer it. I think our new dog got it. He eats paper of all kinds, including a check from 20th Century Fox for residuals. Anyhow, send me another precis of the abstracts so far in. Mine is nearly done.

ALSO: send me another copy of our original letter. The copies you sent before were missing p. 2 — only pps 1 & 3 were there.

Did I send you porters abstract before? It is enclosed. Also one from Gregg Edwards, Rice PhD in physics & NSF officer.

I got a letter from Beverly Jarrett, managing editor at LSU Press, praising my contribution to the new Voegelin book — said it was the best essay in the book. That is a plus for _our_ book. Let's take our time, get all our abstracts in, & then I'll see if I can get a commitment.

Please write, giving me the substance of your last letter. I will not let the dog get this one.

Sincerely,
Bill

10 July 77

Dear Dick,

Here is the redrafted letter. Let's try to get
something from Mel & Tom, & hopefully
from Mr. Brooks before we submit to LSU,
but failing that, we'll have to go. I
think I'll make an "unofficial" submission
to Beverly Jarrad at LSU _prior_ to actually
sending stuff in for determination by the
press committee. If she likes the idea, we
can add an introduction to give the
committee something to hold on to, & see
how it goes.

Let me hear from you.

Bill

P.S. Your re-write of Jim Counahan's
abstract is fine. I wonder, if you have a
secretary, could you have all the abstracts
retyped on single pages before we submit
them? We will add the bios & bibliographies
at the end.

LAW OFFICES

STEVEN R. PLOTKIN
OWEN J. BRADLEY
JAMES C. AZCONA
JOSEPH M. SINGERMAN
JOHN WILLIAM CORRINGTON
JONATHAN M. LAKE
MARTIN L. BROUSSARD, JR.

8·2·77

Dear Dick,

Thanks for yours of 2 February 77. It crossed my last.
I've been in Washington for a few days. The whole place
seems expectant, waiting to see what my countryman,
Jimmy, is fixing to do.

Niemeyer's abstract looks very good. So does Vondungs. I
think we may have the materials of a good book by
the time we get all the abstractions. Did you get Wiser's?
I'll send a copy. Opps! I see you _did_ get it.

I'd hope not to have to use any padding in the book. If it
came out _too_ short, I'd rather use either the work of
contributors we have not yet read, or possibly new
pieces by us. It is a long time to September, so of course,
our dates are not sacramental.

I would speculate that about 8 to 9 thousand would cover
the expenses of participants (20) plus various publicity, etc.
for a conference. What would you think of using New
Orleans? It seems the hottest convention-thing around.
Moreover, it is barely possible that Voegelin might come,
since he has old students & friends here, & likes to
return to Baton Rouge frequently to see old colleagues

from his days there.

Dale Vree wrote me, & has asked me to review a new book for the New Oxford Review. I am finding the academics in political philosophy to be the most cordial & warmhearted people I've ever encountered. I'm looking forward to a time when I can devote more energy to theoretical work. As you say, of course, you've got to make money. I've just won a large & important case against the State of Louisiana — that is, they felt compelled to settle prior to the appeal being argued. I've also got a movie script working. That keeps me eating, but it doesn't feed the soul. However Wallace Stevens was a great poet & an insurance executive, & Heinrich Schliemann discovered Troy despite business. I shouldn't complain. I'm usually aware of God's will moving inchoately behind me, so I try to work & live & not ask too many questions.

We're moving along with Joachim's Tractatus, & Jim Counahan thinks there is money in a fund administered by the Catholic philosophical society for subsidizing publication. It would be hard to imagine a medieval work for which a better case for publication could be made. I'll have to get my gnostic paper revised soon for our book, so that I can start on the Joachim introduction. Jim will do the early Joachitic influence, & I will show the modern. Joachim is still going strong. He is an important figure in John Passmore's the perfectability of Man, Scribner's, 1970 — despite the fact that not one of Joachim's works is available in English. Incredible.

Sincerely, Bi...

John William Corrington
1724 Valence Street
New Orleans, Louisiana 70115

15 August 77

Dear Dick,

Just got back from two weeks fishing
in the swamps. It was great, &
came back not anxious to go to law, but
in excellent fettle for scholarship.
You'll be glad to know I'm 100 pages
into the rough draft of my paper.
I think it will show the indisputable
nexus between gnosticism, magic,
hermeticism, & alchemy. The draft is
very rough, it seems, but it will
shake down well enough. I fear
you may not approve the Jungian
theory involved, & I will get a
copy of the first typescript to you
as soon as possible, since I do not
wish, even inadvertently, to be one
of those, as Voegelin has it, "arguing
against gnosticism in the language
of gnosticism."
I'm relieved at being able to get so
much work done despite the legal
business. I'm tired in the evening,

but I put on some Bach, to go at it, I feel
the need of a larger library with lots of
recent books, but I'm using a fair
amount of the Church Fathers, & standard
texts like Reeves on Joachim, which I have,
so I can get by. Anyhow, most libraries
aren't much on Gnostic texts or medieval
stuff.

I'm interested in seeing Webb's paper, I'm
sending sets of the abstracts to Brooks,
& am hoping to hear that he is ready
to write.

Sometime in the next several weeks
I'll be going to Baton Rouge & will
see Beverley at the press. I just got
my proofs for my piece in the
book on Voegelin. It will be in
production next month.

Let me hear how your symposium
plans progress, & I'll send word
on my discussion with LSU press
folks.

Sincerely,
—Bill

John William Corrington
1724 Valence Street
New Orleans, Louisiana 70115

27 August 77

Dear Dick,

I should never have started this damned paper. It is now 150 pages, & not quite done. How the hell will I cut that down to a size we can use?

Me? Not in a swamp? I forgive you because of your Sicilian heritage (your name is Sicilian, isn't it?) But Tom should know better. I love fishing & the best is back in the dark water where the fish are not disturbed.

I haven't heard from Tom or from Dallas. The chancellor doesn't seem to think answering letters addressed to him as chairman of the Search Committee is one of his duties. I hate boorishness.

My view of the Dallas situation is that they would have to make the job most attractive. I've got a very real possibility of university professor (one of two) at Old Dominion University in Norfolk, Virginia, plus the Florida thing pending, plus

2

the fact that I can survive at law until I find
something worthwhile. I am quite suspicious of
catholic institutions. I find them, like the _ancien regeme_,
forgetting nothing, learning nothing. That is a sad
prospect. I would about as soon deal with
Ramsey Clark as a "literated" priest. The church
as inquisitor is unpleasant; the church as
faddist is wholly repulsive.

Still, Tom & Mel are reason enough to consider
the place. Not fancying coteries & incapable
of supporting boredom, I always make sure
to go where my associates can educate me.

Send me a copy of your book. I trust you'll give
me 1) the discount, 2) a signature with an
appropriate sentiment affixed.

I'll send a copy of our abstracts to Beverly
(I've been holding off, hoping to have an essay
or two to flesh it out — also _vitas_ from
contributors — which, by the way, have you gotten yet?)
and ask for the letter you suggest. But I have
certain doubts about a January 1978 (you
wrote 77; I assume that is 78) date, in that
I doubt most of our people will be ready
for a symposium in 4 to 5 months. I will
be, but what of the others? Of course, we
can presumably put it off a few months,
till people are ready.

3.

Bev should be willing to write a brief personal letter as editor stating interest. The publications Board is the final authority, so her interest is only a first sign.

Why don't you send me your public philosophy essay? I want to do a piece ~~of~~ on Voegelin's essay on law one day soon, & would like to see your view of the public philosophy upon which, one assumes, the law is founded in any community.

By the way, I don't think you should worry about Jim Wiser. We've been in contact, & I'm sure he's still interested in the project.

Cleanth Brooks will be in New Orleans on 5 October, & I will try to prod him. It may be we'll have to go without him, but I hope not. He's a genuine superstar in literature, & I want us to have as much breadth as possible, as I know you do.

Sincerely,
Bill

LAW OFFICES

STEVEN R. PLOTKIN
OWEN J. BRADLEY
JOSEPH M. SINGERMAN
JOHN WILLIAM CORRINGTON
JONATHAN M. LAKE
MARTIN L. BROUSSARD, JR.
JOHN P. COSENTINO

1 Sept 77

Dear Dick,

to my astonishment, I got the letter from Beverly
that you wanted — without even asking for it.
She sent it in reply to my note returning proofs
on my Voegelin article for Steve McKnights
book.

I also got a copy of Webb's piece on ennui, & I
like it.

But: before I submit anything in detail to Bev,
I really think we should get vitas from
everybody. I've received none so far. Maybe
you could coax them along.

Cleanth Brooks will be in New Orleans 5 October,
& I'll try to get him accelerated on his piece.
Since Brooks is one of LSU's greatest luminaries,
his presence in the collection would be helpful
in convincing the Press to publish the book.

P.T.O.

9TH FLOOR, BARONNE BUILDING / NEW ORLEANS, LOUISIANA 70112 / 504 524-1393

Keep me posted on the grant situation.

Bill

John William Corrington
1724 Valence Street
New Orleans, Louisiana 70115

12 Sept 77

Dear Dick,

I am in receipt of your sudden spurt of activity, & like it very well. I'm now of the opinion that those contributors who are serious can probably be ready for winter.

Enclosed is a later communique from Beverley, who adds some proof of interest to her previous letter, but also certain cautionary observations which we'll have to consider.

I don't know if it matters, but LSU hasn't done all my books. Take a look at the vita which, as you requested, I enclose.

I've sent a note to professor Brooks, & expect to see him in October. His being a contributor isn't, I think, crucial to the publication by LSU, but it would be a real plus.

p. T. O.

I read the proposal with interest, & have only one request: I'd very much appreciate it if you'd drop Canavan from those invited. My reasons are both personal & professional, but they are considerable. If you want to know them, I'll tell you.

My paper, vastly over-long, needs only editing in order to make it ready for your initial oversight. It will, I fear, be controversial even amongst the scholars named in the proposal, but I'd want you & McKnight to see it first.

With the Lord's grace, I'll be done within 3 weeks. The only intervention, outside the practice of law (a nasty hobby) might be a new job for 20th century Fox. Go & I might have a "polish" to do on a script done by someone else.

Let me hear from you.

John William Corrington
1724 Valence Street
New Orleans, Louisiana 70115

Dear Dick,

At long last, here is my abstract.
I'm also into the writing of the
piece itself — using the old paper
as a kind of matrice, but going
well beyond it, based on a more
exhaustive look at the documents.

Do you reckon it's time to begin stirring
people up, so we can get on with
both publishing & symposium plans?

Lemme hear,
Bill

Dear Dirk,

I spoke to Paul as I promised, but he'd already talked to you.

We're all three excited by the venture. It seems exactly what we'd like to do. Our present situations pay well, but are essentially meaningless. The chance to make use of our skills for something useful & valuable would be much desired.

Paul said you all will meet this weekend. I'm sure he'll be able to give you plenty of insight into the nature of production. There is no better or more intelligent producer working today. Moreover, his skill at achieving desired effects within strict budget constraints has always amazed Joyce & me.

Knowing Kirk's work generally, I'm sure _Roots_ is a first-class book. I'll try to get a copy, but if you have access to one, please send it.

It would be helpful if we could establish the narrators before any writing was done. Paul said you mentioned Gregory Peck & Charlton Heston as possibilities. Both are excellent — as would be Alestair Cook. In any case, writing-style should reflect the character of the story-teller

I'm enclosing a copy of my vita, which contains all the film & TV stuff as well as academic & published work.

We'll be looking forward to hearing from you. If you can make the deal, please let us know as soon as possible, since we'd need to adjust our schedule to do the work, & to arrange for necessary meetings with you & paul, &, I assume, with Mr. Kirk.

Sincerely,

Bill

Appendix B

The material dealing with the Uroboros, or Cosmic Serpent, is quite large.[1] In this note, I will simply list a number of its occurrences and some commentary upon it.

> The procreation element in any body was the psyche,[2] which appeared in the form of serpent. Okeanos was, as may now be seen, the primeval[3] psyche and this[4] would be conceived as a serpent in relation to procreative liquid. . . . Thus we may see, for Homer, who refers allusively to the conception shared by his contemporaries, the universe had the form of an egg girt about by "Okeanos, who is the generation of All" . . . . We can perhaps also better understand . . . why in (the)[5] Orphic version the serpent was called Chronos, and why, when asked what Chronos was, Pythagoras answered that it was the psyche of the universe.[6]

Ontogenetically, the Uroborotic symbol seems to refer to the pre-conscious state, imaginatively expressed as compact, undifferentiated, androgynous, a unity. Phylogenetically, the symbolism refers to an original pre-creational perfection in which end and beginning are still one as represented in the circle, the rotundum, the round of the alchemist. In both modes, the symbolism expresses the once and future "perfect state in which the opposites are unified[7]—the perfect beginning because the opposites have not yet flown apart and the world has not yet begun, the perfect end because in it the opposites have come together again in a synthesis and the world is once more at rest."[8]

---

1   Editor's note: This appendix was originally footnote 4 in "Structure of Gnostic Consciousness."

2   This term, like several other terms Corrington uses (e.g., Okeanos), are in Greek in the original. In these instances, Corrington might be quoting or summarizing a translator who was quoting the original Greek, in this instance the text of Onians.

3   Onians writes "primal."

4   Onians writes "thus."

5   Onians writes "this."

6   Corrington's note: "P. B. Onians, The Origins of European Thought About the Body, the Mind, the Soul, the World, Time, and Fate, 2nd ed. (Cambridge: Cambridge University Press, 1954), 249f."

7   Neumann writes "united."

8   Corrington's note: "Erich Neumann, The Origins and History of Consciousness (Princeton, NJ: Princeton

The serpent Uroboros-Okeanos-Chronos figures as source and protector, as life and limit of both cosmos and cosmion. In Hermetic literature, the world-egg is encircled by the serpent as "Mighty Power;" in the Theurgic Hermes cult, the "Greatest God" is addressed as "the mighty serpent, the chief of all the gods, O thou who dost possess Egypt's beginning and the end of all the world."[9]

In archaic Greek thought, the serpent encircles the *umphalos*, the navel of the world, and surrogate tomb of heroes, the place from which *cosmoi* arise and to which they return. In a number of mythopoetic traditions the serpent, dragon, or sea-monster partakes of this role. "It symbolizes the involution, the pre-formal modality, of the universe, the undivided 'One' of pre-Creation." The parting or breaking of the Uroboros, symbolized as the Parting of the World-Parents, of the two "sides" of the symbolism which are male and female sexually and yet sexlessly one in the serpent-form forces the embryonic consciousness to reach for an "unnatural" state, an excited state which is "specifically human."[10]

In the *Pistis Sophia*, chapter 126, the Serpent is a fundamental symbolism: "The outer darkness is a huge dragon whose tail is in its mouth." In the *Acts of Thomas*, another passage explicates the symbol: "I am the offspring of the serpent-nature and a corrupter's son. I am the son of him who . . . sits on the throne and has dominion over the creation beneath the heavens, . . . who encircles the sphere, . . . who is outside (around) the ocean, whose tail lies in his mouth."[11]

In the Jewish apocryphal *Acts of Kyriakos and Julitta*, cited in Hans Jonas, we find the dragon described as king of worms of the earth, whose tail lies in his mouth.[12] This is the serpent that led astray through passions the angels from on high; this is the serpent that led astray the first Adam and expelled him from Paradise.

In the *Sephirah di Zenouthia*,[13] The Book of Concealment, purported to represent an early stratum of Kabbalistic literature, we find description of a primeval chaos and the evolution of the universe compared to an uncoiling serpent: "Extending hither and thither, its tail in its mouth, the head twisting on its neck, it is enraged and angry. . . . It watches and conceals itself. Every thousand days it is manifested."[14]

Giorgio de Santillana specifically connects the Okeanos-Chronos serpent symbolism with the Apeiron of Anaximander in his study of myth, apparently

---

University Press, 1954), 8."

9   Corrington's note: "G.R.S. Mead, Thrice-Greatest Hermes (London: J. M. Watkins, 1964), II:21; I:67." According to Mead's book, this is line 8 of a "Prayer of Consecration."

10   Corrington's note: "Mircea Eliade, The Myth of the Eternal Return (Princeton, NJ: Princeton University Press, 1971), 37–42, esp. 40n70. Also 55–60."

11   Corrington's note: "Cited in Hans Jonas, The Gnostic Religion (Boston: Beacon Press, 1963), 116."

12   Corrington's note: "Jonas, Gnostic Religion, 117."

13   Corrington misspells the text Sephirah di Zenouthia. The proper title is Siphrah Dzeniouta, in which the passage on the serpent is cited as the same book and line number cited by Corrington: 1, sec. 16.

14   Corrington's note: "Siphrah Dzeniouta, 1, sec. 16."

supposing that the Uroboros was the mythopoetic precursor of the noetic circle of creation and dissolution.[15]

---

15   Corrington's note: "See Hamlet's Mill (Boston: David R. Godine Publisher, 1977), 188."

Appendix C

These handwritten notes to "Gnosticism and Modern Thought: A Way You'll Never Be" are included here as an appendix because they are thematically distinct from the essay proper. They discuss, for instance, Corrington's belief that a typology of universal experiences finds perennial expression in texts or symbols in different times and places.

\

Real difference between McKnight & myself.
More than semantic. "Semantic quibbles" are carried
on by those who know the provinance & meaning of
words. As Camus wrote a German friend at the
outbreak of war, "we will fight & kill for fine
distinctions.

I believe that there is a fundamental underlying
pneumopathology which invades human thought
& action, converting both from rational courses
into fantasies at odds not only with the logos
of human nature, but frequently with physical
reality as well.

I believe that this infection has two basic forms,
both springing from an identical root. Since ⎯experience
this root is itself wholly at odds with noetic
thought, it must be described by reference to
the mythopoetic symbols which most nearly
approximate the root experience. the root-
experience is a horror of the world as it is,
of physis, being revealed, standing in the
light, alethia, being comprehended in things.

86/-979/

the symbol of choice at this point is that of the
Uroboros, old Leviathan-Okeanos which marks the
Horos or limit of the structure of existence. All
that lies on the existential side of the dragon with
its tail in its mouth is of the world. It is evil,
deficient, imprisoning, corrupt. Beyond the serpent
lies the pleroma, the treasure, the true reality.

Now to know so much constitutes in itself the beginning of the Gnosis.
whether that knowledge derives from a mythic savior,
an established school, a teacher, a vagrant monk,
a führer, or a commisar is of no moment ~~theoretically~~.
the temporal & cultural fixtures do not, of themselves,
have theoretical relevance.

to say that there are distinctions between Hermeticism,
~~Neo-platonism, North~~ Kabballah, alchemy, & magic
is indisputably correct — so long as we confine the
field of discussion to the level of ~~doctrinal the~~
temporal & cultural fixtures. As to that, there
are rather substantial distinctions between
the Neo-platonisms of plotinus, pico & the
Cambridge platonists. For that matter, there are

substantial distinctions to be noted between the Gnosticism of Valentinius, the Naassenes, & Montanus. But I maintain, in the lawyer's phrase, that these are, theoretically considered, distinctions without differences. If the obvious distinctions in the details of the variety of Gnostic mythoi reported by the Church Fathers are taken to be substantive differences from a theoretical perspective, I would propose that, logically, there is no such thing as "Gnosticism" & once again the victory belongs to the Nominalists & their positivistic progeny. By analogy, no two legal cases are, or possibly can be, much alike in their details, much less identical. Yet the very process of judicial decision insists on a very large degree of [perceived] identity between cases, however distinguishable, which are perceived as "the same" within the theoretical overview of law.

What I am proposing, then, is that there is an irreducible corpus of experiences, sentiments, attitudes & symbols which appear again & again within history (history conceived as the growth & differentiation of consciousness). the experiences are essentially the same for any human

4

being anywhere at any time, the sentiments &
the symbols which embody them may or
may not be similar or distinct. the manner
in which those symbols are manipulated will
be largely determined by the empirical circumstances in which they arise.

I emphatically do not hold any theory of cultural diffusion or
connexity between either these experiences or
their symbolizations. Such relationships exist.
When they are proven, they are to be acknowledged. But no such source-tracing is relevant
to the idea that certain classes of experience
& symbolizations arise spontaneously under
certain ~~and~~ historical conditions. If there is a
constellation of experiences, sentiments, & symbols
which must be considered as theoretically
similar regardless of the time or place of their
appearance, the ultimate source must reside
within the structure of human consciousness
itself. I believe that it does.

the Gnostic horror of concrete existence, & ~~the~~ the
need to escape it or alter it is without warrant
in noetic thought. While reason reveals a certain
flexibility in the structure of nature, both physical
& human, that flexibility is limited, & knowledge
of those limits is fundamental to noetic thought.

Mythopoetic thought, on the contrary, is less prone
to such recognition. the possibility of escape
from _physis_ into pleromatic unity, or that
of creating a pleromatic aeon here on earth
is not alien to mythopoetic thought. Myth is
the "narrative philosophy" of ~~Lessing~~ Schelling. In it,
Transmutation of reality is commonplace.

I would propose that the various ideational structures
represented by magic, hermeticism, Kaballah,
alchemy — as well as positivism, scientism,
materialism & such-like — all rest upon
foundations which require a mythopoetic
mode of thought in order to be intelligible.
I do not see neo-platonism as quite so simple.
All neo-platonism is not Gnostic, because
all neo-platonism does not propose the evil or

unreality of existence, ~~a knowl~~ a pleromatic alternative, a knowledge by which the alternative ~~by which it~~ may be reached or created.

the Gnostic groupings, ~~for~~ from ancient to modern times share another aspect not so often stressed, but very important in terms of showing the ~~con~~ theoretical continuity of Gnostic thought. the symbol I have in mind is that of man as God. Virtually every classical Gnostic sect argues that pneumatic man is a spark or part of the unknown god, or of the pleroma. Simon, according to Hippolytus, acknowledged that he was the incarnation of the god; Montanus stated that he was the paraclete, & that all believers were, in faith & in truth, part of the Godhead. Montanus took quite literally St. paul's "new man" of Collosians 3:10 & Ephesians 4:24, & the symbolism became, over the millenia, together with Montanus' chiliastic expectations, the vector along which, from a psychological perspective, took place the shift from passive, classical gnosis in which the divinity of man was held, to the active modern gnosis in which knowledge became power — the power to assert man's

divinity in the world itself. the "New man" of
Paul becomes the "godded man" of the
English Ranters, the "Saint" of the Fifth Monarchy
men, Nietzsche's "superman," Marx's "New
Socialist man," & the ruthless "blond beast"
of National Socialism. the final theoretical step in
the shift from classical to modern gnosticism
is made on principle, by Ludwig Feuerbach,
by way of his
whose theory of the pleromatic constellation as
a "projection" of human consciousness which
must be "drawn back" into humanity in order
to allow the completion of man & establishment
of heaven on earth.

the detailed & exhaustive comparison between
sects, factions, new departures & varieties of
Gnostic thought of both the classical & modern
types remains to be done. the theoretical basis
upon which such studies can be made
already exists.

B

I would add only a footnote: in the New Science of Politics, professor Voegelin seems to take for granted the identity of classical to modern Gnosticism. He passes in some four pages from the initiation of the primitive Christian community to the work of Joachim of Flora. Moreover, there is little or no discussion of the characteristic experiences of classical gnosis.

I find no difficulty in this procedure. The missing commentary is easy enough to fill in, & the inclusion of Jewish apocalyptic & messianic writings as Gnostic simply pushes back the date for the fundamental sources of modern conquest gnosis.

Finally, let me point out that neither my paper nor my present comments are to be taken as a spirited defense of the use of the term "Gnostic" to denominate the experiences, ~~symbol~~ sentiments, & symbols we are discussing.

9

I find the terminology of Gnosticism, gnostic, & gnosis quite satisfactory to describe the pneumo-pathology in question. It has the advantage of being somewhat established, & we are all aware of the cultural & professional difficulties of establishing a working theoretical vocabulary.

I find the concept of magic, hermeticism, alchemy, positivism, scientism, & ideology in general as merely sub-genres of Gnosticism both coherent & convenient. But if someone wishes to propose an alternative terminology, I will not, on principle, quarrel with it.

I will maintain that the fundamental stratum underlying all the ideational structures & symbolic constellations we have discussed is one, & that an attempt to establish each of the entities noted as an independent, & possessing a distinct structure & provenance when considered theoretically, will not withstand detailed analysis.

Appendix D

R eal difference between McKnight and myself. More than semantic. "Semantic quibbles" are carried on by those who know the provenance and meaning of words. As Camus wrote a German friend at the outbreak of war, "We will fight and kill for fine distinctions."

I believe there is a fundamental and underlying pneumopathology which invades human thought and action, converting both from rational courses into fantasies at odds with not only the logos of human nature, but frequently with physical reality as well.

I believe that this infection has two basic forms, both springing from an identical root experience.[1] Since this root is itself wholly at odds with noetic thought, it may be described by reference to the mythopoetic symbols which most nearly approximate the root experience. The root experience is a horror of the world as it is, of *physis*, being revealed, standing in the light, *alethia*, being comprehended in things.

The symbol of choice at this point is the Uroboros, old Leviathan-Okeanos, which marks the Horos or limit of the structure of existence. All that lies on the existential side of the dragon with its tail in its mouth is of the world. It is evil, deficient, imprisoning, corrupt. Beyond the serpent lies the Pleroma, the treasure, the true reality.

Now to know so much constitutes in itself the beginning of the Gnosis. Whether that knowledge derives from a mystic savior, an established school, a teacher, a führer, or a commissar is of no moment. The temporal and cultural fixtures do not, of themselves, have theoretical relevance.

To say that there are distinctions between Hermeticism, Kabbalah, alchemy, and magic is indisputably correct—so long as we confine the field of discussion to the level of temporal and cultural fixtures. As to that, there are rather substantial distinctions between the Neo-platonism[2] of Plotinus, Pico, and the Cambridge

---

1   Corrington later added the word "experience" to the manuscript.
2   This word appears to be plural in the manuscript.

Platonists. For that matter, there are substantial distinctions to be noted between the Gnosticism of Valentinus, the Naassenes, and Montanus. But I maintain, in the lawyer's phrase, that these are, theoretically considered, distinctions without differences. If the obvious distinctions in the details of the variety of Gnostic mythoi reported by the Church Fathers are taken to be substantive differences from a theoretical perspective, I would propose that, logically, there is no such thing as "Gnosticism" and once again the victory belongs to the Nominalists and their positivistic progeny. By analogy, no two legal cases are, or possibly can be, much alike in their details, much less identical. Yet the very process of judicial decision insists on a very large degree of perceived identity between cases, however distinguishable, which are perceived as "the same" within the theoretical overview of law.

What I am proposing, then, is that there is an irreducible corpus of experiences, sentiments, attitudes, and symbols which appear again and again within history (history conceived as the growth and differentiation of consciousness). The expressions are essentially the same for any human being anywhere at any time. The sentiments and the symbols which embody them may or may not be similar or distinct. The manner in which those symbols are manipulated will be largely determined by the empirical circumstances in which they arise.

I emphatically *do not* hold any theory of cultural diffusion or connection between either these experiences or their symbolizations. Such relationships exist. When they are proven, they are to be acknowledged. But no such source-tracing is relevant to the idea that certain classes of experience and symbolizations arise spontaneously under certain historical conditions. If there is a constellation of experiences, sentiments, and symbols which must be considered as theoretically similar regardless of the time or place of their appearance, the ultimate source must reside within the structure of human consciousness itself. I believe that it does.

The Gnostic horror of concrete existence, the need to escape it or alter it, is without warrant in noetic thought. While reason reveals a certain flexibility in the structure of nature, both physical and human, that flexibility is limited, and knowledge of those limits is fundamental to noetic thought.

Mythopoetic thought, on the contrary, is less prone to such recognition. The possibility of escape from *physis* into a pleromatic unity, or that of creating a pleromatic aeon here on earth, is not alien to mythopoetic thought. Myth is the "narrative philosophy" of Schelling. In it, transmutation of reality is commonplace.

I would propose that the various ideational structures represented by magic, Hermeticism, Kabbalah, alchemy—as well as positivism, scientism, materialism and such-like—all rest upon foundations which require a mythopoetic mode of thought in order to be intelligible. I do not see Neo-platonism as quite so simple.

All Neo-platonism is not Gnostic, because all Neo-platonism does not propose the evil or unreality of existence, a pleromatic alternative, a knowledge by which the alternative may be reached or created.

The Gnostic groupings, from ancient to modern times, share another aspect not so often stressed, but very important in terms of showing the theoretical continuity of Gnostic thought. The symbol I have in mind is that of man as God. Virtually every classical Gnostic sect argues that pneumatic man is a spark or part of the unknown god or of the pleroma. Simon, according to Hippolytus, acknowledged that he was the incarnation of the god; Montanus stated that he was the Paraclete, and that all believers were, in faith and in truth, part of the Godhead. Montanus took quite literally St. Paul's "new man" of Colossians 3:10 and Ephesians 4:24, and the symbolism became, over the millennia, together with Montanus's chiliastic expectations, the vector along which, from a psychological perspective, took place the shift from passive classical gnosis in which the divinity of man was held, to the active modern gnosis in which knowledge became power—the power to assert man's divinity in the world itself. The "new man" of Paul becomes the "godded man" of the English Ranters, the "Saint" of the Fifth Monarchy men, Nietzsche's "superman," Marx's "New Socialist Man," and the ruthless "blond beast" of National Socialism. The final theoretical step in the shift from classical to modern Gnosticism is made on principle by Ludwig Feuerbach, by way of his theory of the pleromatic constellation as a "projection" of human consciousness which must be "drawn back" into humanity in order to allow the completion of man and establishment of heaven on earth.

The detailed and exhaustive comparison between sects, factions, new departures, and varieties of Gnostic thought of both the classical and modern types remains to be done. The theoretical basis upon which such studies can be made already exists.

I would add only a footnote: in *The New Science of Politics*, Professor Voegelin seems to take for granted the identity of classical and modern Gnosticism. He passes in some four pages from the initiation of the primitive Christian community to the work of Joachim of Fiore. Moreover, there is little or no discussion of the characteristic experiences of classical gnosis.

I find no difficulty in this procedure. The missing commentary is easy enough to fill in, and the inclusion of Jewish apocalyptic and messianic writings as Gnostic simply pushes back the date for the fundamental sources of modern conquest gnosis.

Finally, let me point out that neither my paper nor my present comments are to be taken as a spirited defense of the use of the term "Gnostic" to denominate the experiences, sentiments, and symbols we are discussing.

I find the terminology of Gnosticism, gnostic, and gnosis quite satisfactory to describe the pneumopathology in questions. It has the advantage of being somewhat established, and we are all aware of the cultural and professional difficulties of establishing a working theoretical vocabulary.

I find the concept of magic, hermeticism, alchemy, positivism, scientism, and ideology in general as merely sub-genres of Gnosticism both coherent and convenient. But if someone wishes to propose an alternative terminology, I will not, in principle, quarrel with it.

I will maintain that the fundamental stratum underlying all the ideational structures and symbolic constellations we have discussed is one, and that an attempt to establish each of the entities noted as independent, and possessing a distinct structure and provenance when considered theoretically, will not withstand detailed analysis.

BIBLIOGRAPHIES

Selected Bibliography

Altizer, Thomas J. J. *The Gospel of Christian Atheism.* Philadelphia: Westminster Press, 1966.

Ambrose. *Hexameron.*

Arendt, Hannah. *The Origins of Totalitarianism.* New York: Harcourt, Brace, Jovanovich, 1973.

Aristotle. *Physica.*

Baker, Herschel. *The Image of Man.* New York: Harper Torchbooks, 1961.

Breasted, H. *A History of Egypt from the Earliest Times to the Persian Conquest.* New York: C. Scribner's Sons, 1909.

Cicero, *De Re Publica.* Loeb Classical Library. London: Heinemann, Ltd., 1922.

Cochrane, Charles N. *Christianity and Classical Culture: A Study of Thought and Action from Augustus to Augustine.* London: Oxford University Press, 1944.

Cohn, Norman. *The Pursuit of the Millennium.* Rev. ed. New York: Oxford University Press, 1970.

Cornford, F. M. *Plato's Cosmology: The Timaeus of Plato.* New York: Harper and Row, 1957.

———. *From Religion to Philosophy: A Study in the Origins of Western Speculation.* New York: Harper and Row, 1957.

———. "Mysticism and Science in the Pythagorean Tradition," *Classical Quarterly* 16 (1922): 137–50.

Corrington, John William. "Order and Consciousness/Consciousness and History: The New Program of Eric Voegelin." In *Voegelin's Search for Order in History.* Edited by Stephen McKnight. Baton Rouge, LA: Louisiana State University Press, 1977.

Dickens, Charles. *Bleak House.* 1853.

Dylan, Bob. "Blowin' in the Wind." 1962.

———. "The Times They Are A-Changin.'" 1963.

Efros, Israel. *Studies in Medieval Jewish Philosophy.* New York: Columbia University Press, 1974.

Eggeling, Julius. *The Satapatha Brahmana,* in *The Sacred Books of the East,* edited by F. Max Müller. Oxford: Clarendon Press, 1882.

Eliade, Mircea. *The Myth of the Eternal Return.* Princeton, NJ: Princeton University Press, 1971.

Fiore, Joachim of. *"Tractatus Super Quartuor Evangelia."* Translated by James Counahan. Unpublished manuscript.

Foerster, Werner. *Gnosis: A Selection of Gnostic Texts.* Vol. 1 *Patristic Evidence.* Edited by R. McLachlan Wilson. Oxford: Clarendon Press, 1972.

Forrest, Nathan Bedford. "Letter to D. C. Trader." May 23, 1862.

Franck, Adolphe. *The Kabbalah: The Religious Philosophy of the Hebrews.* New Hyde Park, NY: University Books, 1967.

Frankfort, Henri, et al. *The Intellectual Adventure of Ancient Man.* Chicago: University of Chicago press, 1946.

Freeman, Kathleen. *Ancilla to the Pre-Socratic Philosophers.* Oxford: Blackwell, 1962.

Gaon, Saadia. *The Book of Beliefs and Opinions.* Translated by Samuel Rosenblatt. New Haven: Yale University Press, 1948.

Gonda, Jan. *Notes on Brahman.* Utrecht: J. L. Beyers, 1950.

Grant, Robert M. *Gnosticism and Early Christanity.* New York: Columbia University Press, 1966.

Guignebert, Charles. *The Jewish World in the Time of Jesus.* New Hyde Park, NY: University Books, 1954.

Harnack, Adolph von. *History of Dogma.* Translated by Neil Buchanan. 7 vols. Reprint, New York: Russell & Russell, 1958.

Heidegger, Martin. *An Introduction to Metaphysics.* New Haven: Yale University Press, 1959.

Heisenburg, Werner. *Physics and Beyond.* Translated by Arnold J. Pomerans. New York: Harper & Row, 1972.

———. *Physics and Philosophy: The Revolution in Modern Science.* New York: Harper and Row, 1962.

Hennecke, Edgar, ed. *Gospels and Related Writings.* Vol. 1 of *New Testament Apocrypha.* Translated by R. McLachlan Wilson. London: Lutterworth Press, 1963.

Herodotus. *Histories I.*

Homer. *Iliad.*

Jaeger, Werner. *Paideia: The Ideals of Greek Culture.* New York: Oxford University Press, 1945.

James, M. R. *The Apocryphal New Testament.* Oxford: Clarendon Press, 1924.

Fiore, Joachim of, and Ernesto Buonaiuti. *Tractatus Super Quatuor Evangelia.* Translated by James Counahan.

———. *Psalterium decem cordarum abbatis Joachim.* Venice: s.n., 1527. Quoted in Frank Manuel, *Shapes of Philosophical History.* Stanford, CA: Stanford University Press, 1965.

———. Preface to *Liber Concordie.* Venice: Simon de Luere, 1519.

Jonas, Hans. *The Gnostic Religion: The Message of the Alien God and the Beginnings of Christianity.* Boston: Beacon Press, 1963.

Jung, C. G. "Aion." Vol. 9, pt. 2 of *The Collected Works of C. G. Jung.* London: Routledge & Kegan Paul, 1968.

———. "Psychology and Alchemy." Vol. 12 of *The Collected Works of C. G. Jung.* London: Routledge & Kegan Paul, 1968.

———. "The Archetypes and the Collective Unconscious." Vol. 9, pt. 1 of *The Collected Works of C. G. Jung.* London: Routledge & Kegan Paul, 1958.

Kirk, G. S., and J. E. Raven, eds. *The Presocratic Philosophers.* Cambridge: Cambridge University Press, 1957.

Löwith, Kurt. *Meaning in History: The Theological Implications of the Philosophy of History.* Chicago: University of Chicago Press, 1949.

Lubac, Henri de. *The Drama of Atheist Humanism.* New York: World Publishing, 1963.

MacDonell, Arthur A. *A History of Sanskrit Literature.* New York: Haskell House Publishers, Ltd., 1968.

Manuel, Frank. *Shapes of Philosophical History.* Stanford, CA: Stanford University Press, 1965.

Marcel, Gabriel. *The Mystery of Being.* Vol. 1. Chicago: Henry Regnery, 1960.

Mead, G. R. S. *Fragments of a Faith Forgotten.* Reprint, New Hyde Park, New York: University Books, 1960.

Midrash Rabbah, ed. Freedman, Harry, et al. Vol. 10. London: Soncino Press, 1939.

Milman, Henry H. *History of Latin Christianity.* 6 vols. London: John Murray, 1854.

Neill, Stephen. *The Interpretation of the New Testament: 1861-1961.* London: Oxford University Press, 1964.

Neumann, Erich. *The Origins and History of Consciousness*. Translated by R. F. C. Hull. Bollingen Series, no. 42. Princeton: Princeton University Press, 1954.

O'Flaherty, Wendy Doniger. *The Rig Veda*. New York: Finland books, 1981.

Pelikan, Jaroslav. "The Emergence of the Catholic Tradition (100–600)," vol. 1 of *The Christian Tradition*. Chicago: University of Chicago Press, 1971.

Plato. *Theaetetus*.

Plotinus. *The Enneads*. Translated by Stephen MacKenna. With an introduction by Paul Henry. New York: Pantheon Books, n.d.

Proust, Marcel. *Swann's Way*. Translated by C. K. Scott-Moncrieff. Vol. 1 of *In Search of Lost Time Or Remembrance of Things Past*.

Puech, Henri-Charles. "Gnosis and Time." In *Man and Time*, edited by Joseph Campbell, Bollingen Series, vol. 30, no. 3. Princeton, NJ: Princeton University Press, 1957.

Radhakrishanan, S. *The Principal Upanishads*. London: George Allen and Unwin, 1953.

Rainy, Robert. *The Ancient Catholic Church*. New York: Scribner, 1902.

Reeves, Marjorie and Beatrice Hirsch-Reich. *The Figurae of Joachim of Fiore*. Oxford: Clarendon Press, 1972.

Reeves, Marjorie. *The Influence of Prophecy in the Later Middle Ages*. Oxford: Clarendon Press, 1969.

Rexroth, Kenneth. "Thou Shalt Not Kill" (A Memorial for Dylan Thomas).

Roberts, Alexander, and James Donaldson, eds. *The Ante-Nicene Fathers: Translations of the Writings of the Fathers down to AD 325*. 10 vols. Grand Rapids, MI: W. B. Eerdmans, 1967.

Runciman, Steven. *The Medieval Manichee: A Study of the Christian Dualist Heresy*. Cambridge: Cambridge University Press, 1955.

Sandoz, Ellis. *Eric Voegelin's Thought: A Critical Appraisal* (Durham, NC: Duke University Press, 1982).

———. *The Voegelinian Revolution: A Biographical Introduction*. Baton Rouge, LA: Louisiana State University Press, 1981.

Saint Ambrose. *Hexameron*.

Scholem, Gershom G. *On the Kabbalah and Its Symbolism*. New York: Schocken Books, 1969.

Seligman, Paul. *The Apeiron of Anaximander*. London: University of London, 1962.

Spengler, Oswald. *Decline of the West*. Translated by Charles Francis Atkinson. 2 vols. London: George Allen and Unwin, 1932.

Thomas, Dylan. *Collected Poems, 1934–1952*. New York: New Directions, 2003.

Thorndike, Lynn. "During the First Thirteen Centuries of Our Era." Vol. 1 of *History of Magic and Experimental Science*. New York: Columbia University Press, 1923.

Tillich, Paul. *Systematic Theology*. Vol. 3. Chicago: University of Chicago Press, 1963.

Toynbee, Arnold. *A Study of History*. London: Oxford University Press, 1934.

Trotsky, Leon. *Literature and Revolution*. 1924.

Tucker, Robert. *Philosophy and Myth in Karl Marx*. Cambridge: Cambridge University Press, 1972.

Voegelin, Eric. "Autobiographical Sketch." Unpublished manuscript.

———. *The Collected Works of Eric Voegelin*. Columbia, MO: University of Missouri Press, 2000.

———. *The Collected Works of Eric Voegelin, Vol. 25,* History of Political Ideas, Volume VII: The New Order and Last Orientation. Columbia, MO: University of Missouri Press, 1999.

———. *Order and History*. 5 vols. Baton Rouge, Louisiana: Louisiana State University Press, 1956–1987.

———. *From Enlightenment to Revolution*. Durham, NC: Duke University Press, 1975.

———. *Science, Politics, and Gnosticism*. Chicago: Henry Regnery, 1968.

———. "Immortality: Experience and Symbol." *Harvard Theological Review* 60, no. 3 (1967).

———. *The New Science of Politics: An Introduction*. Chicago: University of Chicago Press, 1952, 1953.

Waite, Arthur Edward. *Azoth; or, The Star in the East*. Secaucus, NY: University Books, 1973.

———. *The Holy Kabbalah: A Study of the Secret Tradition in Israel as Unfolded by Sons of the Doctrine for the Benefit and Consolation of the Elect Dispersed through the Lands and Ages of the Greater Exile*. New Hyde Park, NY: University Books, 1960.

Wolfe, Thomas. *Thomas Wolfe: An Illustrated Biography*. Edited by Ted Mitchell. New York: Pegasus Books, LLC, 2006.

Youngbloods. "Get Together". Composed by Chet Powers. 1967, 1969

The Collected Works of Eric Voegelin

In his references to the works of Eric Voegelin, John William Corrington cited the early editions available to him. However, the University of Missouri Press has since published *The Collected Works of Eric Voegelin* in numbered volumes. These volumes are listed below to offer contemporary readers reference to Voegelin's works that are currently in print and available.

Volume 1 *On The Form of the American Mind*, ed. Jürgen Gebhardt and Barry Cooper (1995).

Volume 2 *Race and State*, ed. Klaus Vondung, trans. Ruth Hein (1997).

Volume 3 *The History of the Race Idea*, ed. Klaus Vondung, trans. Ruth Hein (1998).

Volume 4 *The Authoritarian State*, ed. Gilbert Weiss, trans. Ruth Hein, collaborator Erika Weinzierl (1999).

Volume 5 *Modernity Without Restraint*, ed. Manfred Henningsen (1999).

Volume 6 *Anamnesis*, ed. David Walsh, trans. Gerhart Niemeyer and M. J. Hanak (2002).

Volume 7 *Published Essays, 1922—1928*, ed. Thomas W. Heilke and John von Heyking, trans. M. J. Hanak (2003).

Volume 8 *Published Essays, 1929—1933*, ed. Thomas W. Heilke and John von Heyking, trans. M. J. Hanak and Jodi Cockerill (2003).

Volume 9 *Published Essays, 1934—1939*, ed. Thomas W. Heilke, trans. M. J. Hanak (2001).

Volume 10 *Published Essays, 1940—1952*, ed. Ellis Sandoz (2000).

Volume 11 *Published Essays, 1953—1965*, ed. Ellis Sandoz (2000).

Volume 12 *Published Essays, 1966—1985*, ed. Ellis Sandoz (1990).

Volume 13 *Selected Book Reviews*, ed. Barry Cooper, trans. Jodi Cockerill (2002).

Order and History, (Vols 1-5)

Volume 14 *Israel and Revelation*, ed. Maurice P. Hogan (2001).

Volume 15 *The World of the Polis*, ed. Athanasios Moulakis (2000).

Volume 16 *Plato and Aristotle*, ed. Dante Germino (1999).

Volume 17 *The Ecumenic Age*, ed. Michael Franz (2000).

Volume 18 *In Search of Order*, ed. Ellis Sandoz (2000).

History of Political Ideas, (Vols 1-8)

Volume 19 *Hellenism, Rome and Early Christianity*, ed. Athanasios Moulakis (1997).

Volume 20 *The Middle Ages to Aquinas*, ed. Peter von Sivers (1998).

Volume 21 *The Later Middle Ages*, ed. David Walsh (1998).

Volume 22 *Renaissance and Reformation*, ed. David L. Morse and William M. Thompson (1998).

Volume 23 *Religion and the Rise of Modernity*, ed. James L. Wiser (1998).

Volume 24 *Revolution and the New Science*, ed. Barry Cooper (1999).

Volume 25 *The New Order and Last Orientation*, ed. Jürgen Gebhardt and Thomas A. Hollweck (1999).

Volume 26 *Crisis and the Apocalypse of Man*, ed. David Walsh (1999).

Volume 27 *The Nature of the Law*, ed. Robert Anthony Pascal, James Lee Babin, and John William Corrington (1991).

Volume 28 *What is History?*, ed. Thomas A. Hollweck and Paul Caringella (1990).

Volume 29 *Selected Correspondence: 1924-1949*, ed. Jürgen Gebhardt, trans. William Petropulos (2009).

Volume 30 *Selected Correspondence: 1950-1984*, ed. Thomas A. Hollweck, trans. Sandy Adler, Thomas A. Hollweck, and William Petropulos (2007).

Volume 31 *Hitler and the Germans*, ed. and trans. Detlev Clemens and Brendan Purcell (1999).

Volume 32 *The Theory of Governance and other Miscellaneous Papers, 1921-1938*, ed. William Petropulos and Gilbert Weiss, trans. Sue Bollans, Jodi Cockerill, M. J. Hanak, Ingrid Heldt, and Elizabeth von Lochner (2004).

Volume 33 *The Drama of Humanity and other Miscellaneous Papers, 1939-1985*, ed. William Petropulos and Gilbert Weiss (2004).

Volume 34 *Autobiographical Reflections*, Glossary and Index, ed. Ellis Sandoz (2006).

Corrington's Publications

1. Books

Where We Are (Poetry), The Charioteer Press, Washington, D. C., 1962. (hardback and paperback)

The Anatomy of Love and Other Poems (Poetry), Roman Books, Ft. Lauderdale, Florida, 1964. (hardback and paperback)

Mr. Clean and Other Poems (Poetry), Amber House Press, San Francisco, California, 1964.

And Wait for the Night (Novel), G. P. Putnam's Sons, New York, N. Y., 1964; Anthony Blond, Ltd., London, 1964; Pocket Books, Inc., New York, N. Y., 1965; Panther Books, Ltd., London, 1967.

Lines to the South and Other Poems (Poetry), Louisiana State University Press, Baton Rouge, Louisiana, 1965.

Southern Writing in the Sixties: Fiction (Anthology), ed. with Miller Williams, Louisiana State University Press, Baton Rouge, Louisiana, 1966. (hardback and paperback)

Southern Writing in the Sixties: Poetry (Anthology), ed. with Miller Williams, Louisiana State University Press, Baton Rouge, Louisiana, 1967. (hardback and paperback)

The Upper Hand (Novel), G. P. Putnam's Sons, New York, N. Y., 1967; Anthony Blond, Ltd., London, 1968; Berkeley Books, New York, N. Y., 1968; Panther Books, London, 1969.

The Lonesome Traveler and Other Stories (Short Fiction),G. P. Putnam's Sons, New York, N. Y., 1968.

The Bombardier (Novel), G. P. Putnam's Sons, New York, N. Y., 1970; Lancer Books, New York, N. Y., 1972.

The Actes and Monuments (Short Fiction), University of Illinois Press, Urbana, Illinois, 1978. (hardback and paperback)

The Southern Reporter Stories (Short Fiction), Louisiana State University Press, Baton Rouge, Louisiana, 1981.

Shad Sentell (Novel), Congdon & Weed, Inc., New York, N. Y., 1984; (Shad) Macmillan, London, 1984; (Shad) Grafton Books, London, 1986.

So Small a Carnival, (Novel, with Joyce H. Corrington), Viking/Penguin, New York, 1986; Ballantine Books, New York, 1987; (Karneval med doden) Nyt Nordisk Forlag Arnold Busck A/S, Kobenhavn, Denmark, 1988;Hayakawa Publishing, Inc, Japan, 1988; (New Orleans Carneval) Wilhelm Heyne Verlag, Munchen, Germany, 1988; (Carnaval de Sangue) Editora Best Seller, Sao Paulo, Brazil, 1988; Mysterious Press, London, UK, 1989; (Carnaval de Sangue) Editora Nova Cultural Ltda., Sao Paulo, Brazil, 1990.

A Project Named Desire, (Novel, with Joyce H. Corrington),Viking/Penguin, New York, 1987; (*Das Desire-Projekt*) Wilhelm Heyne Verlag, Munchen, Germany, 1987; Ballantine Books, New York, 1988; (*Dannys sidste sang*) Nyt Nordisk Forlag Arnold Busck, Kobenhavn, Denmark, 1988; Hayakawa Publishing, Inc., Japan, 1988; (*Una Canzone Per Morire*) Arnoldo Mondadori Editore S.p.A., Milano, Italy; (*Um Projecto Chamado Desejo*) Editora Nova Cultural Ltda., Sao Paulo, Brazil, 1990; (*Um Projecto Chamado Desejo*) Circulo do Livro, Sao Paulo, Brazil, 1990; (*Um Projecto Chamado Desejo*) Editora Best Seller, Sao Paulo, Brazil, 1990.

A Civil Death, (Novel, with Joyce H. Corrington), Viking/Penguin, New York, 1987; (*Begrabnis Erster Klasse*) Wilhelm Heyne Verlag, Munchen, Germany, 1988; Ballantine Books, New York, 1989; Hayakawa Publishing, Inc., Japan, 1989; (*Finche Odio Ci Separi*) Arnoldo Mondadori Editore S.p.A., Milano, Italy, 1989.

All My Trials, (2 Short Novels, "Decoration Day" and "The Risi's Wife"), University of Arkansas Press, Fayetteville, Arkansas, 1987. (hardback and paperback)

The White Zone, (Novel with Joyce Corrington),Viking/Penguin, New York, 1990.

The Collected Stories of John William Corrington, ed. by Joyce Corrington, University of Missouri Press, Columbia, Missouri, 1990.

The Collected Works of Eric Voegelin, Volume 27, The Nature of the Law, and Related Legal Writings, ed. with Robert Anthony Pascal, James Lee Babin, Louisiana State University Press, Baton Rouge, Louisiana, 1991.

2. Screenplays and Television (All with Joyce H. Corrington)

Von Richthofen and Brown (retitled *The Red Baron*), Solo Credit, The Corman Company/United Artists, 1969.

The Omega Man, Solo Credit, Walter Seltzer Productions/ Warner Brothers, 1970.

Boxcar Bertha, Solo Credit, The Corman Company/American International Productions, 1971.

The Arena (retitled *Naked Warriors*), Solo Credit, La Honda Productions/New World Pictures, 1972.

The Battle for the Planet of the Apes, Solo Credit, Apjac Productions/20th Century Fox, 1973.

The Killer Bees, Solo Credit, RSO Productions, ABC Movie of the Week, 1974.

Search for Tomorrow, Head Writer episodes #6949-7426, Proctor & Gamble Productions/CBS Daytime Serial, 1978-80.

Another World, Co-Head Writer episodes #4058-4081, Proctor & Gamble Productions/NBC Daytime Serial, 1980.

Texas, Creator and Head Writer episodes #1-147, Proctor & Gamble Productions/NBC Daytime Serial, 1980-81.

General Hospital, Head Writer episodes #(1982) 52-106, ABC Television Network Daytime Serial, 1982.

Capitol, Head Writer episodes #104-271, John Conboy Productions/CBS Daytime Serial, 1982-83.

One Life to Live, Head Writer episodes #4122-4219, ABC Television Network Daytime Serial, 1984.

Superior Court, Head Writer/Producer episodes #1001-1170, 2001-2170, 3001-3170, Ralph Edwards/Stu Billett Productions, Syndicated Serial, 1986-89.

3. Contributions to Books

"Charles Bukowski in Mid-Flight," critical introduction to *It Catches My Heart in Its Hands*, Charles Bukowski, Loujon Press, New Orleans, 1963.

"Communique," in *Poets of Today*, ed. Walter Lowenfels, International Publishers, New York, N. Y. 1964.

"Lawrence Ferlinghetti and the Painter's Eye," in *Nine Essays in Modern Literature*, ed. Donald E. Stanford, Louisiana State University Press, Baton Rouge, Louisiana, 1965.

"Nuestro Hombre en Gomorra," in *19 Poetas de Hoy en Los Estados Unidos*, ed. Miller Williams, Departmento de Cultura de Chile, Santiago, Chile, 1966.

"To Carthage Then I Came," in *American Literary Anthology*, Volume 1, (National Endowment for the Arts Awards in Literature), Farrar, Straus and Geroux, New York, N. Y., 1968.

"The Sisters," in *James Joyce's Dubliners: Critical Essays*, ed. Clive Hart, Faber and Faber, London, 1969; Viking Press, New York, N. Y., 1969.

"Alabama Tenants: 1937," in *Black and White in America*, (Anthology from the Massachusetts Review), University of Massachusetts Press, n.p., 1969.

"Pastoral," in *Mandala*, ed. Wilfred L. Guerin, Earle Labor, Lee Morgan, and John R. Willingham, Harper & Row, New York, N. Y., 1970.

"Reunion," in *The Southern Experience in Short Fiction*, ed. Allen F. Stein and Thomas N. Walters, Scott, Foresman & Company, Glenview, Illinois, 1970.

"The Retrievers," in *The Southern Experience in Short Fiction*, ed. Allen F. Stein and Thomas N. Walters, Scott, Foresman & Company, Glenview, Illinois, 1970.

"James Dickey's Poems 1957-1967: A Personal Appraisal," in *Contemporary Literary Criticism*, Volume 1, ed. Phyllis Carmel Mendelson and Dedria Bryfonski, Gale Reserach Company, Detroit, Michigan, 1970.

"Communique," in *The United States*, ed. Richard Hofstadter, William Miller, and Daniel Aaron, Prentice-Hall, Inc., Englewood Cliffs, New Jersey, 1972.

"For A Woods-Colt Miscarried," in *Contemporary Poetry in America*, ed. Miller Williams, Random House, New York, N.Y., 1972.

"Guevera with Minutes to Go," in *Contemporary Poetry in America*, ed. Miller Williams, Random House, New York, N.Y., 1972.

"On My Eighteenth Birthday," in *Contemporary Poetry in America*, ed. Miller Williams, Random House, New York, N.Y., 1972.

"Old Men Dream Dreams, Young Men See Visions," in *Best American Short Stories, 1972*, ed. Martha Foley, Houghton-Mifflin, Boston, Mass., 1973.

"A Trip to Omaha: Normandy 6.VI.44," in *Poems in Context*, ed. Lee A. Jacobus and William T. Moynihan, Harcourt Brace Jovanovich, New York, N.Y., 1974.

"Mr. Clean," in *Poetry: Points of Departure*, ed. Henry Taylor, Winthrop Publishers, Inc., Cambridge, Mass., 1974.

"The Second Coming," in *How Does A Poem Mean?*, ed. John Ciardi and Miller Williams, Houghton Mifflin, Boston, Mass., 1975.

"The Actes and Monuments," in *Prize Stories 1975, The O. Henry Awards*, ed. William Abraham, Doubleday and Company, Garden City, N. Y., 1976.

"The Actes and Monuments," in *Best American Short Stories, 1975*, ed. Martha Foley, Houghton Mifflin, Boston, Mass., 1976.

"Old Men Dream Dreams, Young Men See Visions," in *The Wrought Response*, ed. Ray Kytle and Juanita Lyons, Dickenson Publishing Co., Encino, California, 1976.

"Charles Bukowski at Mid-Flight," in *Modern American Literature: A Library of Literary Criticism*, Volume IV, ed. Dorothy Nyren, Maurice Kramer, and Elaine Fialka, Frederick Ungar Publishing Co., New York, N.Y., 1976.

"Pleadings," in *Best American Short Stories, 1977*, ed. Martha Foley, Houghton Mifflin, Boston, Mass., 1977.

"Stones from the Rubble by Marion Montgomery," in *Contemporary Literary Criticism*, Volume 7, ed. Phyllis Carmel Mendelson and Dedria Bryfonski, Gale Research Company, Detroit, Michigan, 1977

"Order and Consciousness/Consciousness and History: The New Program of Voegelin," in *Eric Voegelin's Search for Order in History*, ed. Stephen A. McKnight, Louisiana State University Press, Baton Rouge, Louisiana, 1978.

"For A Woods-Colt Miscarried," in *Contemporary Southern Poetry*, ed. Guy Owen and Mary C. Williams, Louisiana State University Press, Baton Rouge, Louisiana, 1979.

"Pastoral," in *Contemporary Southern Poetry*, ed. Guy Owen and Mary C. Williams, Louisiana State University Press, Baton Rouge, Louisiana, 1979.

"Lines to the South," in *Contemporary Southern Poetry*, ed. Guy Owen and Mary C. Williams, Louisiana State University Press, Baton Rouge, Louisiana, 1979.

"The Recovery of the Humanities," in *Politics, Society, and the Humanities*, University of Tennessee, Chattanooga, 1985.

"Pastoral," in *LIT*, Wilfred Guerin, et al., eds. Harper & Row, New York, 1986.

"Creeley's For Love," in *Robert Creeley's Life and Work*, John Wilson, ed, University of Michigan Press, Ann Arbor, 1986.

"Every Act Whatever of Man," in *The Short Story in Louisiana*, Center for Louisiana Writing, Lafayette, Louisiana, 1986.

"Heroic Measures/Vital Signs," in *New Stories from the South*, ed. Shannon Ravenel, Chapel Hill, 1987.

"For a Woods-Colt Miscarried," in *The Made Thing*, ed. Leon Stokesbury, University of Arkansas Press, Fayetteville, Arkansas, 1987.

"On the Flesh of Christ," in *The Made Thing*, ed. Leon Stokesbury, University of Arkansas Press, Fayetteville, Arkansas, 1987.

"The Actes and Monuments," in *Prime Number: Seventeen Stories from Illinois Short Fiction*, University of Illinois Press, Urbana, Illinois, 1988.

"Pleadings," in *Selected Stories from the Southern Review*, 1965-1985, ed. Lewis P. Simpson, et al, Louisiana State University Press, Baton Rouge, 1988

"Reunion," in *Something in Common, Contemporary Louisiana Stories*, ed. Ann Brewster Dobie, Louisiana State University Press, Baton Rouge, 1991.

"Pleadings," *Louisiana Short Stories*, ed. Ben Forkner, Pelican Publishing Co., Gretna, Louisiana, 1990.

"Pleadings," Stories of the Modern South, ed. Ben Forkner andPatrick Samway, S.J., Penguin Books, New York, New York, 1995.

4. Critical Articles, Essays, and Reviews

"The Anatomy of Love," Introductory Essay, *The Mill*, Rice University, Houston, Texas, Fall 1958. 14ff.

"A Portrait of the Artist as a Young Label," *Trace*, No. 42, Hollywood, California, Summer 1961. 146ff.

"A Poet's Credo," *Midwest*, Chicago, Illinois, No. 2, Summer 1961. 17.

"Little Magazines for Classrooms," *Trace*, Hollywood, California, No. 4, Autumn 1961. 226.

"Merwin's Poetry," *Midwest*, Chicago, Illinois, No. 3, Winter 1961-62. 33ff.

"Hedley: A Negative View," *Midwest*, Chicago, Illinois, No. 4, Summer 1962. 34ff.

"Charles Bukowski: Three Poems," *The Outsider*, New Orleans, Louisiana, Vol. 1, No. 3, Spring 1963. 93ff.

"Patriotic Gore, by Edmund Wilson," *The Georgia Review*, Athens, Georgia, Vol. 17, No. 1, Spring 1963. 93ff.

"Denise Levertov: The Jacob's Ladder," *Midwest*, Chicago, Illinois, No. 5/6, Spring 1963. 14ff.

"Little Magazines in America: Symposium," *Mainstream*, New York, N.Y., Vol. 16, No. 6, June 1963. 38ff.

"For Love: Poems 1950-60, by Robert Creeley," *The Northwest Review*, Eugene, Oregon, Vol. 6, No. 3, Summer 1963. 106ff.

"Introduction," *A Modern Miscellany*, Roman Books, Ft. Lauderdale, Florida, 1963. 1ff.

"Charles Bukowski and the Savage Surfaces," T*he Northwest Review*, Eugene, Oregon, Vol. 6, No. 4, Fall 1963. 123ff.

"An American Look at Canada's Governor-General Award Books," *Evidence*, Toronto, Canada, No. 8, 1964. 36ff.

"A Circle of Stone, by Miller Williams," *The Georgia Review*, Athens, Georgia, Vol. 19, No. 2, Summer 1965. 29ff.

"William Faulkner of Oxford," *The Georgia Review*, Athens, Georgia, Vol. 19, No. 4, Winter 1965. 485ff.

"Graduate Literary Study in Britain and America," *Motive*, Nashville, Tennessee, Vol. 25, No. 8, May 1965. 6ff.

"An American Dreamer," *The Chicago Review*, Chicago, Illinois, Vol. 18, No. 1, Summer 1965. 58ff.

"From Another Country," *Today*, Chicago, Illinois, Vol. 21, No. 3, December 1965. 4ff.

"Isolation as Motif in 'A Painful Case,'" *James Joyce Quarterly*, Vol. 3, No. 3, Spring 1966. 182ff.

"Rocks and Bones and Wine," *The Northwest Review*, Eugene, Oregon, Vol. 7, No. 3, Spring 1966. 107ff.

"Nouveau Gnomic Poetry?" *The Northwest Review*, Eugene, Oregon, Vol. 7, No. 3, Spring 1966. 111ff.

"Views from a Ferris-Wheel," *The Georgia Review*, Athens, Georgia, Vol. 20, No. 3, Fall 1966. 374f.

"Where The Music Was, by Charles East," *The Georgia Review*, Athens, Georgia, Vol. 21, No, 1, Spring 1967. 133ff

"Stones from the Rubble, by Marion Montgomery," *The Georgia Review*, Athens, Georgia, Vol. 21, No. 1, Spring 1967. 135ff.

"History and Fiction," *Louisiana Studies*, Nachitoches, Louisiana, Vol. 6, No. 1, Spring 1967. 27ff.

"Thomas Wolfe, by Andrew Turnbull," *The National Observer*, Silver Spring, Maryland, 26 February 1968. 27ff.

"James Dickey's Poems 1957-1967: A Personal Appraisal," *The Georgia Review*, Athens, Georgia, Vol. 22, No. 1, Spring 1968. 12ff.

"Thomas Altizer Talks with NOR's Editor-at-Large," *The New Orleans Review*, Vol. 1, No. 1, Fall 1968. 26ff

"The Klansman, by William Bradford Huie," *The National Observer*, Silver Spring, Maryland, 31 August 1968. 27.

"Outer Dark, by Cormac McCarthy," *The National Observer*, Silver Spring, Maryland, 11 November 1968. 23.

"Three Books about a Southern Romantic," *The Southern Literary Journal*, Vol. 1, No. 1, Autumn 1968. 98ff.

"Nelson Algren Talks with NOR's Editor-at-Large," *The New Orleans Review*, New Orleans, Louisiana, Vol. 1, No. 3, Winter 1969. 130.

"Homage to Kenneth Patchen," *The Outsider*, No. 4/5, Tucson, Arizona, Winter 1969. 113ff.

"The Feast of St. Barnabas, by Jesse Hill Ford," *The National Observer*, Silver Spring, Maryland, 3 March 1969. 22.

"Wallace Stevens and the Problem of Order," *The Arlington Quarterly*, Arlington, Texas, Vol. 1, No. 4, Summer 1968. 50ff.

"Hodding Carter Talks to NOR's Editor-at-Large," *The New Orleans Review*, New Orleans, Louisiana, Vol. 2, No. 1, Autumn 1969. 81ff.

"A Writer's Legacy," *The National Observer*, Silver Spring, Maryland, 5 May 1969. 20.

"Ernest Hemingway: A Life Story, by Carlos Baker," *The New Orleans Review*, New Orleans, Louisiana, Vol. 2, No. 1, Autumn 1969. 81ff.

"Escape into Myth: The Long Dying of Bayard Sartoris," *Recherches Anglaises et Americaines*, Strausbourg, France, No. 4, 1971. 31ff.

"Cassirer's Curse, Keats's Urn, and the Poem Before the Poem," *Forum*, Houston, Texas, Vol. 10, No. 2, Summer-Fall 1972. 10ff.

"The Law and the Prophets," *The Forum*, Tulane University School of Law, New Orleans, Louisiana, October, 1973. 5.

"The Philosophies of History: An Interview with Eric Voegelin," *The New Orleans Review*, New Orleans, Louisiana, Volume 3, No. 2, 1973. 135.

"The New Physics vs. The Old Gnosis," *The New Orleans Review*, New Orleans, La., Vol. 4, No. 2, 1974. 99ff.

"Beyond Literature: A Review of Norman O. Brown's Closing Time," *The Denver Quarterly*, Denver, Colorado, Vol. 9, No. 2, Summer 1974. 97ff

"Charles Reich and the Gnostic Vision," *The New Orleans Review*, New Orleans, La., Vol. 5, No. 2, 1975. 3ff.

"The Rights and Duties of the Lessor in Louisiana Law," *The Tulane Civil Law Forum*, New Orleans, Louisiana, 1975. 26f.

"A Symposium on Eric Voegelin," (editor and contributor), *The Denver Quarterly*, Denver, Colorado, Vol. 10, No. 3, Autumn 1975. 93ff.

"Utopia in Revolution by Melvin Lasky," *New Oxford Review*, Volume 44, No. 7, 1977. 23.

"Horribles, Hitchikers and Faith Healers," a review of *Ballads Blues & Swan Songs* by William Wiser. *The Washington Post Book World*, Washington, D. C., 14 March 1983. 4.

"Fifi's Flights of Fancy," a review of *Ancient Lights* by David Grubb. *The Washington Post Book World*, Washington, D. C., 24 July 1982. 3.

"A Rebirth of Philosophical Thought," *The Southern Review*, Baton Rouge, Louisiana, Vol. 20, No. 3, Summer 1984. 738.

"Are Southerners Different?" *The Southern Partisan*, Columbia, South Carolina, Vol. 4, No. 1, Winter 1984. 16.

"Interview with John William Corrington" by William Parrill, *Louisiana Literature*, Hammond, Louisiana, Fall, 1985. 4ff.

Those Who Blink by William W. Mills, *Los Angeles Times Book Review*, Los Angeles, California, 22 June 1986, 3.

5. Short Fiction

"An Excerpt from the Novel Suffer, Little Children," *The Rectangle*, Wayne, Nebraska, Vol. 30, No. 2, Autumn, 1954. 42ff.

"Excerpts from a Novel: Suffer, Little Children," *Janus*, Houston, Texas, March 1960. 4ff.

"The Journal of a Purchased Person," *The New Idea*, Madison, Wisconsin, Fall 1960. 24ff.

"Union in the Rain," *The Georgia Review*, Athens, Georgia, Vol. 16, No. 2, Summer 1962. 141ff.

"Reunion," *The Southwest Review*, Dallas, Texas, Vol. 48, No, 3, Summer 1963. 200ff.

"Legend," *The Chicago Review*, Chicago, Illinois, Vol. 16, No. 3, Autumn 1963. 94ff.

"First Blood," *The Georgia Review*, Athens, Georgia, Vol. 19, No. 1, Spring 1965. 16ff.

"Dr. Aorta," *Motive*, Nashville, Tennessee, Vol. 26, No. 2, November 1965. 12ff.

"To Carthage Then I Came," *The Southwest Review*, Dallas, Texas, Vol. 51, No. 2, Spring 1966. 110ff.

"A Time to Embrace," *The Denver Quarterly*, Denver, Colorado, Vol. 2, No. 4, Winter 1968. 43ff.

"The Lonesome Traveler," *The Arlington Quarterly*, Vol. 1, No. 2, Winter 1968. 5ff.

"The Retrievers," *The Arlington Quarterly*, Arlington, Texas, Vol. 1, No. 3, Spring 1968. 183ff.

"The Night School," *The Massachusetts Review*, Amherst, Massachusetts, Vol. 9, No. 3, Summer 1968. 463ff.

"Keep Them Cards and Letters Comin' In," *The Sewanee Review*, Sewanee, Tennessee, Vol. 78, No. 1, Winter 1970. 60ff.

"A Chapter from The Disintegrator," *The New Orleans Review*, New Orleans, Louisiana, Vol. 2, No. 3, 1970. 247ff.

"Old Men Dream Dreams, Young Men See Visions," *The Sewanee Review*, Sewanee, Tennessee, Vol. 80, No. 1, Winter 1972. 73ff.

"The Door," *The Denver Quarterly*, Denver, Colorado, Vol. 8, No. 3, Autumn 1973. 87ff.

"From The Disintegrator," *The Barataria Review*, New Orleans, Louisiana, Vol. 1, No. 1, Winter 1975. 48ff.

"The Actes and Monuments," *The Sewanee Review*, Sewanee, Tennessee, Vol. 83, No. 1, Winter 1975. 61ff.

"Pleadings," *The Southern Review*, Baton Rouge, Louisiana, Vol. 12, No. 1, Winter 1976. 168ff.

"Every Act Whatever of Man," *The Southern Review*, Baton Rouge, Louisiana, Vol. 14, No. 3, Summer 1978. 517ff.

"Nothing Succeeds," *The Southern Review*, Baton Rouge, Louisiana, Vol. 16, No. 1, Winter 1980. 177ff.

"Heroic Measures/Vital Signs," *The Southern Review*, Baton Rouge, Louisiana, Vol. 22, No. 4, Fall 1986, 804ff.

6. Poetry

"Yesterday They Knew the River," *The Rectangle*, Wayne, Nebraska, Vol. 31, No. 1, Spring 1955. 281f.

"Suffer, Little Children," *The Rectangle*, Wayne, Nebraska, Vol. 31, No. 2, Autumn 1955. 19f.

"A Sonnet for Carolyn," *The Mill*, Houston, Texas, Fall 1957. 4.

"Take a Letter," *The Mill*, Houston, Texas, Fall 1957. 4.

"Orate, Fratres," *Venture*, New York, N. Y., Vol. 2, No. 4, Winter 1957-58. 42.

"The Anatomy of Love," *The Mill*, Houston, Texas, Fall 1958, 14ff.

"Symmetrical Romance," *Descant*, Fort Worth, Texas, Vol. 3, No. 3, Spring 1959. 19.

"The Gamblers," *Descant*, Fort Worth, Texas, Vol. 3, No. 3, Spring 1959. 19.

"A Sonnet for Carolyn," *Literary Calendar*, Shreveport, Louisiana, Spring 1959. 9.

"Effete," *Quicksilver*, Forth Worth, Texas, Vol. 12, No. 2, Summer 1959. 4.

"Reformation," *The Fiddlehead*, Fredricton, N.B., Canada, No. 41, Summer 1959. 13.

"An Act of Attrition," *Flame*, Alpine, Texas, Vol. 6, No. 2, Summer 1959. 13.

"What Are You Talking About?" *The American Weave*, Cleveland, Ohio, Vol. 24, No. 1, Summer 1959. 16f.

"The Garden of Delight," *The Forum*, Houston, Texas, Vol. 3, No. 3, Fall 1959. 19.

"The Functions of a Complex Variable," *Descant*, Fort Worth, Texas, Vol. 4, No. 1, Fall 1959. 30.

"[An Exemplary History] Unser Kampf," *Descant*, Forth Worth, Texas, Vol. 4, No. 1, Fall 1959. 31.

"An Exemplary Romance," *Odyssey*, Chicago, Illinois, Vol. 1, No. 4, Winter 1959. 11.

"Horn," *The San Francisco Review*, San Francisco, California, Vol. 1, No. 4, March 1960.

"The Gamblers," *The International Poetry Review*, Paterson, N. J., Vol. 1, No. 1, March 1960. 76.

"Homage to a Patriot," *Janus*, Houston, Texas, March 1960. 7.

"Public Enemy," *The Cresset*, Valparaiso, Indiana, Vol. 23, No. 7, May 1960. 27.

"Protoepithalamion I," *Quagga*, Austin, Texas, Vol. 1, No. 2, May 1960. 12.

"Protoepithalamia," *Epos*, Crescent City, Florida, Vol. 12, No. 2, Winter 1960. 28.

"Stick Em Up," *The Dalhousie Review*, Halifax, Canada, Vol. 40, No. 1, Spring 1960. 87.

"The Medusa," *The Dalhousie Review*, Halifax, Canada, Vol. 40, No. 1, Spring 1960. 87.

"Crescendo," *Epos*, Crescent City, Florida, Vol. 11, No. 3, Spring 1960. 20.

"The Poetics," *Epos*, Crescent City, Florida, Vol. 11, No. 3, Spring 1960. 21.

"The Classical Stance," *The Fiddlehead*, Fredricton, N.B., Canada, No. 45, Summer 1960. 41.

"An Exemplary Fiction," *Epos*, Crescent City, Florida, Vol. 11, No. 4, Summer 1960. 12.

"Protoepithalamion III," *Choice*, Madison, Wisconsin, No. 3, Fall 1960. 16.

"Here, Boy," *Point West*, Phoenix, Arizona, Vol. 2, No. 10, October 1960. 19.

"A Tribute to Laura," *Flame*, Alpine, Texas, Vol. 7, No. 4, Winter 1960. 11.

"The Fifth Horseman," *The Claremont Quarterly*, Claremont, California, Vol. 7, No. 2, Winter 1960. 42.

"An Exemplary Biography," *Patterns*, Burlington, Vermont, Vol. 3, No. 2, Winter 1960. 10.

"Footnote," *Inland*, Salt Lake City, Utah, Vol. 3, No. 3, Winter 1960. 34.

"Monterrey: 4.IV.52," *The Grecourt Review*, Northampton, Massachusetts, Vol. 4, No. 1, December 1960. 35.

"The Praesidion Cafe: Munich, 12.VI.58," *The Grecourt Review*, Northampton, Massachusetts, Vol. 4, No. 1, December 1960. 35.

"Pastoral," *The San Francisco Review*, San Francisco, California, Vol. 1, No. 8, Spring 1961. 39.

"uncle david," *Venture*, New York, N. Y., Vol. 4, No. 1, Spring 1961. 48.

"Magnificat," *Venture*, New York, N. Y., Vol. 4, No. 1, Spring 1961. 49.

"Objet d'Art," *Targets*, Sandia Park, New Mexico, No. 5, Spring 1961. 27.

"Professor Murk," *Targets*, Sandia Park, New Mexico, No. 5, Spring 1961. 26.

"On War," *Signet*, Alamo, California, Vol. 1, No. 3, March 1961. 12.

"Droodle," *Signet*, Alamo, California, Vol. 1, No. 3, March 1961. 11.

"The Orient Hotel," *The Poetry Dial*, South Bend, Indiana, Vol. 1, No. 2, Spring 1961. 37.

"Tribute II," *The Sparrow*, Flushing, N. Y., April 1961. 25.

"At Recess," *The Grecourt Review*, Northampton, Massachusetts, Vol. 4, No. 3, May 1961. 44.

"Summit," *Mutiny*, New York, N. Y., Vol. 3, No. 3, Summer 1961. 243.

"Viajera," *The Chicago Review*, Chicago, Illinois, Vol. 15, No. 1, Summer 1961. 58.

"Note from a Dead City," *Midwest*, Chicago, Illinois, No. 2, Summer 1961. 15.

"Ship Ahoy," *Midwest*, Chicago, Illinois, No. 2, Summer 1961. 16.

"I Love a Mystery," *Epos*, Crescent City, Florida, Vol. 12, No. 4, Summer 1961. 25.

"this is sombodies weather," *Choice IV*, Madison, Wisconsin, Summer 1961. 16.

"Limiting Factor," *Choice IV*, Madison, Wisconsin, Summer 1961. 15.

"Protoepithalamion IV," *The Galley Sail Review*, San Francisco, California, Vol. 3, No. 1, June 1961. 33

"Protoepithalamion II," *The Galley Sail Review*, San Francisco, California, Vol. 3, No. 1, June 1961. 33.

"Poem," *Targets*, Sandia Park, New Mexico, No. 6, June 1961.8.

"Novus Ordo Saeclorum," *Targets*, Sandia Park, New Mexico, No. 6, June 1961. 6.

"Hard Man," *The Outsider*, New Orleans, Louisiana, Vol. 1, No. 1, Fall 1961. 85.

"Where Do We Go From Here," *The Georgia Review*, Athens, Georgia, Vol. 15, No. 3, Fall 1961. 323.

"For The Army of Northern Virginia: 1861-1961," *Descant*, Fort Worth, Texas, Vol. 6, No. 1, Fall 1961. 15.

"For My Daughter Nine Months Old," *Descant*, Forth Worth, Texas, Vol. 6, No. 1, Fall 1961. 14.

"Tribute III: to Laura," *Renaissance*, San Francisco, California, Vol. 1, No. 1, Fall 1961. 66.

"Tomorrow," *Four Quarters*, Philadelphia, Pennsylvania, Vol.11, No. 1, November 1961. 27.

"Man of War," *Discourse*, Moorhead, Minnesota, Vol. 4, No. 1, Winter 1961. 70.

"Police Report," *Discourse*, Moorhead, Minnesota, Vol. 4, No. 1, Winter 1961. 69.

"Protoepithalamion VI," *Epos*, Crescent City, Florida, Vol. 12, No. 2, Winter 1961. 28.

"Je Suis Galant Sometimes," *Targets*, Sandia Park, New Mexico, No. 8, December 1961. 28ff.

"for charlie..." *Quagga*, Austin, Texas, Vol. 1, No. 3, Winter 1961. 11.

"Middleman," *Descant*, Fort Worth, Texas, Vol. 5, No. 2, Winter 1961. 14.

"An Exemplary Epic," *Descant*, Fort Worth, Texas, Vol. 5, No. 2, Winter 1961. 15

"Homage to a Patriot," *The Dalhousie Review*, Halifax, Canada, Vol. 41, No. 4, Winter 1961-62. 465.

"The Adventures of a Young Man," *Discourse*, Moorhead, Minnesota, Vol. 5, No. 1, Winter 1961-62. 48.

"At Murphy's Diner," *Targets*, Sandia Park, New Mexico, No. 8, December 1961. 26.

"A Man of Terrible Integrity," *Salon 13*, Guatamala City, California, Vol. 2, No. 4, December 1961. 33.

"Summer in South Georgia," *Salon 13*, Guatamala City, California, Vol. 2, No. 4, December 1961. 34.

"Vol de Nuit," *Salon 13*, Guatamala City, California, Vol. 2, No. 4, December 1961. 32.

"Legionaire," *The Grecourt Review*, Northampton, Massachusetts, Vol. 5, No. 1, December 1961. 38ff.

"Libera Nos, Deus," *Sun*, San Francisco, California, No. 3, 1961. 17.

"The Portable Goya," *The Chicago Review*, Chicago, Illinois,Vol. 15, No. 3, Winter-Spring 1962. 61ff.

"The Second Coming," *Southern Poetry Today*, Deland, Florida, Spring 1962. 21.

"Confederate Veteran's Home," *Southern Poetry Today*, Spring 1962. 20.

"A Christmas Carol," *Sun*, San Francisco, California, No. 7, Spring 1962. 13.

"Communique I - Communique IV," *Trace*, Hollywood, California, No. 45, Spring 1962. 117ff.

"Caveat," *Statements*, Iowa City, No. 5, Spring 1962. 1.

"Monte Cassino: 17 February 1944," *Four Quarters*, Philadelphia, Pennsylvania, Vol. 11, No. 2, January 1962. 10.

"It Happens Every Spring," *The San Francisco Review*, San Francisco, California, Vol. 1, No. 11, March 1962. 22f.

"The Anatomy of Love," *El Corno Emplumado*, Mexico D. F., Vol. 1, No. 2, April 1962. 58ff.

"Ah The University," *El Corno Emplumado*, Mexico, D. F.,Vol. 1, No. 2, April 1962. 57.

"Surreal for Lorca," *The Outsider*, New Orleans, Louisiana, Vol. 1, No. 2, Summer 1962. 61.

"Homage to an Artist: Leonardo da Vinci," *The Personalist*, Los Angeles, California, Vol. 43, No. 3, Summer 1962. 337.

"Something for the Kids," *Outcry*, Washington, D.C., Vol. 1, No. 1, Summer 1962. 31.

"Tribute IV," *Outcry*, Washington, D.C., Vol. 1, No. 1, Summer 1962. 32.

"Photo of a Lady," *The Minnesota Review*, Minneapolis, Minnesota, Vol. 2, No. 4, Summer 1962. 458.

"An Exemplary Philosophy," *The Minnesota Review*, Minneapolis, Minnesota, Vol. 2, No. 4, Summer 1962. 459.

"Catabasis," *Renaissance*, San Francisco, California, Vol. 1,No. 3, Summer 1962. 52.

"Contratemps: in a minor," *Renaissance*, San Francisco, California, Vol. 1, No. 3, Summer 1962. 54.

"Legend," *The Black Cat Review*, San Bernardino, California,No. 1, June 1962. 10.

"Antichrist," *The Dubliner*, Dublin, Ireland, Vol. 1, No. 3,May-June 1962. 34.

"C.O.D.," *The Dubliner*, Dublin, Ireland, Vol. 1, No. 3, May-June 1962. 35.

"A Trip to Omaha," *Coastlines*, Santa Monica, California, Vol. 5, No. 3, Fall 1962. 15.

"Stay Where You Are," *The Colorado Quarterly*, Boulder, Colorado, Vol. 11, No. 2, Fall 1962. 135.

"A Memo from Lilith," *The Northwest Review*, Eugene, Oregon,Vol. 5, No. 1, Fall 1962. 68.

"Lines in a Dying-Room," *The Northwest Review*, Eugene, Oregon, Vol. 5, No. 1, Fall 1962. 69f.

"Private Eye," *Discourse*, Moorhead, Minnesota, Vol. 5, No. 4, Autumn 1962. 447.

"Come On In," *Discourse*, Moorhead, Minnesota, Vol. 5, No. 4, Autumn 1962. 448.

"Death Watch," *Discourse*, Moorhead, Minnesota, Vol. 5, No. 4, Autumn 1962. 449f.

"In A Field Near Baton Rouge," *The Southwest Review*, Dallas, Texas, Vol. 47, No. 4, Autumn 1962. 308.

"The Imperial Hotel," *The Watauga Review*, Johnson City, Tennessee, Vol. 1, No. 1, Fall 1962. 37.

"C.O.D.," *The Watauga Review*, Johnson City, Tennessee, Vol.1, No. 1, Fall 1962. 38.

"Clowns Snakes Magic Shills," *Brand X*, New York, New York, No. 5, May 1962.

"Crash," *The Watauga Review*, Johnson City, Tennessee, Vol. 1, No. 1, Fall 1962. 39.

"Letter to a Friend," *Salon 13*, Guatamala City, California, Vol. 3, No. 3, September 1962. 13.

"Some Versions of Pastoral," *Salon 13*, Guatamala City, C.A., Vol. 3, No. 3, September 1962. 14f.

"Woman in a Field," *Salon 13*, Guatamala City, California, Vol. 3, No. 3, September 1962. 16.

"Hollywood: 17.VII.47," *The Fat Abbot*, Boston, Massachusetts, Vol. 1, No. 4, Fall-Winter 1962. 45.

"They Were Killing Us On The Ridge," *Choice*, Chicago, Illinois, Vol. 1, No. 2, Winter 1962. 19.

"The System," *The Northwest Review*, Eugene, Oregon, Vol. 5,No. 1, Winter 1962. 86f.

"Nor Turkish Horse Nor Pangs of Trent," *The Northwest Review*, Vol. 5, No. 1, Winter 1962. 85.

"Inside Job," *The Fiddlehead*, Fredricton, N. B., Canada, No. 51, Winter 1962. 2.

"Reunion," *The Colorado Quarterly*, Boulder, Colorado, Vol. 10, No. 3, Winter 1962. 283.

"Communion," *The Outsider*, New Orleans, Louisiana, Vol. 1, No. 3, Spring 1963. 87.

"Algerien Reveur," *The Chicago Review*, Chicago, Illinois, Vol. 16, No. 1, Winter-Spring 1963. 111f.

"Communique V," *El Corno Emplumado*, Mexico, D.F., Vol. 1, No. 6, Spring 1963. 48ff.

"Bonaparte's Retreat," *Renaissance*, San Francisco, California, Vol. 1, No. 4, Spring 1963. 67f.

"Metaphysician at Huntsville," *The Northwest Review*, Eugene, Oregon, Vol. 6, No. 2, Spring 1963. 114f.

"The Expatriates," *The Dalhousie Review*, Halifax, Canada, Vol. 43, No. 1, Spring 1963. 98.

"Surreal for Lorca," *Motive*, Nashville, Tennessee, Vol. 23, No. 5, February 1963. 15.

"Limiting Factor," *Chat Noir Review*, Chicago, Illinois, Vol. 2, No. 1, February 1963. 6.

"The Mystic," *The Kenyon Review*, Gambier, Ohio, Vol. 25, No. 3, Summer 1963. 516.

"Our Man in Gomorrah," *The Chicago Review*, Chicago, Illinois, Vol. 16, No. 2, Summer 1963. 41ff.

"Maid in the Shade," *The Chicago Review*, Chicago, Illinois, Vol. 16, No. 2, Summer 1963. 44f.

"Rudolph to Greta," *The Chicago Review*, Chicago, Illinois, Vol. 16, No. 2, Summer 1963. 46.

"Death and Transfiguration," *Northeast*, Waterville, Maine, Vol. 1, No. 1, Summer 1963. 49.

"Kritique," *Northeast*, Waterville, Maine, Vol. 1, No. 1, Summer 1963. 48.

"The Late Late Show," *The Massachusetts Review*, Amherst, Massachusetts, Vol. 4, No. 4, Summer 1963. 770.

"Who Goes There," *The Georgia Review*, Athens, Georgia, Vol. 17, No. 3, Fall 1963. 325.

"How Long Do I Have?" *Burning Water*, Princeton, New Jersey,Vol. 1, No. 1, Fall 1963. 50.

"Viva Zapata," *Mainstream*, New York, N.Y., Vol. 16, No. 8, August 1963. 51.

"Poem," *Descant*, Fort Worth, Texas, Vol. 7, No. 2, Winter 1963. 24.

"A Man of Terrible Integrity," *Targets*, Sandia Park, New Mexico, No. 12, Winter 1963. 10.

"Traveling Salesman," *Targets*, Sandia Park, New Mexico, No. 12, Winter 1963, 11.

"On My 18th Birthday," *Targets*, Sandia Park, New Mexico, No.12, Winter 1963. 12.

"Still Life with Fruit," *Targets*, Sandia Park, New Mexico, No. 12, Winter 1963. 13.

"The Man in the Purple Sheet," *Targets*, Sandia Park, New Mexico, No. 12, Winter 1963. 14.

"My Funny Valentine," *Targets*, Sandia Park, New Mexico, No.12, Winter 1963. 15.

"Trust Me Just This Once," *Targets*, Sandia Park, New Mexico, No. 12, Winter 1963. 16.

"Convention," *The Emerson Review*, Hollywood, California, Vol. 1, No. 1, Winter 1963. 49f.

"The Prince," *The Emerson Review*, Hollywood, California, Vol. 1, No. 1, Winter 1963. 48.

"Prayers for a Mass in the Vernacular," *El Corno Emplumado*, Mexico, D.F., Vol. 1, No. 9, Winter 1963-64. 59ff.

"A Phrase for King Oliver," *Choice*, Chicago, Illinois, Vol.1, No. 3, Spring 1964. 86

"Something You Need," *Choice*, Chicago, Illinois, Vol. 1, No. 3, Spring 1964. 86.

"Photo of a Lady," *The Times Literary Supplement*, London, England, No. 3,246, 14 May 1964. 408.

"Debutante," *Evidence*, Toronto, Canada, No. 9, Spring 1965. 46.

"this is somebodies weather," *Evidence*, Toronto, Canada, No. 9, Spring 1965. 47.

"Letter to a Friend," *Evidence*, Toronto, Canada, No. 9, Spring 1965. 48.

"The Grand Inquisitor Continues," *Motive*, Nashville, Tennessee, Vol. 25, No. 6, March 1965. 9.

"What Are You Talking About?" *Chelsea*, New York, N.Y., No. 16, March 1965. 72.

"Count Dracula: An Epilogue," *Chelsea*, New York, N.Y., No.16, March 1965. 72.

"The Physicist," *The Northwest Review*, Eugene, Oregon, Vol.7, No. 2, Fall/Winter 1965. 19.

"Alabama Tenants: 1937," *The Massachusetts Review*, Amherst,Mass., Vol. 7., No. 4, Autumn 1966. 638.

"Memphis: 1939," *The Georgia Review*, Athens, Georgia, Vol. 20, No. 4, Winter 1966. 396.

"On The Self-Immolation of a Monk in Saigon," *Southern Humanities Review*, Vol. 1, No. 1, Spring 1967. 41f.

"Toccata by an Eminent Amateur," *Transatlantic Review*, New York, N. Y., No. 26, Autumn 1967. 104.

"My Funny Valentine," *Poem*, Atlanta, Georgia, No. 1, November 1967. 21.

"Clowns Snakes Magic Shills," *Poem*, Atlanta, Georgia, No. 1, November 1967. 22f.

"You Don't Say," *The Intercollegiate Review*, Vol. 4, No. 1,November-December, 1967. 26.

"The Girl Girl-Watchers Watch," *The Saturday Review*, New York, N. Y., 17 February 1968. 48.

"Guevera with Minutes to Go," *The Saturday Review*, New York, N.Y., 6 July 1968. 48.

"Song About a Mouse," *Folio*, Vol. 4, No. 2, August 1968. 8.

"Saint Sebastian to the Left Bank," *Folio*, Vol. 4, No. 2, August 1968. 8.

"Ikon: Two," *Folio*, Vol. 4, No. 2, August 1968. 9.

"They Call This Quarter French," *The New Orleans Review*, New Orleans, Louisiana, Vol. 1, No. 1, Fall 1968. 48.

"The Son of Frankenstein," *The Daily Californian Weekly Magazine*, Berkeley, California, Vol. 4, No. 6, 5 November 1968. 14.

"A Poem for August," *The Daily Californian Weekly Magazine*,Berkeley, California, Vol. 4, No. 9, 14 January 1969. 13.

"When Grandma Whipped the Nigger Who Flogged His Mule," *The Daily Californian Weekly Magazine*, Berkeley, California, Vol. 4, No. 12, 28 January 1969. 13.

"Notes for an Undelivered Sermon," *The Denver Quarterly*, Denver Colorado, Vol. 3, No. 4, Winter 1969. 73ff.

"Mes Tribulations en Russie," *Prism International*, Vancouver, B.C., Canada, Vol. 9, No. 1, Summer 1969. 24.

"Lib," *PTA Magazine*, Chicago, Illinois, Vol. 67, No. 10, June 1973. 19.

"Absalom on Entropy," *The New Orleans Review*, New Orleans, Louisiana, Vol. 4, No. 1, Spring 1974. 31.

"The Prophet Remembered," *The Barataria Review*, New Orleans, Louisiana, Vol. 1, No. 1, 1975. 70.

"Joe Tolliver Who Mowed Our Lawn," *The Southern Review*, Baton Rouge, Louisiana, Vol. 13, No. 1, Spring 1977. 334.

"I Know a Girl Whose Heart," *The Southern Review*, Baton Rouge, Louisiana, Vol. 13, No. 1, Spring 1977. 336.

"On the Flesh of Christ," *The Southern Review*, Baton Rouge,Louisiana, Vol. 13, No. 1, Spring 1977. 337.

"The Beloved," *The Sewanee Review*, Sewanee, Tennessee, Vol. 85, No. 2, April-June 1977. 207.

"Archaic Torso of Apollo," *The New Orleans Review*, New Orleans, Louisiana, Vol. 5, No. 3, Spring 1977. 234.

"K. 627," *The Southern Review*, Baton Rouge, Louisiana, Vol. 16, No. 1, Winter 1980. 153.

"The Baptist," *The Cimarron Review*, Stillwater, Oklahoma, No. 50. January 1980. 52.

"The Anchorite," *The Cimarron Review*, Stillwater, Oklahoma,No. 50, January 1980. 64.

"The Rainmaker," *The Cimarron Review*, Stillwater, Oklahoma,No. 51, April 1980. 24.

"Francisco Goya Will Now Point Out The Moral of Painting Nudes," *The Cimarron Review*, Stillwater, Oklahoma, No. 51, April 1980. 56f.

"Translations," *The Southern Review*, Baton Rouge, Louisiana, Vol. 24, No. 1, Winter 1988. 150.

"Old Man Among His Flowers," *Pegasus*, Centenary College, Shreveport, Louisiana, 1989. 44.

"Old Man Among His Flowers," *The Southern Review*, Baton Rouge, Louisiana, Vol. 25, No. 3, Summer 1989. 595.

About the Editor

A llen Mendenhall is associate dean and executive director of the Blackstone & Burke Center for Law & Liberty at Faulkner University Thomas Goode Jones School of Law. His previous books include *Literature and Liberty (2014)* and *Oliver Wendell Holmes Jr., Pragmatism, and the Jurisprudence of Agon (2017).* He holds a B.A. in English from Furman University, M.A. in English from West Virginia University, J.D. from West Virginia University College of Law, LL.M. in transnational law from Temple University Beasley School of Law, and Ph.D. in English from Auburn University. He edits the *Southern Literary Review* and has been an adjunct legal associate at the Cato Institute, a Mises Emerging Scholar with the Ludwig von Mises Institute Canada, a Humane Studies Fellow with the Institute for Humane Studies at George Mason University, a policy advisor for the Heartland Institute, a staff attorney to the Chief Justice of the Supreme Court of Alabama, and an assistant attorney general in the State of Alabama Office of the Attorney General. He is an elected member of the Philadelphia Society, an associate of the Abbeville Institute, and the president of the Montgomery Lawyers' Chapter of the Federalist Society. He lives in Auburn, Alabama, with his wife and two children.

www.ingramcontent.com/pod-product-compliance
Lightning Source LLC
Chambersburg PA
CBHW051131030726
47504CB00004B/821